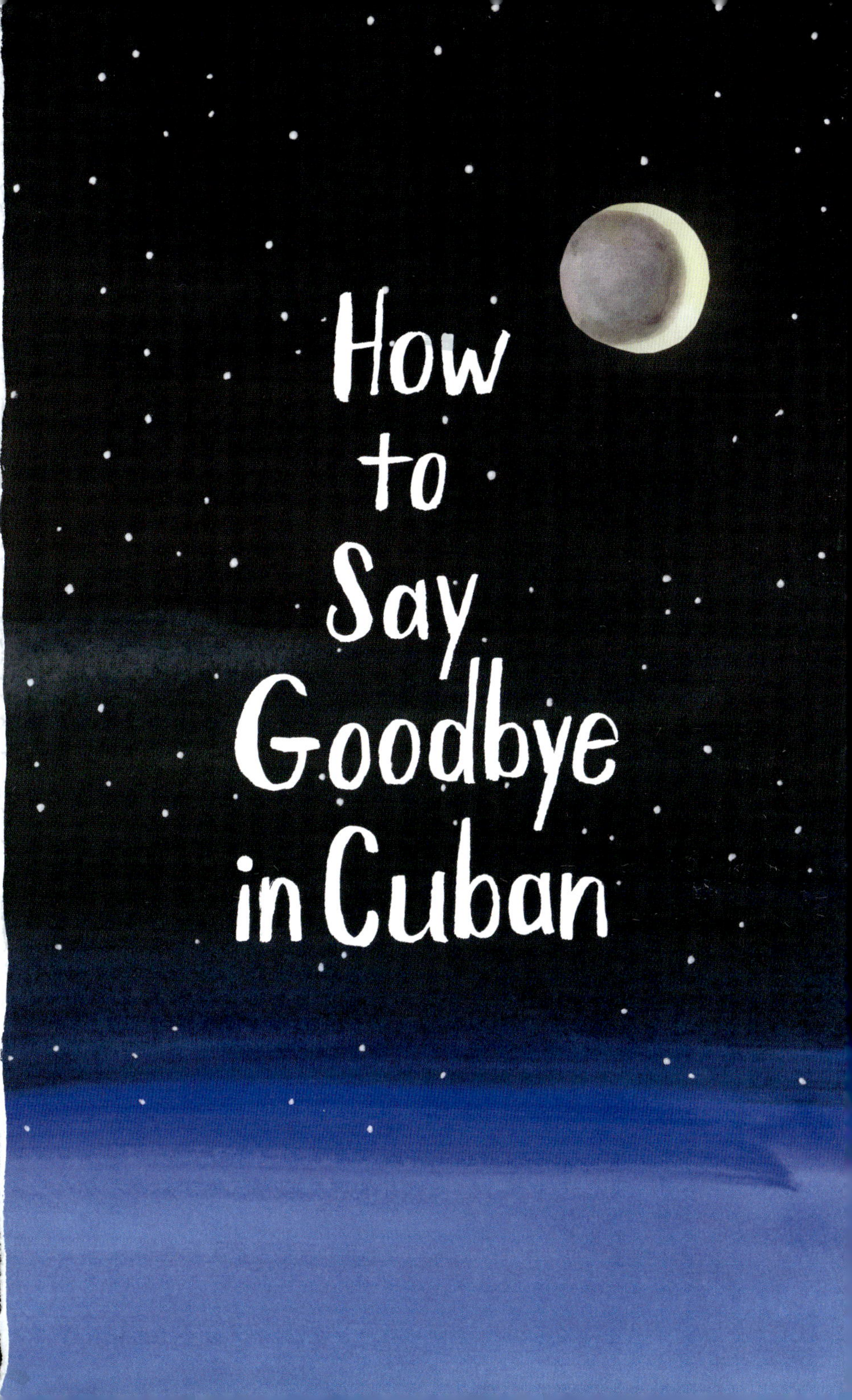
How to Say Goodbye in Cuban

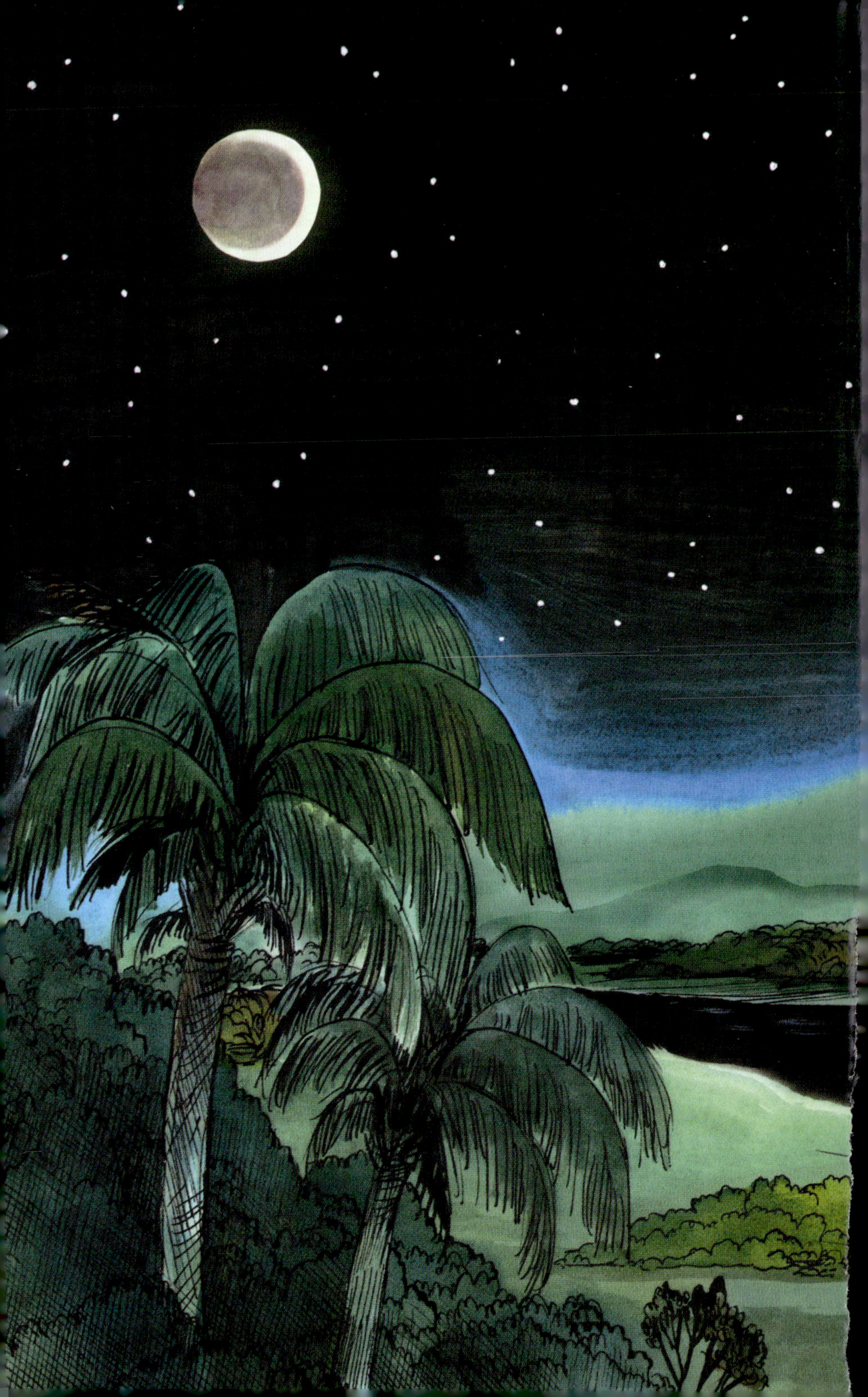

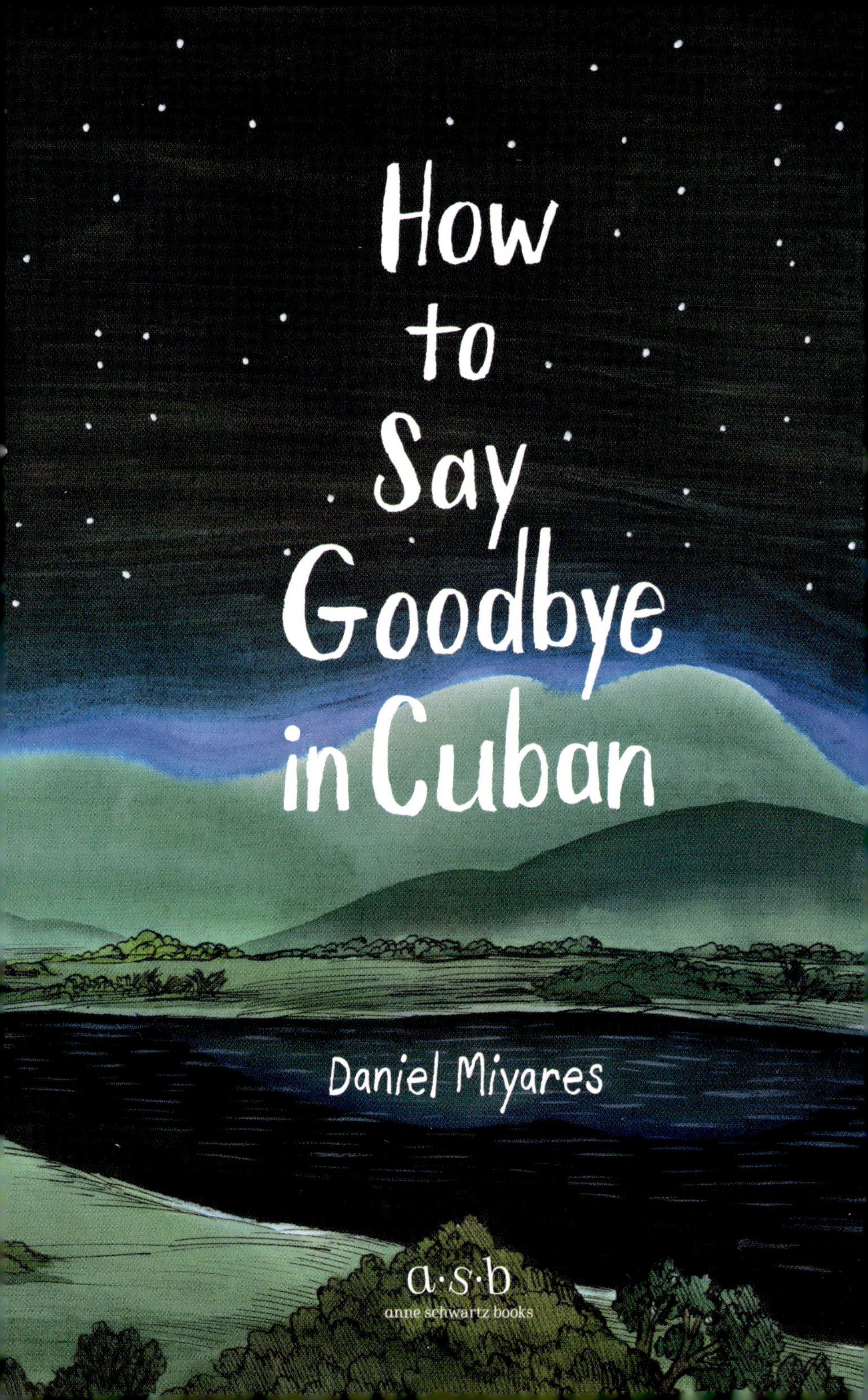
How to Say Goodbye in Cuban
Daniel Miyares
a·s·b
anne schwartz books

Copyright © 2025 by Daniel Miyares

All rights reserved. Published in the United States by Anne Schwartz Books, an imprint of Random House Children's Books, a division of Penguin Random House LLC, 1745 Broadway, New York, NY 10049.

Anne Schwartz Books and the colophon are trademarks of Penguin Random House LLC.

penguinrandomhouse.com
rhcbooks.com

Library of Congress Cataloging-in-Publication Data is available upon request.

ISBN 978-0-593-56829-3 (hardcover) — ISBN 978-0-593-56830-9 (trade pbk.) — ISBN 978-0-593-56831-6 (lib. bdg.) — ISBN 978-0-593-56832-3 (ebook)

The text of this book is set in 6-point Miyares Handwriting.

The illustrations were rendered in ink and watercolor.

Book design by Juliet Goodman

MANUFACTURED IN CHINA

10 9 8 7 6 5 4 3 2 1

First Edition

The authorized representative in the EU for product safety and compliance is Penguin Random House Ireland, Morrison Chambers, 32 Nassau Street, Dublin D02 YH68, Ireland, https://eu-contact.penguin.ie.

Random House Children's Books supports the First Amendment and celebrates the right to read.

Penguin Random House values and supports copyright. Copyright fuels creativity, encourages diverse voices, promotes free speech, and creates a vibrant culture. Thank you for buying an authorized edition of this book and for complying with copyright laws by not reproducing, scanning, or distributing any part of it in any form without permission. You are supporting writers and allowing Penguin Random House to continue to publish books for every reader. Please note that no part of this book may be used or reproduced in any manner for the purpose of training artificial intelligence technologies or systems.

For Dad, Abuela, Abuelo, Maggie, Lázaro, and Isaura.
Thank you for making your journey so I could make mine.

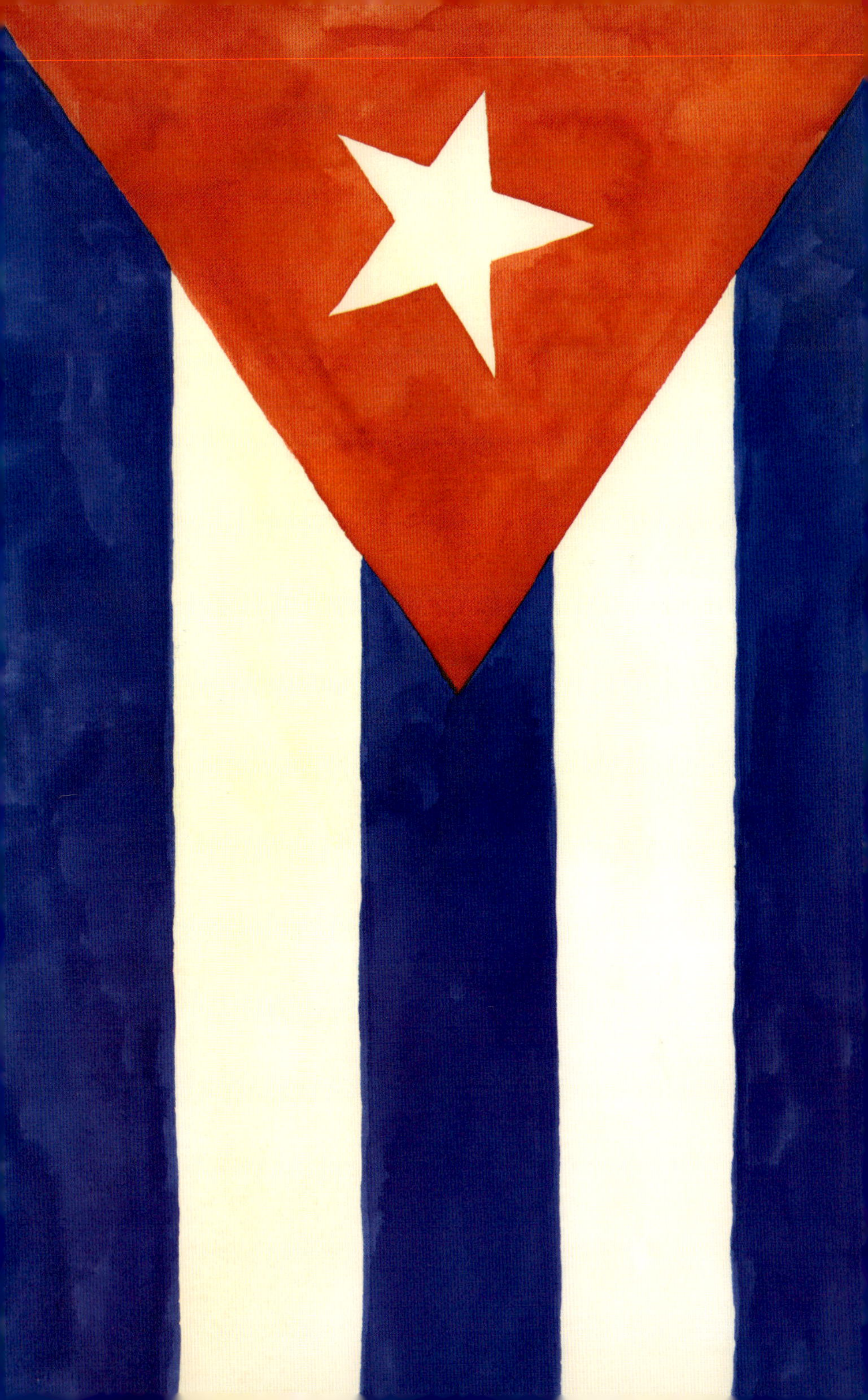

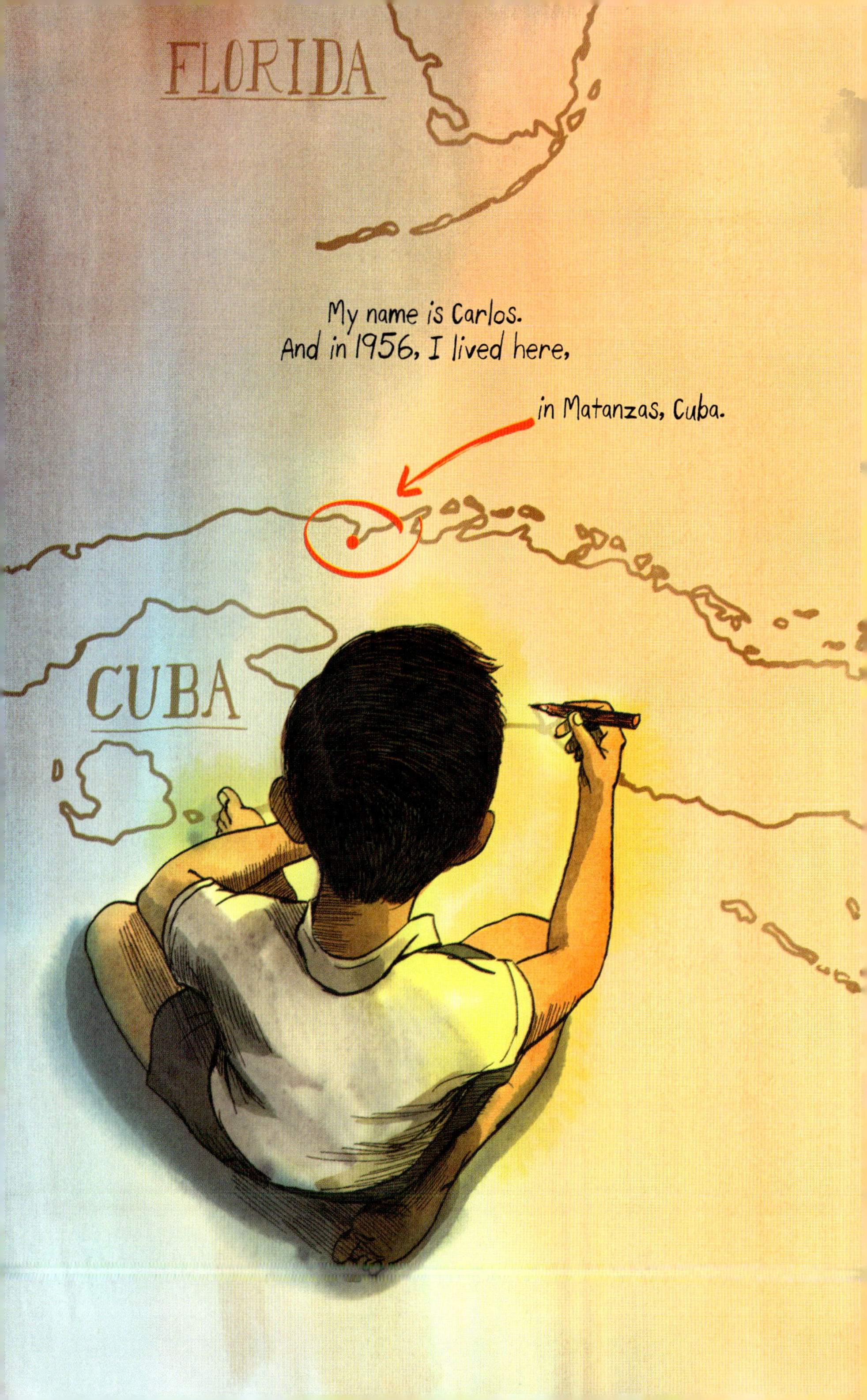
FLORIDA
My name is Carlos.
And in 1956, I lived here,
in Matanzas, Cuba.
CUBA

Well, actually here...

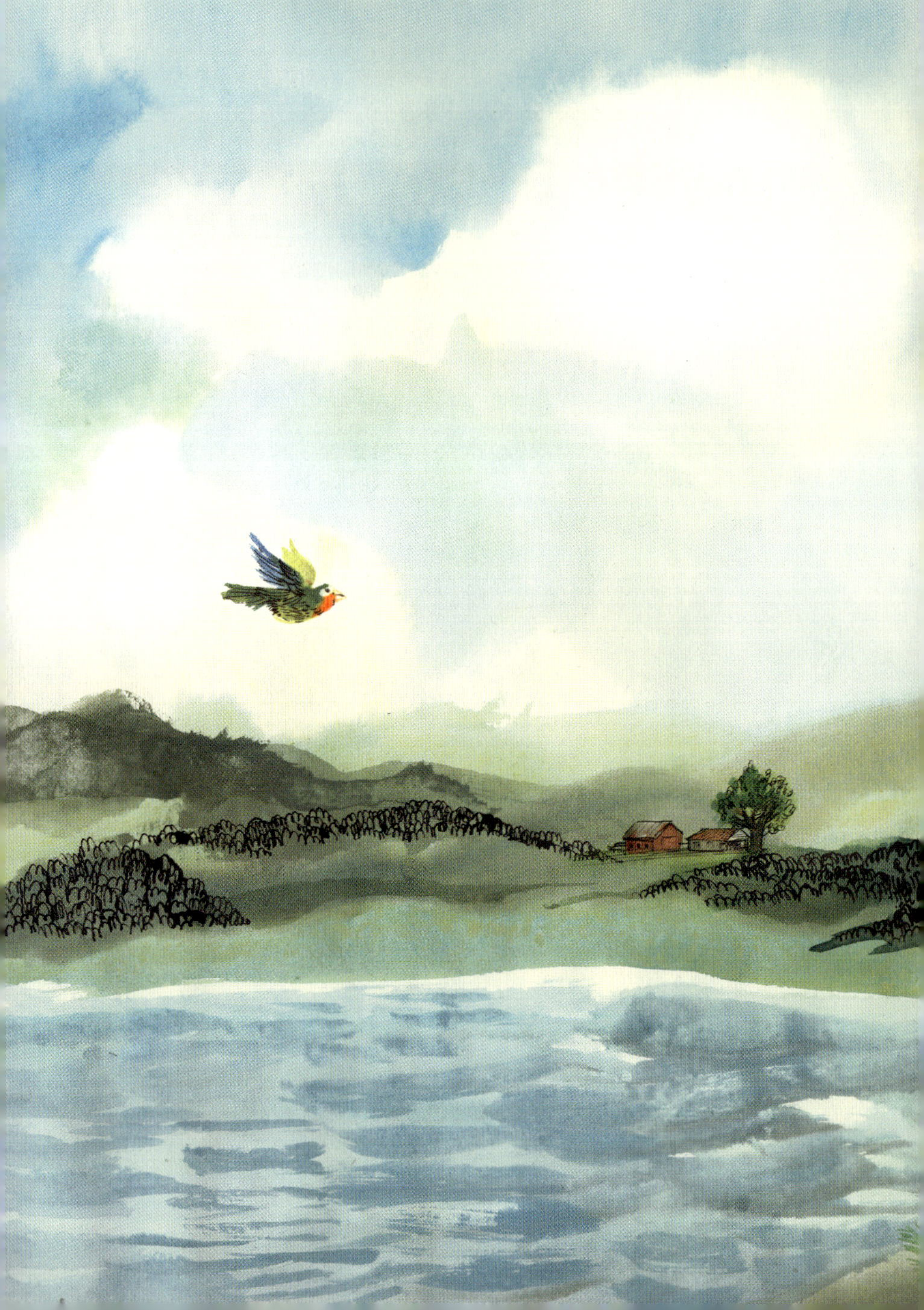

in the countryside just outside the city
in a place called Ceiba Mocha.

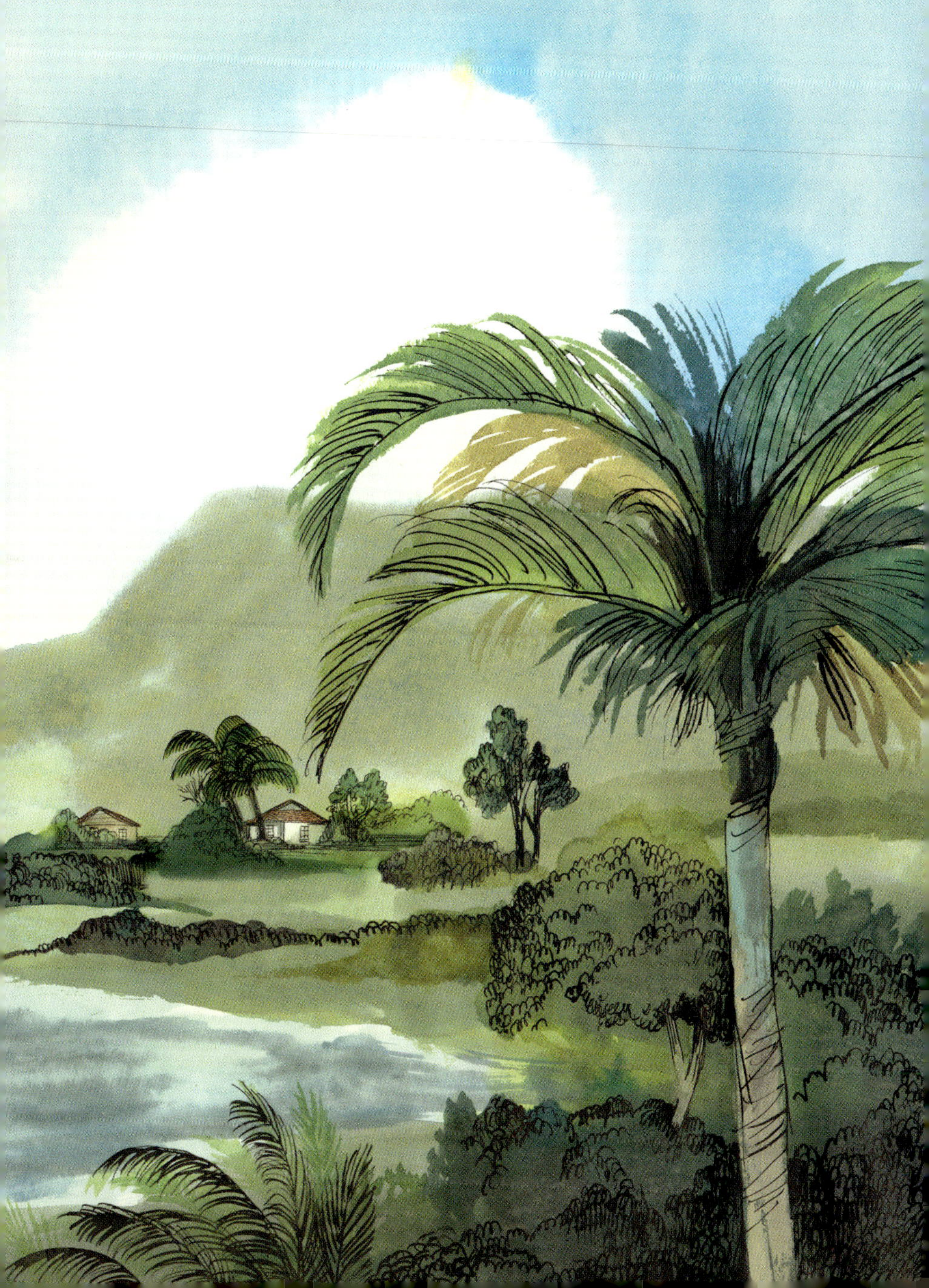

Me, my brother Lázaro, my sisters Maggie and Isaura, and Mamá and Papi's house was on the corner.

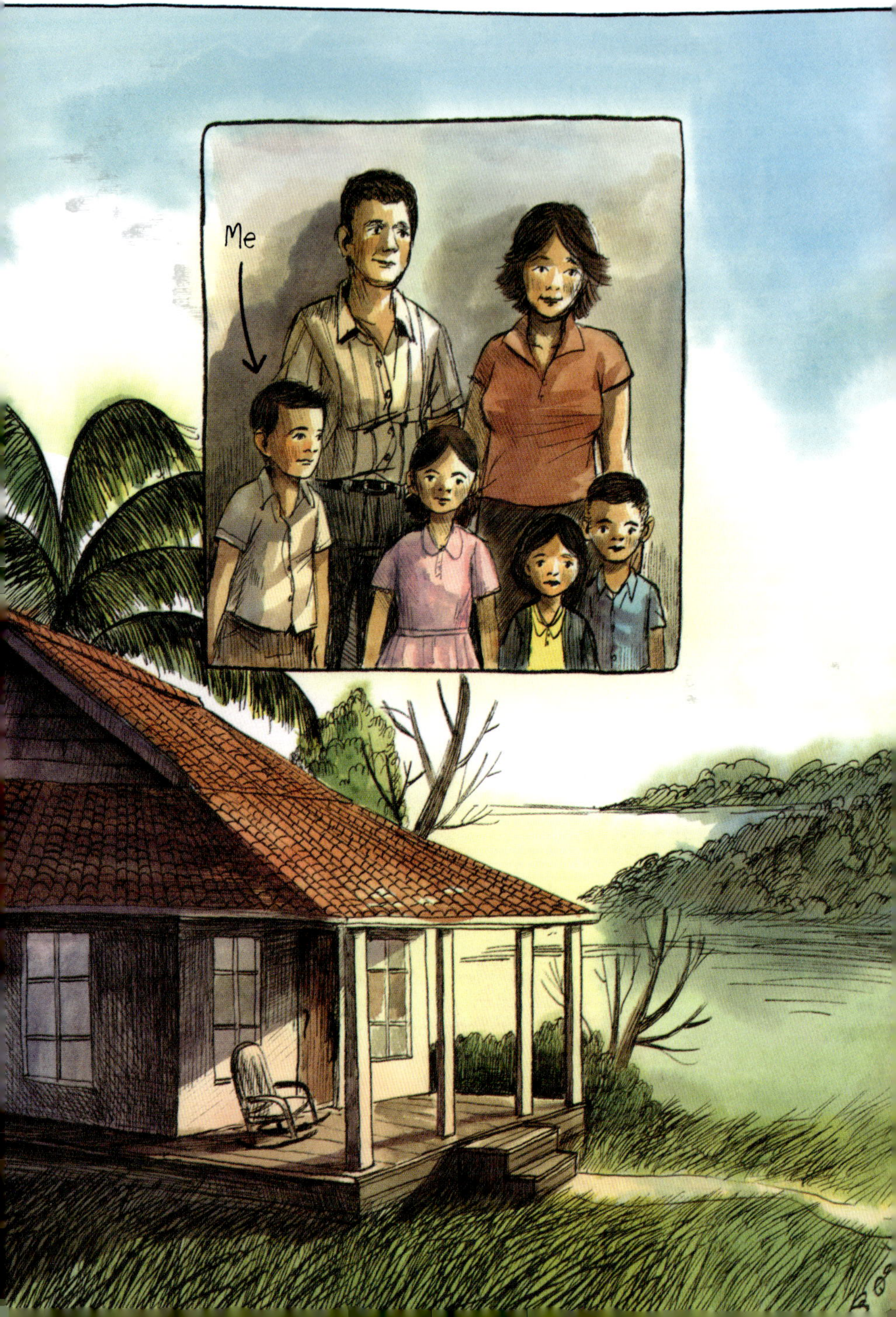
Me

Down the way was my tía's house, and across the road, our abuelos' sugarcane farm.

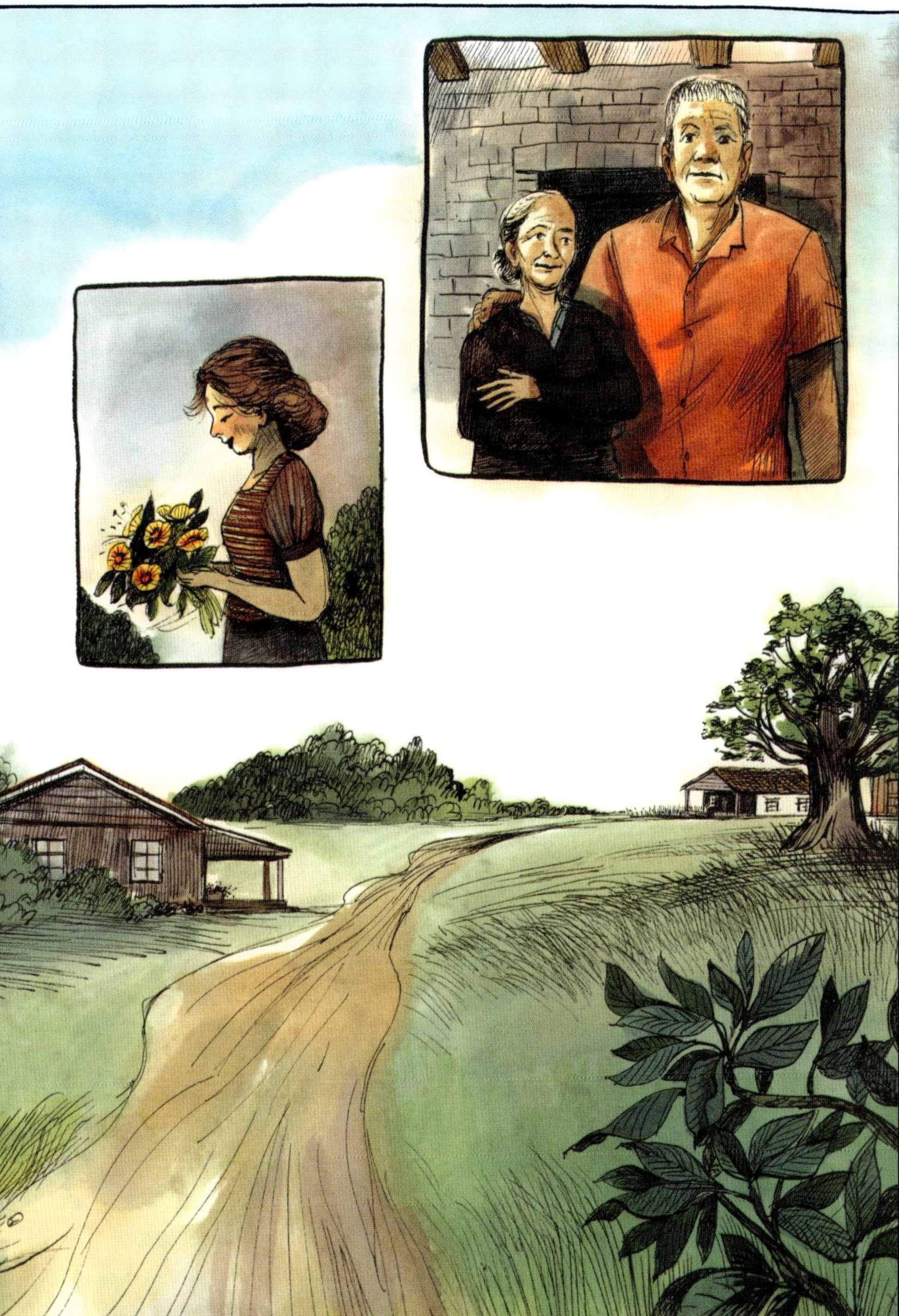

Fidel Castro and eighty-one other rebels return to Cuba aboard a sixty-foot yacht called Granma after a year in exile. Their plan? To overthrow Cuba's president, Fulgencio Batista.

Ceiba Mocha

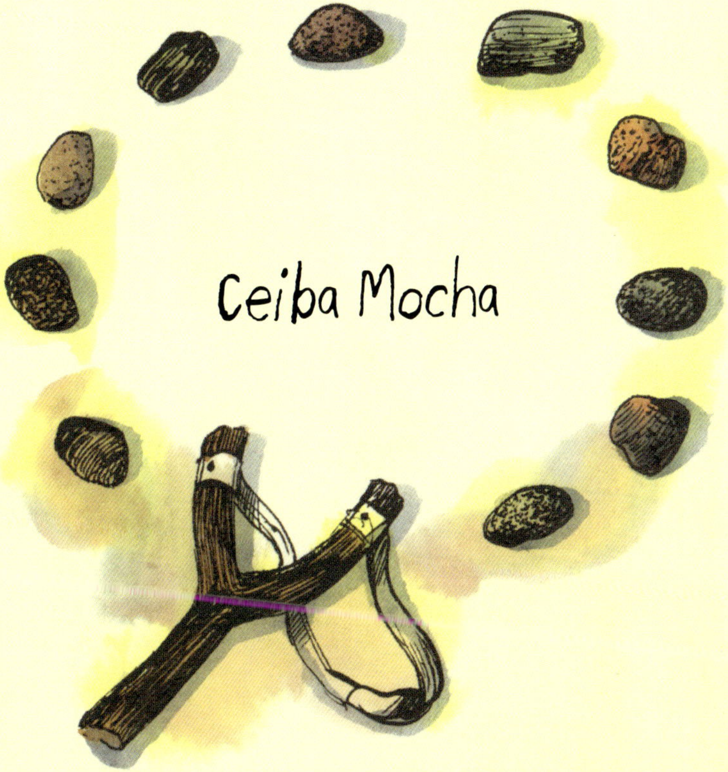

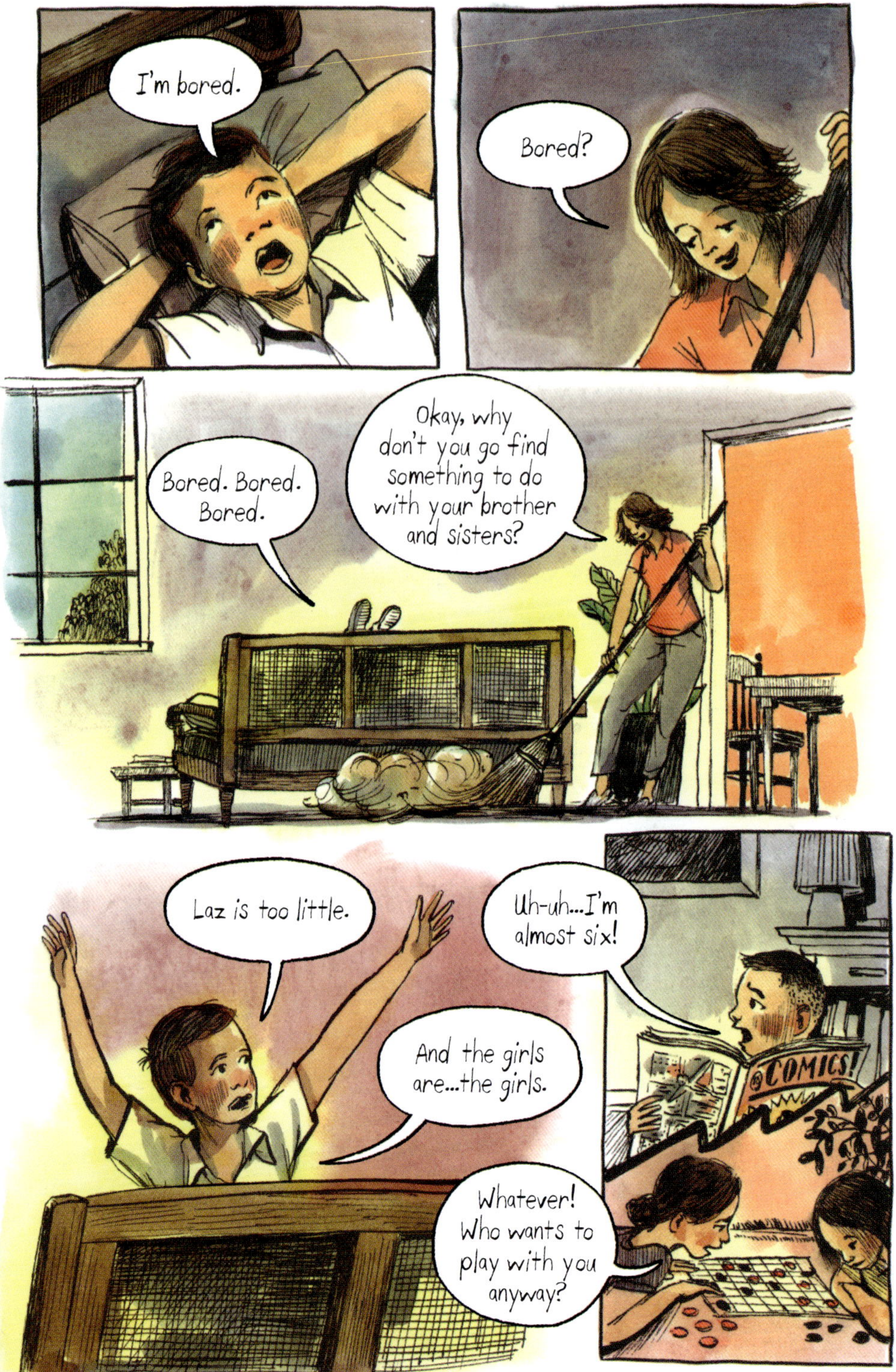
I'm bored.
Bored?
Bored. Bored. Bored.
Okay, why don't you go find something to do with your brother and sisters?
Laz is too little.
Uh-uh...I'm almost six!
COMICS!
And the girls are...the girls.
Whatever! Who wants to play with you anyway?

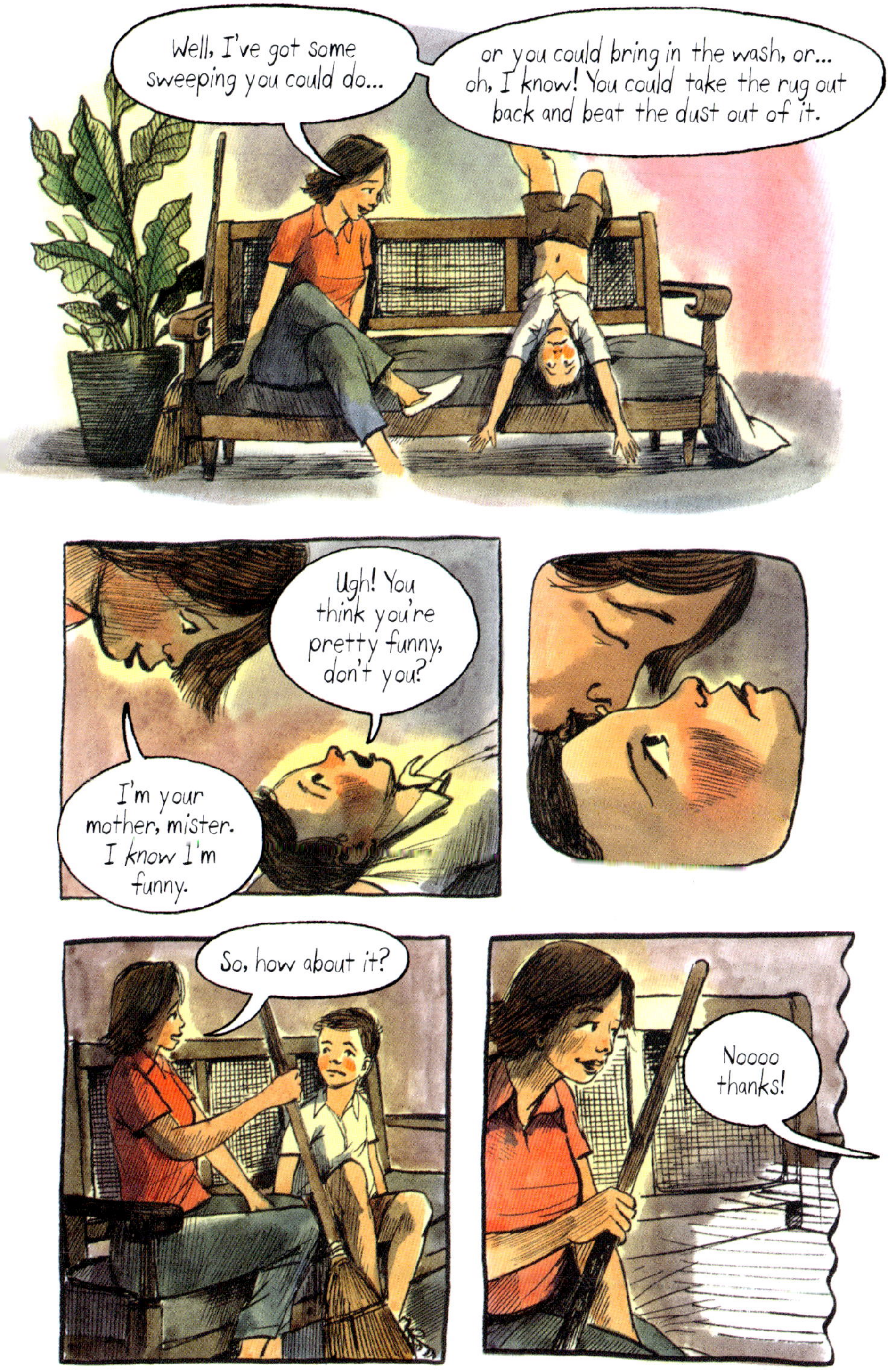
Well, I've got some sweeping you could do...
or you could bring in the wash, or... oh, I know! You could take the rug out back and beat the dust out of it.
Ugh! You think you're pretty funny, don't you?
I'm your mother, mister. I know I'm funny.
So, how about it?
Noooo thanks!

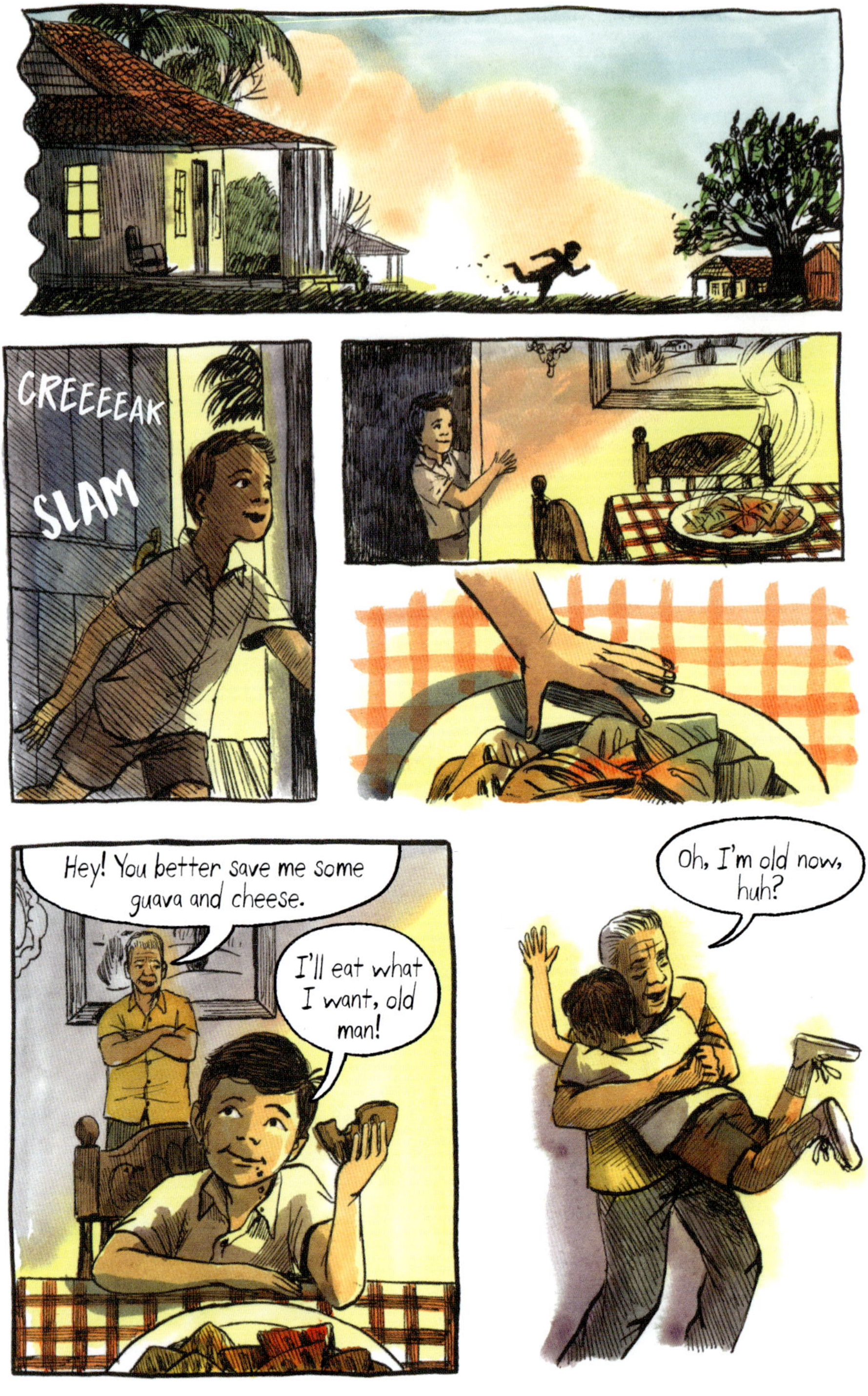
CREEEEAK
SLAM
Hey! You better save me some guava and cheese.
I'll eat what I want, old man!
Oh, I'm old now, huh?

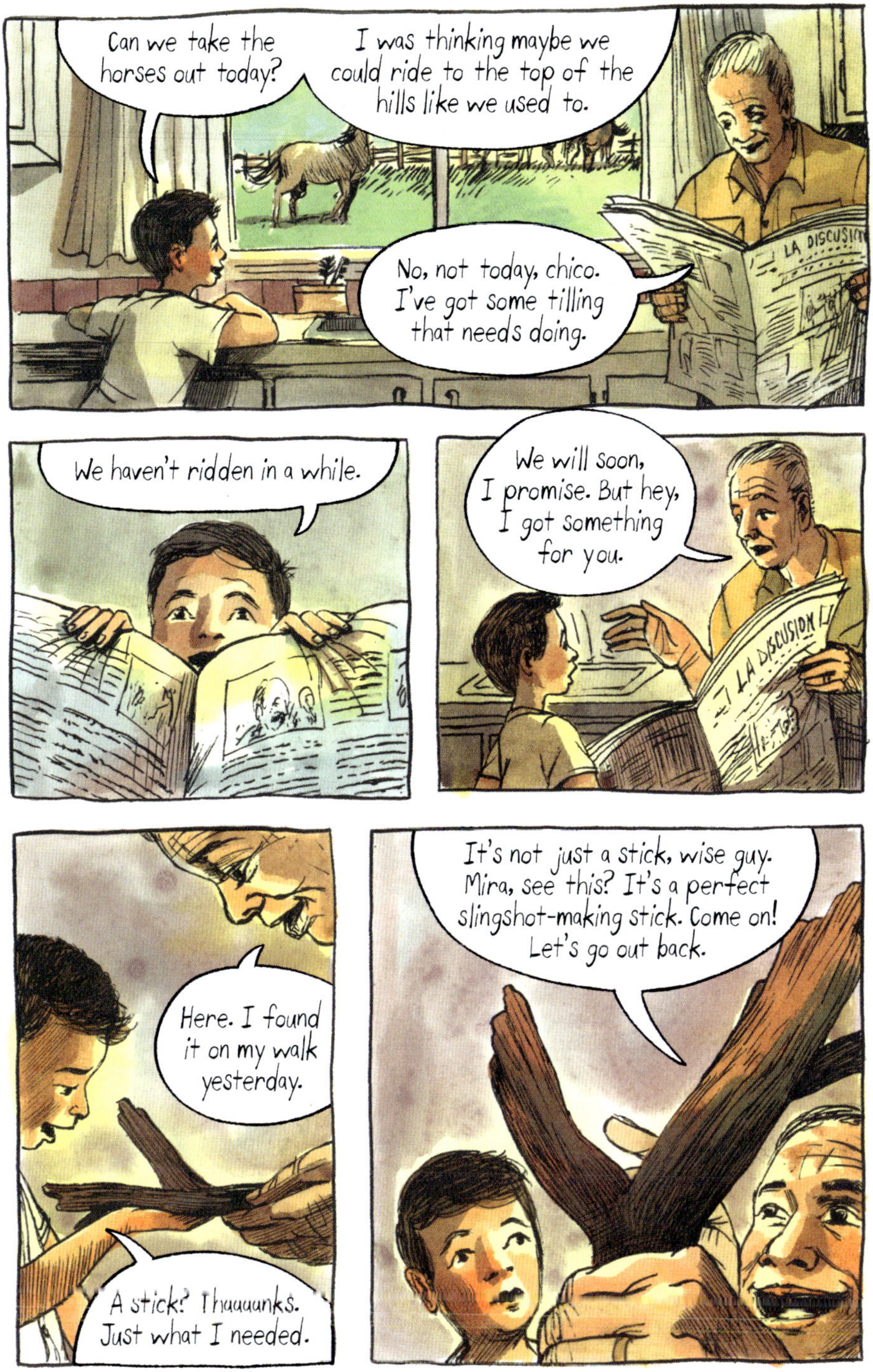
Can we take the horses out today?
I was thinking maybe we could ride to the top of the hills like we used to.
No, not today, chico. I've got some tilling that needs doing.
LA DISCUSION
We haven't ridden in a while.
We will soon, I promise. But hey, I got something for you.
LA DISCUSION
Here. I found it on my walk yesterday.
A stick? Thauuunks. Just what I needed.
It's not just a stick, wise guy. Mira, see this? It's a perfect slingshot-making stick. Come on! Let's go out back.

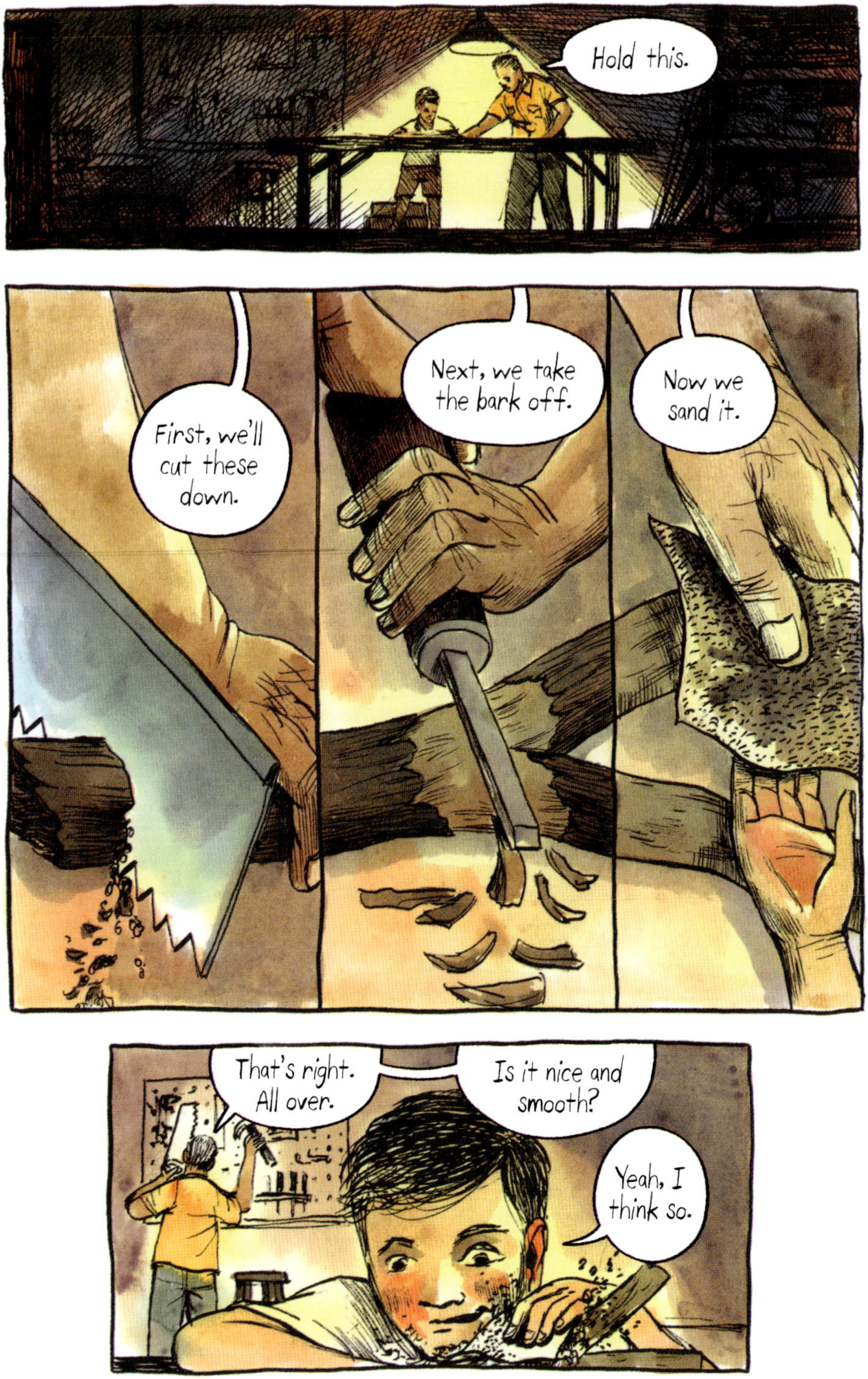
Hold this.
First, we'll cut these down.
Next, we take the bark off.
Now we sand it.
That's right. All over.
Is it nice and smooth?
Yeah, I think so.

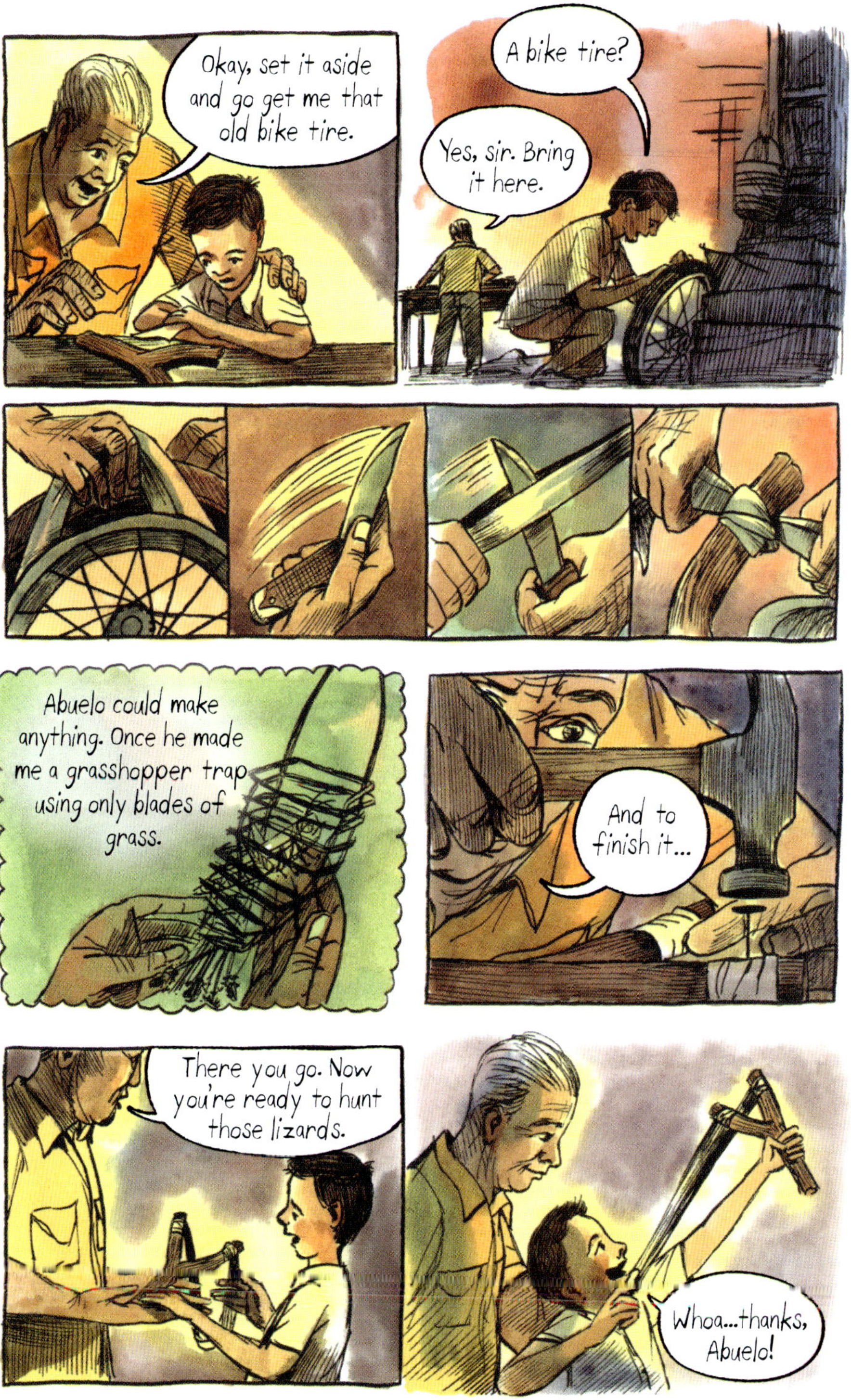
Okay, set it aside and go get me that old bike tire.
A bike tire?
Yes, sir. Bring it here.
Abuelo could make anything. Once he made me a grasshopper trap using only blades of grass.
And to finish it...
There you go. Now you're ready to hunt those lizards.
Whoa...thanks, Abuelo!

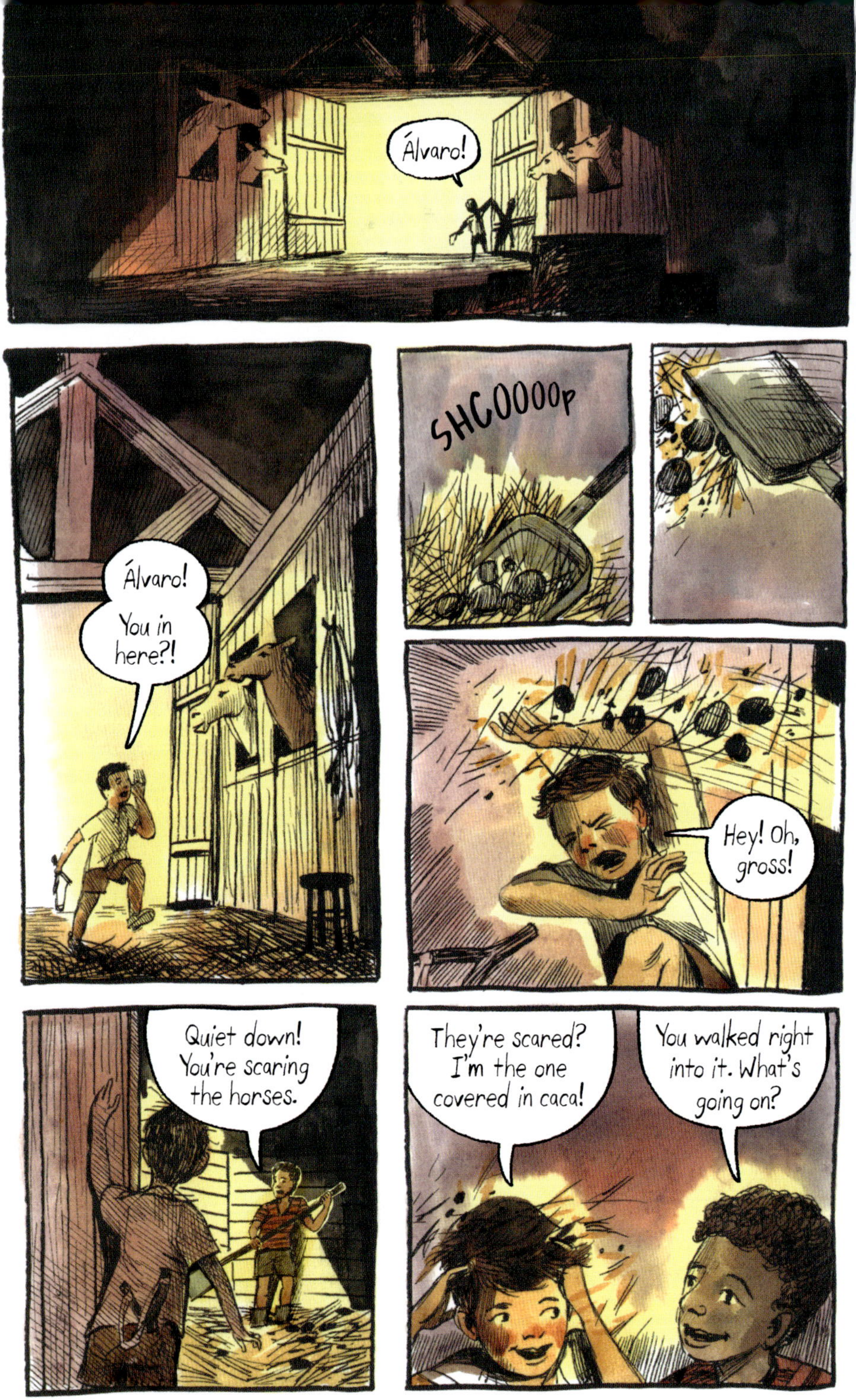
Álvaro!
Álvaro! You in here?!
SHCOOOOp
Hey! Oh, gross!
Quiet down! You're scaring the horses.
They're scared? I'm the one covered in caca!
You walked right into it. What's going on?

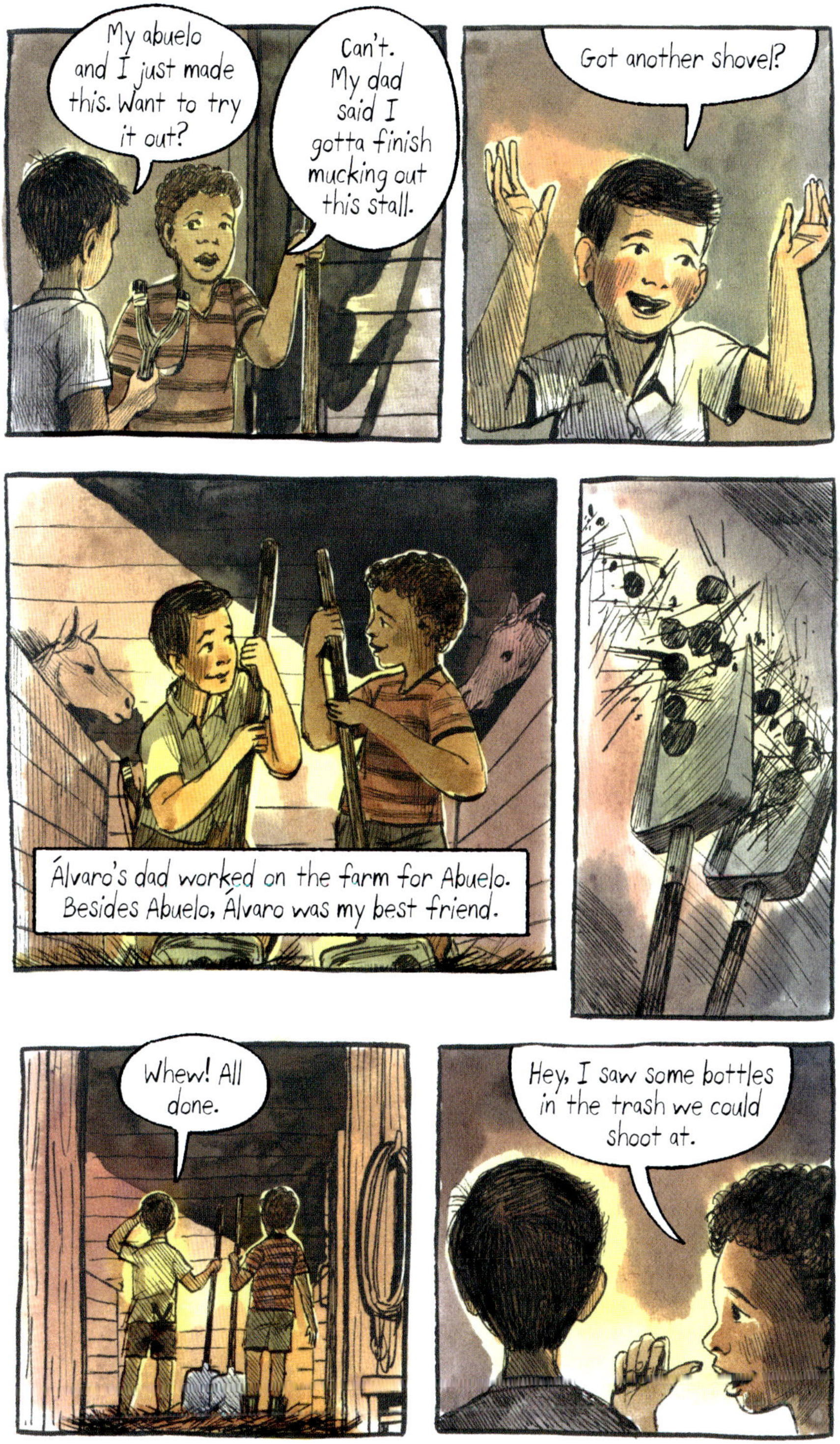
My abuelo and I just made this. Want to try it out?
Can't. My dad said I gotta finish mucking out this stall.
Got another shovel?
Álvaro's dad worked on the farm for Abuelo. Besides Abuelo, Álvaro was my best friend.
Whew! All done.
Hey, I saw some bottles in the trash we could shoot at.

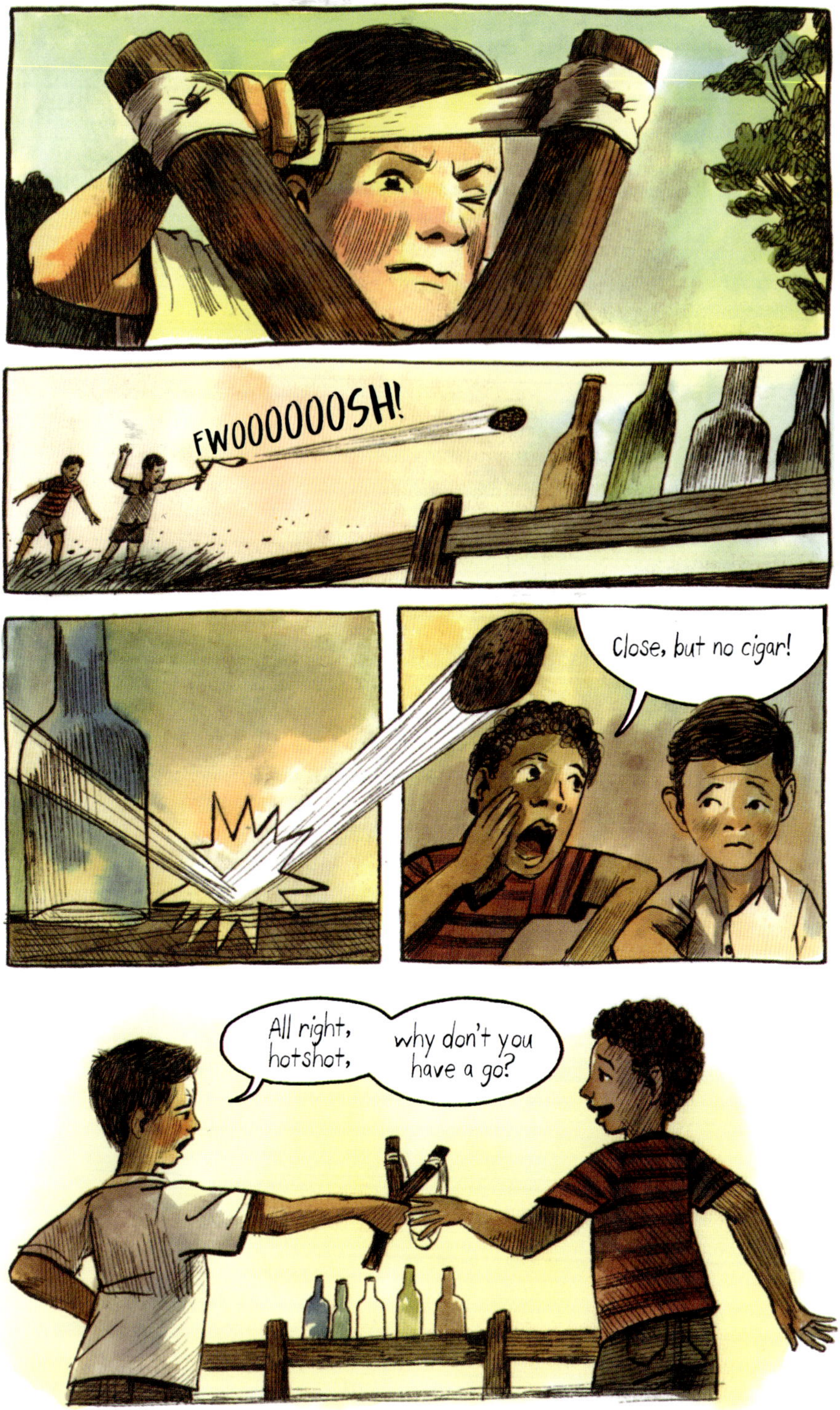
FWOOOOOOSH!
Close, but no cigar!
All right, hotshot,
why don't you have a go?

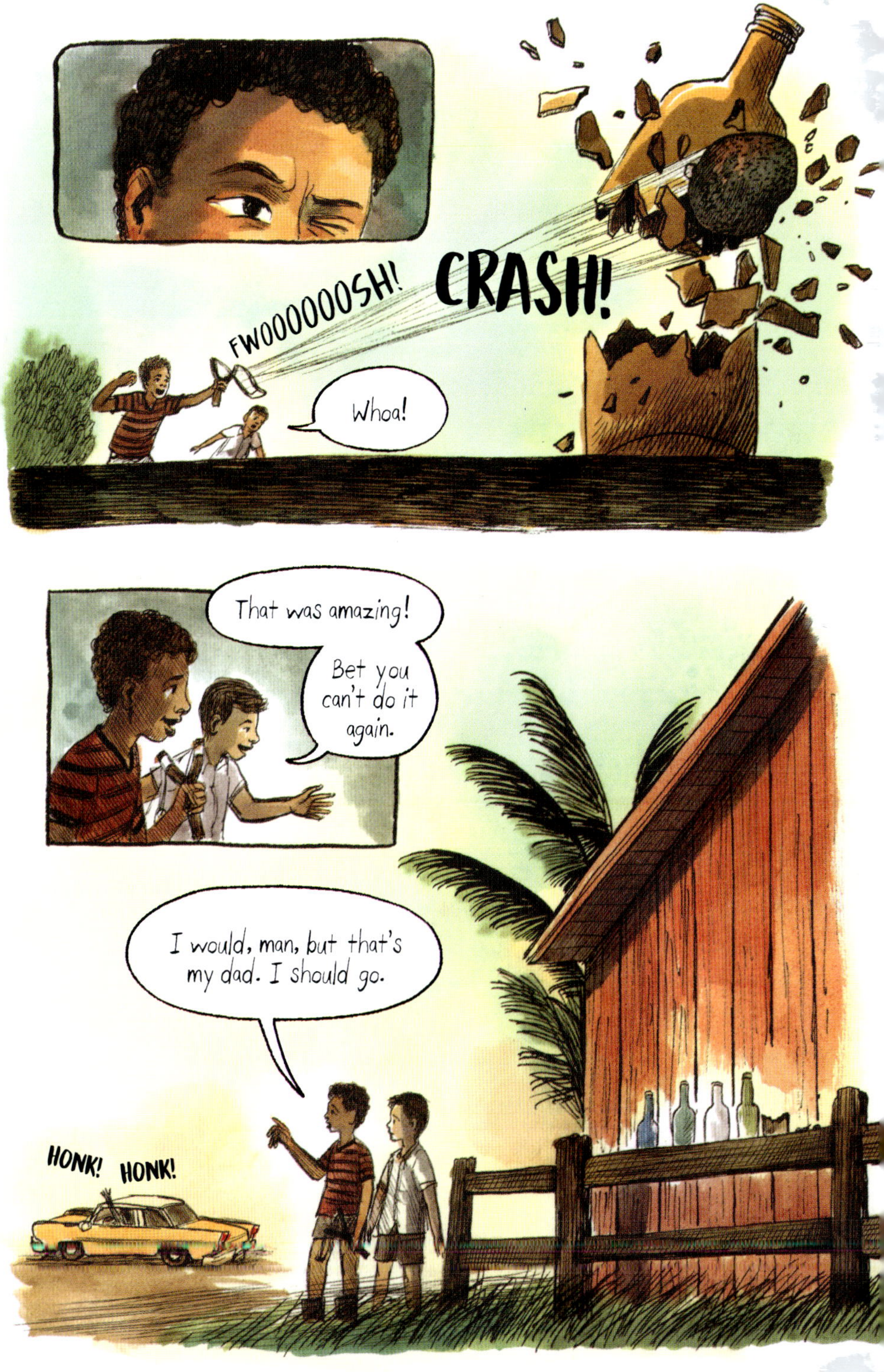
FWOOOOOOSH!
CRASH!
Whoa!
That was amazing!
Bet you can't do it again.
I would, man, but that's my dad. I should go.
HONK! HONK!

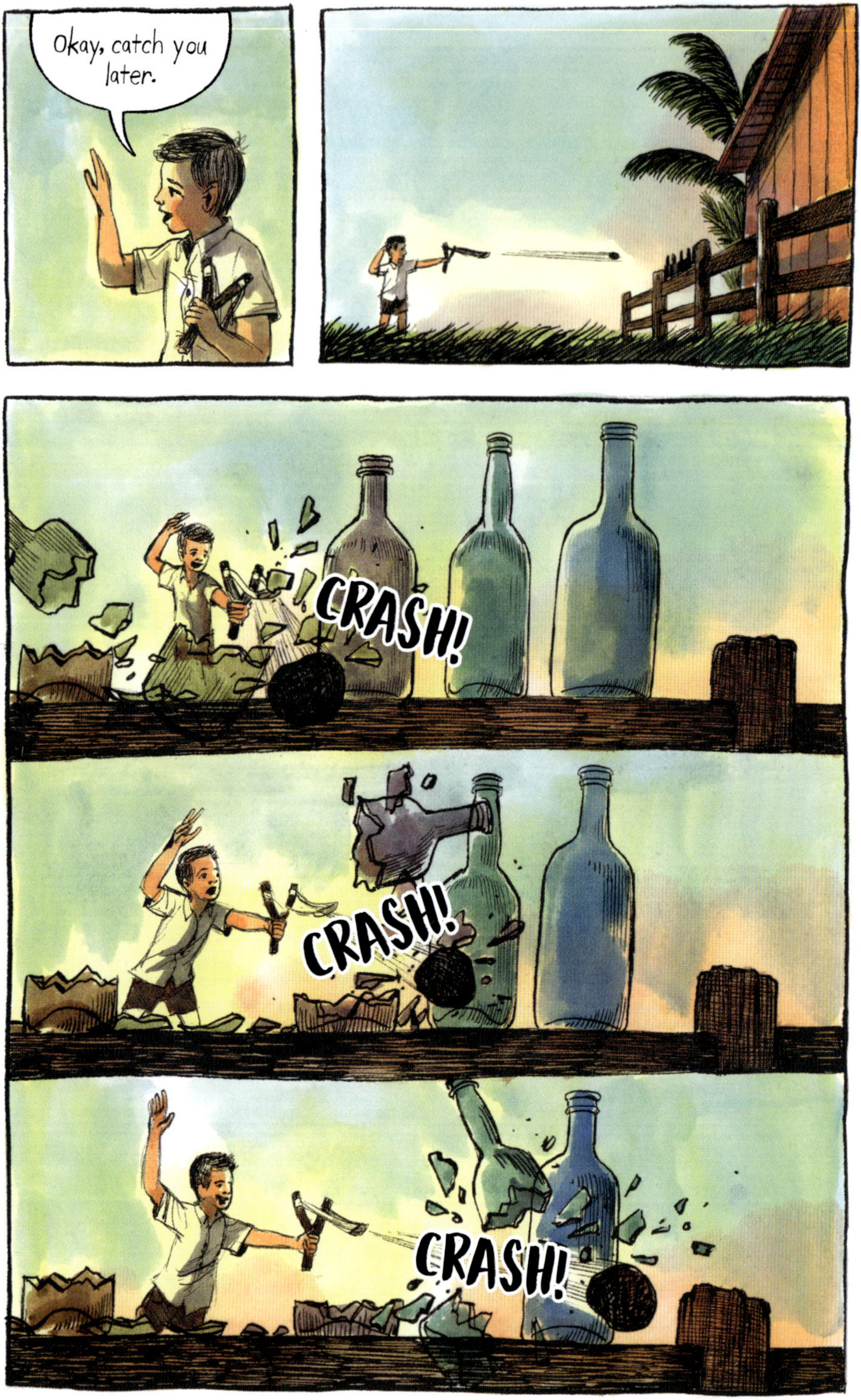
Okay, catch you later.
CRASH!
CRASH!
CRASH!

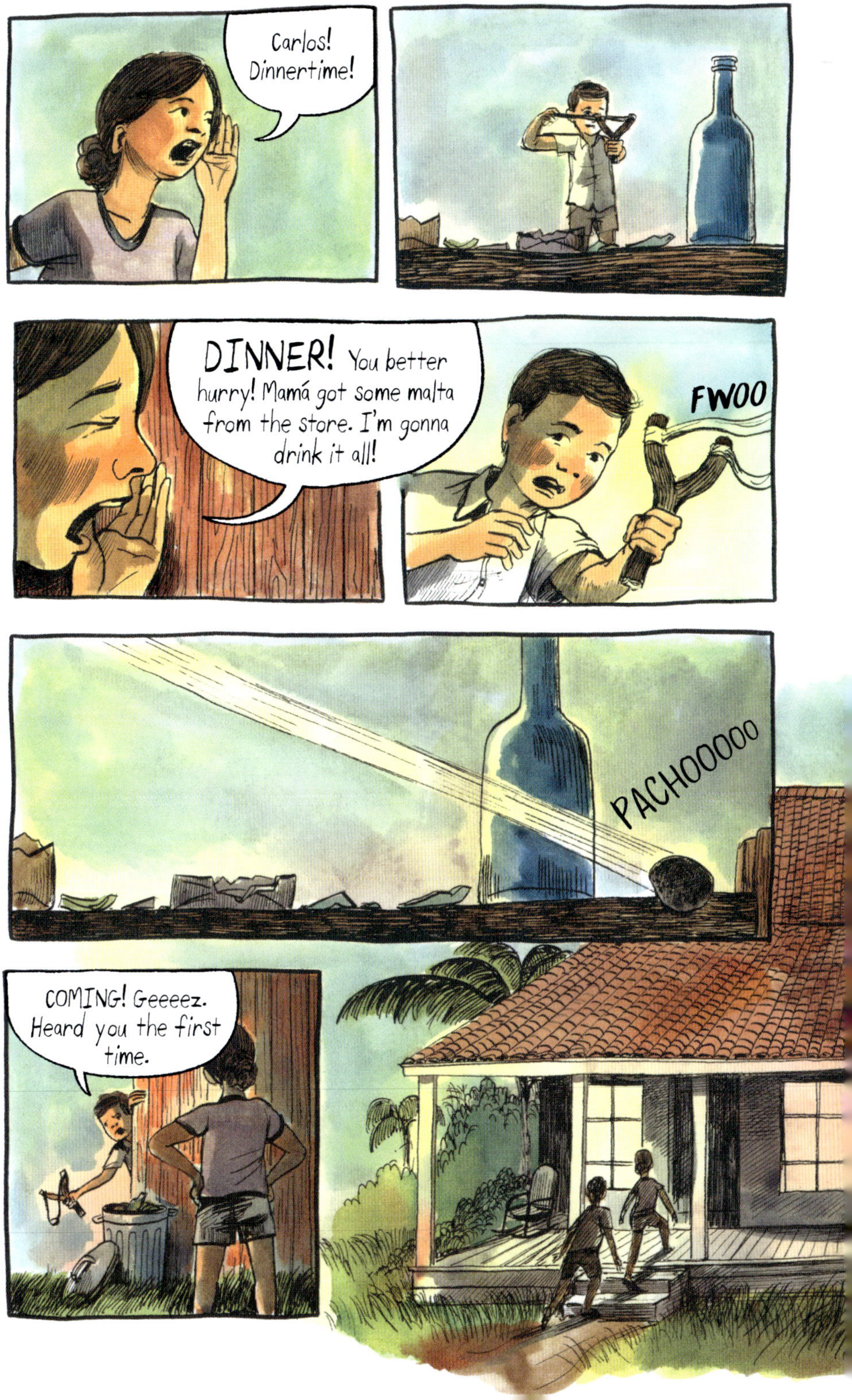
Carlos! Dinnertime!
DINNER! You better hurry! Mamá got some malta from the store. I'm gonna drink it all!
FWOO
PACHOOOOO
COMING! Geeeez. Heard you the first time.

Castro's small invading force is ambushed by President Batista's military. More than half are killed or captured, and the rest flee with the help of local farmers.

Dinnertime

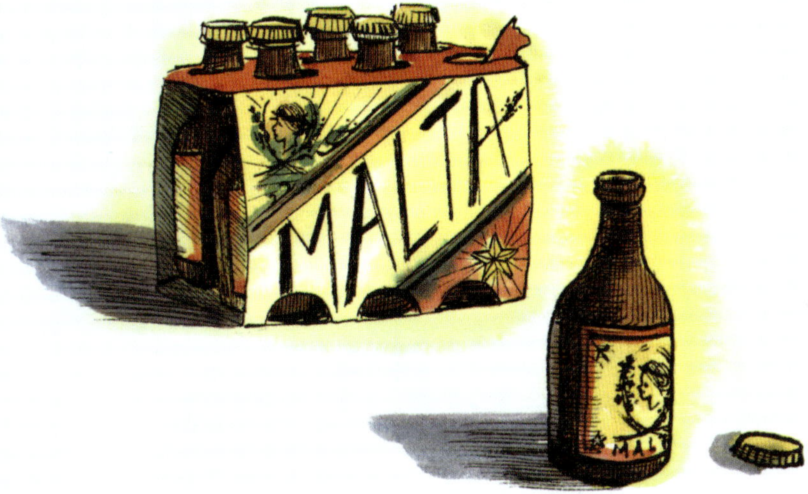
MALTA
MAL

Dinner was a time for the whole family to be together. Mamá would buzz around the kitchen, then place all the food on the table as if it were no big deal, but I had smelled the lechón asado cooking even before I'd woken up that morning!

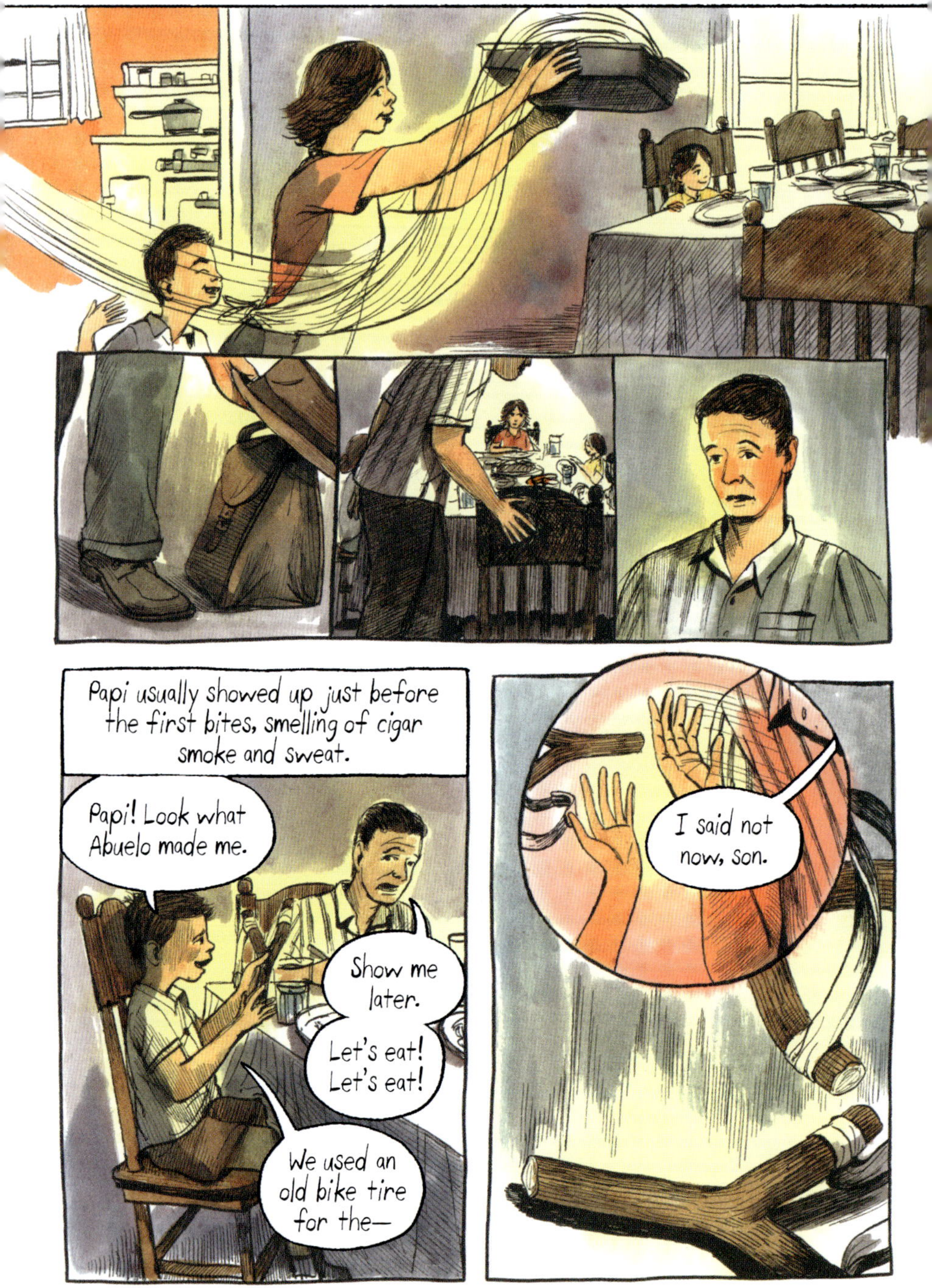
Papi usually showed up just before the first bites, smelling of cigar smoke and sweat.
Papi! Look what Abuelo made me.
Show me later.
Let's eat! Let's eat!
We used an old bike tire for the—
I said not now, son.

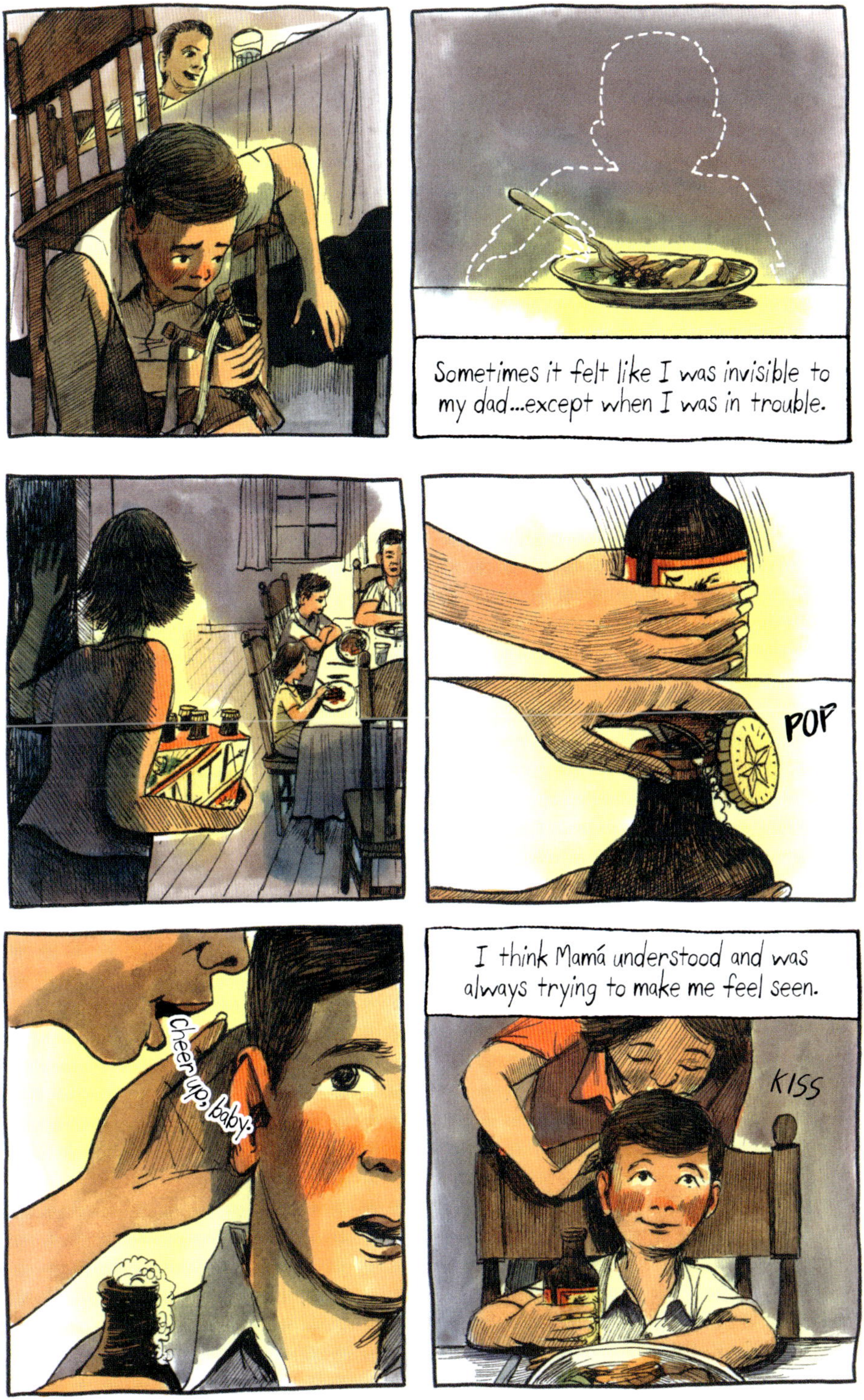
Sometimes it felt like I was invisible to my dad...except when I was in trouble.
POP
Cheer up, baby.
I think Mamá understood and was always trying to make me feel seen.
KISS

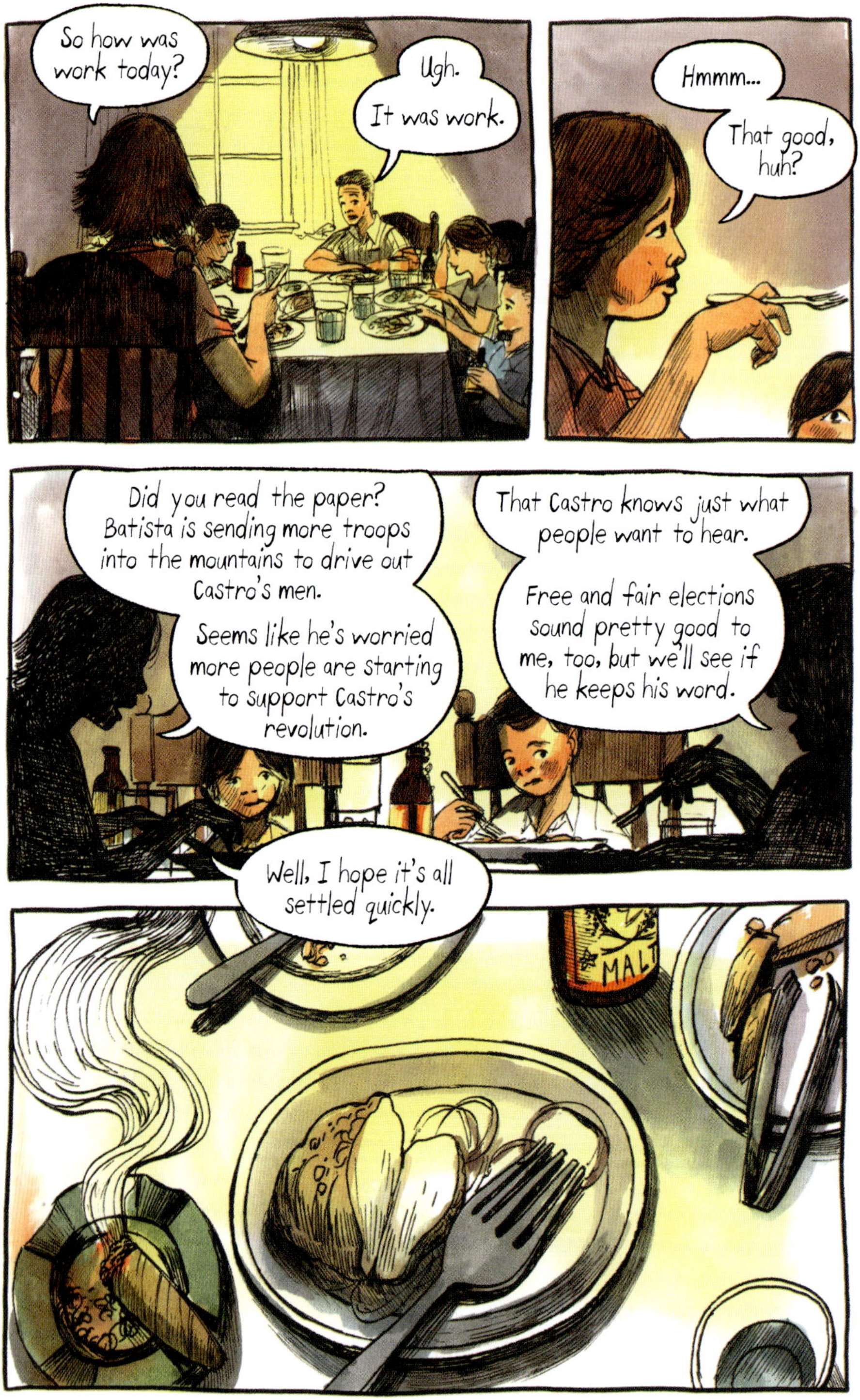
So how was work today?
Ugh.
It was work.
Hmmm...
That good, huh?
Did you read the paper? Batista is sending more troops into the mountains to drive out Castro's men.
Seems like he's worried more people are starting to support Castro's revolution.
That Castro knows just what people want to hear.
Free and fair elections sound pretty good to me, too, but we'll see if he keeps his word.
Well, I hope it's all settled quickly.
MALT

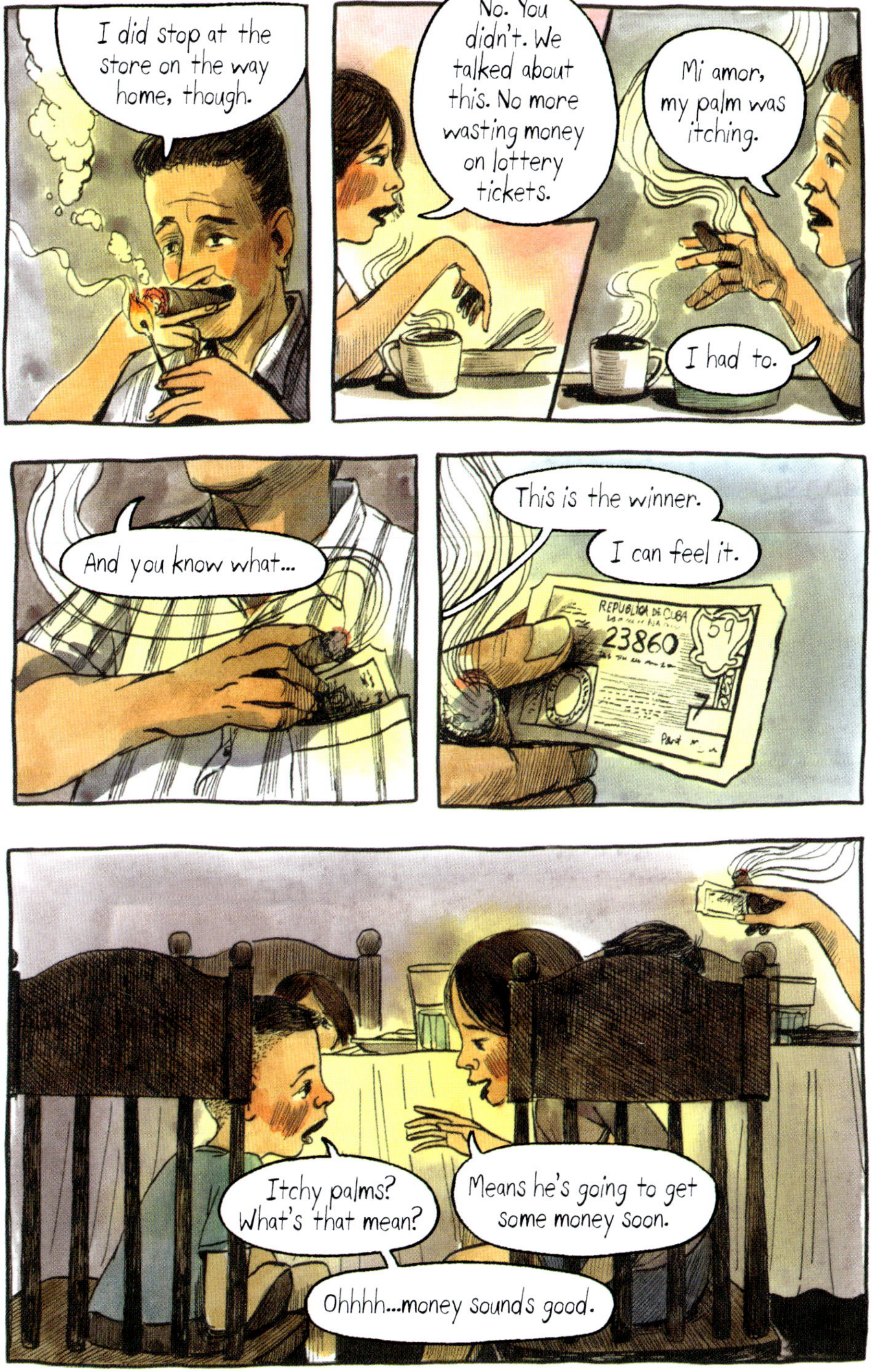
I did stop at the store on the way home, though.
No. You didn't. We talked about this. No more wasting money on lottery tickets.
Mi amor, my palm was itching.
I had to.
And you know what...
This is the winner.
I can feel it.
REPÚBLICA DE CUBA
23860
59
Itchy palms? What's that mean?
Means he's going to get some money soon.
Ohhhh...money sounds good.

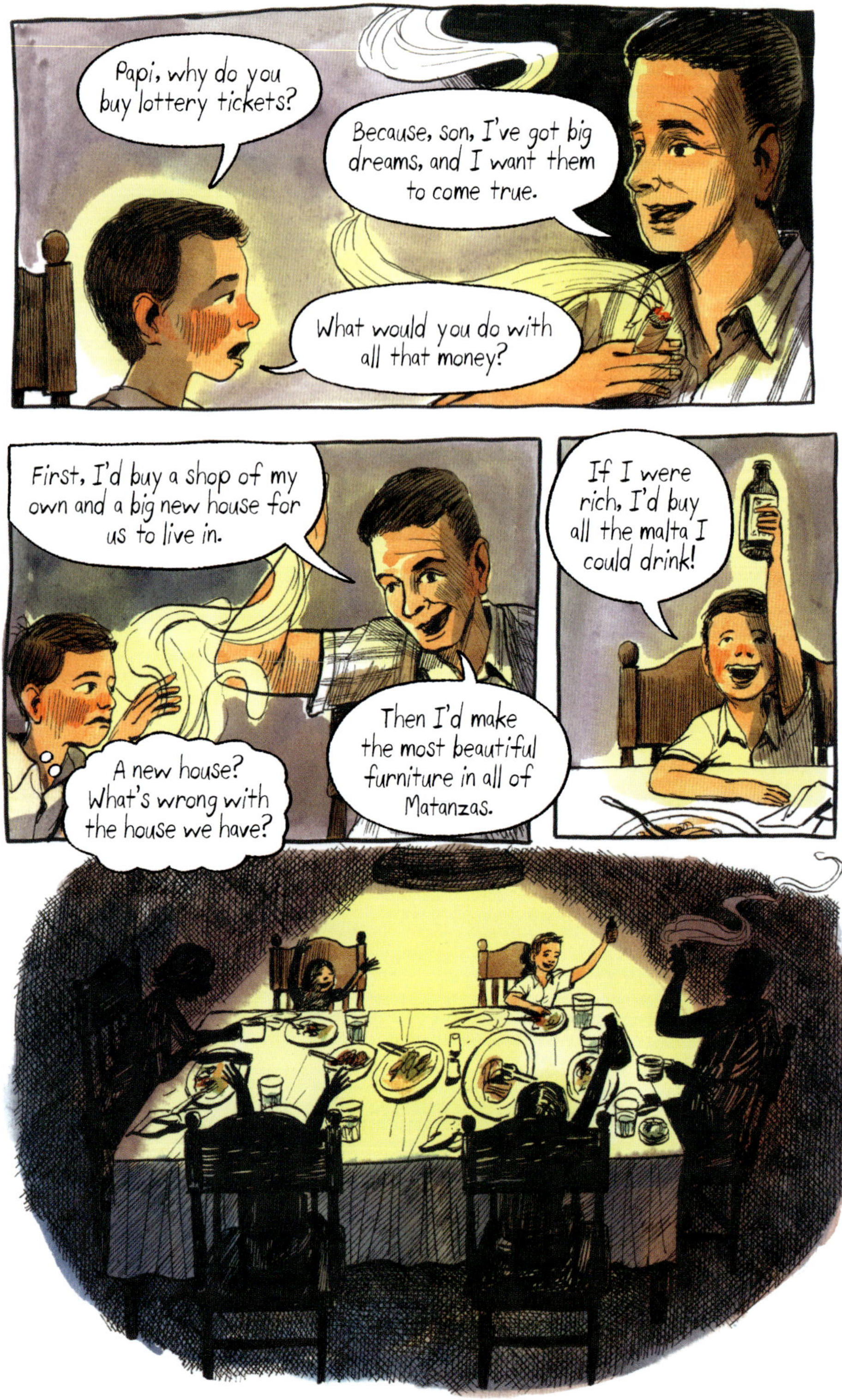
Papi, why do you buy lottery tickets?
Because, son, I've got big dreams, and I want them to come true.
What would you do with all that money?
First, I'd buy a shop of my own and a big new house for us to live in.
A new house? What's wrong with the house we have?
Then I'd make the most beautiful furniture in all of Matanzas.
If I were rich, I'd buy all the malta I could drink!

Castro and his guerrilla fighters regroup and set up camp in the Sierra Maestra mountains. Their numbers begin to grow. Soon they overtake a military post in La Plata—their first victory over Batista's troops.

Saturday

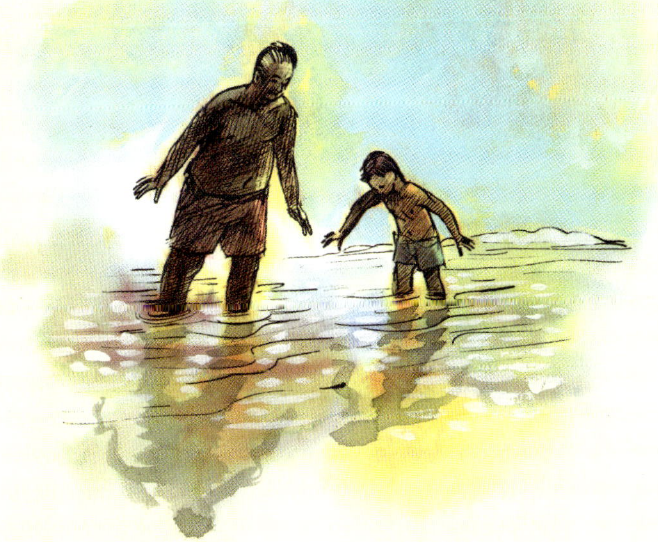

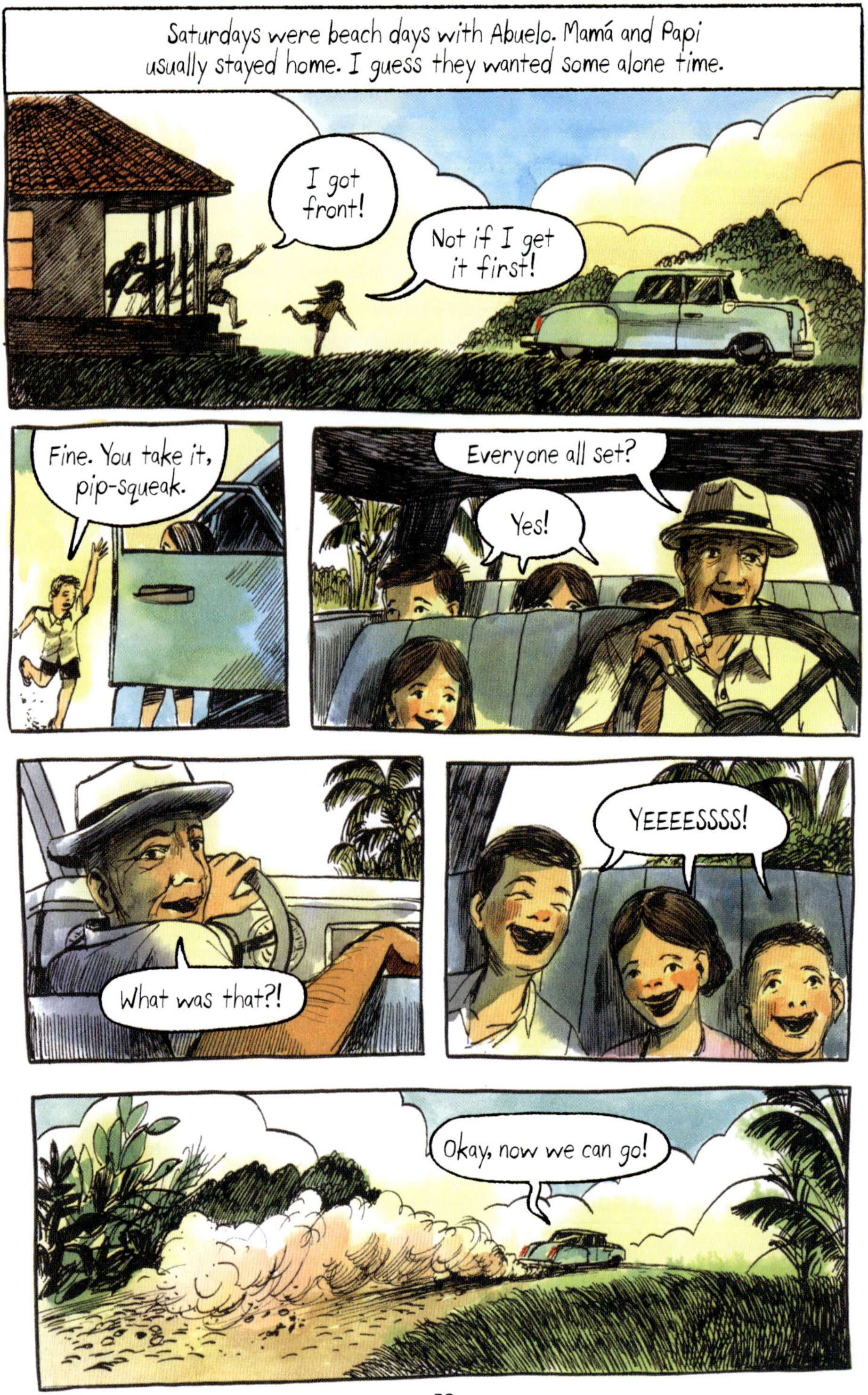
Saturdays were beach days with Abuelo. Mamá and Papi usually stayed home. I guess they wanted some alone time.
I got front!
Not if I get it first!
Fine. You take it, pip-squeak.
Everyone all set?
Yes!
What was that?!
YEEEESSSS!
Okay, now we can go!

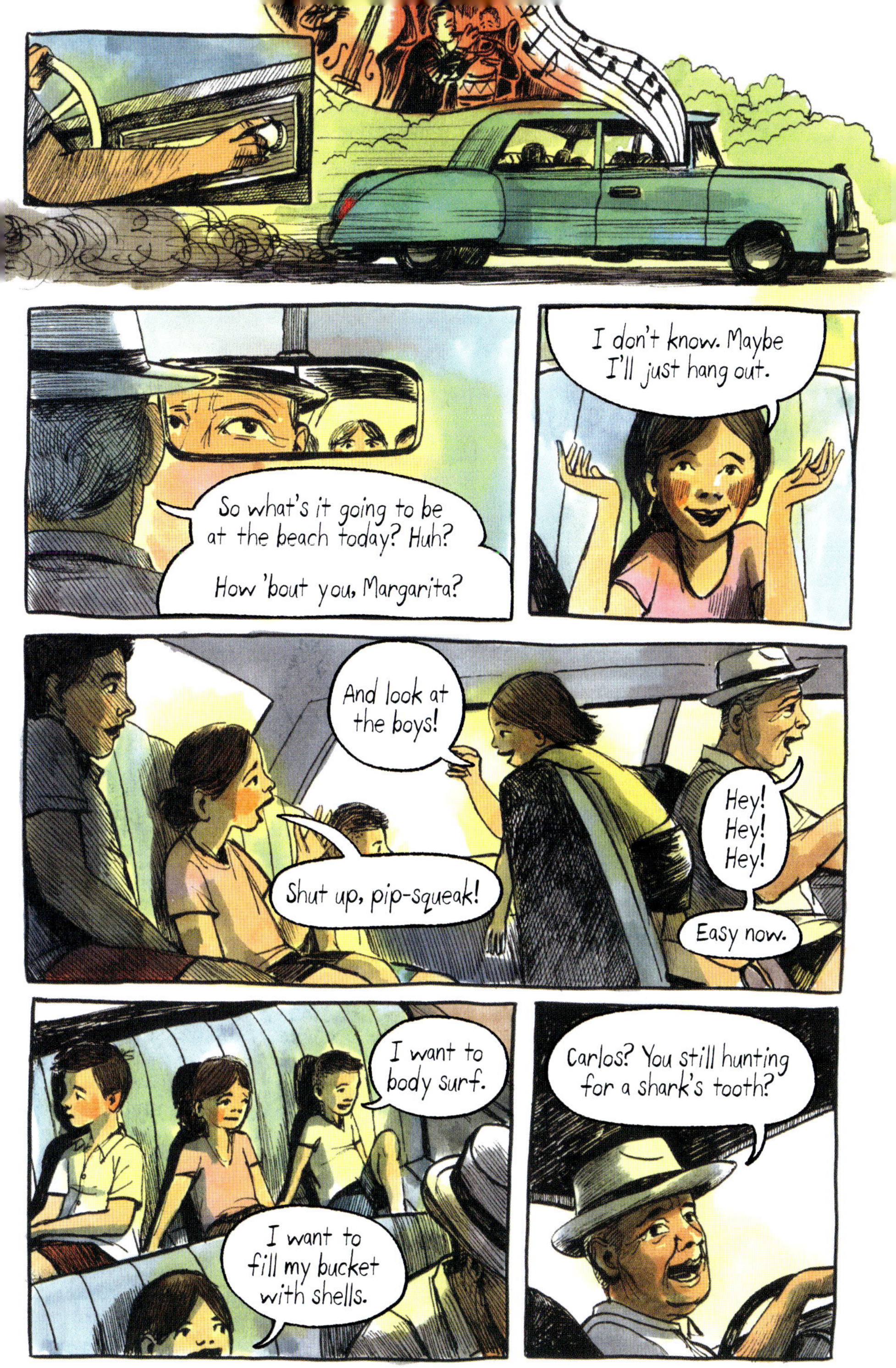

So what's it going to be at the beach today? Huh?
How 'bout you, Margarita?
I don't know. Maybe I'll just hang out.
And look at the boys!
Shut up, pip-squeak!
Hey! Hey! Hey!
Easy now.
I want to body surf.
I want to fill my bucket with shells.
Carlos? You still hunting for a shark's tooth?

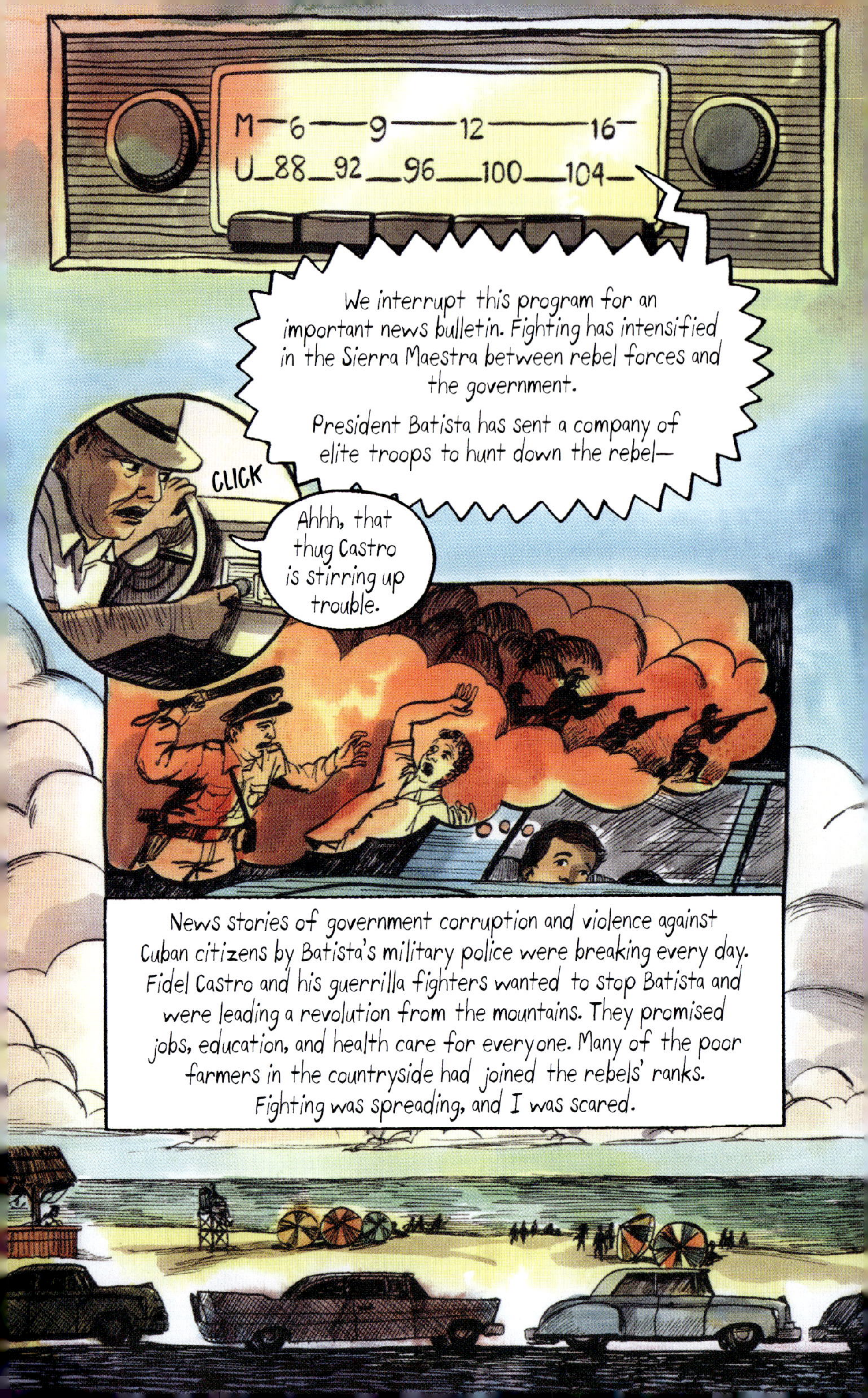

M—6—9—12—16—
U_88_92_96_100_104_
We interrupt this program for an important news bulletin. Fighting has intensified in the Sierra Maestra between rebel forces and the government.
President Batista has sent a company of elite troops to hunt down the rebel—
CLICK
Ahhh, that thug Castro is stirring up trouble.
News stories of government corruption and violence against Cuban citizens by Batista's military police were breaking every day. Fidel Castro and his guerrilla fighters wanted to stop Batista and were leading a revolution from the mountains. They promised jobs, education, and health care for everyone. Many of the poor farmers in the countryside had joined the rebels' ranks. Fighting was spreading, and I was scared.

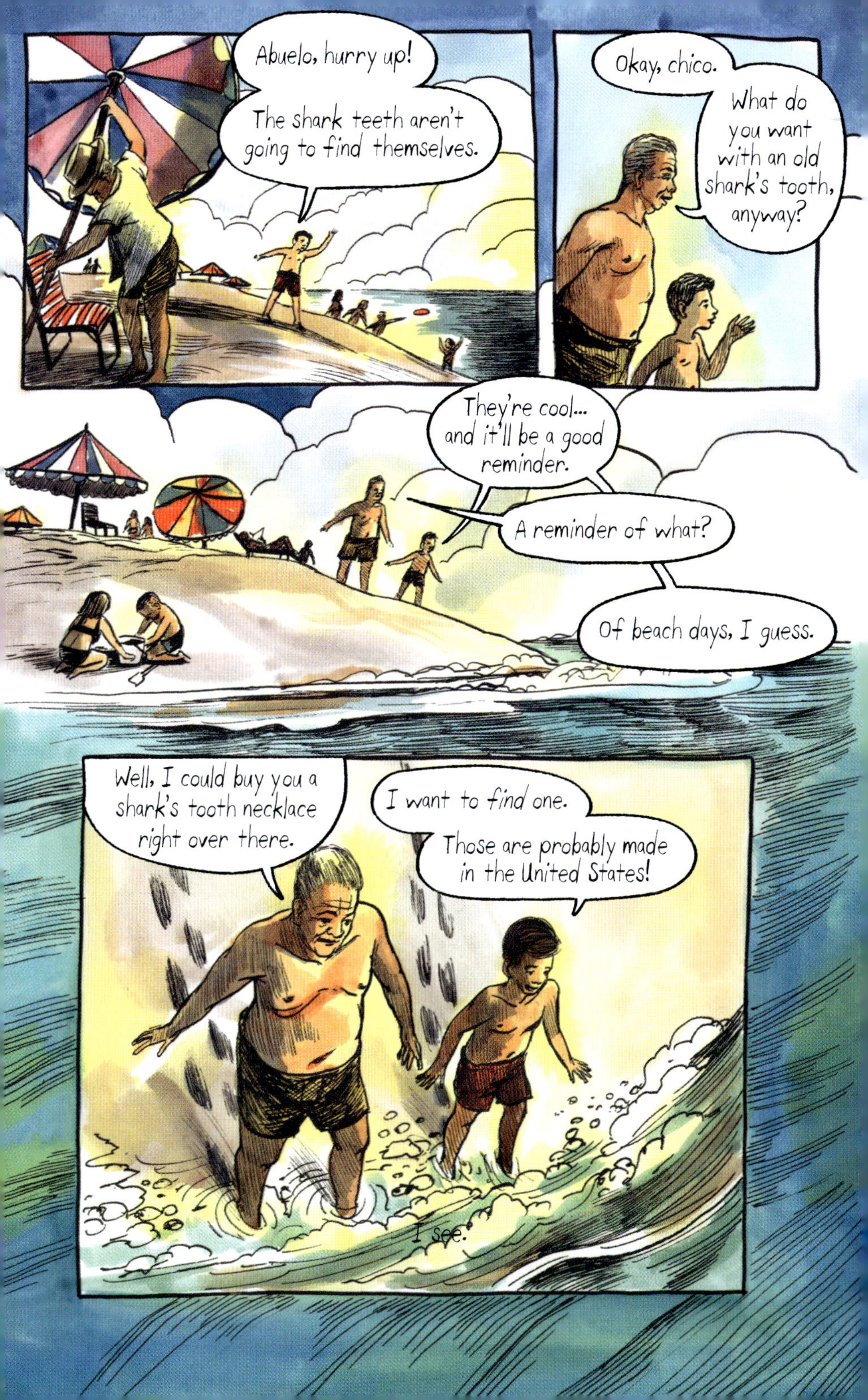
Abuelo, hurry up!
The shark teeth aren't going to find themselves.
Okay, chico.
What do you want with an old shark's tooth, anyway?
They're cool... and it'll be a good reminder.
A reminder of what?
Of beach days, I guess.
Well, I could buy you a shark's tooth necklace right over there.
I want to find one.
Those are probably made in the United States!
I see.

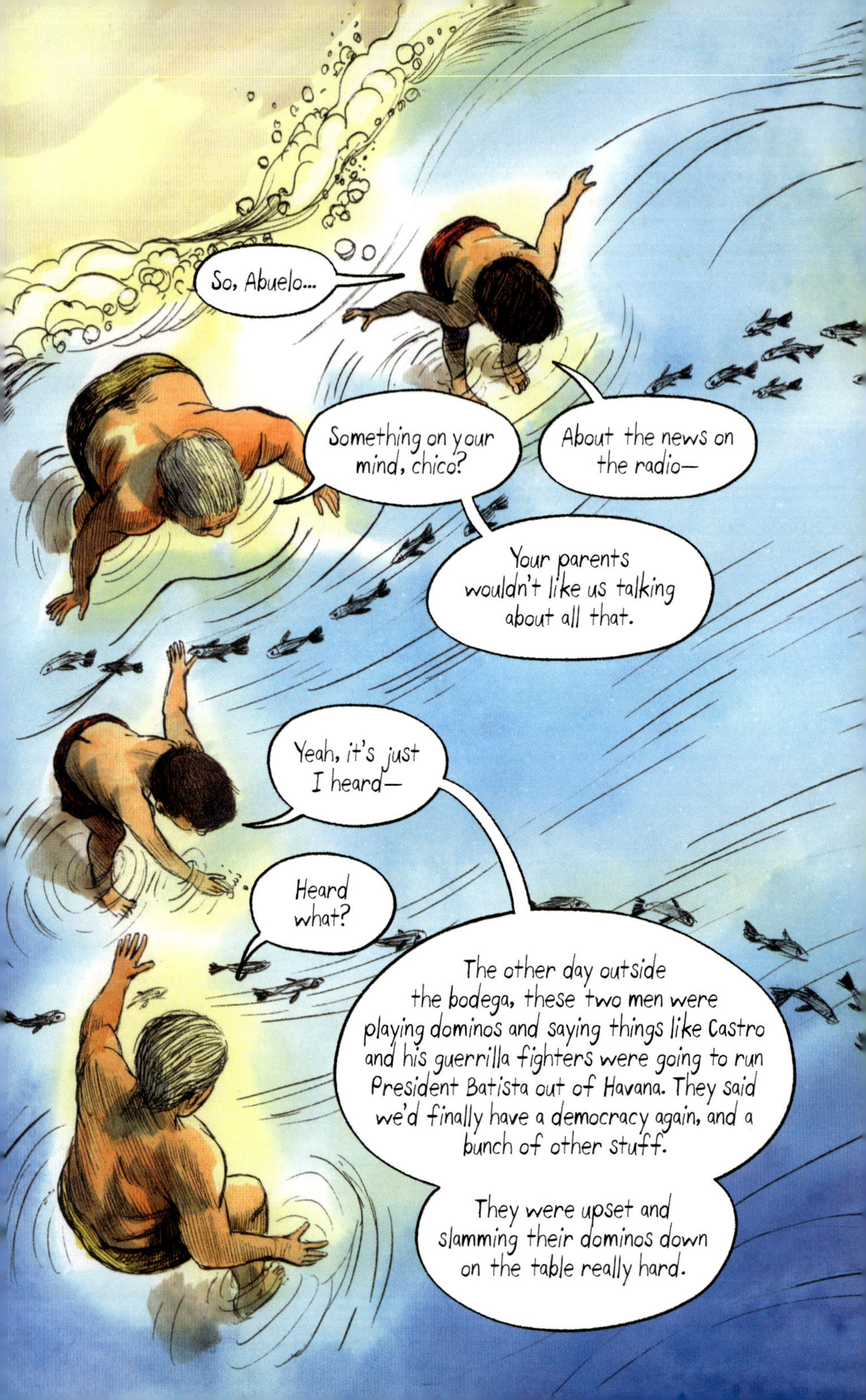
So, Abuelo...
Something on your mind, chico?
About the news on the radio—
Your parents wouldn't like us talking about all that.
Yeah, it's just I heard—
Heard what?
The other day outside the bodega, these two men were playing dominos and saying things like Castro and his guerrilla fighters were going to run President Batista out of Havana. They said we'd finally have a democracy again, and a bunch of other stuff.
They were upset and slamming their dominos down on the table really hard.

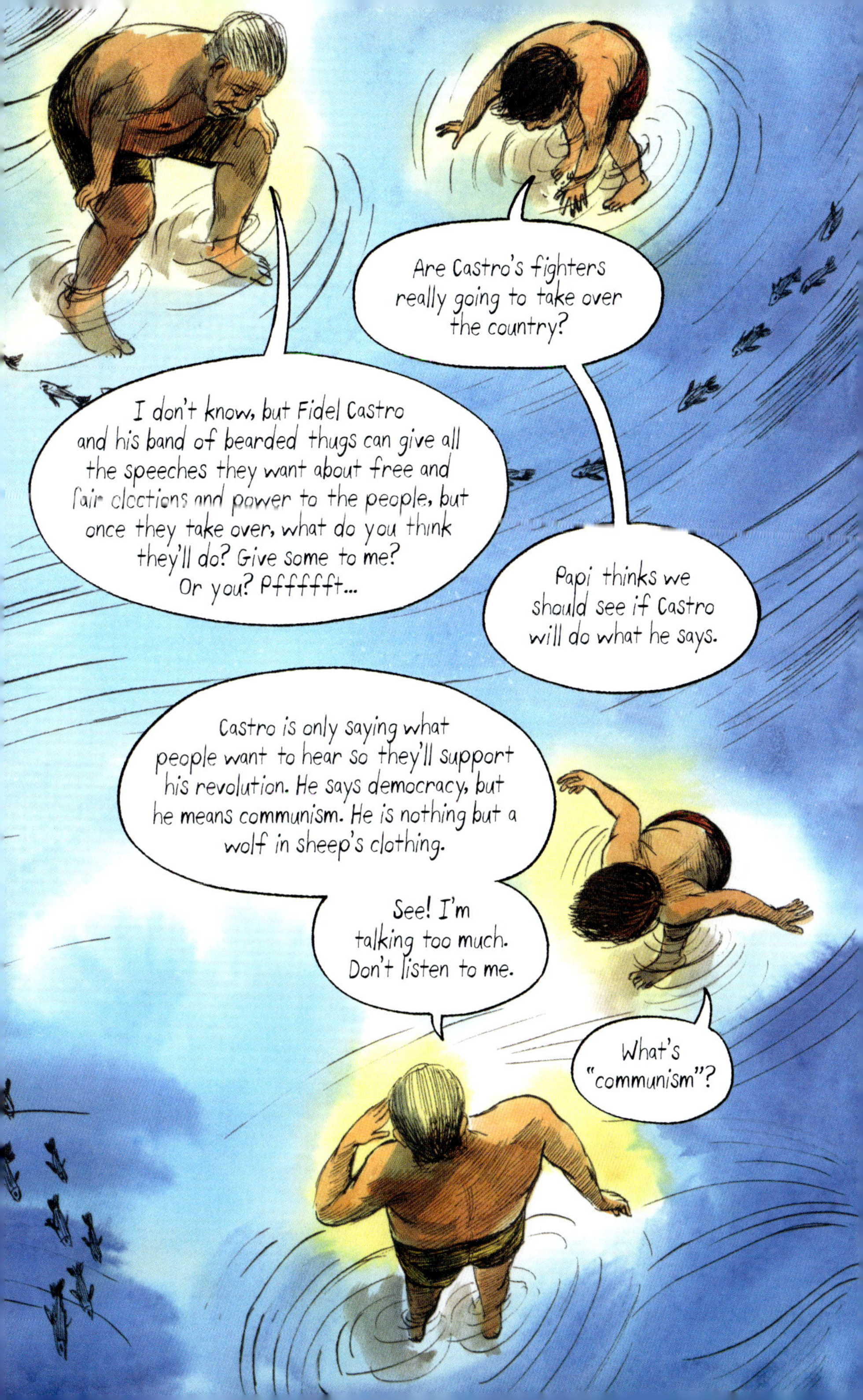
Are Castro's fighters really going to take over the country?
I don't know, but Fidel Castro and his band of bearded thugs can give all the speeches they want about free and fair elections and power to the people, but once they take over, what do you think they'll do? Give some to me? Or you? Pffffft...
Papi thinks we should see if Castro will do what he says.
Castro is only saying what people want to hear so they'll support his revolution. He says democracy, but he means communism. He is nothing but a wolf in sheep's clothing.
See! I'm talking too much. Don't listen to me.
What's "communism"?

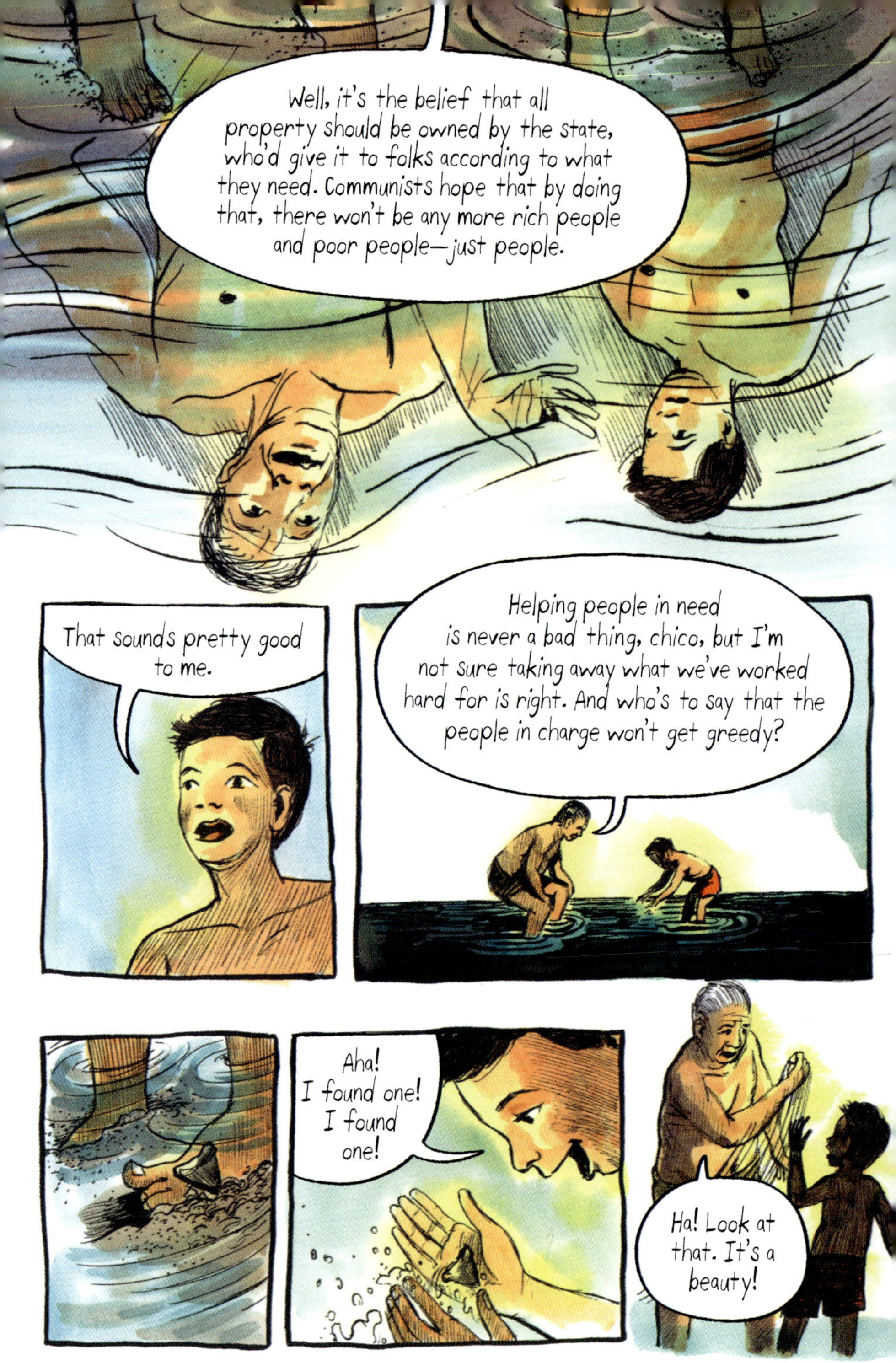
Well, it's the belief that all property should be owned by the state, who'd give it to folks according to what they need. Communists hope that by doing that, there won't be any more rich people and poor people—just people.
That sounds pretty good to me.
Helping people in need is never a bad thing, chico, but I'm not sure taking away what we've worked hard for is right. And who's to say that the people in charge won't get greedy?
Aha! I found one! I found one!
Ha! Look at that. It's a beauty!

"Hey! That's mine! I found it."

"Uh-uh, it's the state's tooth now."

"To be used as the state sees fit."

Abuelo wasn't one for subtlety.

"That's not funny. Give it back."

SNATCH!

"Soldiers, communists, and guerrilla fighters? I don't want anyone to take our home."

Castro's rebels attack one of Batista's army barracks and win a major victory. News of the battle spreads, inspiring many Cubans to join the revolution.

Lucky Numbers

One week later...

"What colors are we going to pick for the walls of our rooms at the new house?"

"Or better yet, what kind of dress is Mamá going to buy to go out dancing in on Friday nights?"

"That's enough, you!"

"Your little ticket hasn't won anything yet. Don't go filling our heads with these ideas. This house is just fine..."

My thoughts exactly!

"...and I have plenty of good dresses already. Food's getting cold."

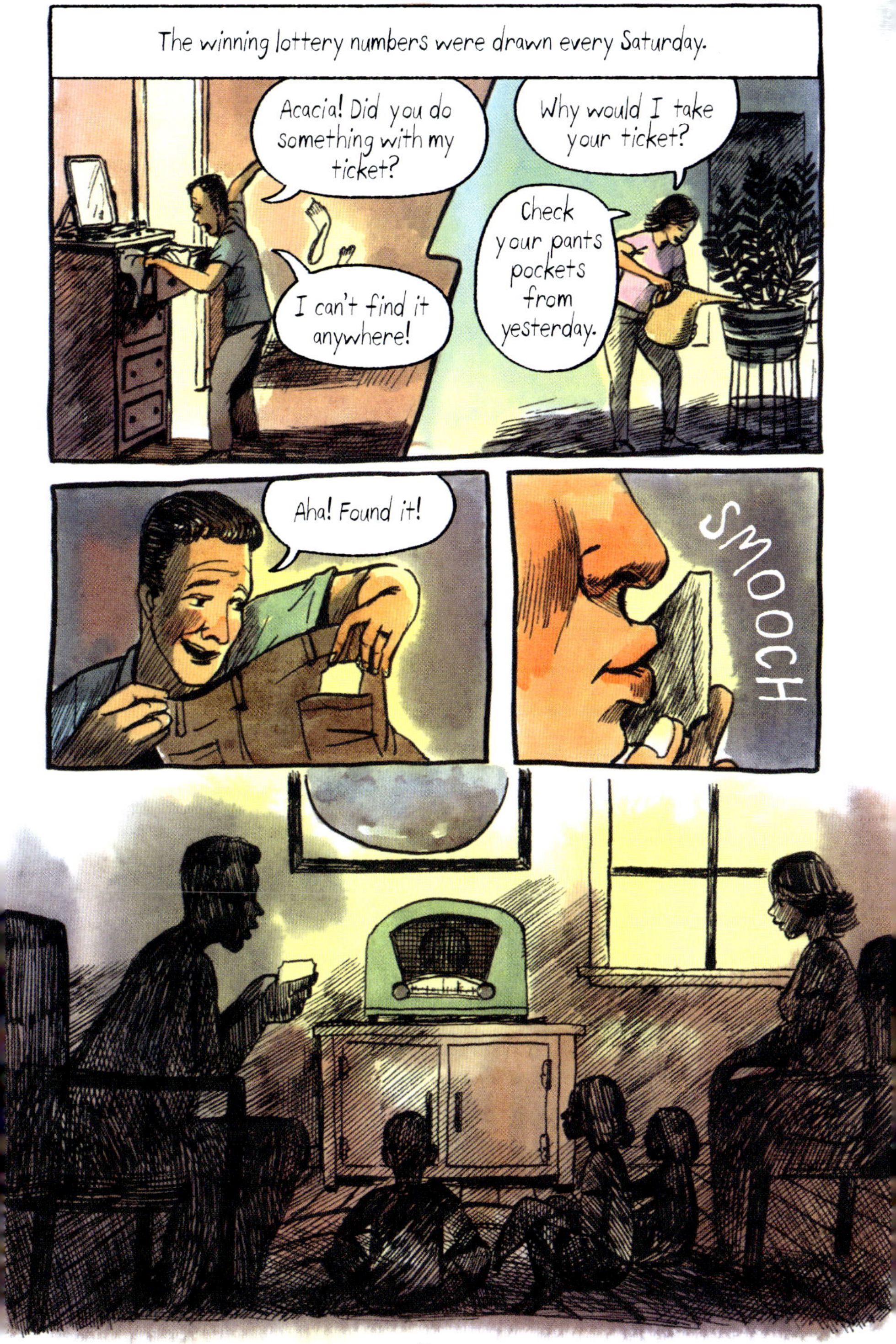
The winning lottery numbers were drawn every Saturday.
Acacia! Did you do something with my ticket?
Why would I take your ticket?
I can't find it anywhere!
Check your pants pockets from yesterday.
Aha! Found it!
SMOOCH

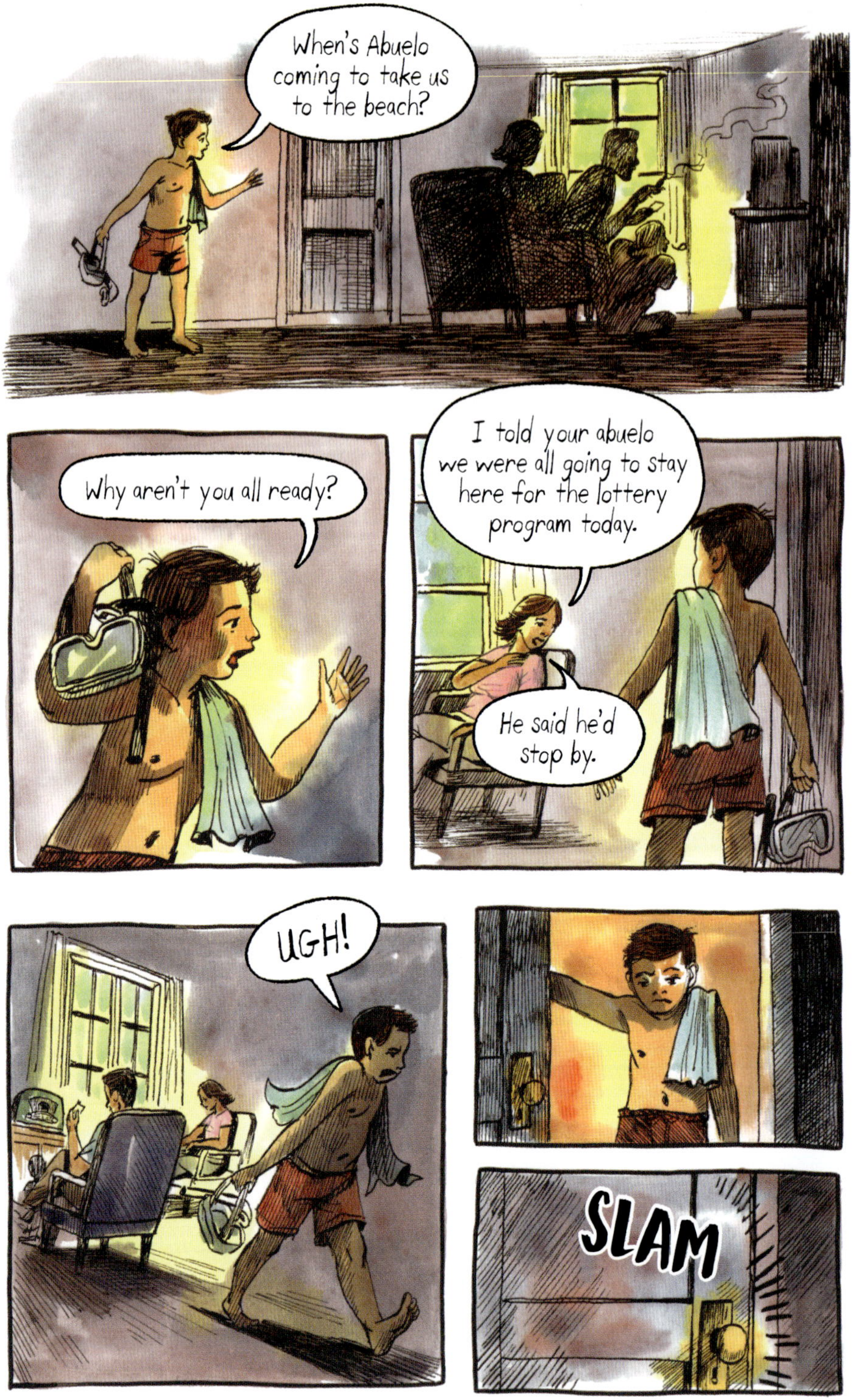
When's Abuelo coming to take us to the beach?
Why aren't you all ready?
I told your abuelo we were all going to stay here for the lottery program today.
He said he'd stop by.
UGH!
SLAM

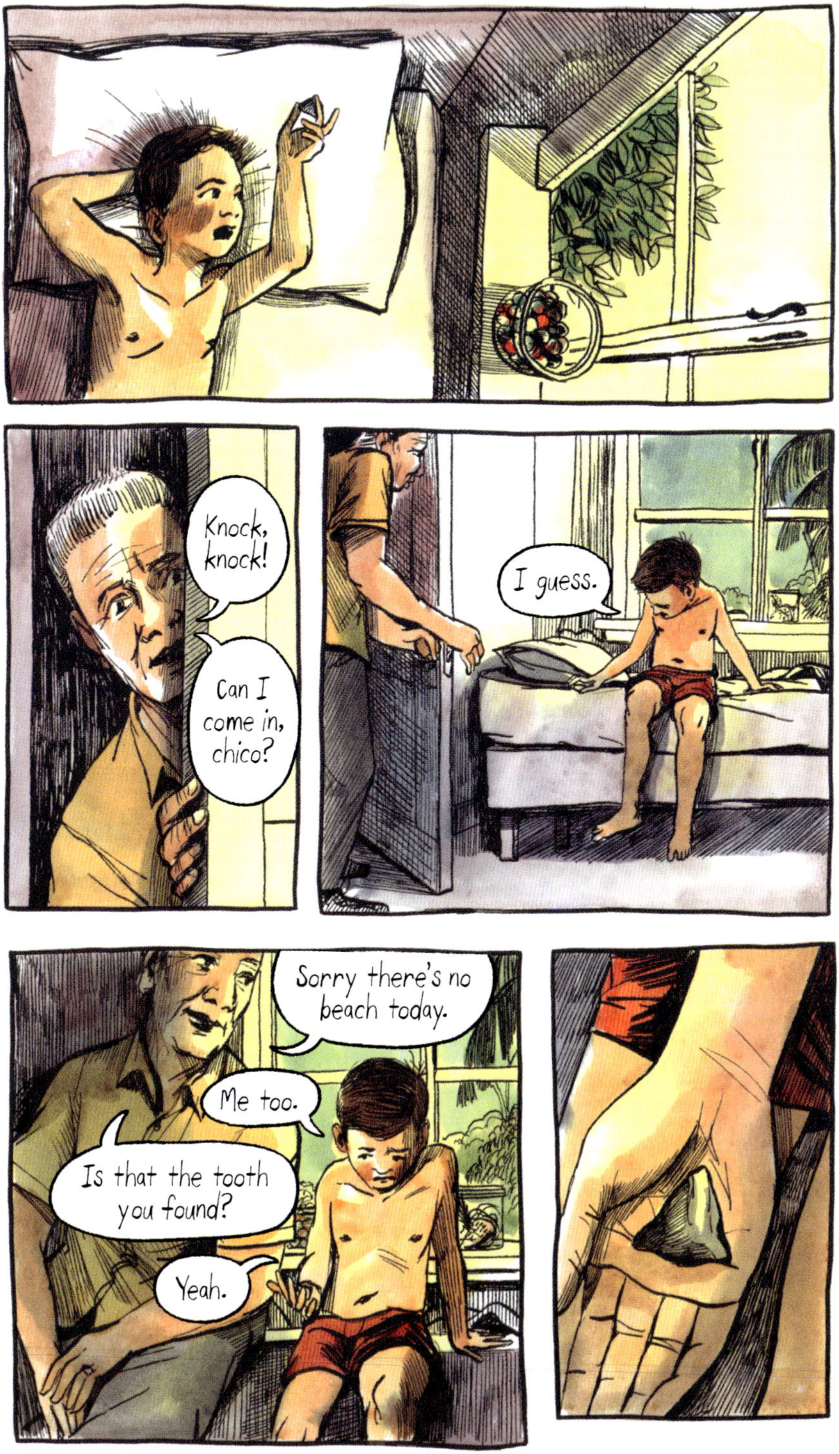
Knock, knock!
Can I come in, chico?
I guess.
Sorry there's no beach today.
Me too.
Is that the tooth you found?
Yeah.

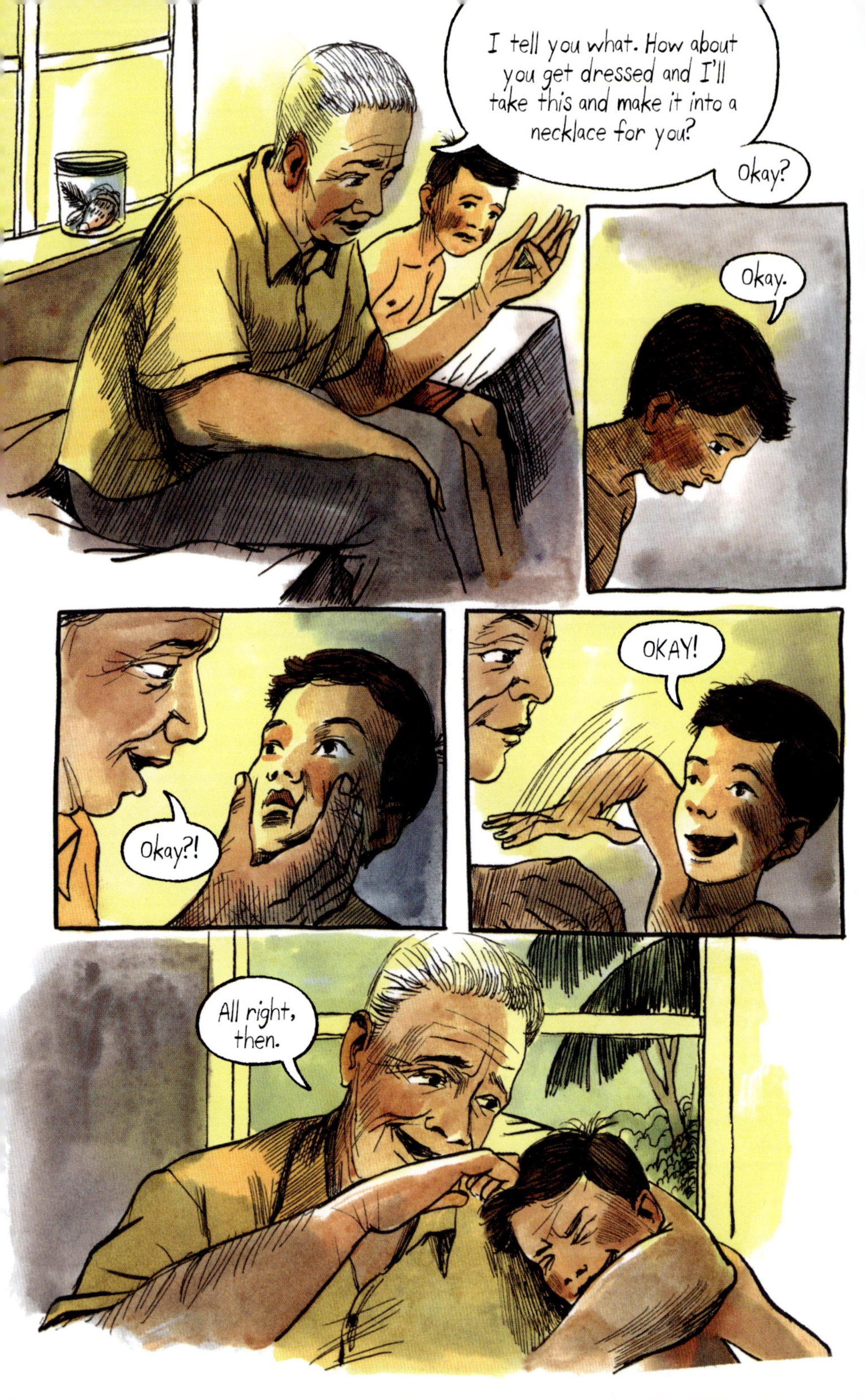
I tell you what. How about you get dressed and I'll take this and make it into a necklace for you?
Okay?
Okay.
Okay?!
OKAY!
All right, then.

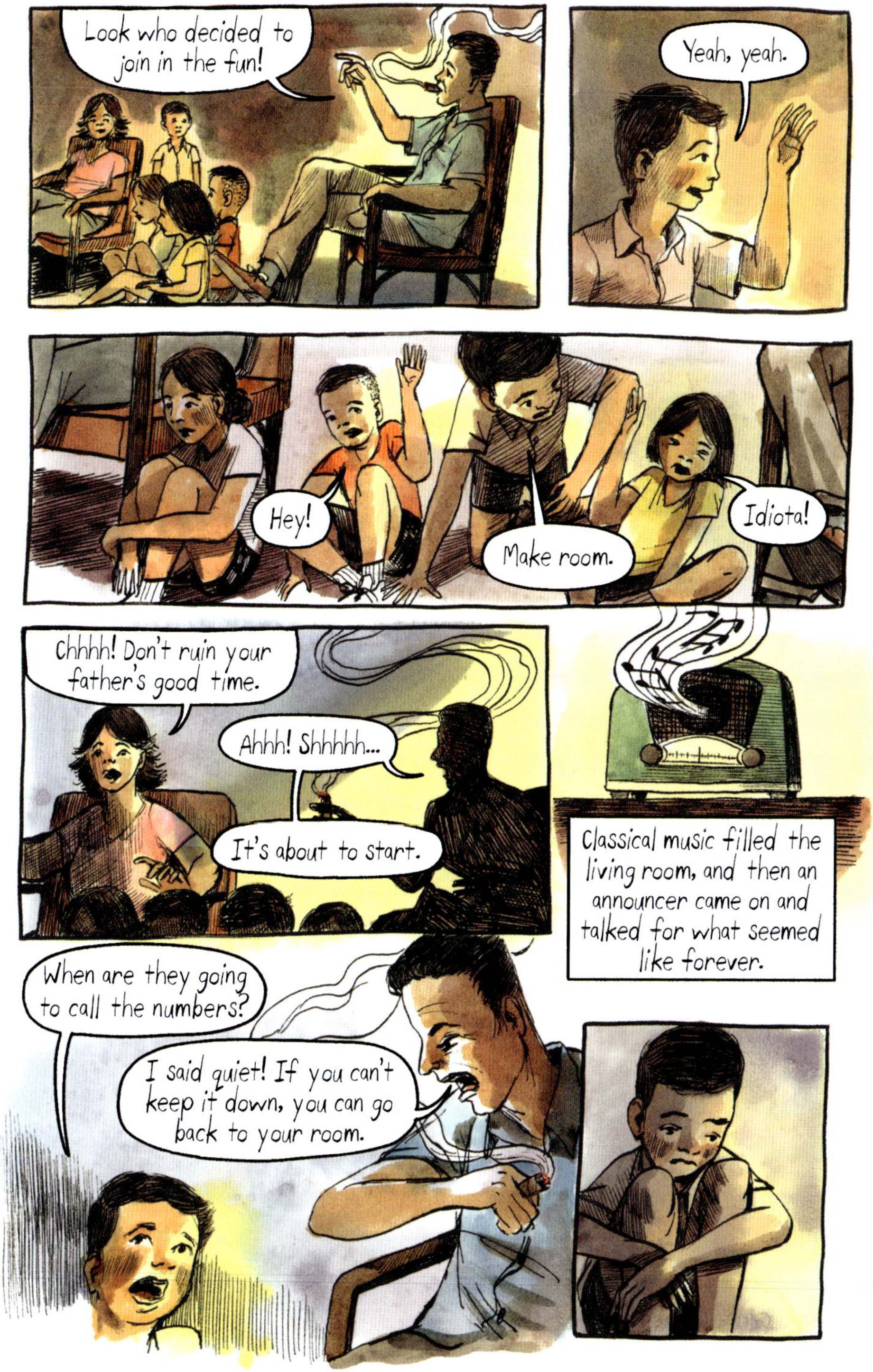
Look who decided to join in the fun!
Yeah, yeah.
Hey!
Make room.
Idiota!
Chhhh! Don't ruin your father's good time.
Ahhh! Shhhhh...
It's about to start.
Classical music filled the living room, and then an announcer came on and talked for what seemed like forever.
When are they going to call the numbers?
I said quiet! If you can't keep it down, you can go back to your room.

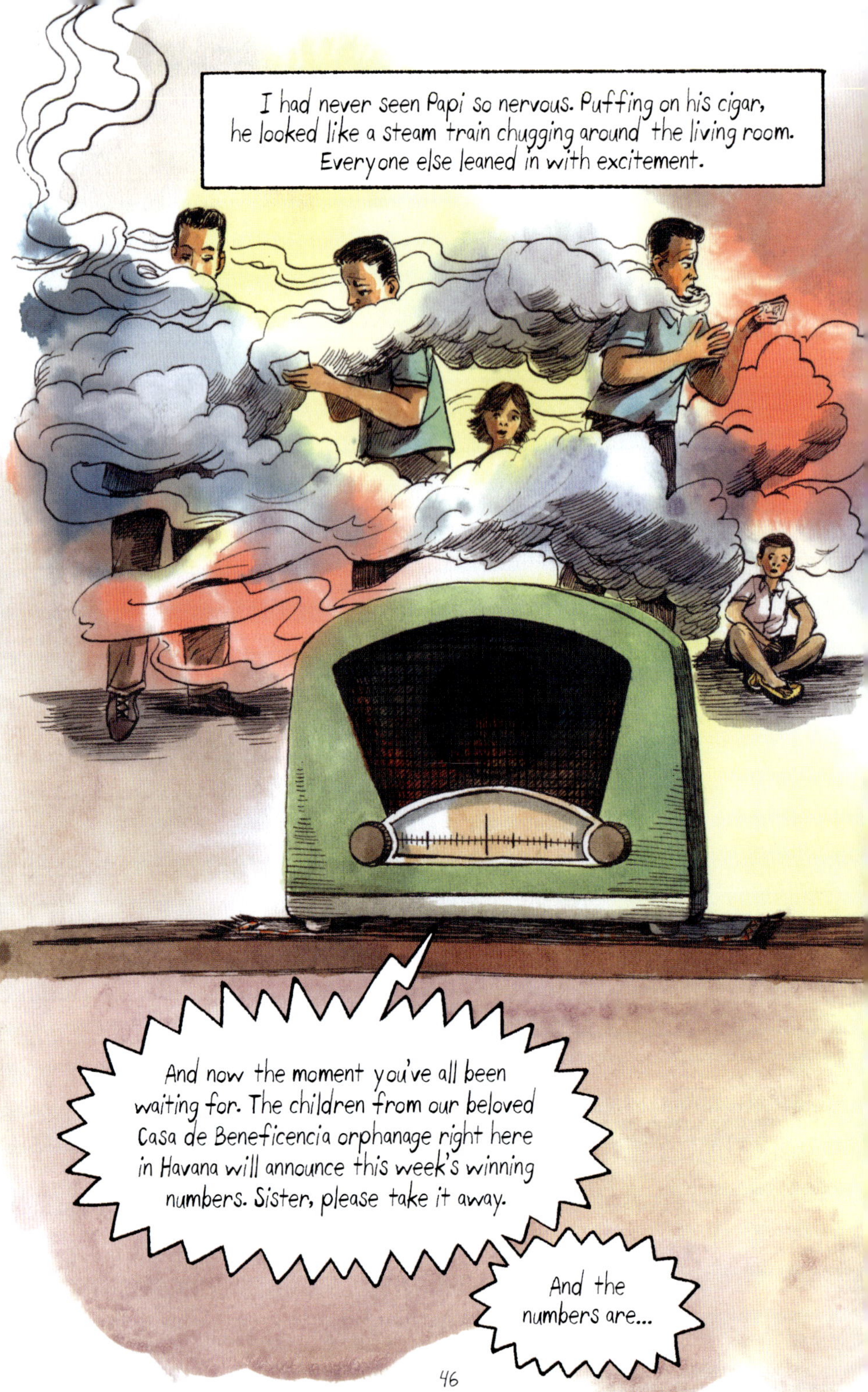
I had never seen Papi so nervous. Puffing on his cigar, he looked like a steam train chugging around the living room. Everyone else leaned in with excitement.
And now the moment you've all been waiting for. The children from our beloved Casa de Beneficencia orphanage right here in Havana will announce this week's winning numbers. Sister, please take it away.
And the numbers are...

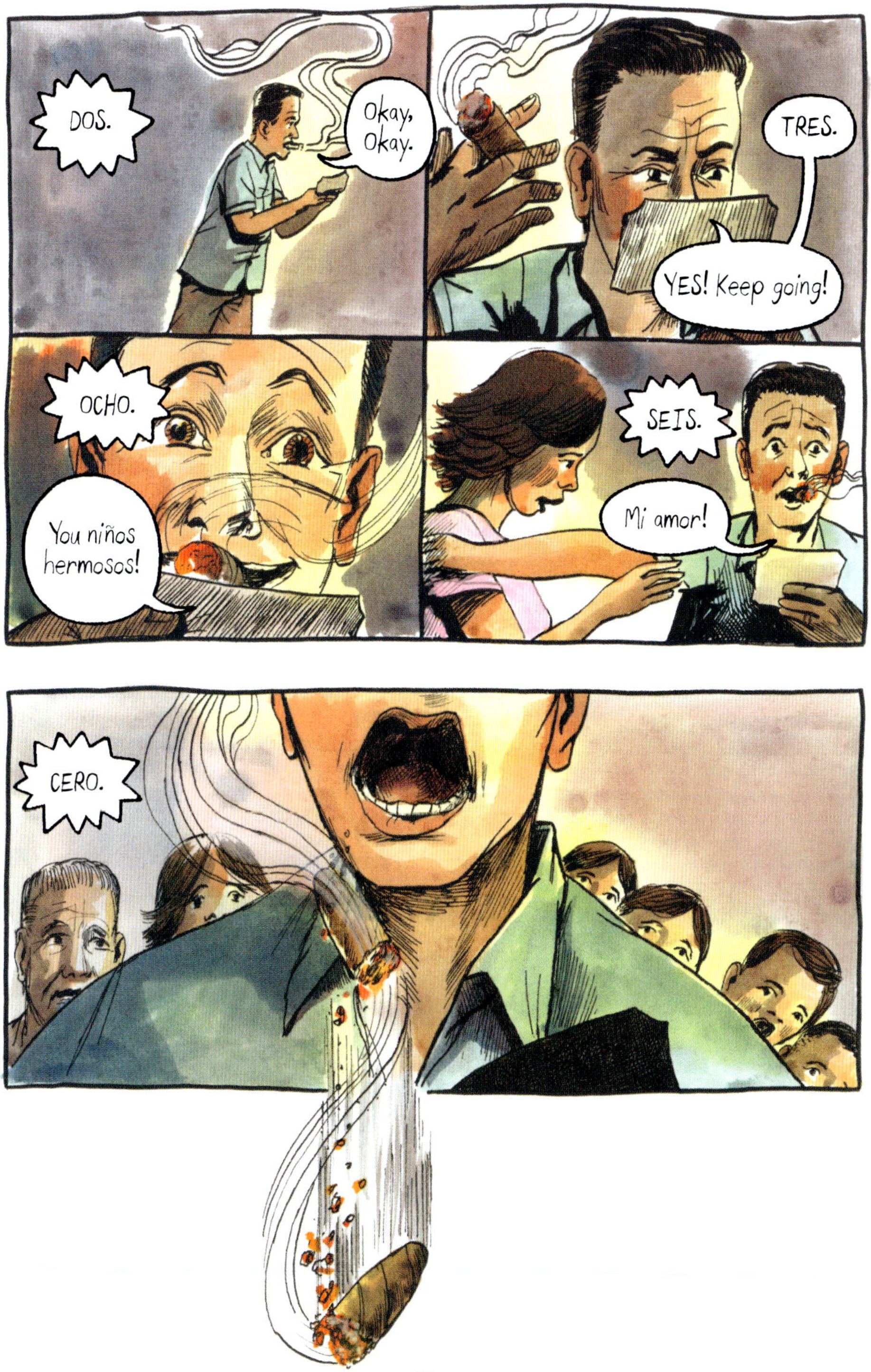
DOS.
Okay, Okay.
TRES.
YES! Keep going!
OCHO.
You niños hermosos!
SEIS.
Mi amor!
CERO.

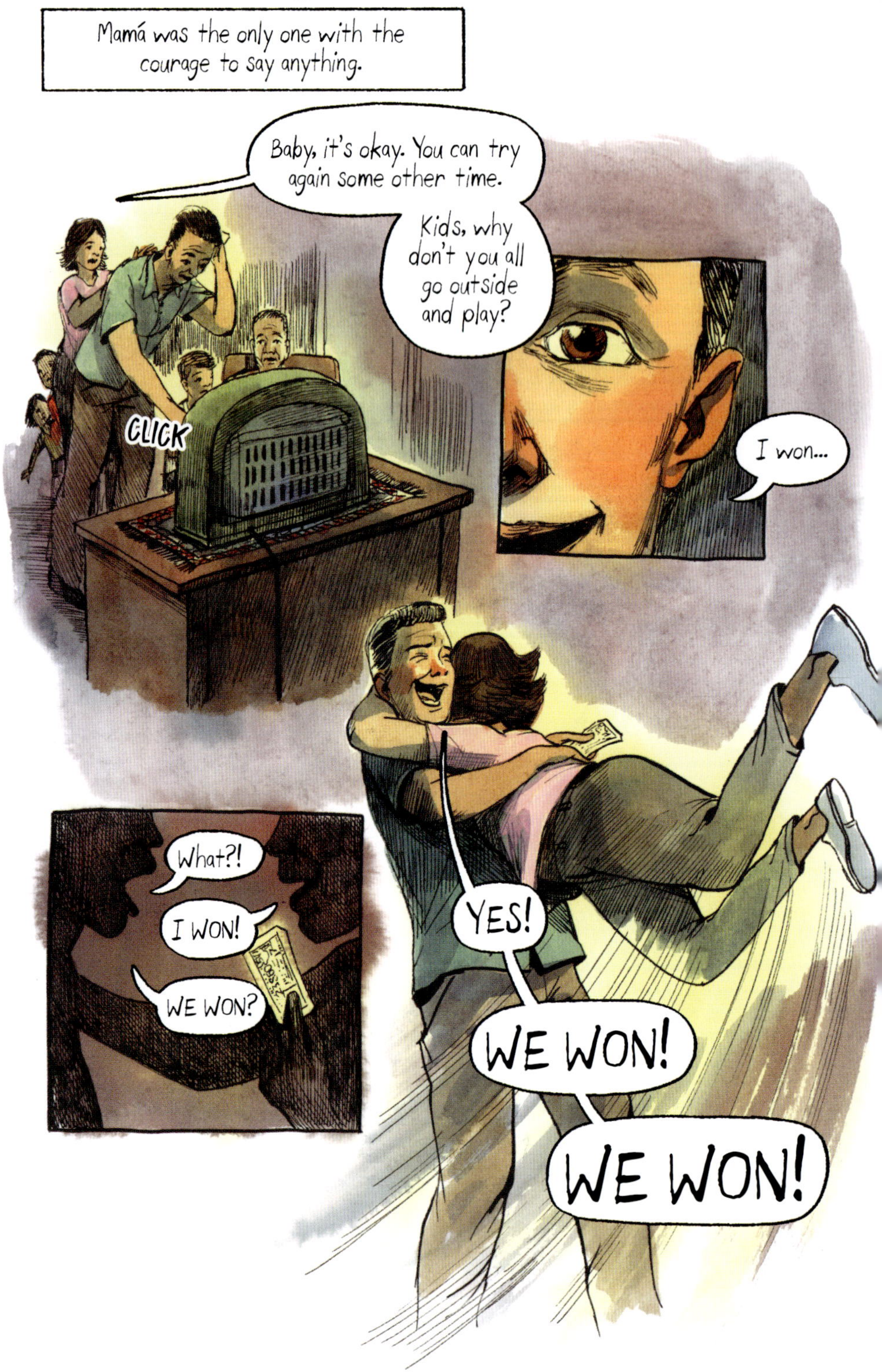

Mamá was the only one with the courage to say anything.
Baby, it's okay. You can try again some other time.
Kids, why don't you all go outside and play?
CLICK
I won...
What?!
I WON!
WE WON?
YES!
WE WON!
WE WON!

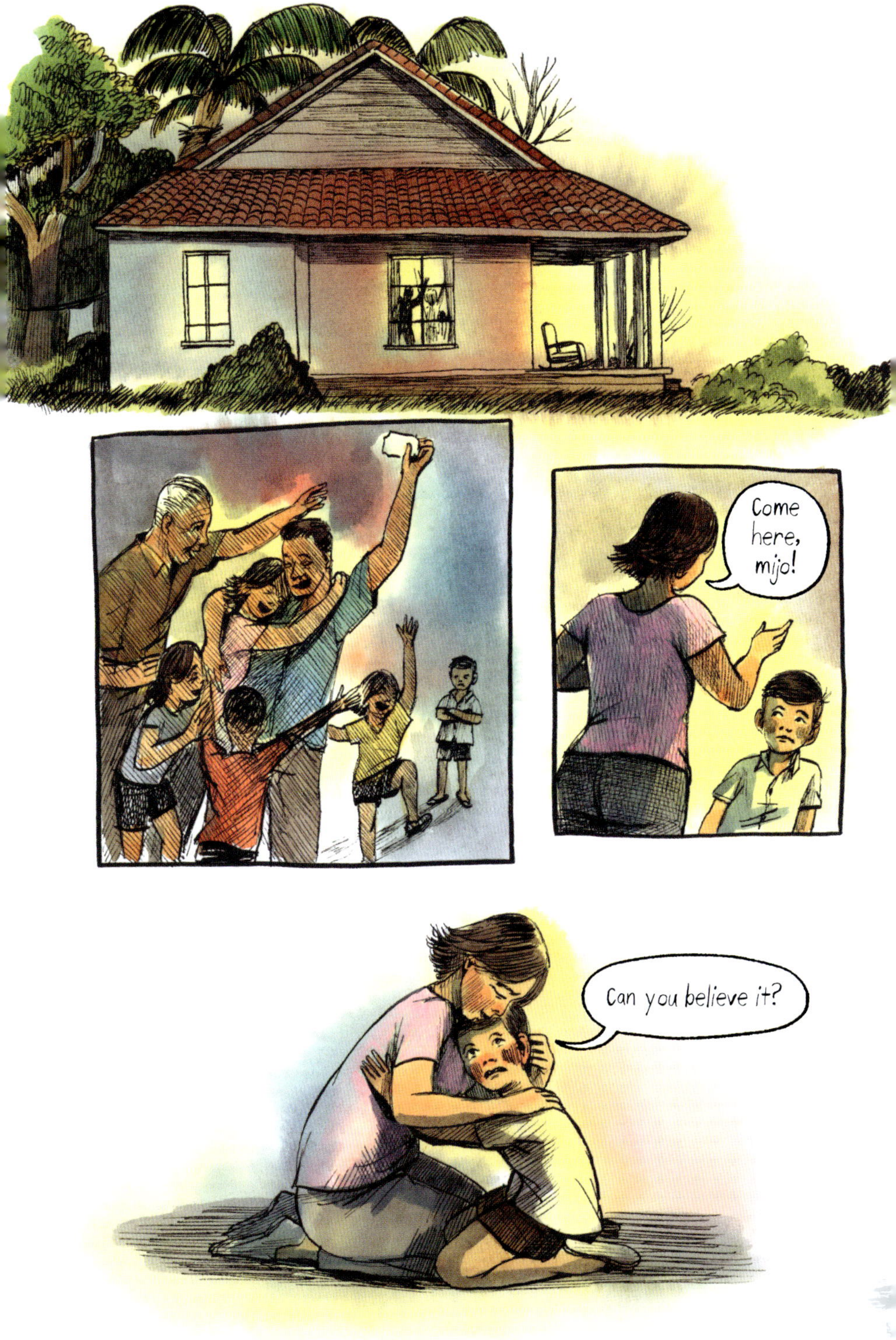
Come here, mijo!
Can you believe it?

Castro's forces attack civilian targets like sugar plantations, and even cabarets and movie theaters.

Winnings

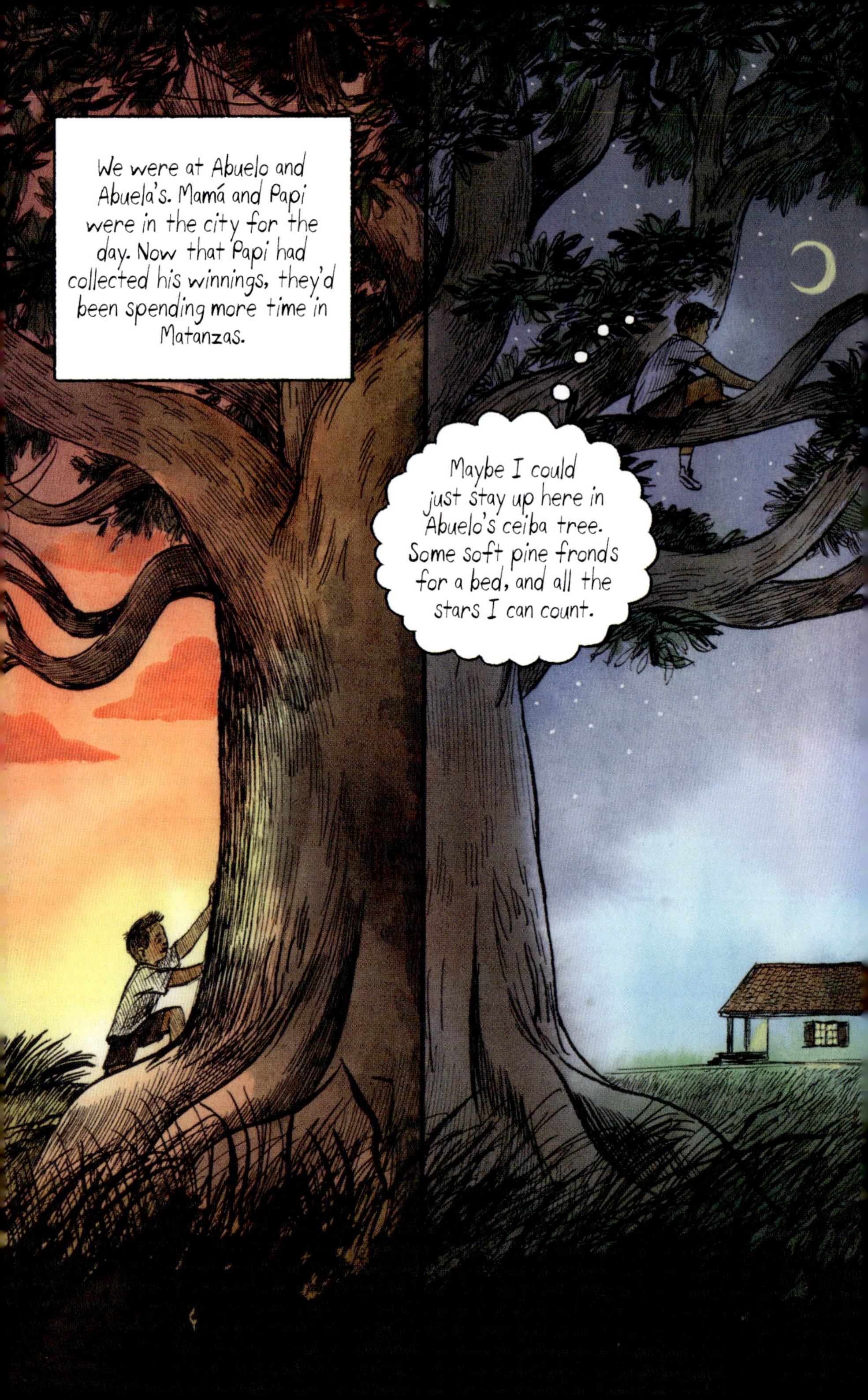
We were at Abuelo and Abuela's. Mamá and Papi were in the city for the day. Now that Papi had collected his winnings, they'd been spending more time in Matanzas.
Maybe I could just stay up here in Abuelo's ceiba tree. Some soft pine fronds for a bed, and all the stars I can count.

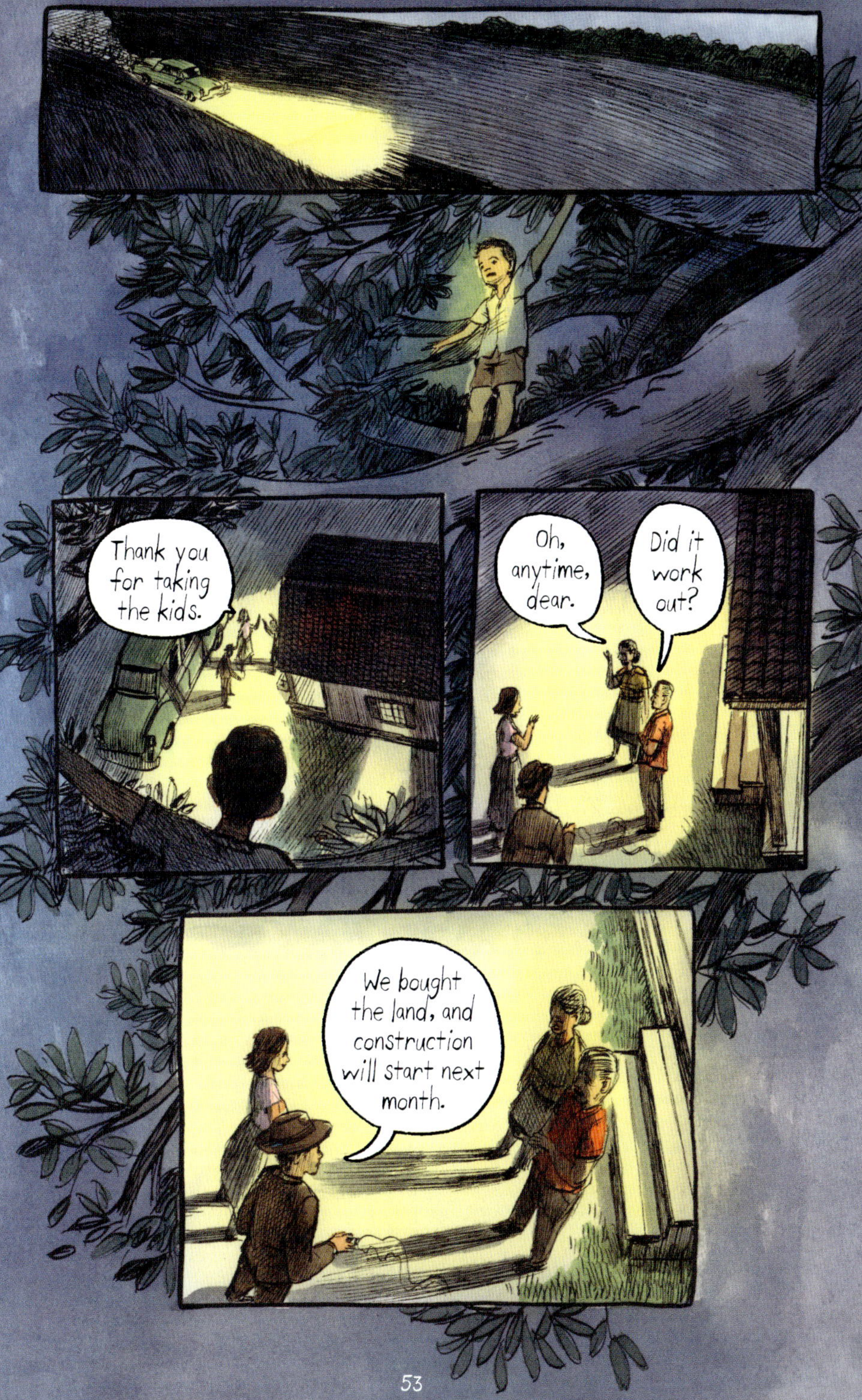
Thank you for taking the kids.
Oh, anytime, dear.
Did it work out?
We bought the land, and construction will start next month.

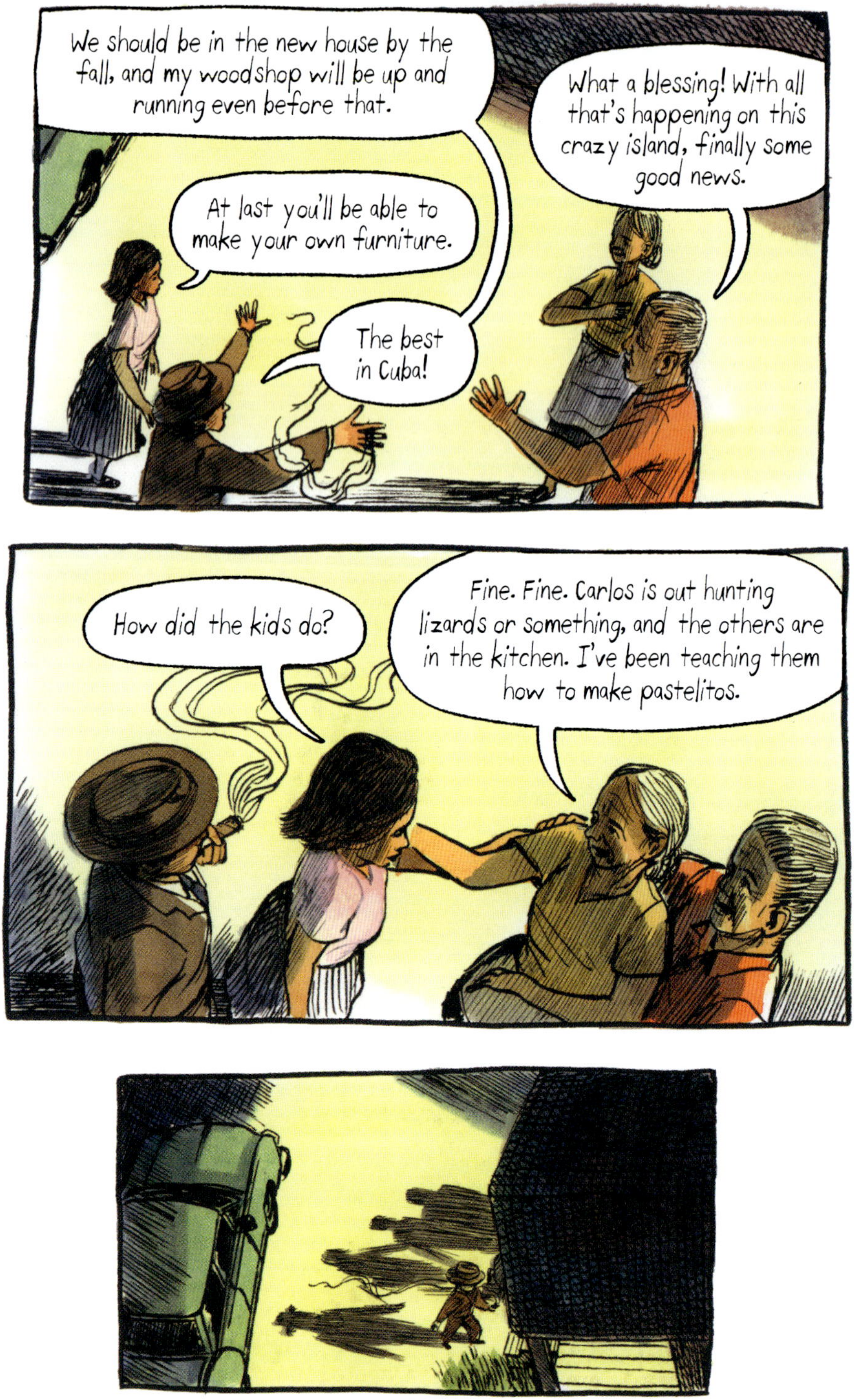
We should be in the new house by the fall, and my woodshop will be up and running even before that.
What a blessing! With all that's happening on this crazy island, finally some good news.
At last you'll be able to make your own furniture.
The best in Cuba!
How did the kids do?
Fine. Fine. Carlos is out hunting lizards or something, and the others are in the kitchen. I've been teaching them how to make pastelitos.

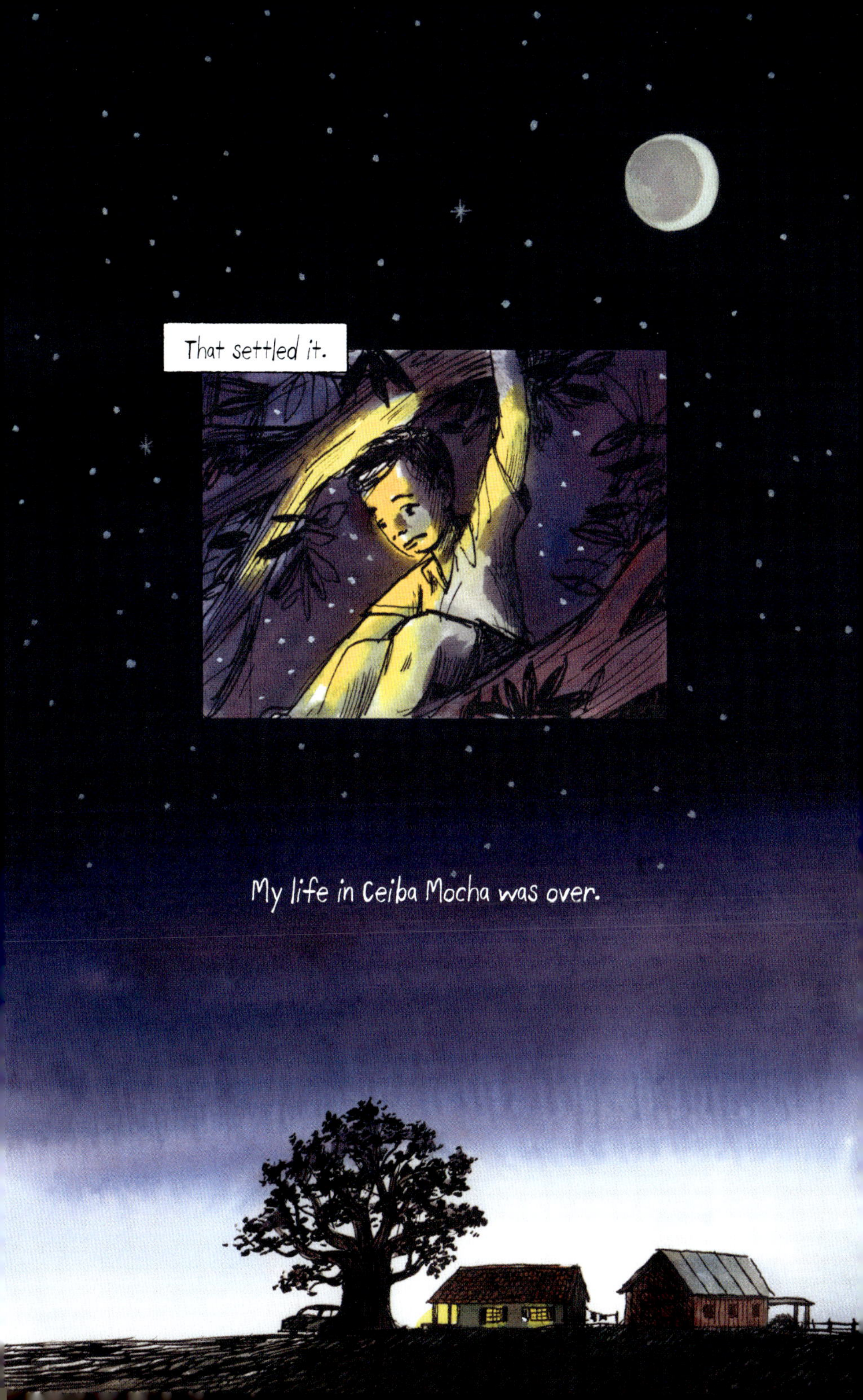
That settled it.
My life in Ceiba Mocha was over.

The Batista government cracks down on anyone it suspects may be a revolutionary. Constitutional rights are suspended, including freedom of speech and freedom of assembly.

Boxed Up

The summer was flying by. Papi was at home more now, but he was always meeting with strangers and talking business. Mamá was boxing up anything that wasn't nailed down.

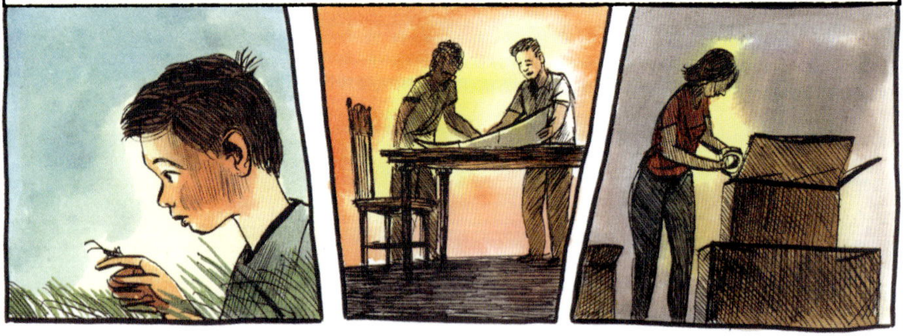

I tried to avoid being in the house as much as possible. Everything there just reminded me that we'd be leaving.

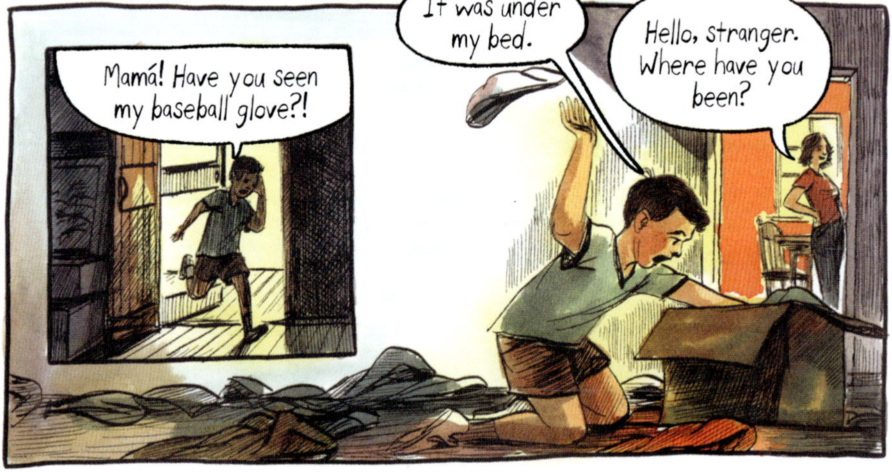

Mamá! Have you seen my baseball glove?!
It was under my bed.
Hello, stranger. Where have you been?

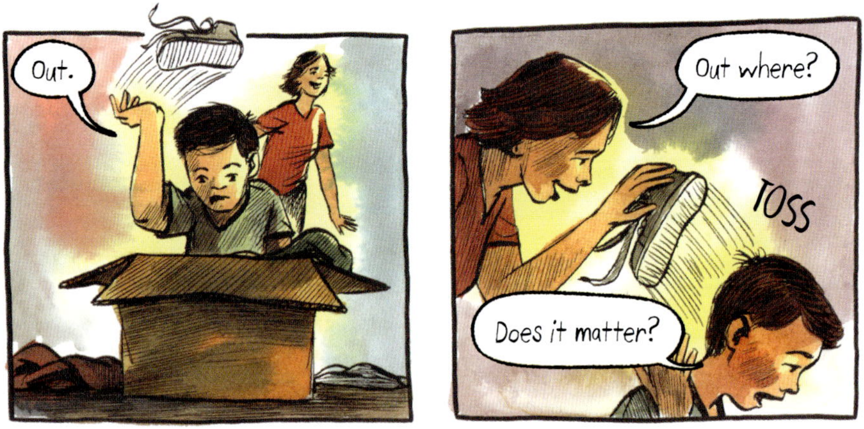

Out.
Out where?
TOSS
Does it matter?

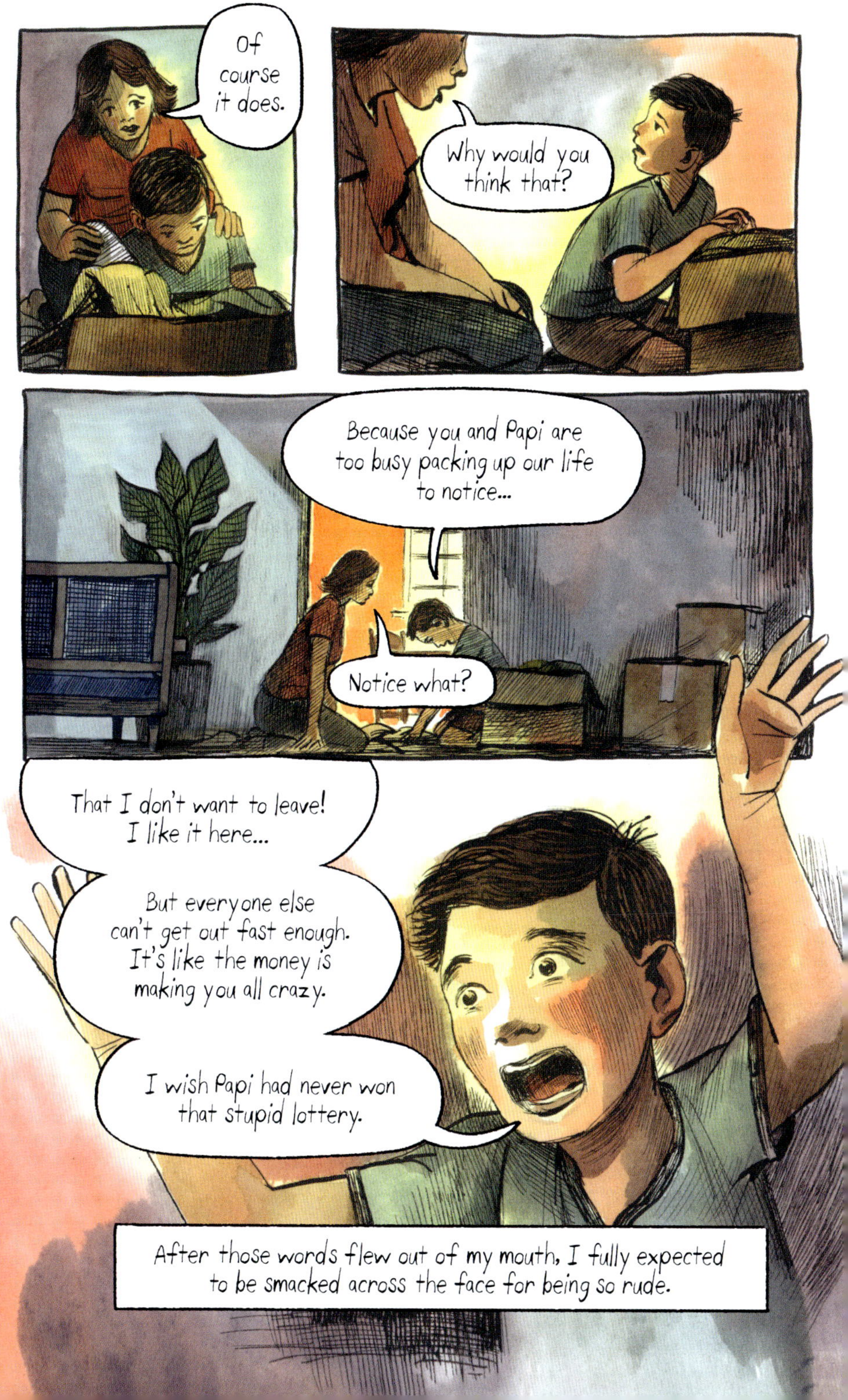
Of course it does.
Why would you think that?
Because you and Papi are too busy packing up our life to notice...
Notice what?
That I don't want to leave! I like it here...
But everyone else can't get out fast enough. It's like the money is making you all crazy.
I wish Papi had never won that stupid lottery.
After those words flew out of my mouth, I fully expected to be smacked across the face for being so rude.

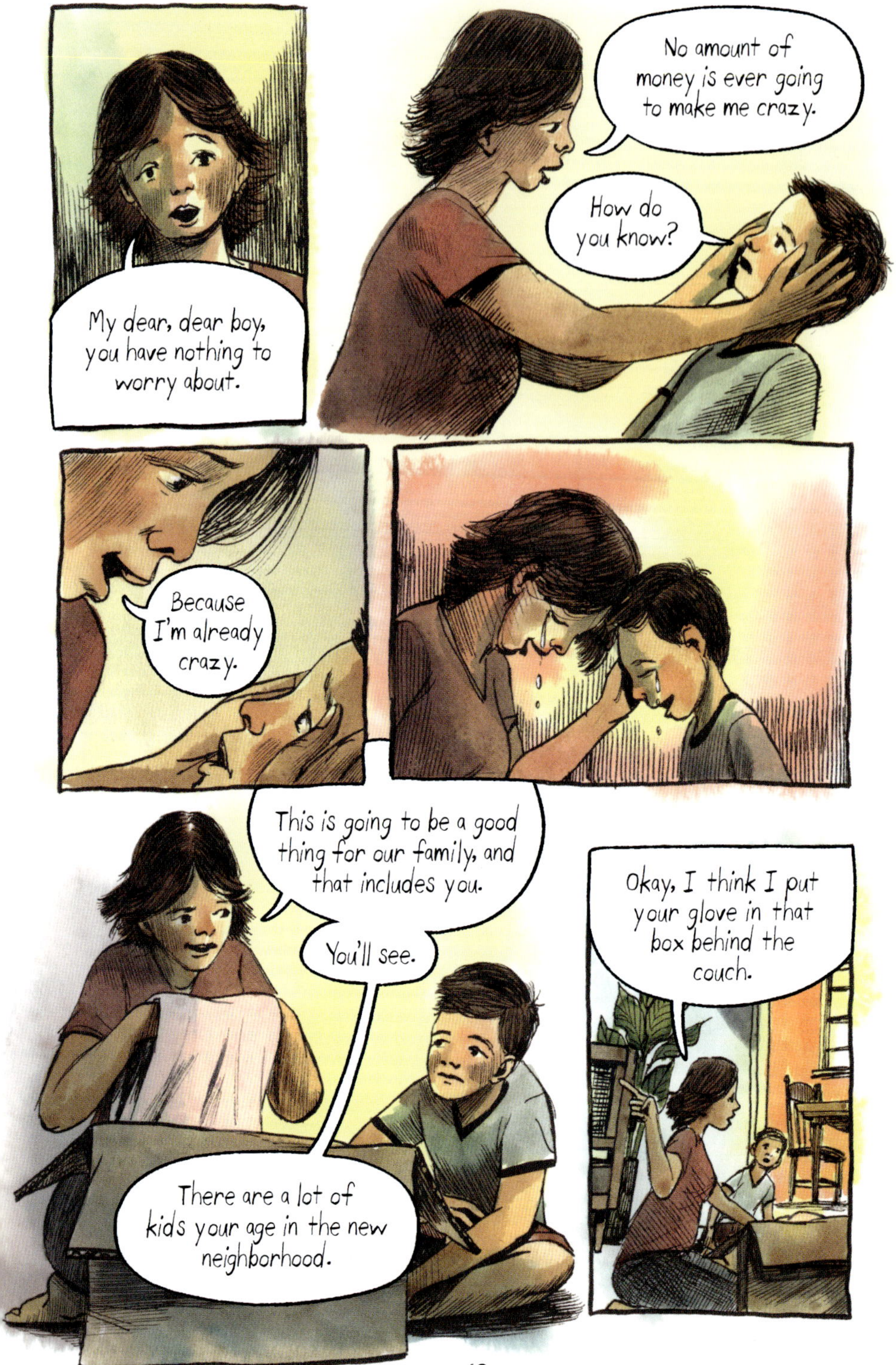
My dear, dear boy, you have nothing to worry about.
No amount of money is ever going to make me crazy.
How do you know?
Because I'm already crazy.
This is going to be a good thing for our family, and that includes you.
You'll see.
There are a lot of kids your age in the new neighborhood.
Okay, I think I put your glove in that box behind the couch.

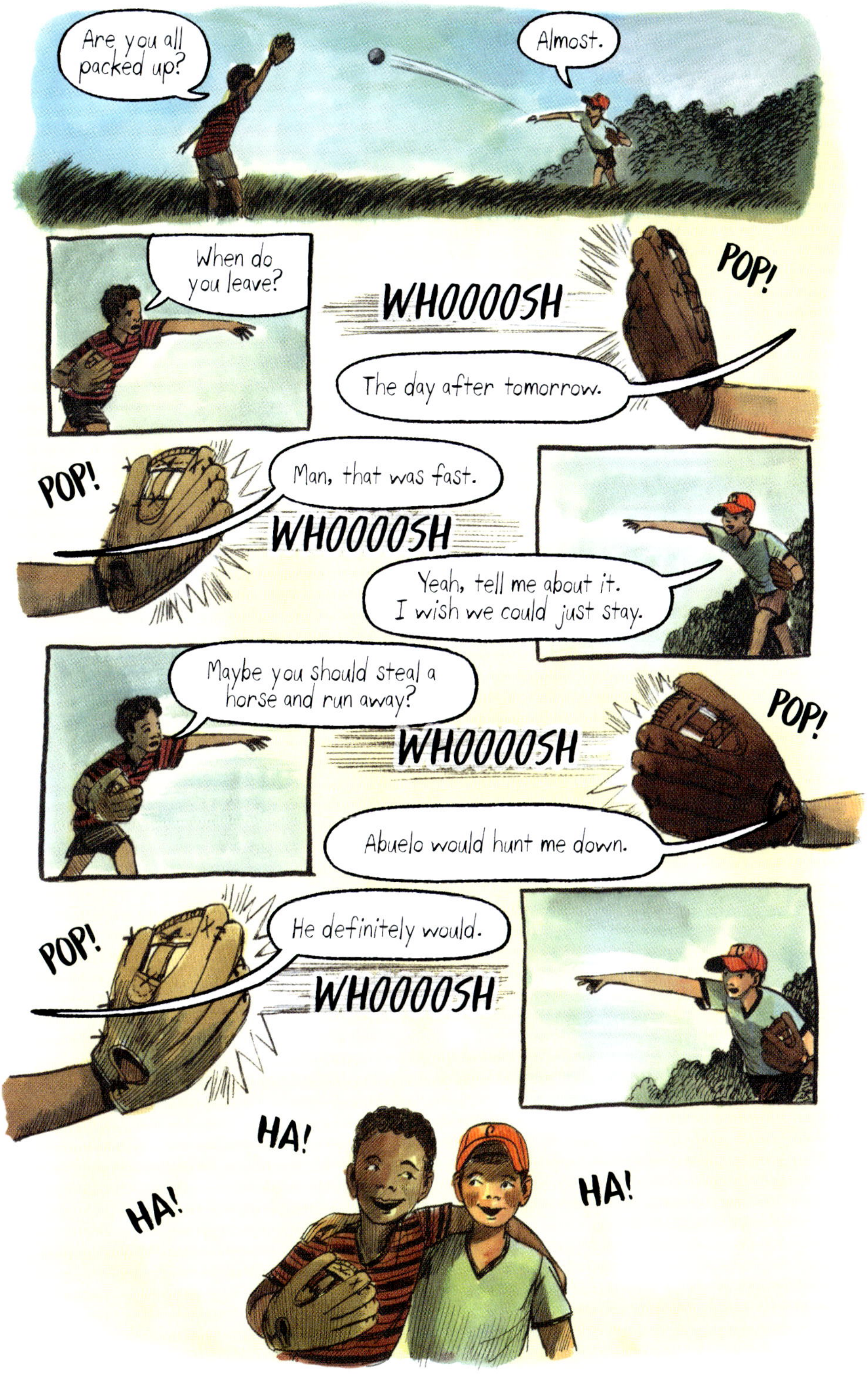
Are you all packed up?
Almost.
When do you leave?
WHOOOOSH
POP!
The day after tomorrow.
POP!
Man, that was fast.
WHOOOOSH
Yeah, tell me about it. I wish we could just stay.
Maybe you should steal a horse and run away?
WHOOOOSH
POP!
Abuelo would hunt me down.
POP!
He definitely would.
WHOOOOSH
HA!
HA!
HA!

Support for Castro continues to grow, with protests breaking out against Batista.

Matanzas

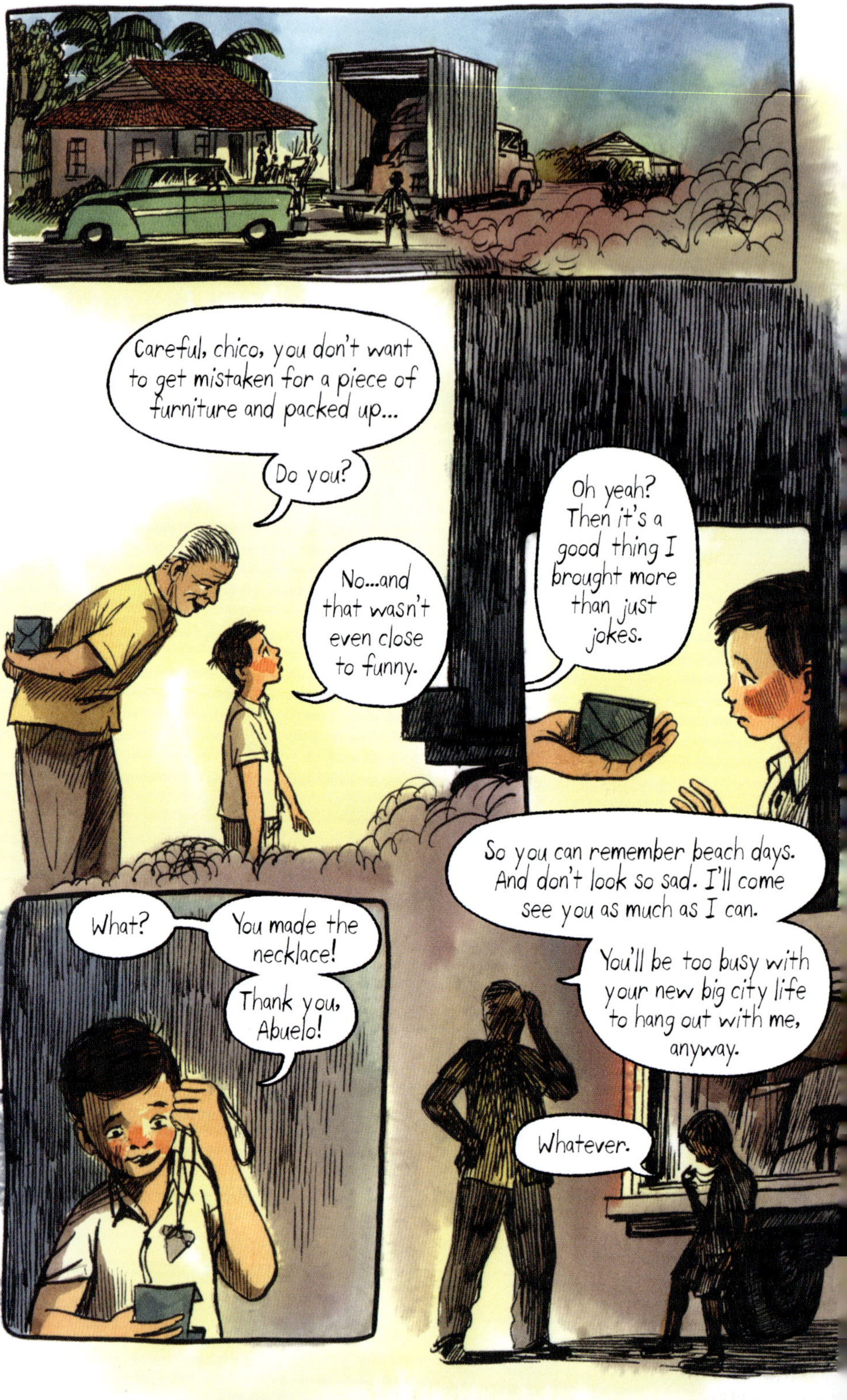
Careful, chico, you don't want to get mistaken for a piece of furniture and packed up...
Do you?
No...and that wasn't even close to funny.
Oh yeah? Then it's a good thing I brought more than just jokes.
What?
You made the necklace!
Thank you, Abuelo!
So you can remember beach days. And don't look so sad. I'll come see you as much as I can.
You'll be too busy with your new big city life to hang out with me, anyway.
Whatever.

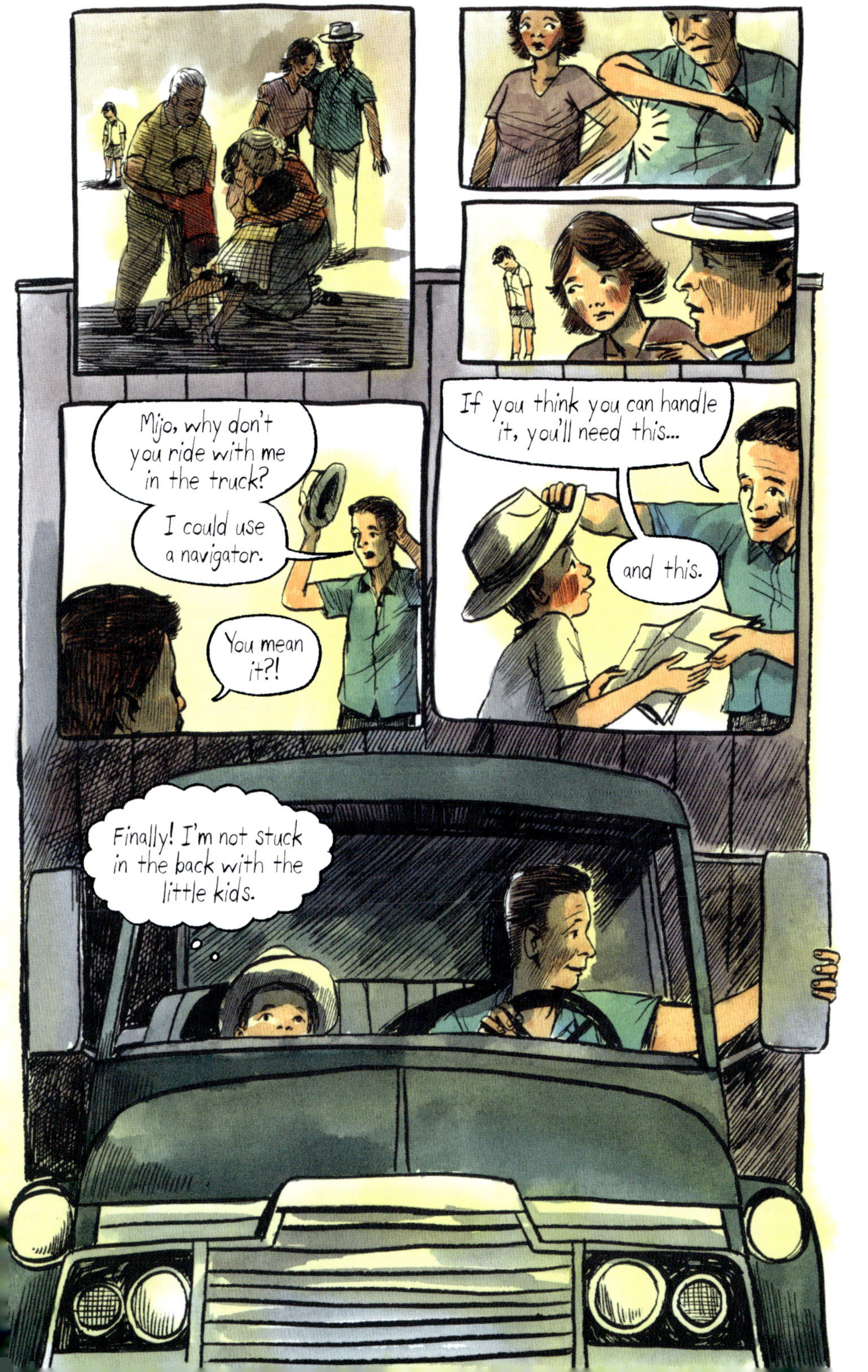
Mijo, why don't you ride with me in the truck?
I could use a navigator.
You mean it?!
If you think you can handle it, you'll need this...
and this.
Finally! I'm not stuck in the back with the little kids.

What do you think you're doing?

I was just going to find some music.

Nope. My truck, my music.

Okay.

Which way should we go? Left or right?

Uh... I think we should... ummm...

HONK HONK
HONK HONK
HONK HONK
HONK
HONK HONK

SWIPE!

Here, it's not that hard. We need to go this way.

66

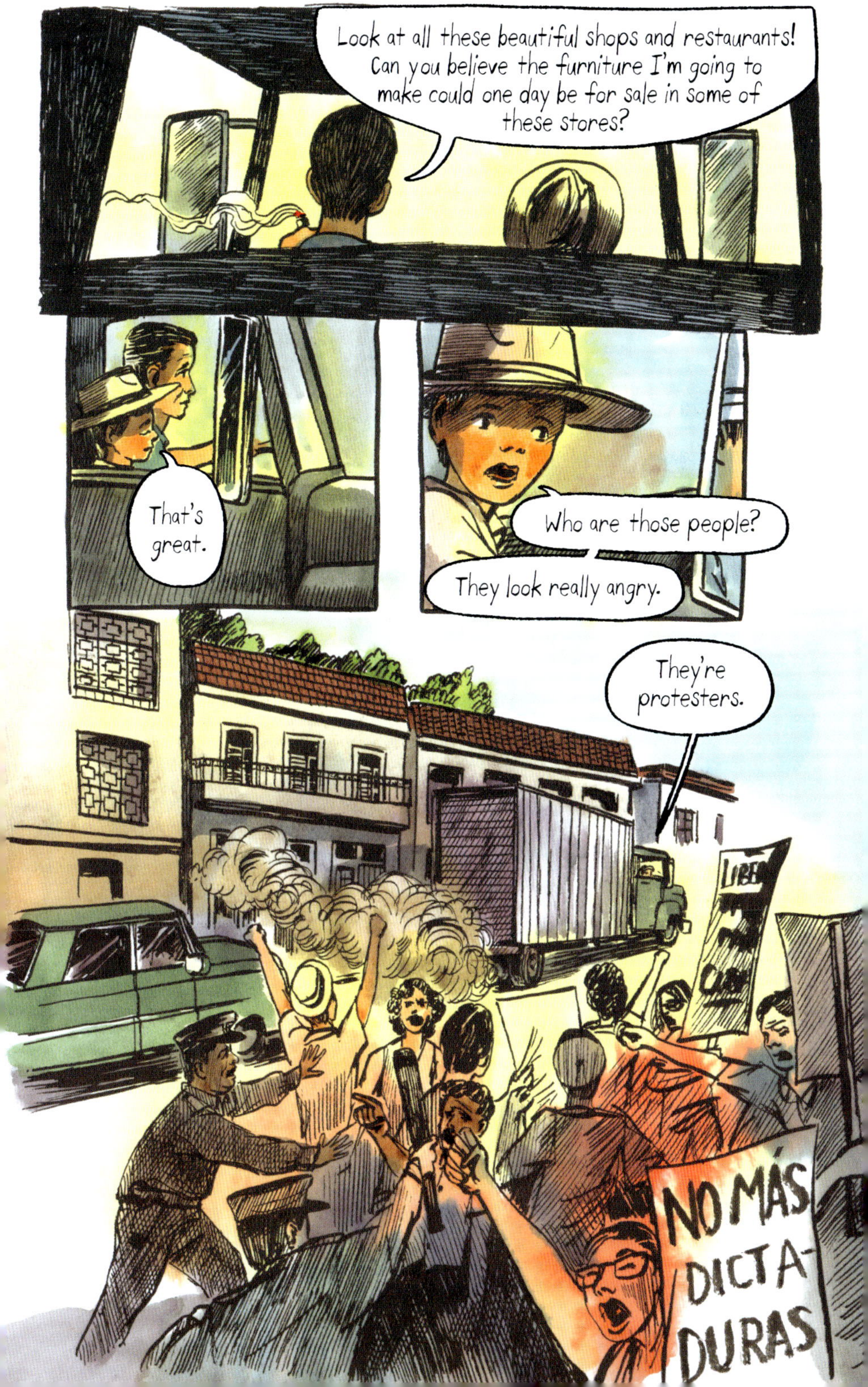
Look at all these beautiful shops and restaurants! Can you believe the furniture I'm going to make could one day be for sale in some of these stores?
That's great.
Who are those people?
They look really angry.
They're protesters.
NO MÁS DICTA-DURAS

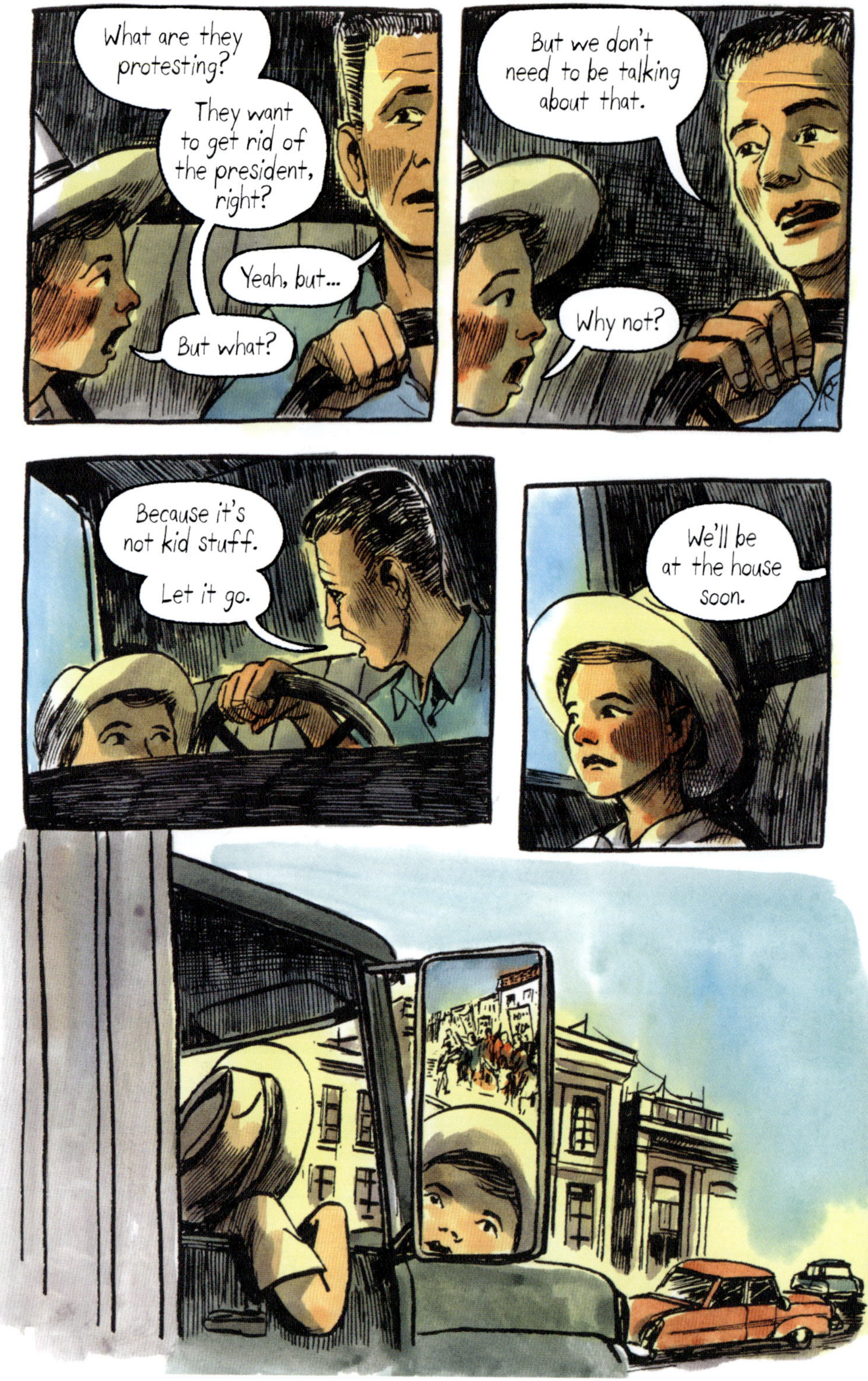
What are they protesting?
They want to get rid of the president, right?
Yeah, but...
But what?
But we don't need to be talking about that.
Why not?
Because it's not kid stuff.
Let it go.
We'll be at the house soon.

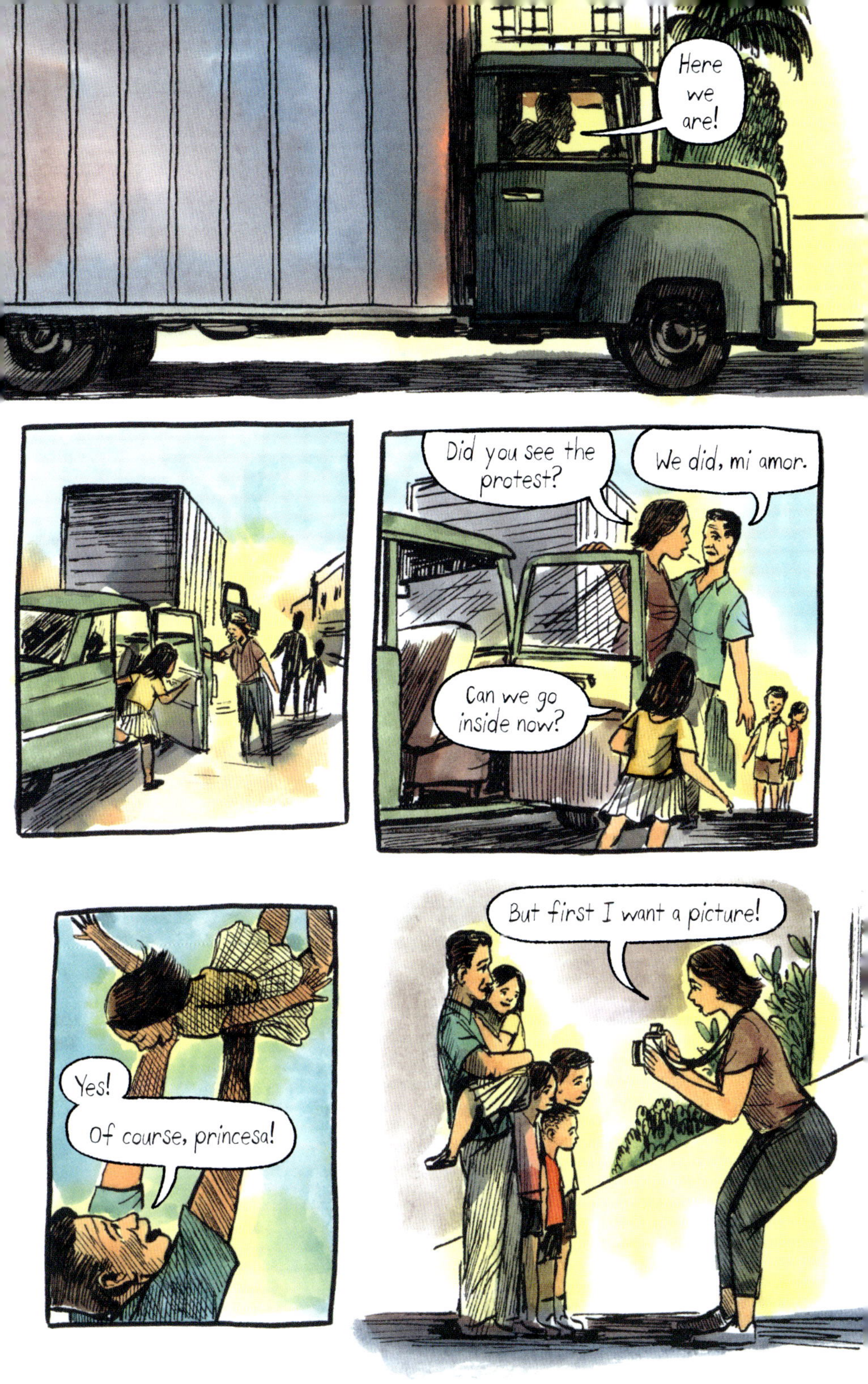
Here we are!
Did you see the protest?
We did, mi amor.
Can we go inside now?
Yes!
Of course, princesa!
But first I want a picture!

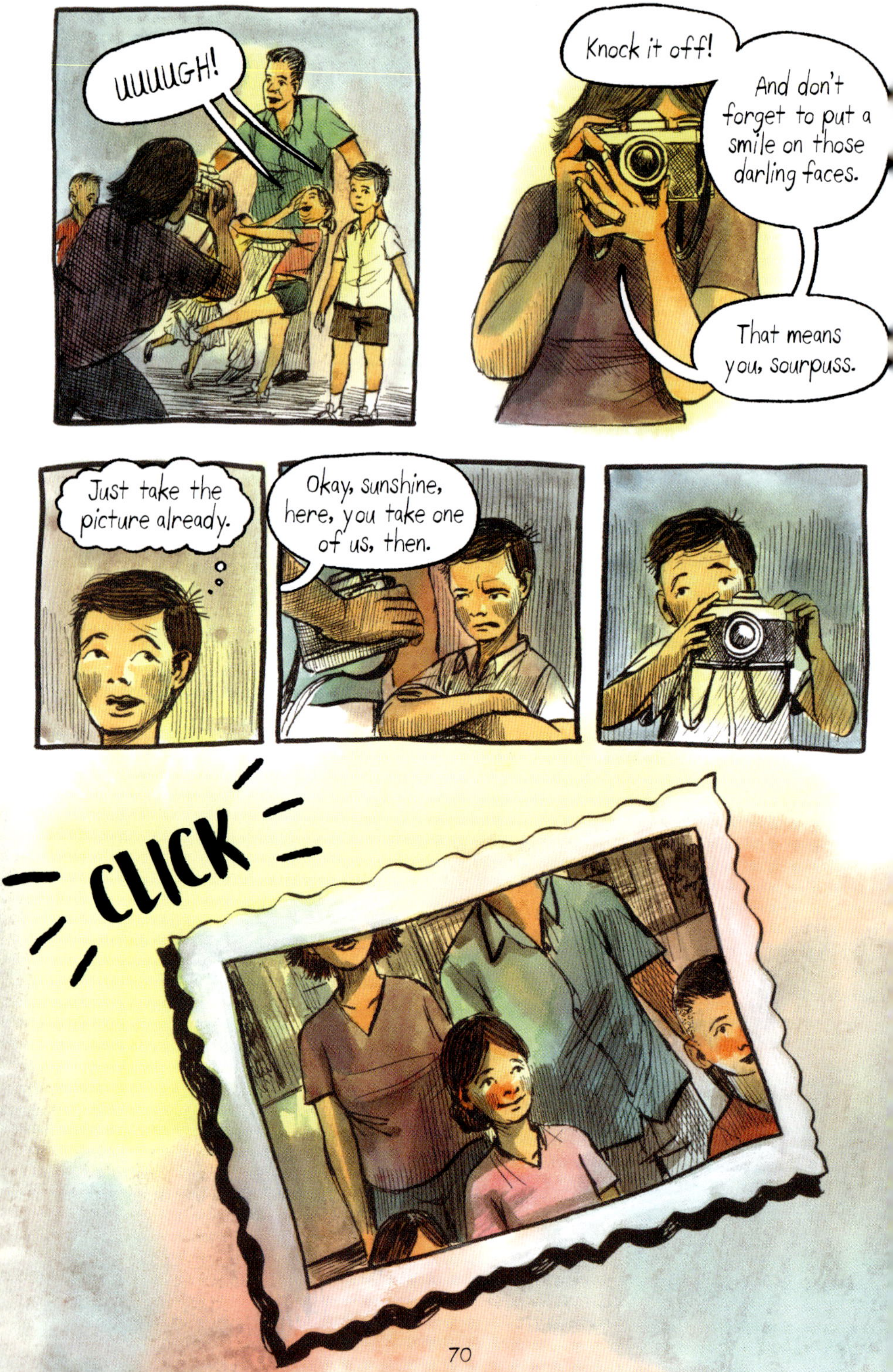
UUUUGH!
Knock it off!
And don't forget to put a smile on those darling faces.
That means you, sourpuss.
Just take the picture already.
Okay, sunshine, here, you take one of us, then.
CLICK

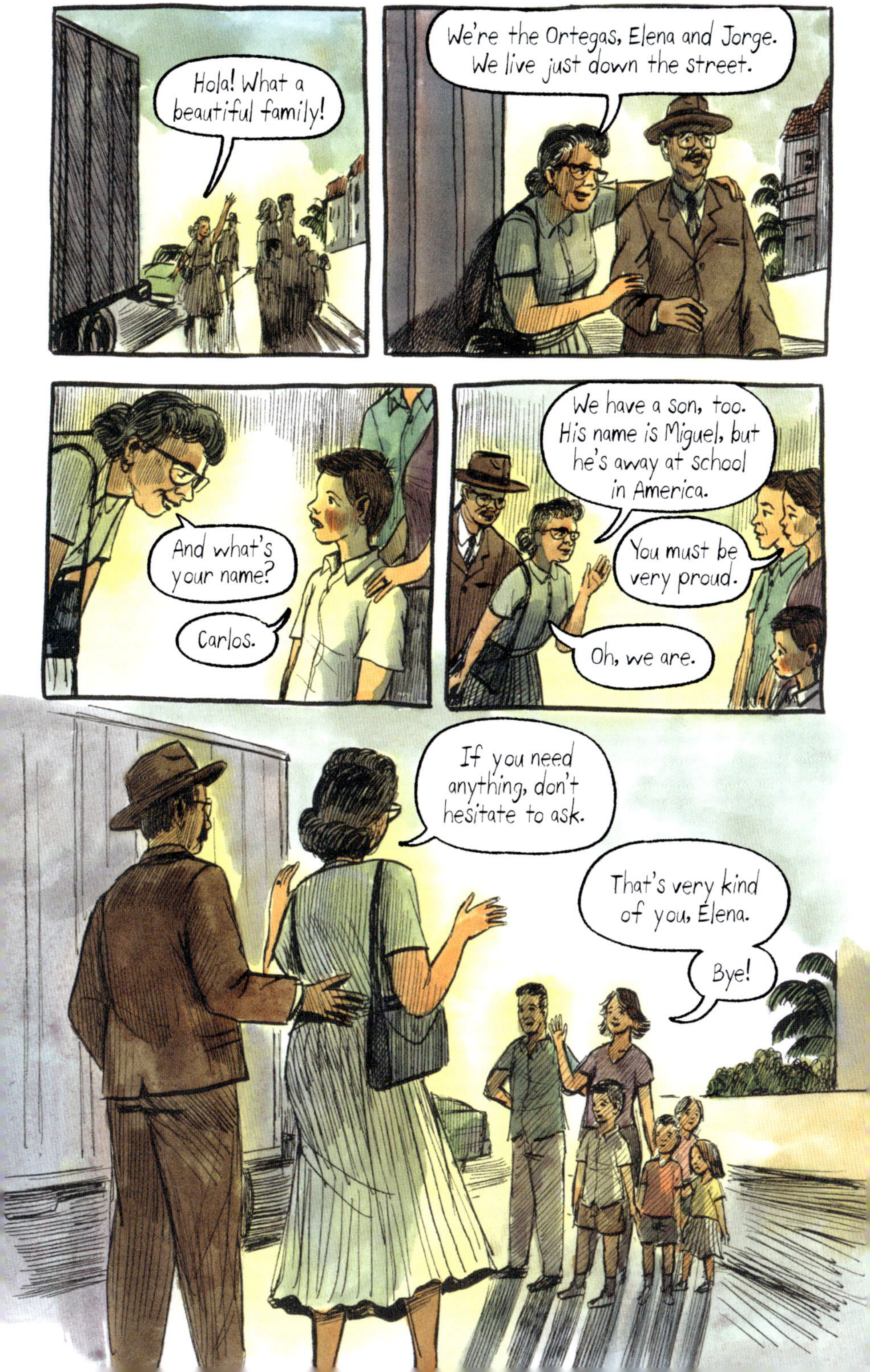
Hola! What a beautiful family!
We're the Ortegas, Elena and Jorge. We live just down the street.
And what's your name?
Carlos.
We have a son, too. His name is Miguel, but he's away at school in America.
You must be very proud.
Oh, we are.
If you need anything, don't hesitate to ask.
That's very kind of you, Elena.
Bye!

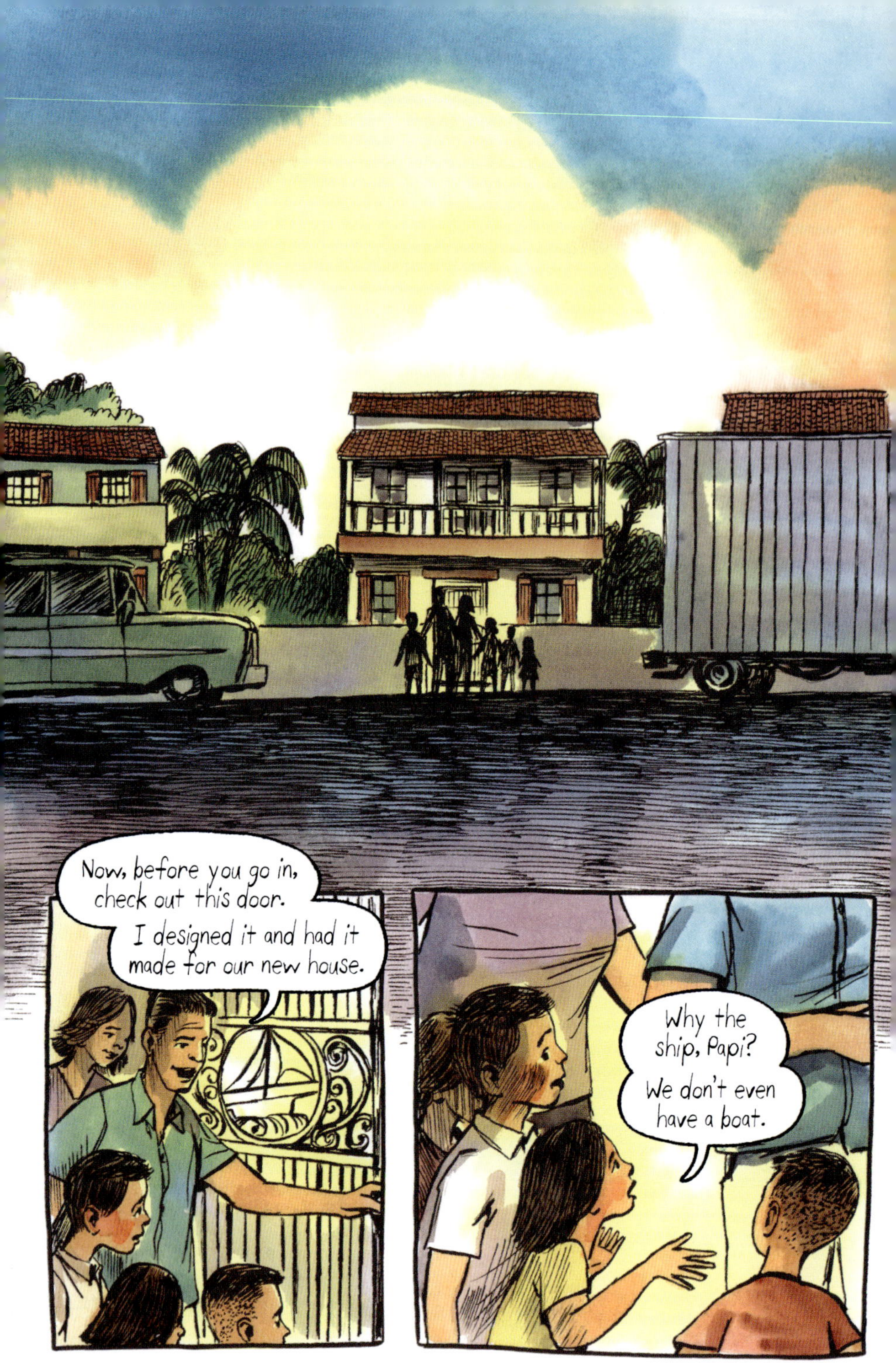
Now, before you go in, check out this door.
I designed it and had it made for our new house.
Why the ship, Papi?
We don't even have a boat.

"Because I want nothing but good fortune and full sails for our family."

"Can we please go in?!"

"Ha! Yes! Go ahead."

"Wipe your feet first."

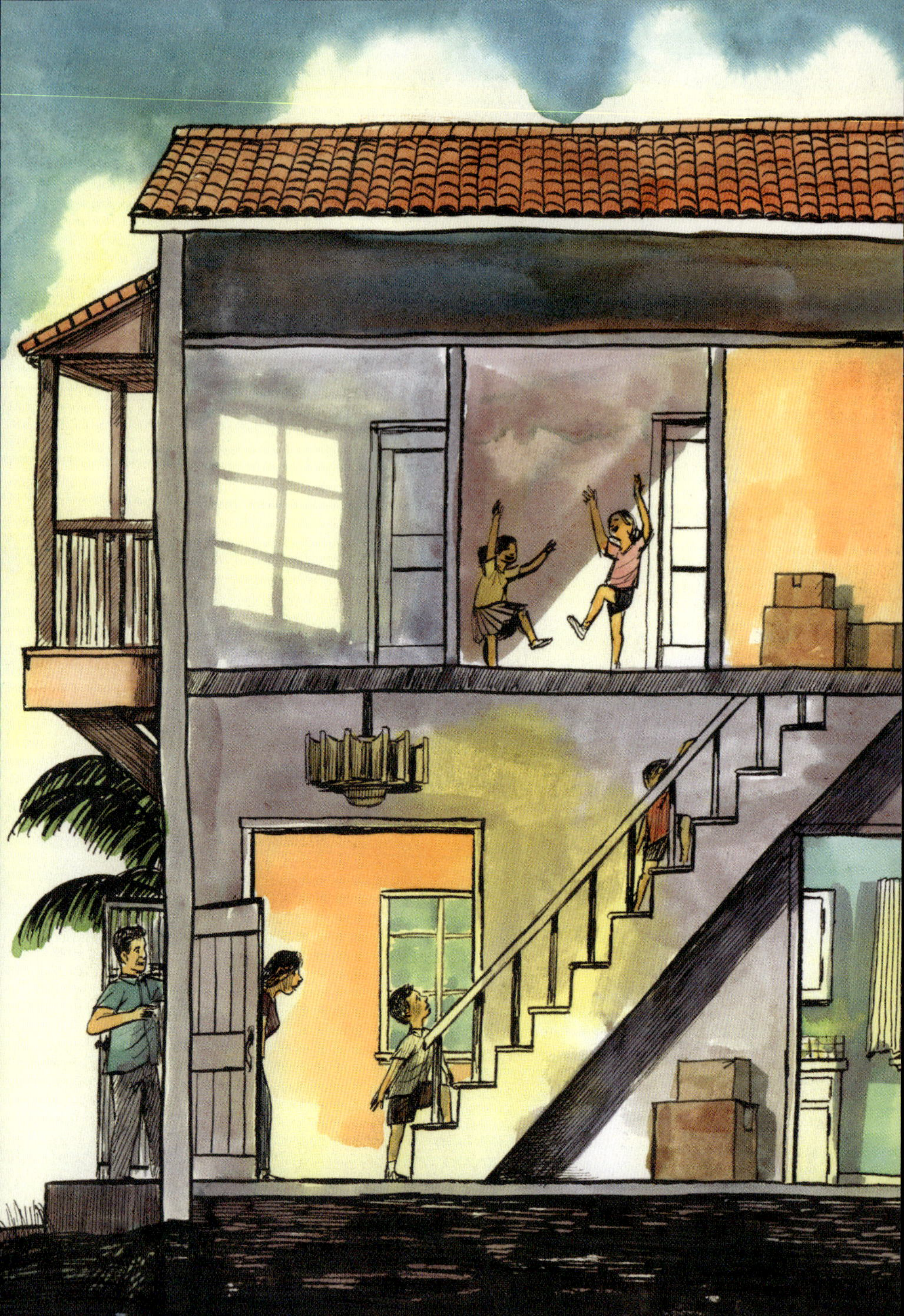

It felt strange having neighbors who weren't our family.

"Hey!"

"Hey."

"Are you moving in?"

"Yeah, we just got here."

"I'm Carlos."

"I'm Diego, and he's Luis. We live up the street. Want to hang out?"

"Let me put this down."

"We could explore the woods."

"Sure!"

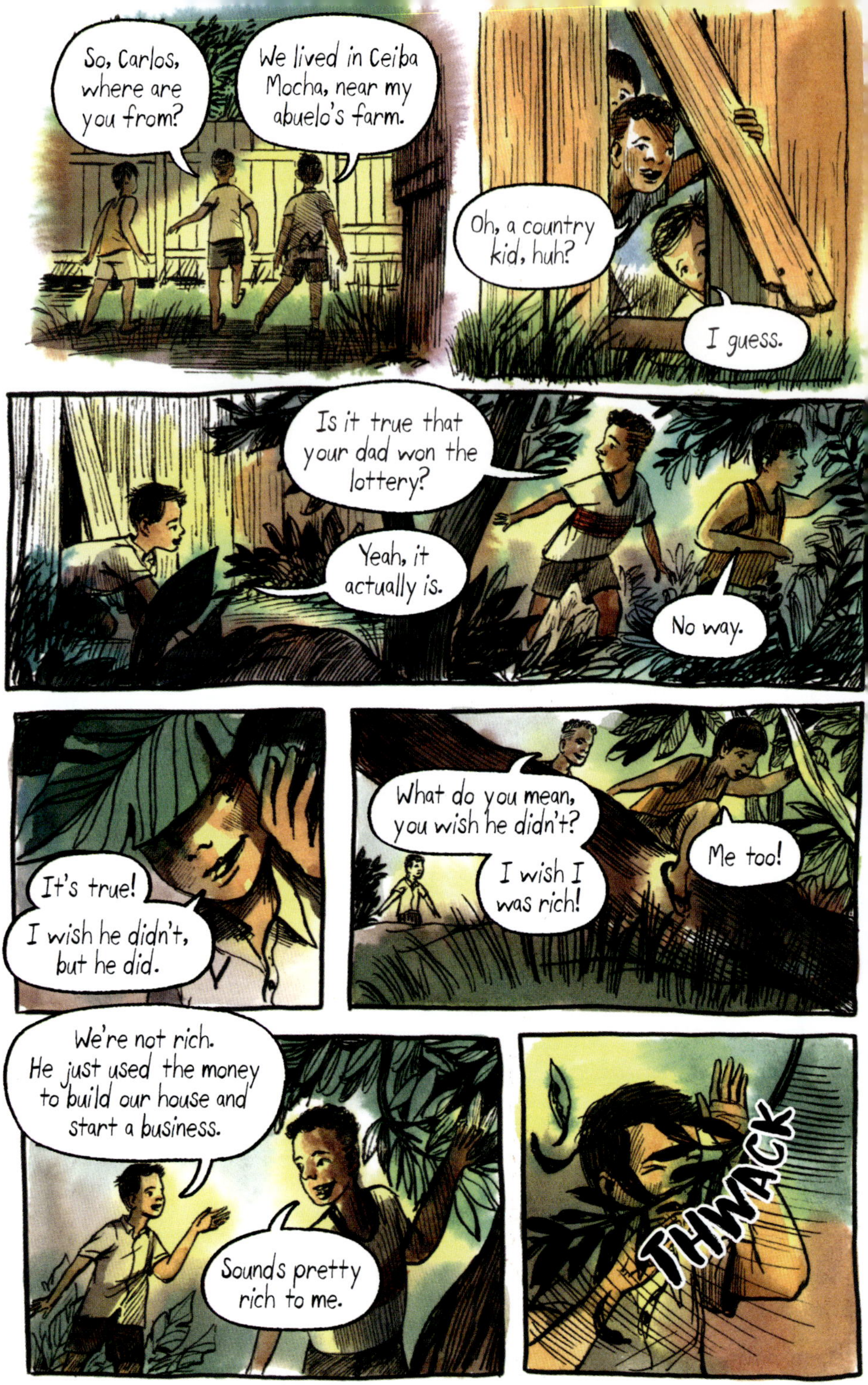
So, Carlos, where are you from?
We lived in Ceiba Mocha, near my abuelo's farm.
Oh, a country kid, huh?
I guess.
Is it true that your dad won the lottery?
Yeah, it actually is.
No way.
It's true!
I wish he didn't, but he did.
What do you mean, you wish he didn't?
I wish I was rich!
Me too!
We're not rich. He just used the money to build our house and start a business.
Sounds pretty rich to me.
THWACK

"How could I change the stupid subject?"

"Okay, so you guys are city kids, huh?"

"Yeah, what about it?"

"I saw a bunch of angry people on the streets when we were driving in. Is it always like that?"

"Lately there's been more..."

"My dad says they'll keep on protesting until Batista's gone. He calls him an American lapdog."

"American lapdog?"

"Yeah, like he takes money from gangsters and big American companies and does whatever they want. My dad says he needs to be run off the island."

I guess my family isn't the only one with strong opinions.

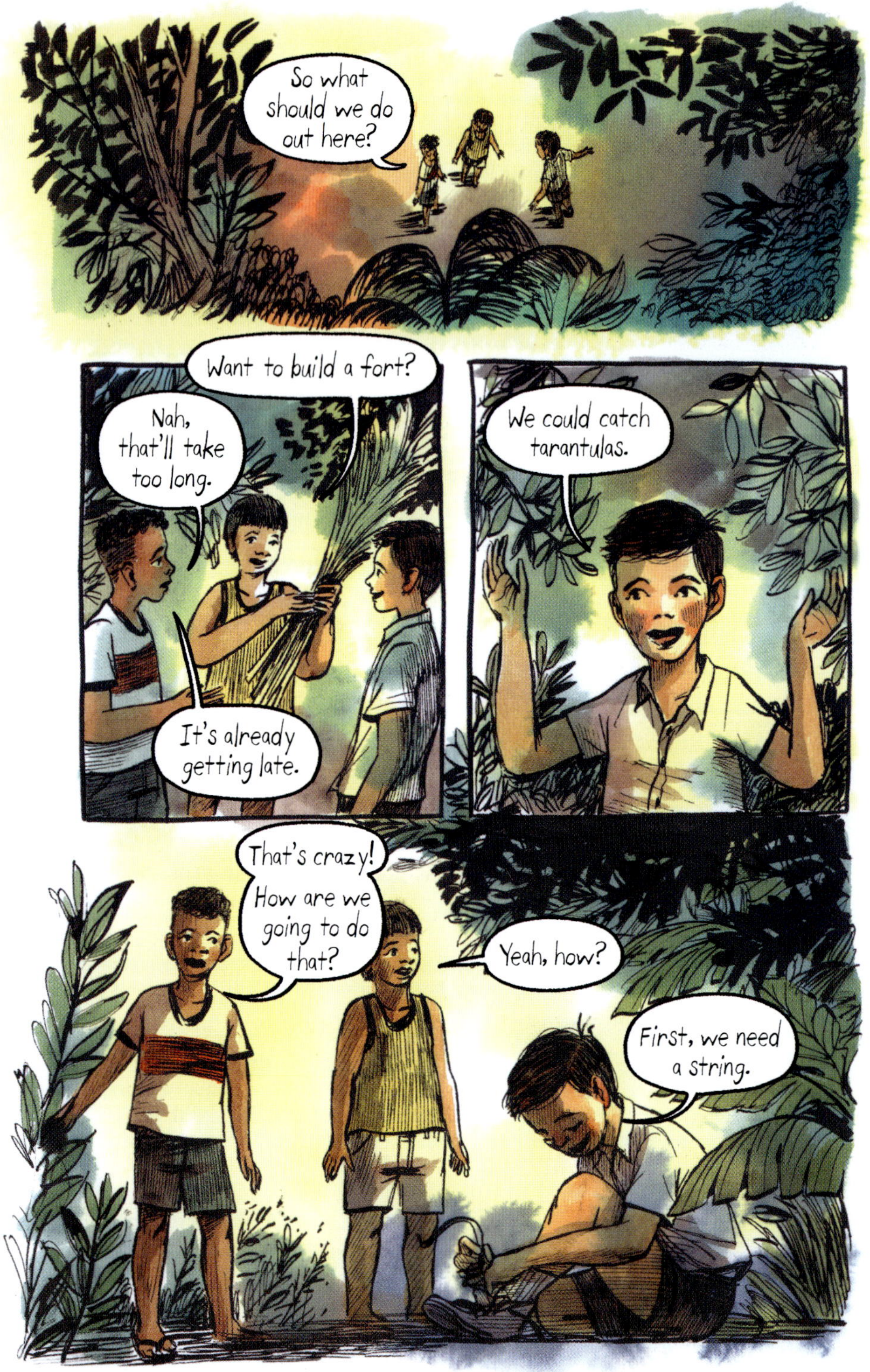
So what should we do out here?
Want to build a fort?
Nah, that'll take too long.
It's already getting late.
We could catch tarantulas.
That's crazy!
How are we going to do that?
Yeah, how?
First, we need a string.

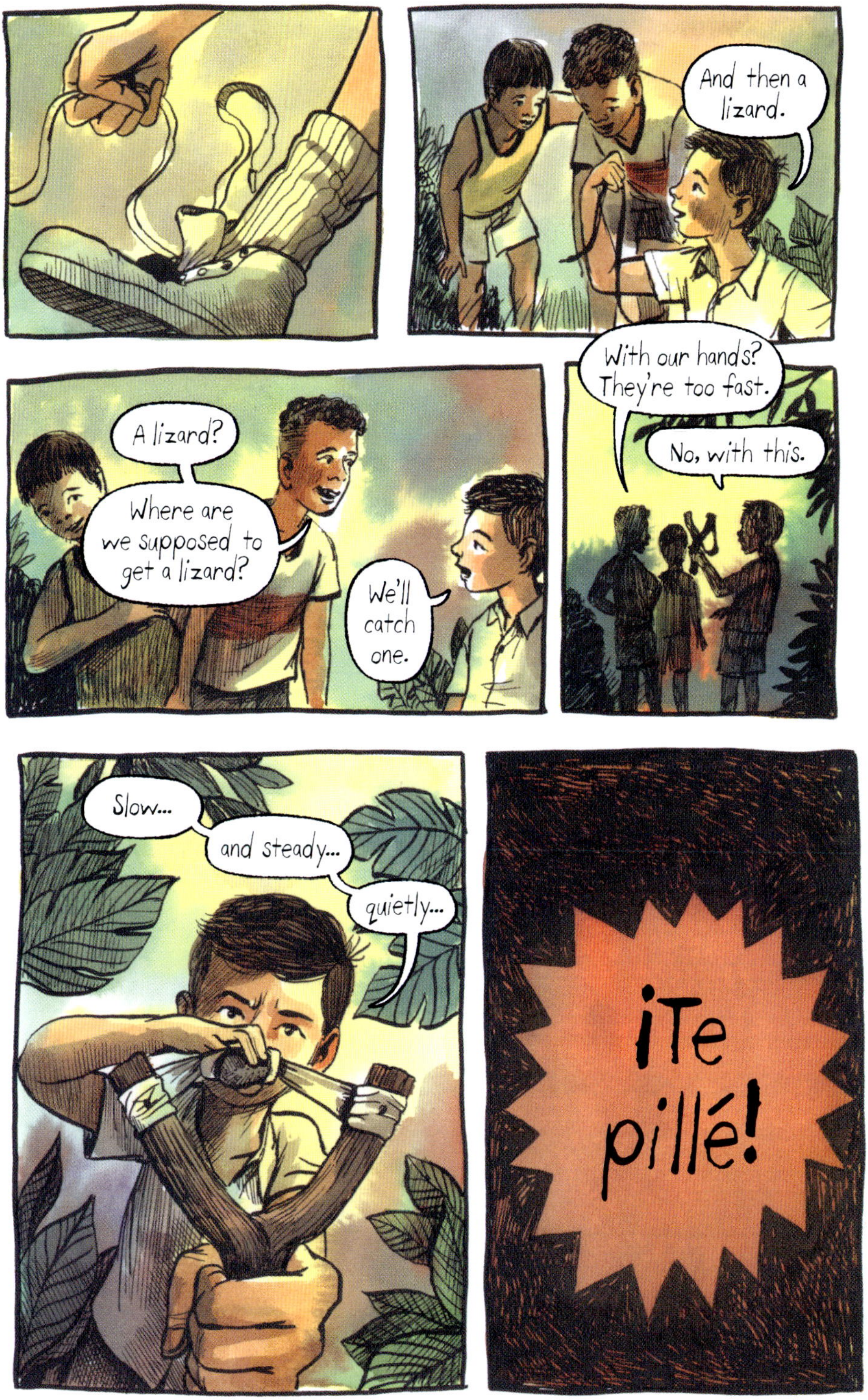
And then a lizard.
A lizard?
Where are we supposed to get a lizard?
We'll catch one.
With our hands? They're too fast.
No, with this.
Slow...
and steady...
quietly...
¡Te pillé!

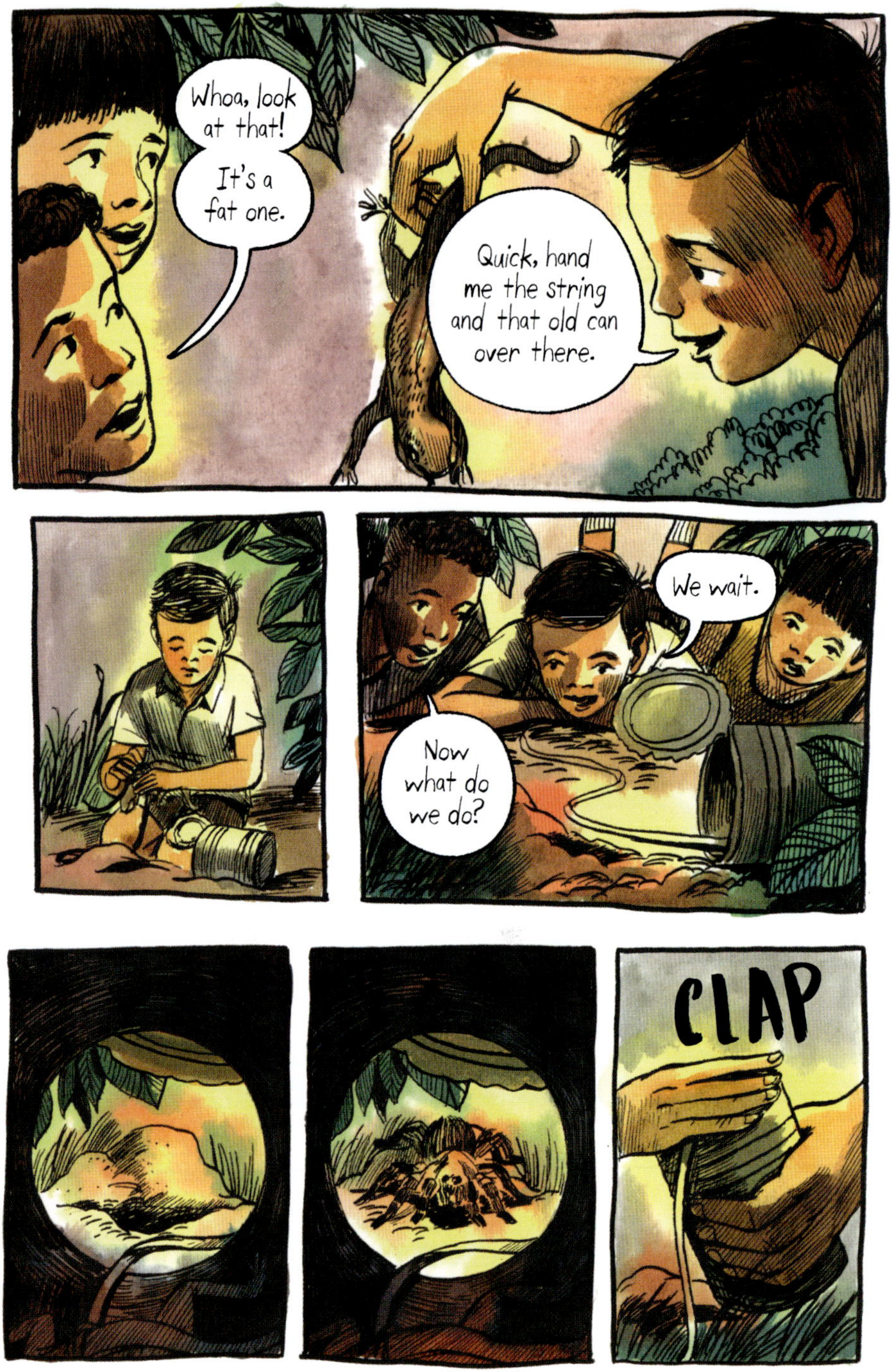
Whoa, look at that!
It's a fat one.
Quick, hand me the string and that old can over there.
We wait.
Now what do we do?
CLAP

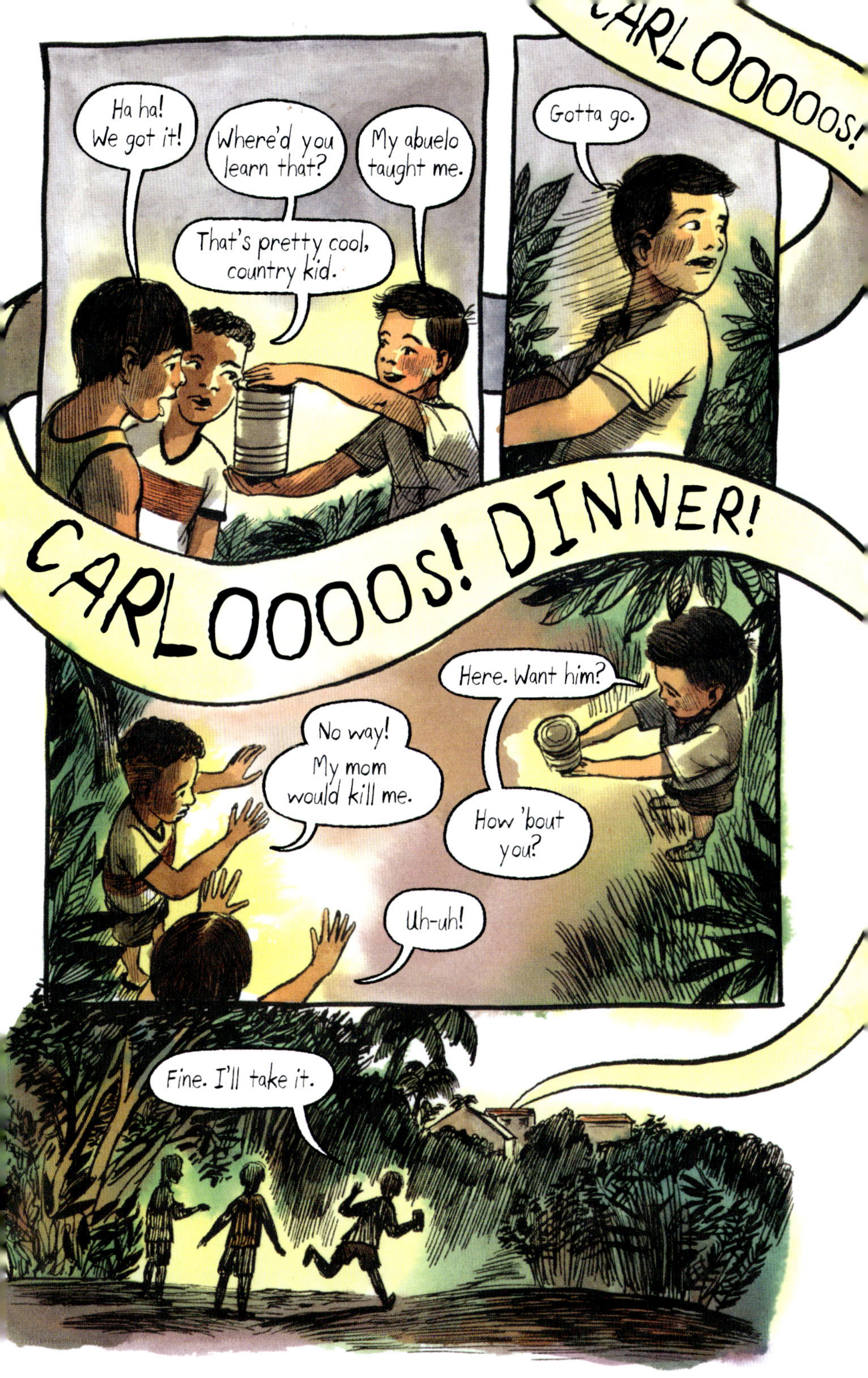
Ha ha! We got it!
Where'd you learn that?
My abuelo taught me.
That's pretty cool, country kid.
CARLOOOOOS!
Gotta go.
CARLOOOOOS! DINNER!
Here. Want him?
How 'bout you?
No way! My mom would kill me.
Uh-uh!
Fine. I'll take it.

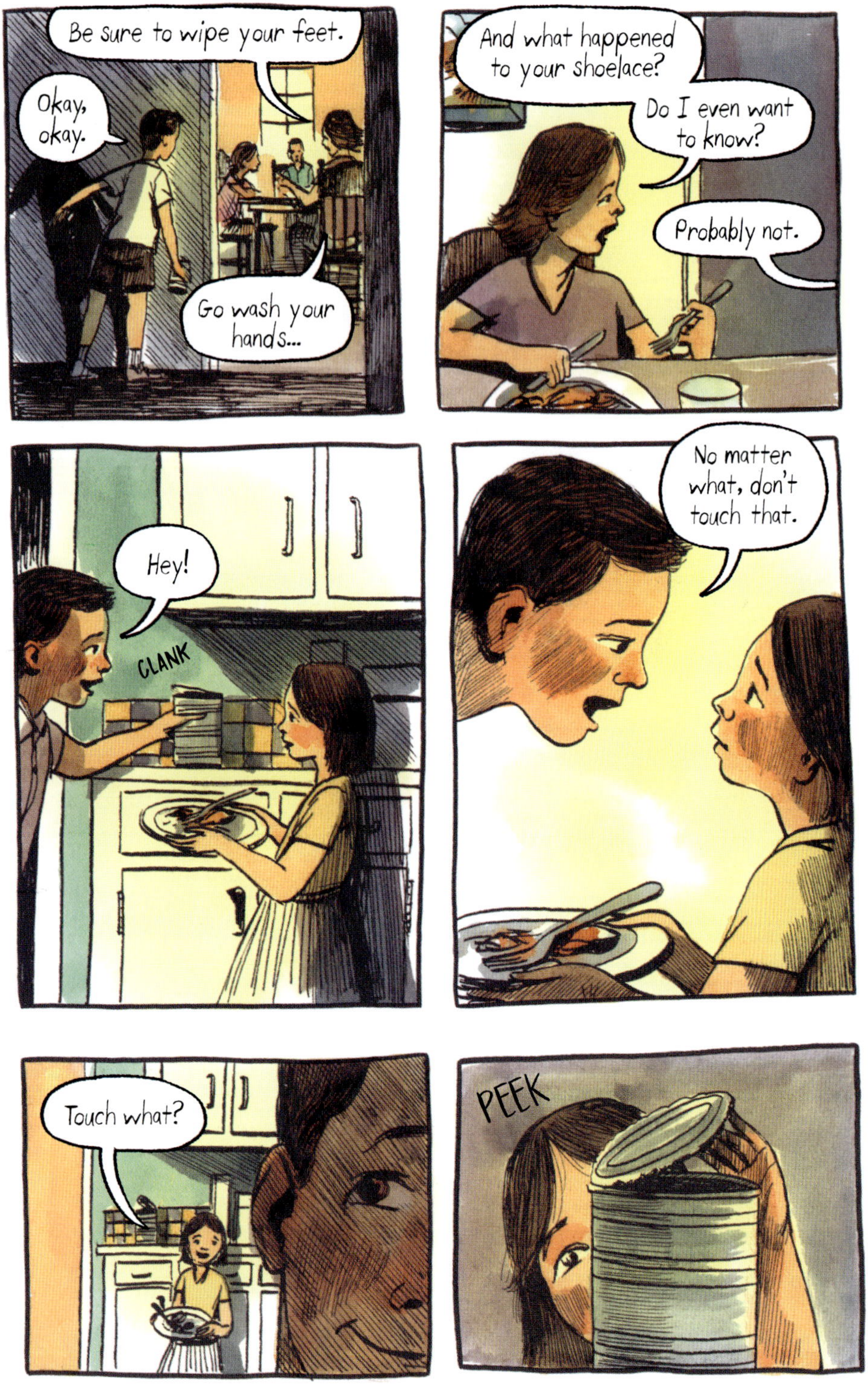
Be sure to wipe your feet.
Okay, okay.
Go wash your hands...
And what happened to your shoelace?
Do I even want to know?
Probably not.
Hey!
CLANK
No matter what, don't touch that.
Touch what?
PEEK

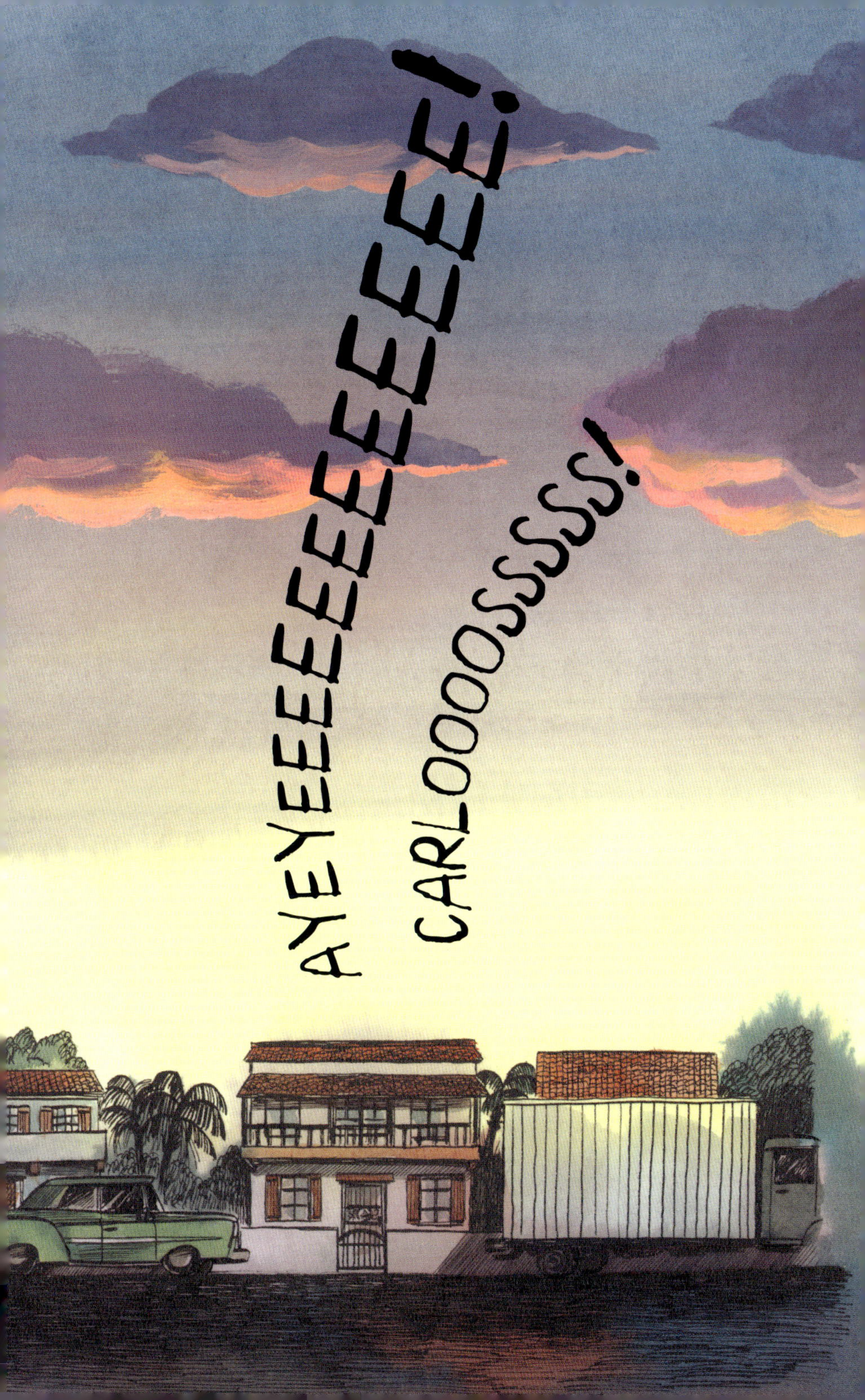

AYEYEEEEEEEEEEEEEEEEE!
CARLOOOOSSSSSS!

Trying to crush the rebellion, Batista's army begins a series of attacks against Castro in the Sierra Maestra mountains. In response, Castro launches his own guerrilla attacks throughout Cuba.

Country Kid

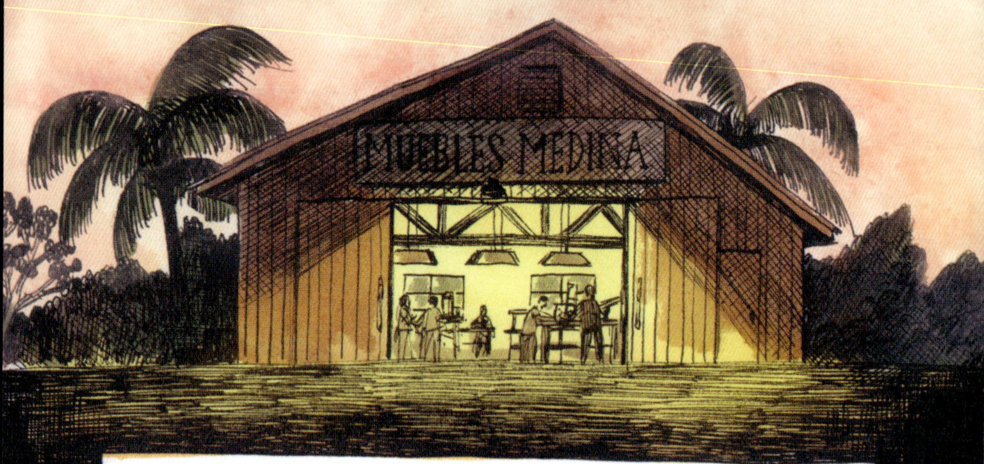
MUEBLES MEDINA

Papi's business was up and running now. It took all of his time.

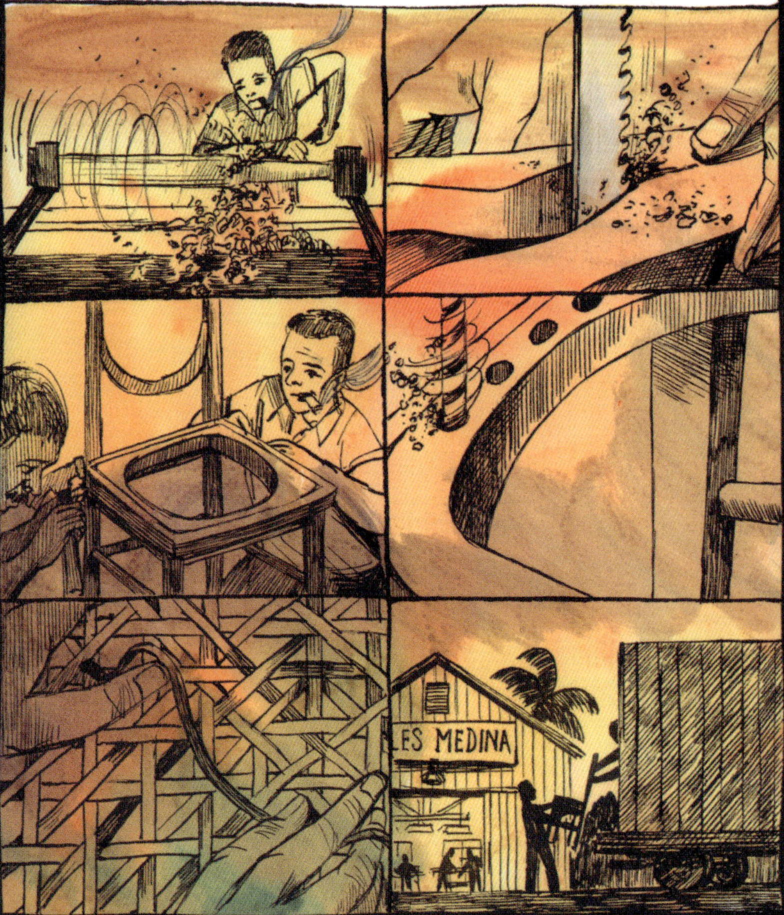
LES MEDINA

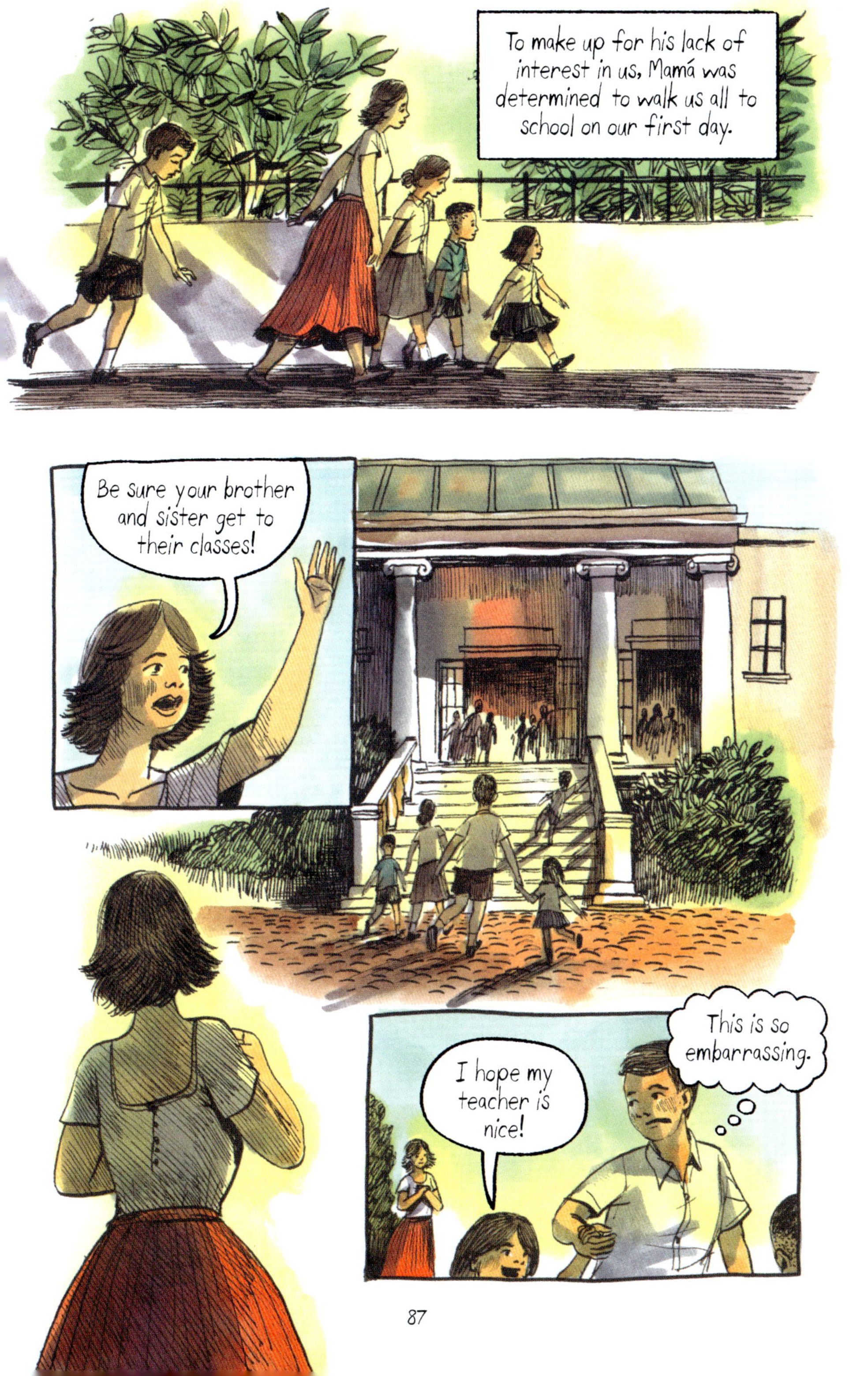
To make up for his lack of interest in us, Mamá was determined to walk us all to school on our first day.
Be sure your brother and sister get to their classes!
This is so embarrassing.
I hope my teacher is nice!

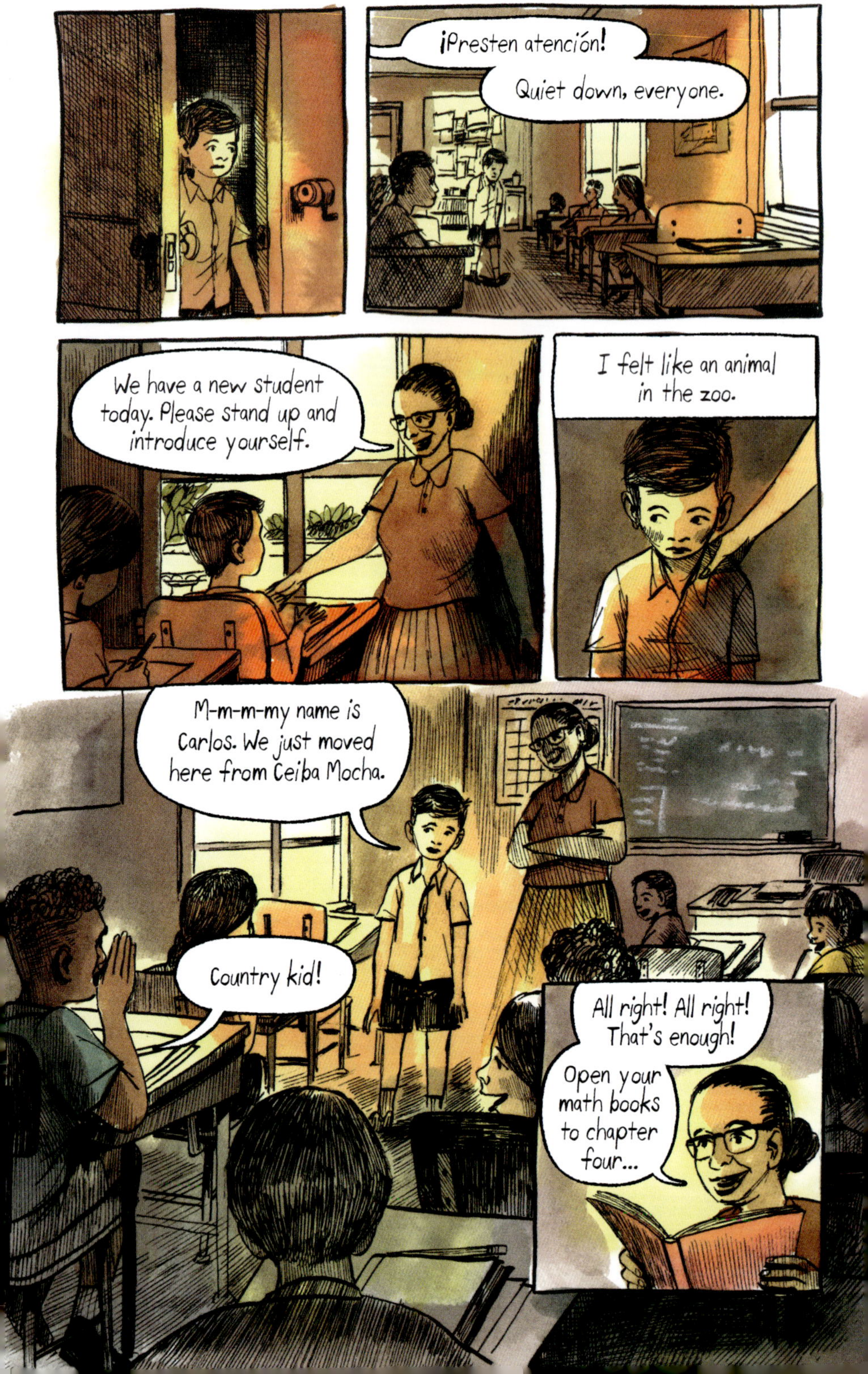
¡Presten atención!
Quiet down, everyone.
We have a new student today. Please stand up and introduce yourself.
I felt like an animal in the zoo.
M-m-m-my name is Carlos. We just moved here from Ceiba Mocha.
Country kid!
All right! All right! That's enough!
Open your math books to chapter four...

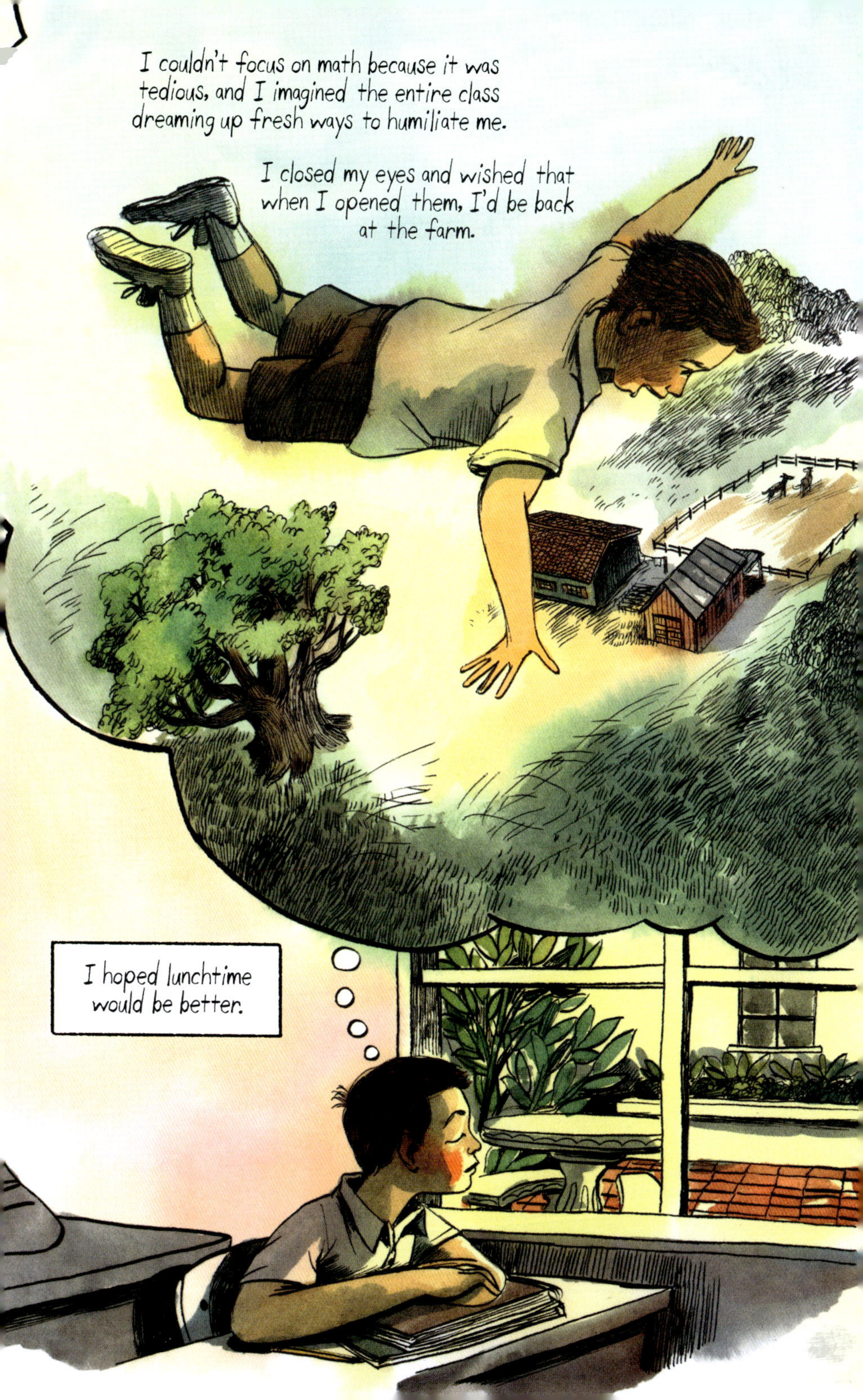
I couldn't focus on math because it was tedious, and I imagined the entire class dreaming up fresh ways to humiliate me.
I closed my eyes and wished that when I opened them, I'd be back at the farm.
I hoped lunchtime would be better.

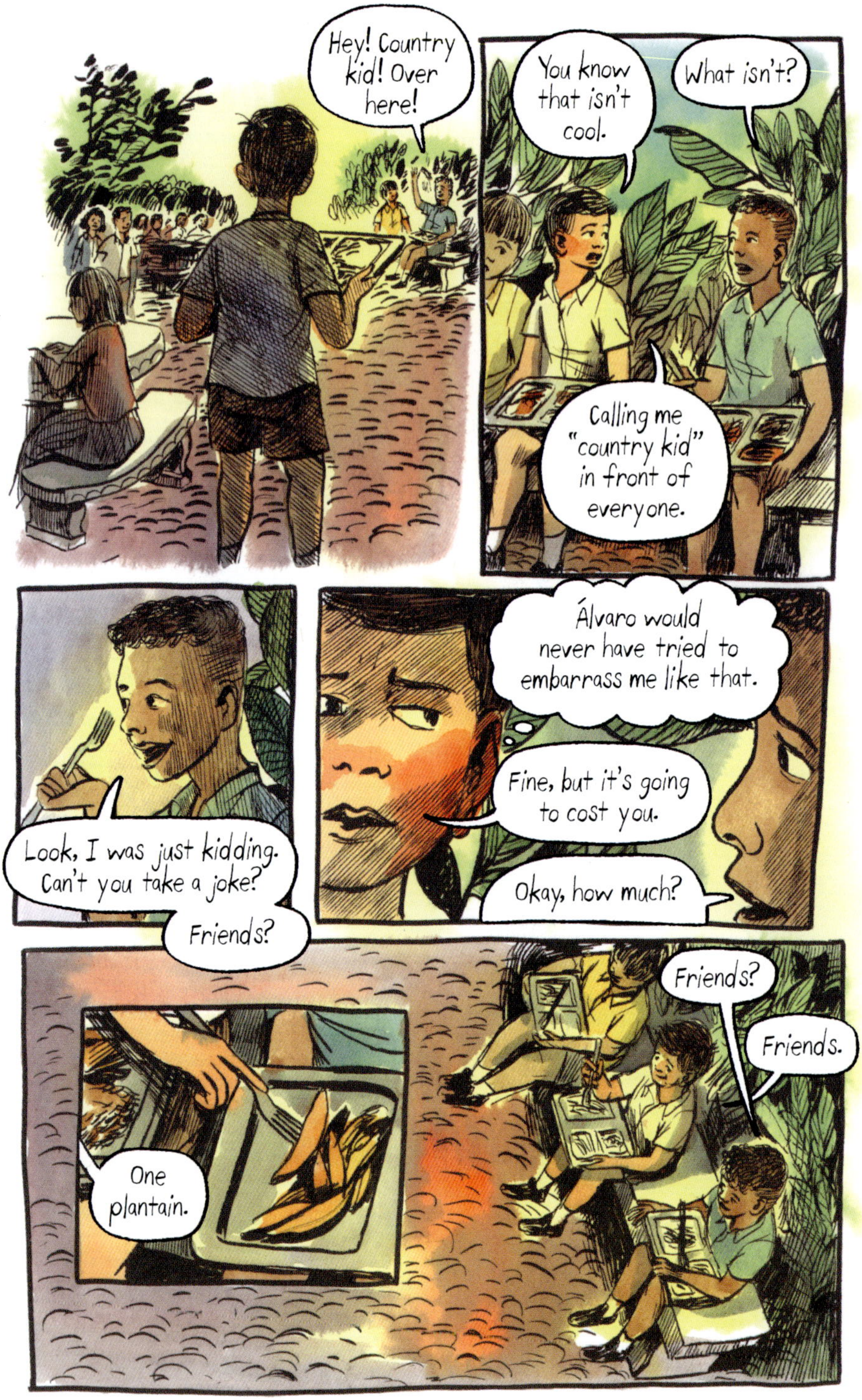
Hey! Country kid! Over here!
You know that isn't cool.
What isn't?
Calling me "country kid" in front of everyone.
Look, I was just kidding. Can't you take a joke?
Friends?
Álvaro would never have tried to embarrass me like that.
Fine, but it's going to cost you.
Okay, how much?
One plantain.
Friends?
Friends.

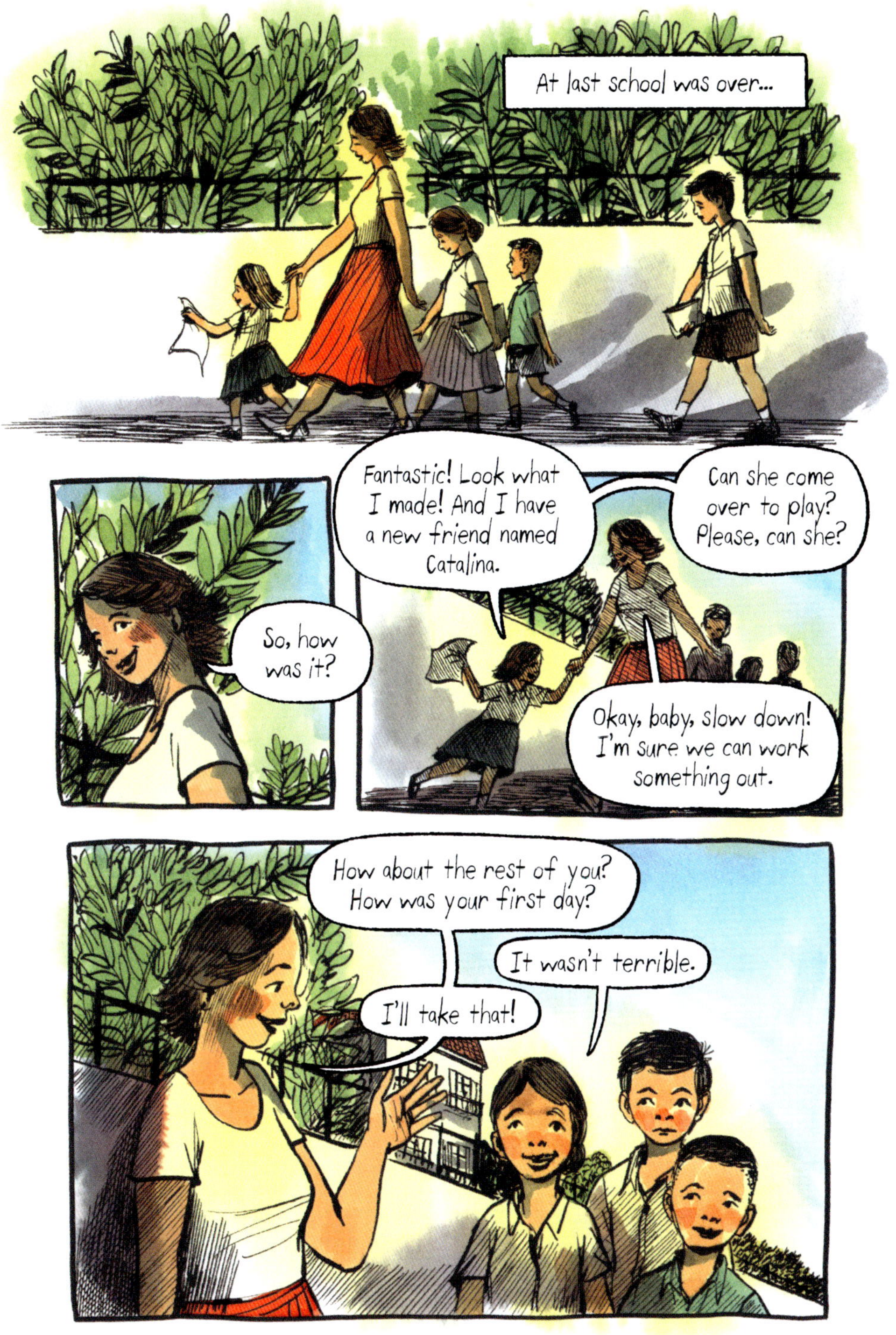

At last school was over...
So, how was it?
Fantastic! Look what I made! And I have a new friend named Catalina.
Can she come over to play? Please, can she?
Okay, baby, slow down! I'm sure we can work something out.
How about the rest of you? How was your first day?
It wasn't terrible.
I'll take that!

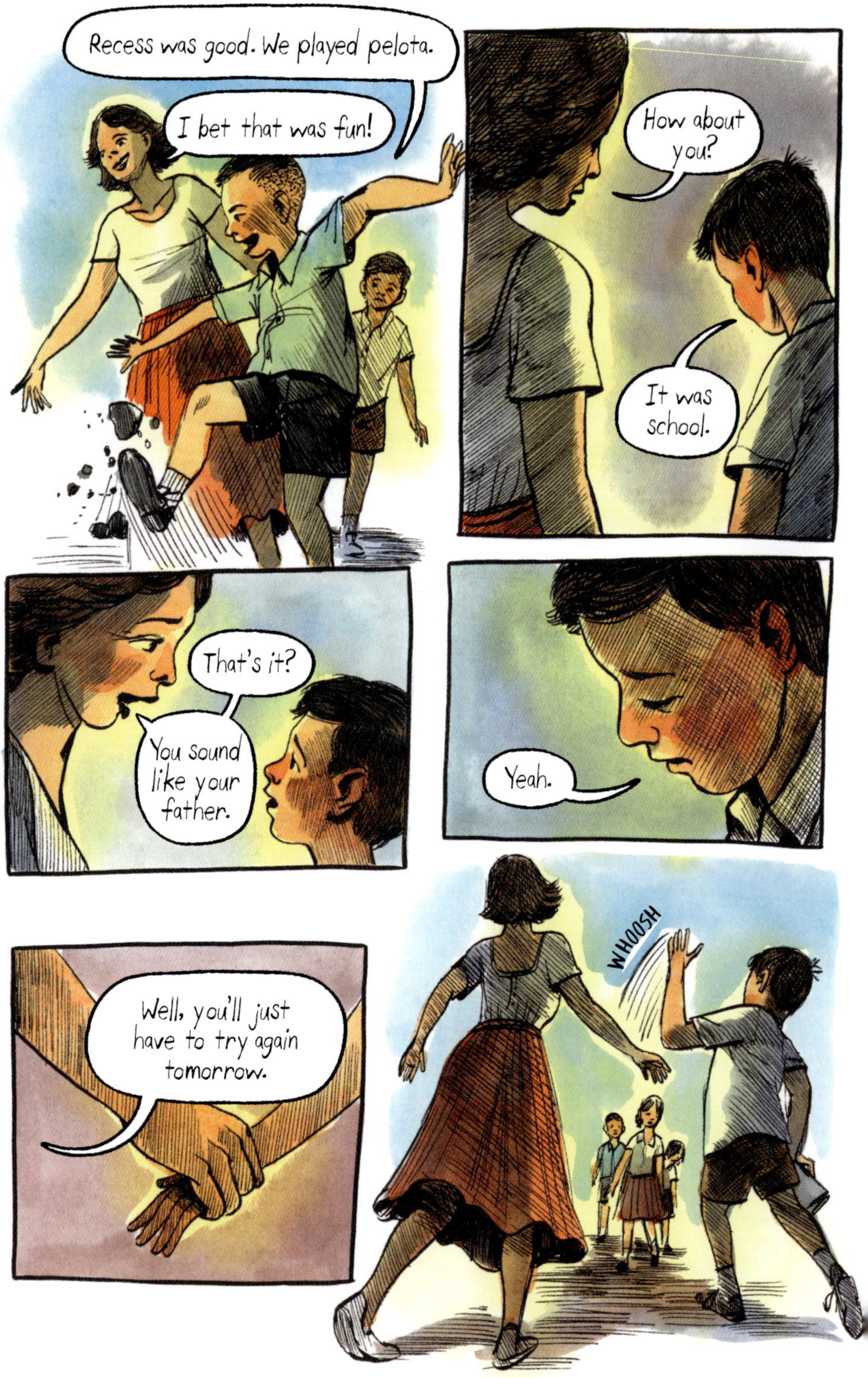
Recess was good. We played pelota.
I bet that was fun!
How about you?
It was school.
That's it?
You sound like your father.
Yeah.
Well, you'll just have to try again tomorrow.
WHOOSH

Tomorrow turned into next week.
And next week into next month.

Math was still tedious, but I discovered that
I liked to draw...

and wasn't half bad at it, either. My teacher said I had a good "visual memory." I think that meant I could hold pictures in my head and put them down on paper later.

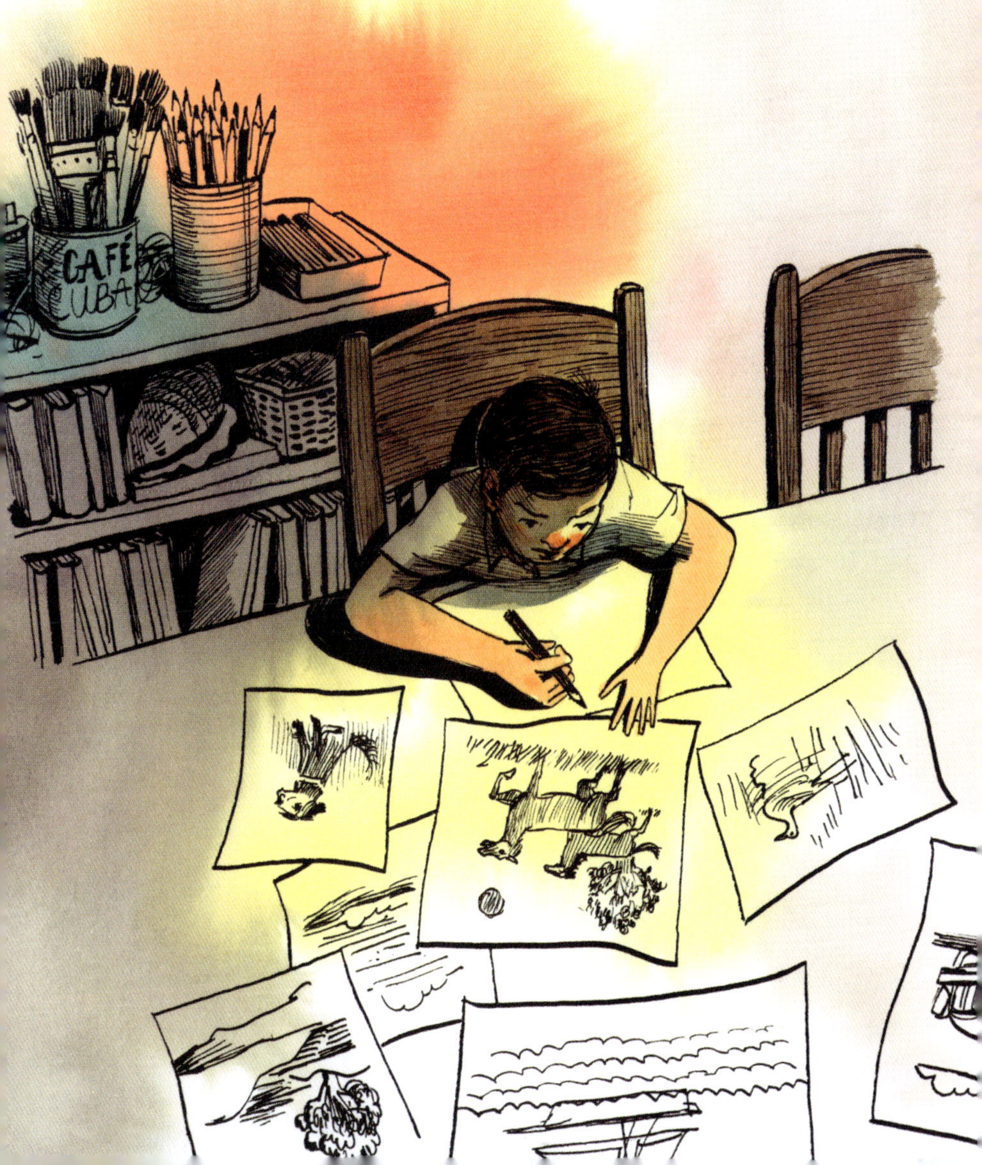
CAFÉ
CUBA

Papi was still up with the sun and didn't come in from the shop until late, but the business was thriving! He even had to hire more carpenters.

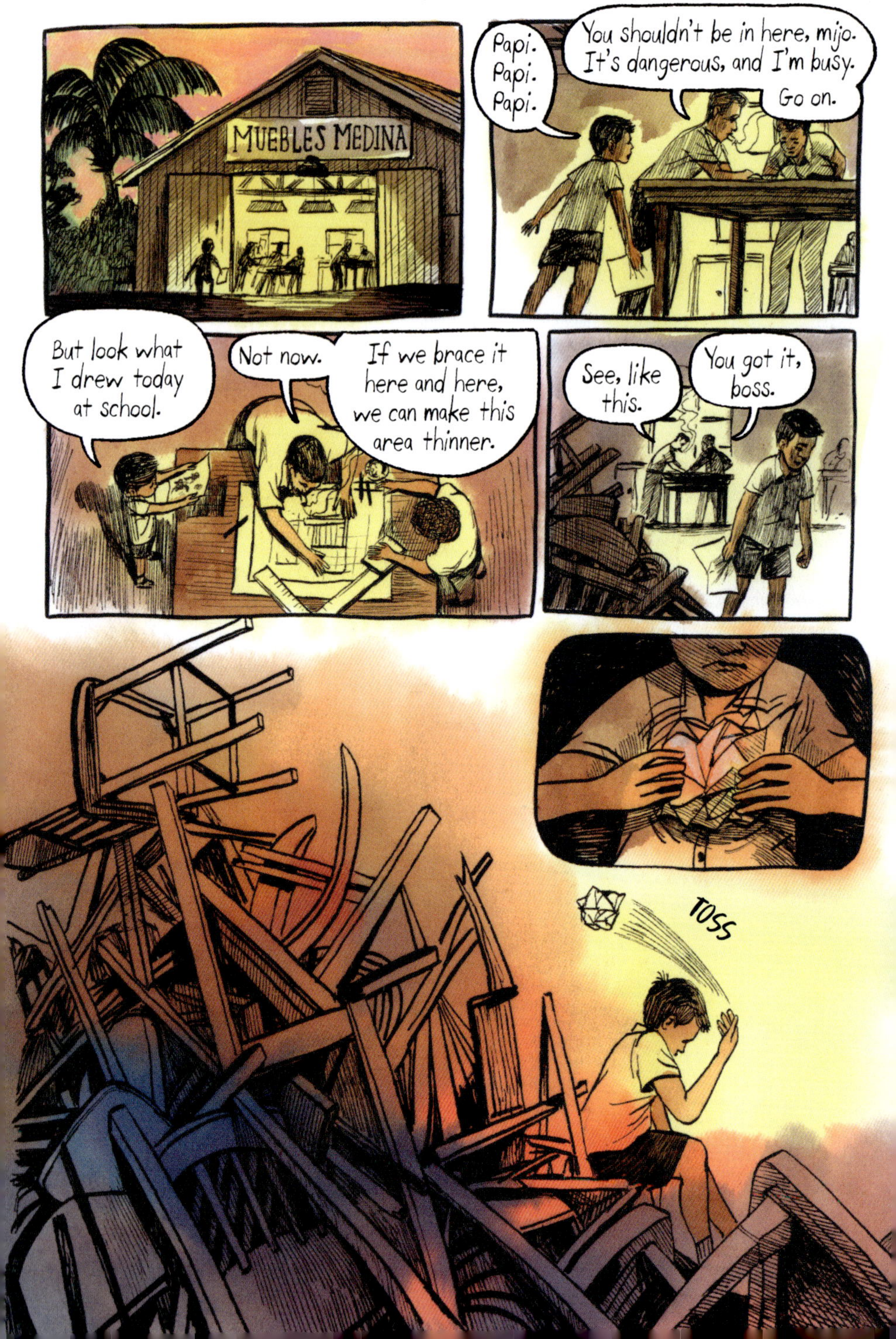
MUEBLES MEDINA
Papi. Papi. Papi.
You shouldn't be in here, mijo. It's dangerous, and I'm busy.
Go on.
But look what I drew today at school.
Not now.
If we brace it here and here, we can make this area thinner.
See, like this.
You got it, boss.
TOSS

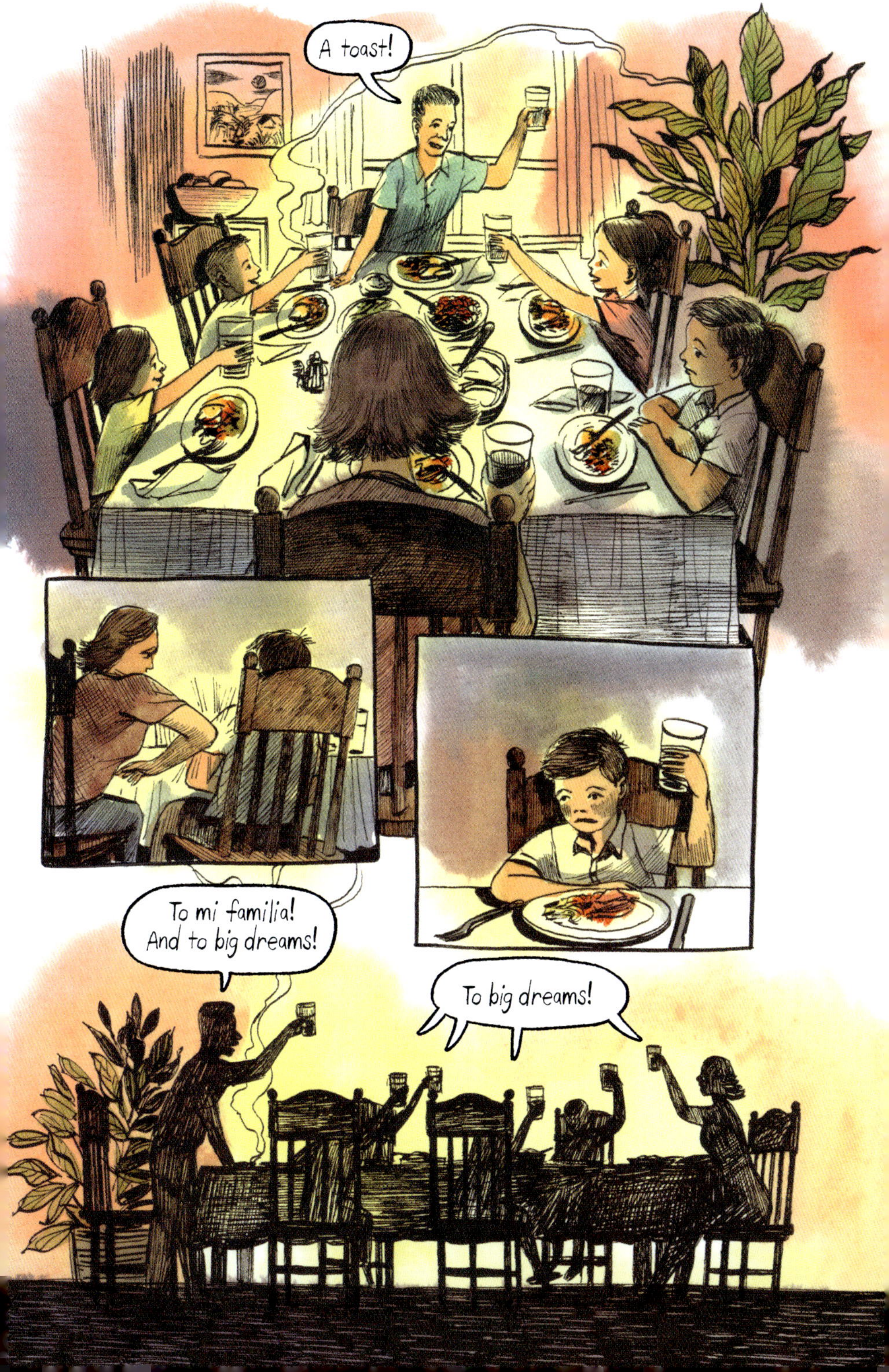
A toast!
To mi familia! And to big dreams!
To big dreams!

After the revolutionaries take a number of cities in central Cuba, Batista flees Havana. One week later, Castro arrives and takes control of the government. He begins to round up and execute people who were loyal to Batista.

New Year's Day 1959

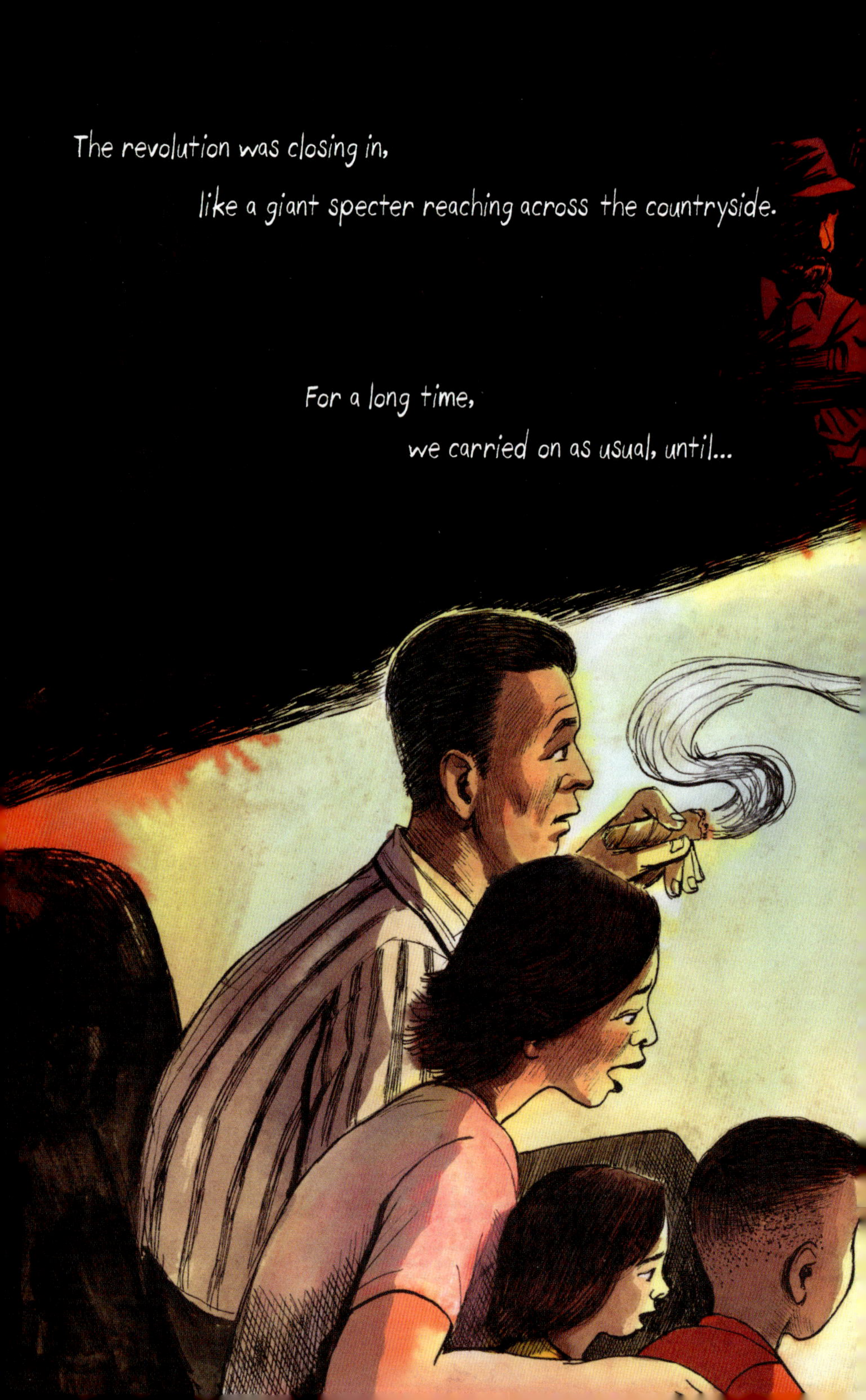
The revolution was closing in,
like a giant specter reaching across the countryside.
For a long time,
we carried on as usual, until...

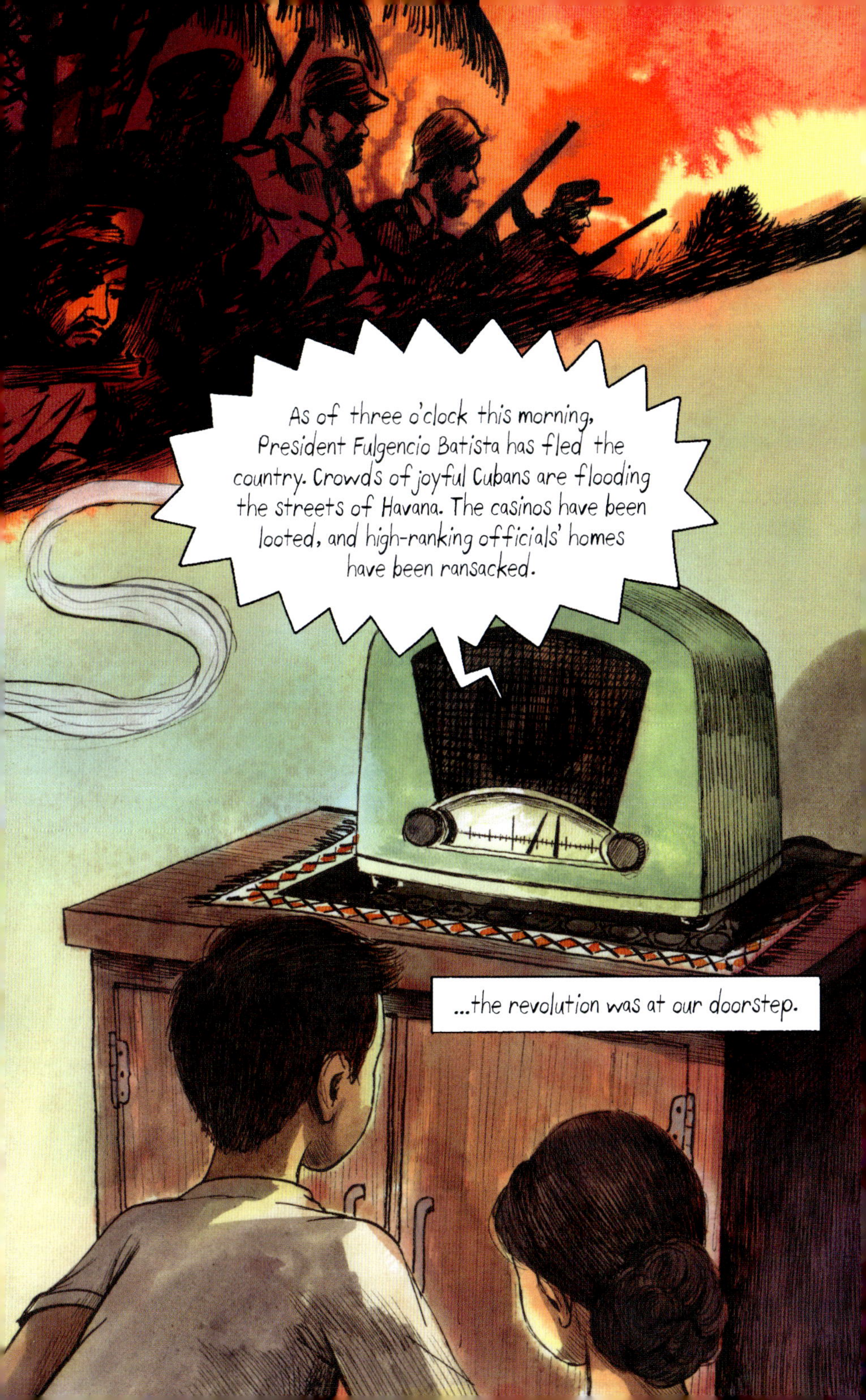
As of three o'clock this morning, President Fulgencio Batista has fled the country. Crowds of joyful Cubans are flooding the streets of Havana. The casinos have been looted, and high-ranking officials' homes have been ransacked.
...the revolution was at our doorstep.

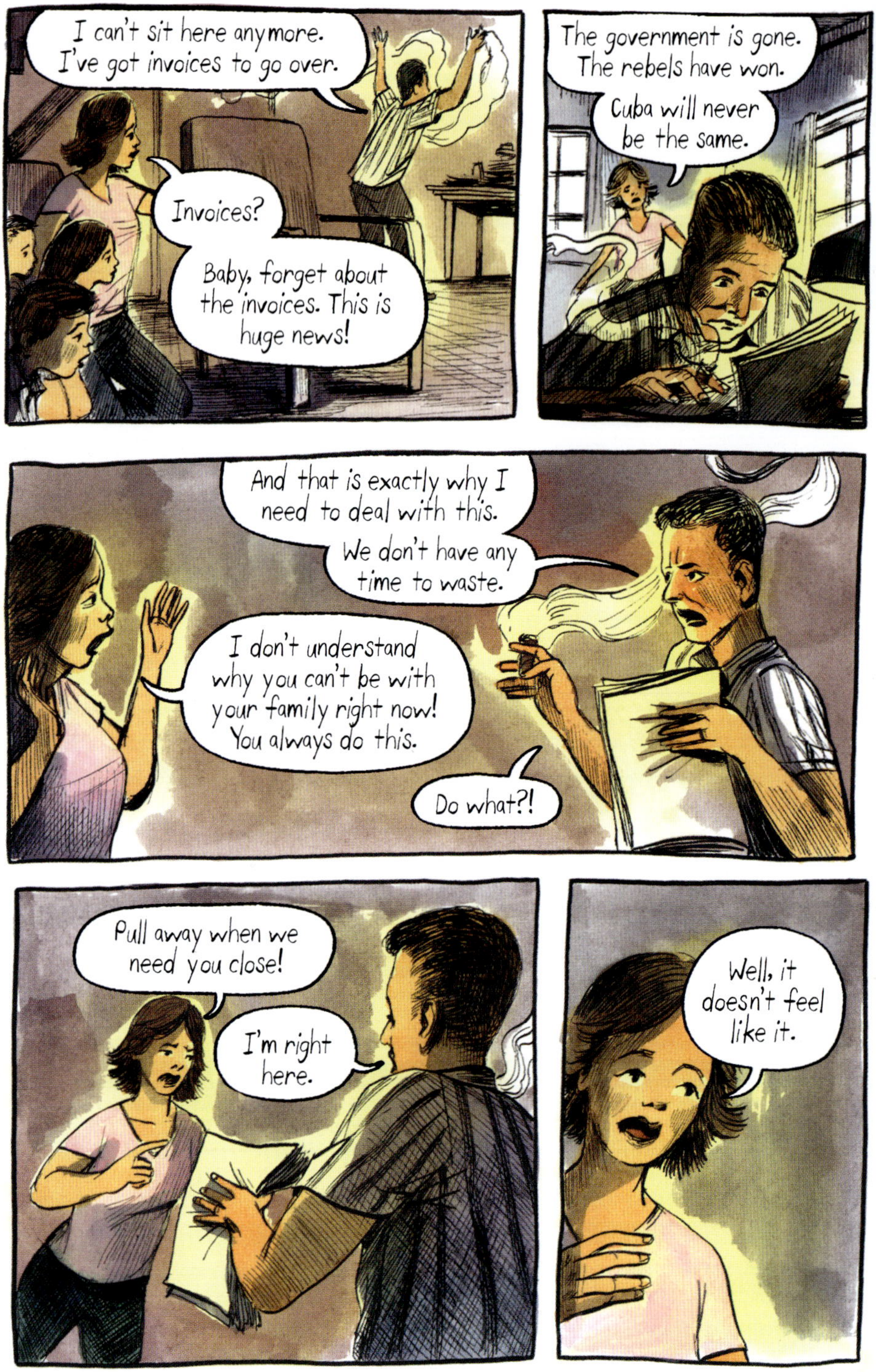
I can't sit here anymore. I've got invoices to go over.
Invoices?
Baby, forget about the invoices. This is huge news!
The government is gone. The rebels have won.
Cuba will never be the same.
And that is exactly why I need to deal with this.
We don't have any time to waste.
I don't understand why you can't be with your family right now! You always do this.
Do what?!
Pull away when we need you close!
I'm right here.
Well, it doesn't feel like it.

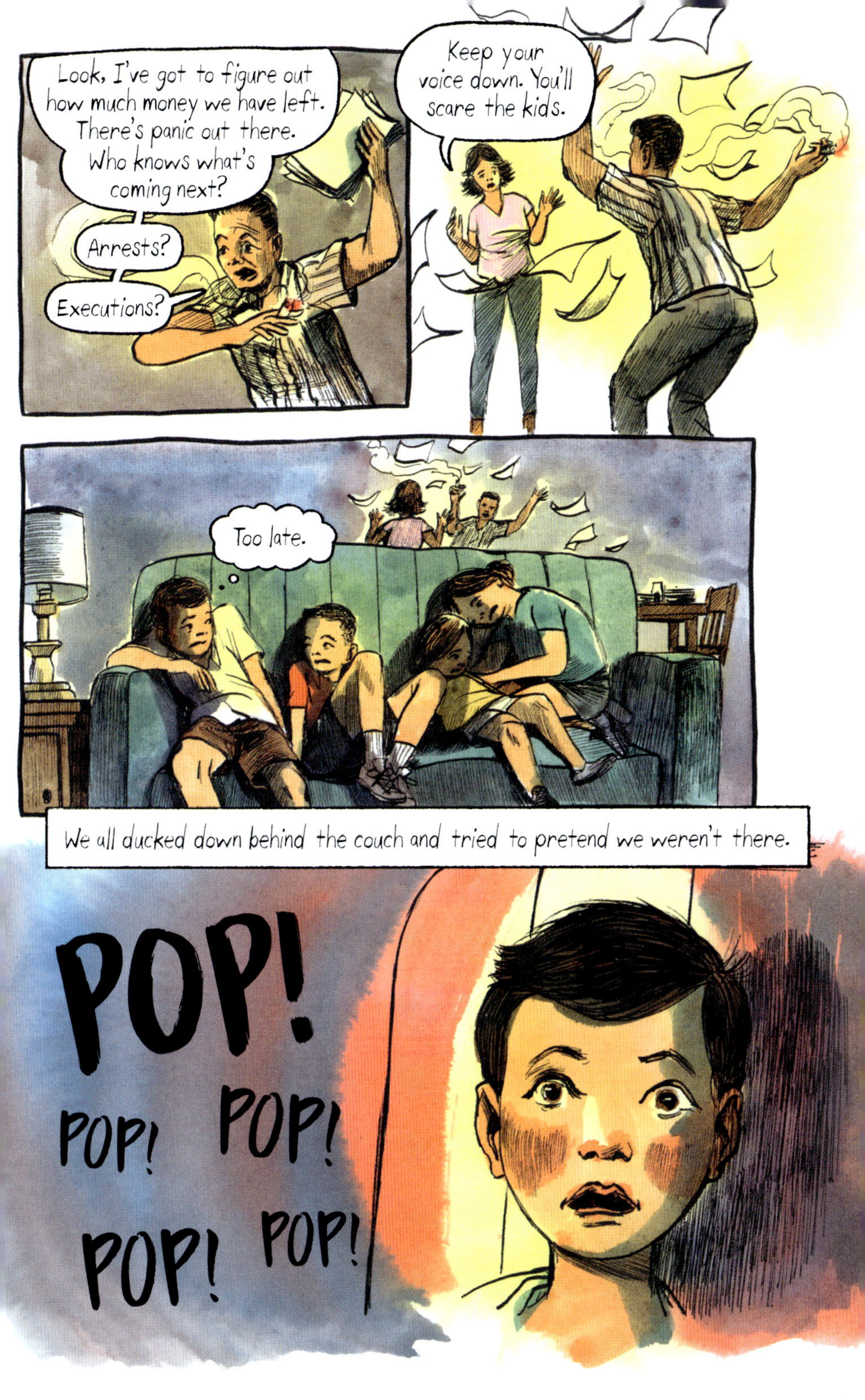
Look, I've got to figure out how much money we have left. There's panic out there. Who knows what's coming next?
Arrests?
Executions?
Keep your voice down. You'll scare the kids.
Too late.
We all ducked down behind the couch and tried to pretend we weren't there.
POP!
POP!
POP!
POP!
POP!

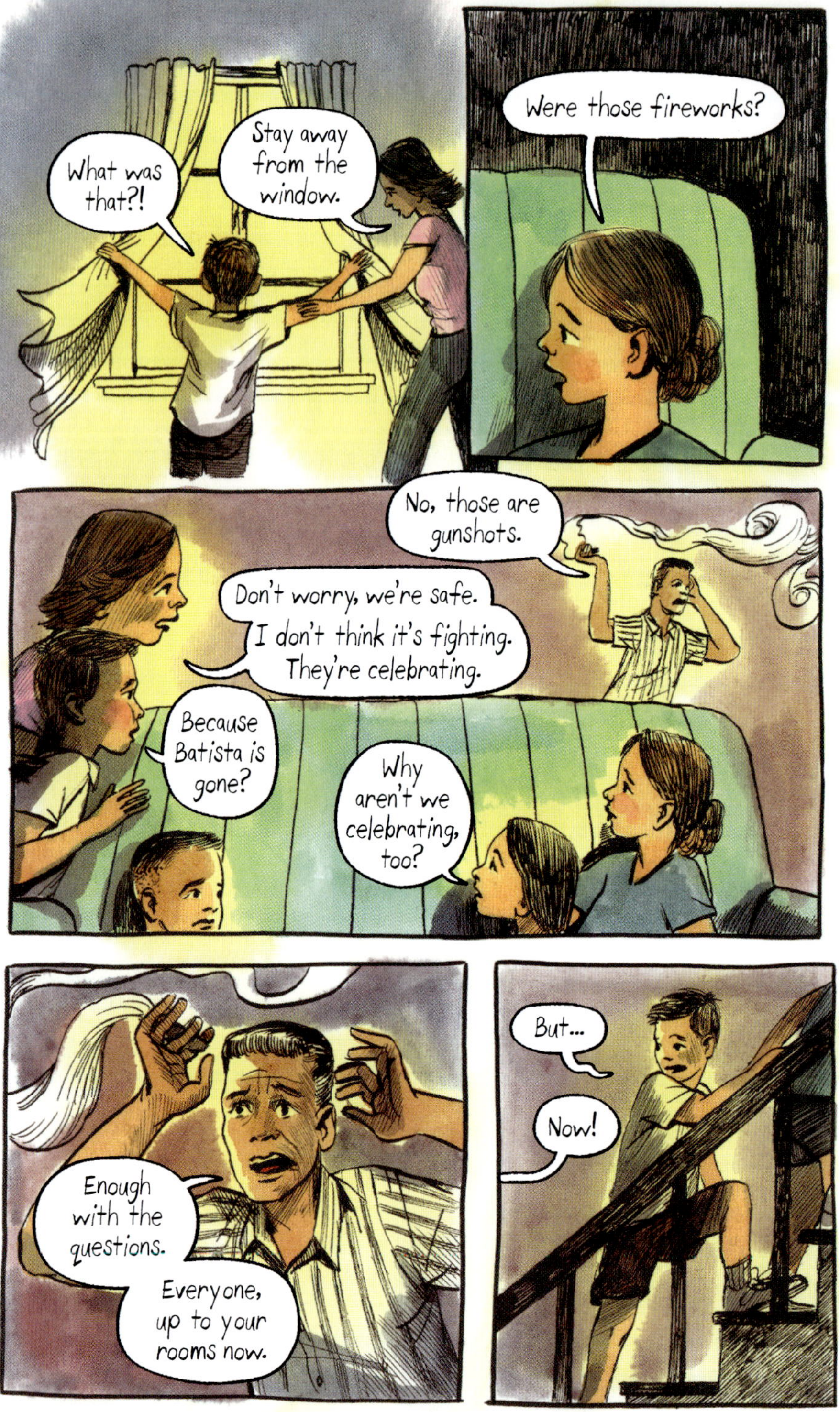
What was that?!
Stay away from the window.
Were those fireworks?
No, those are gunshots.
Don't worry, we're safe. I don't think it's fighting. They're celebrating.
Because Batista is gone?
Why aren't we celebrating, too?
Enough with the questions.
Everyone, up to your rooms now.
But...
Now!

Hey, Carlos.

Yeah, bro?

Do you think we're going to go to school tomorrow?

Sorry, little man, I don't think so.

Good.

HA! HA! HA!

Wait. Shhhh...

Do you hear that?

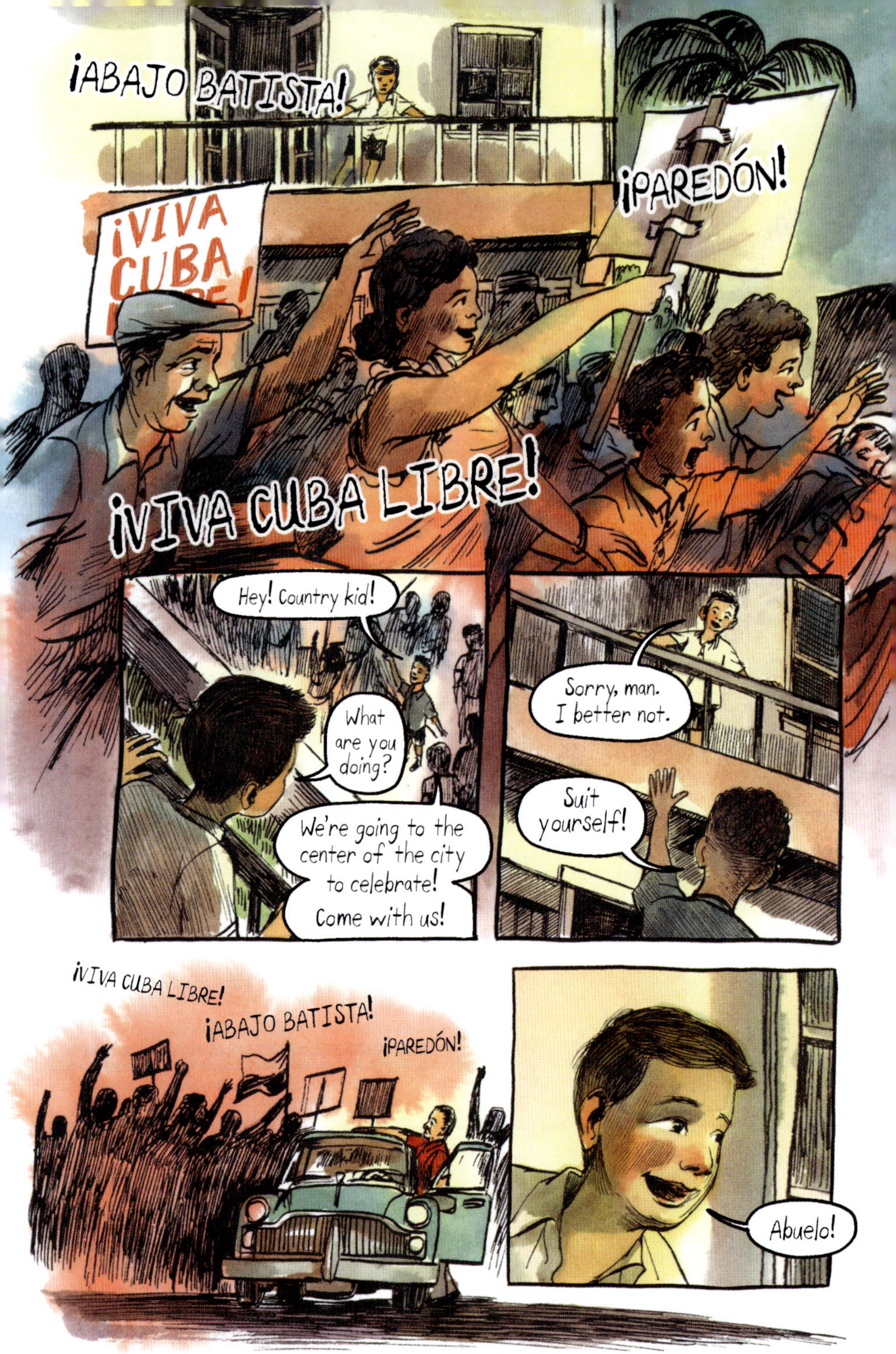
¡ABAJO BATISTA!
¡VIVA CUBA
¡PAREDÓN!
¡VIVA CUBA LIBRE!
Hey! Country kid!
What are you doing?
We're going to the center of the city to celebrate!
Come with us!
Sorry, man. I better not.
Suit yourself!
¡VIVA CUBA LIBRE!
¡ABAJO BATISTA!
¡PAREDÓN!
Abuelo!

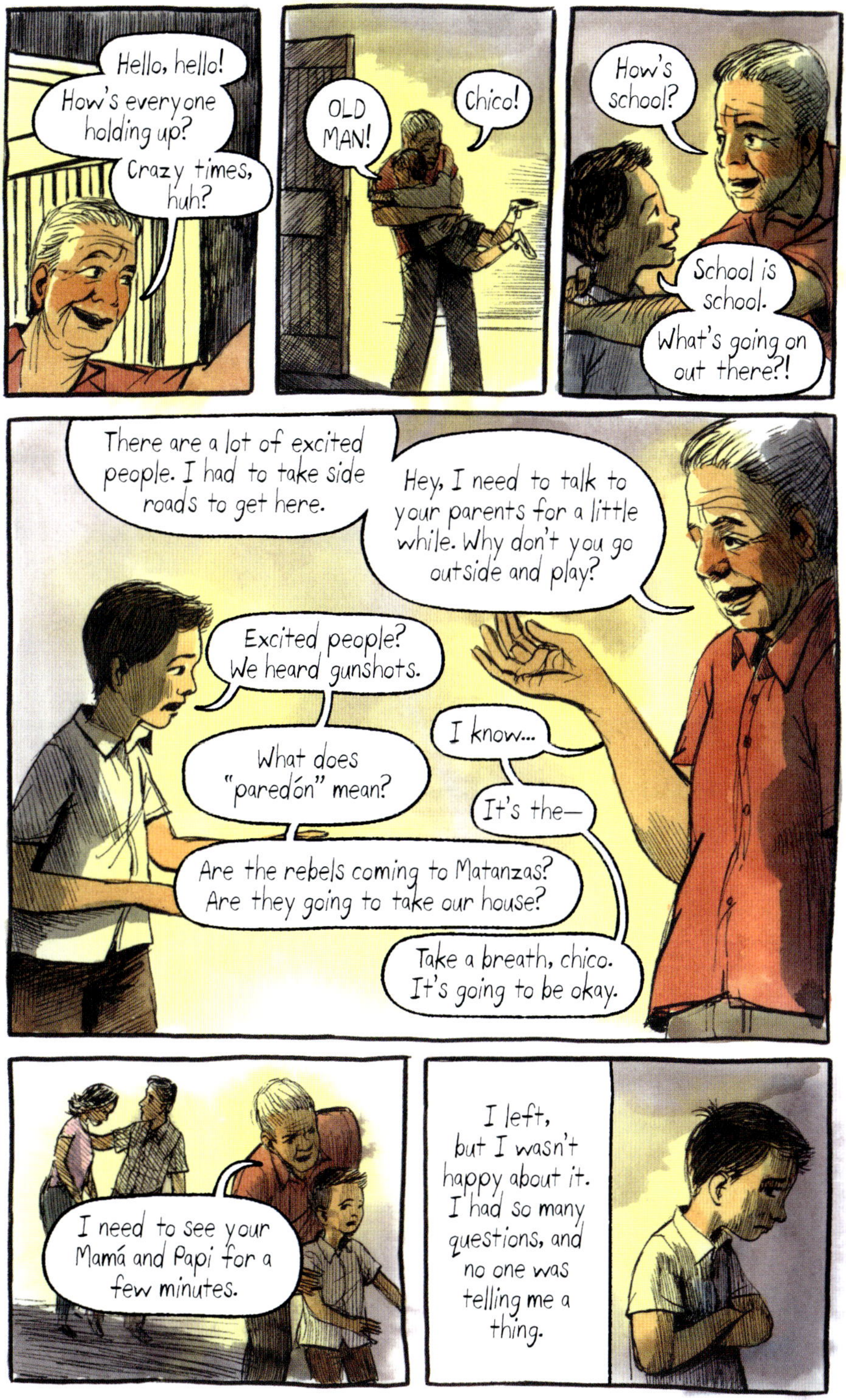
Hello, hello!
How's everyone holding up?
Crazy times, huh?
OLD MAN!
Chico!
How's school?
School is school.
What's going on out there?!
There are a lot of excited people. I had to take side roads to get here.
Hey, I need to talk to your parents for a little while. Why don't you go outside and play?
Excited people? We heard gunshots.
What does "paredón" mean?
I know...
It's the—
Are the rebels coming to Matanzas? Are they going to take our house?
Take a breath, chico. It's going to be okay.
I need to see your Mamá and Papi for a few minutes.
I left, but I wasn't happy about it. I had so many questions, and no one was telling me a thing.

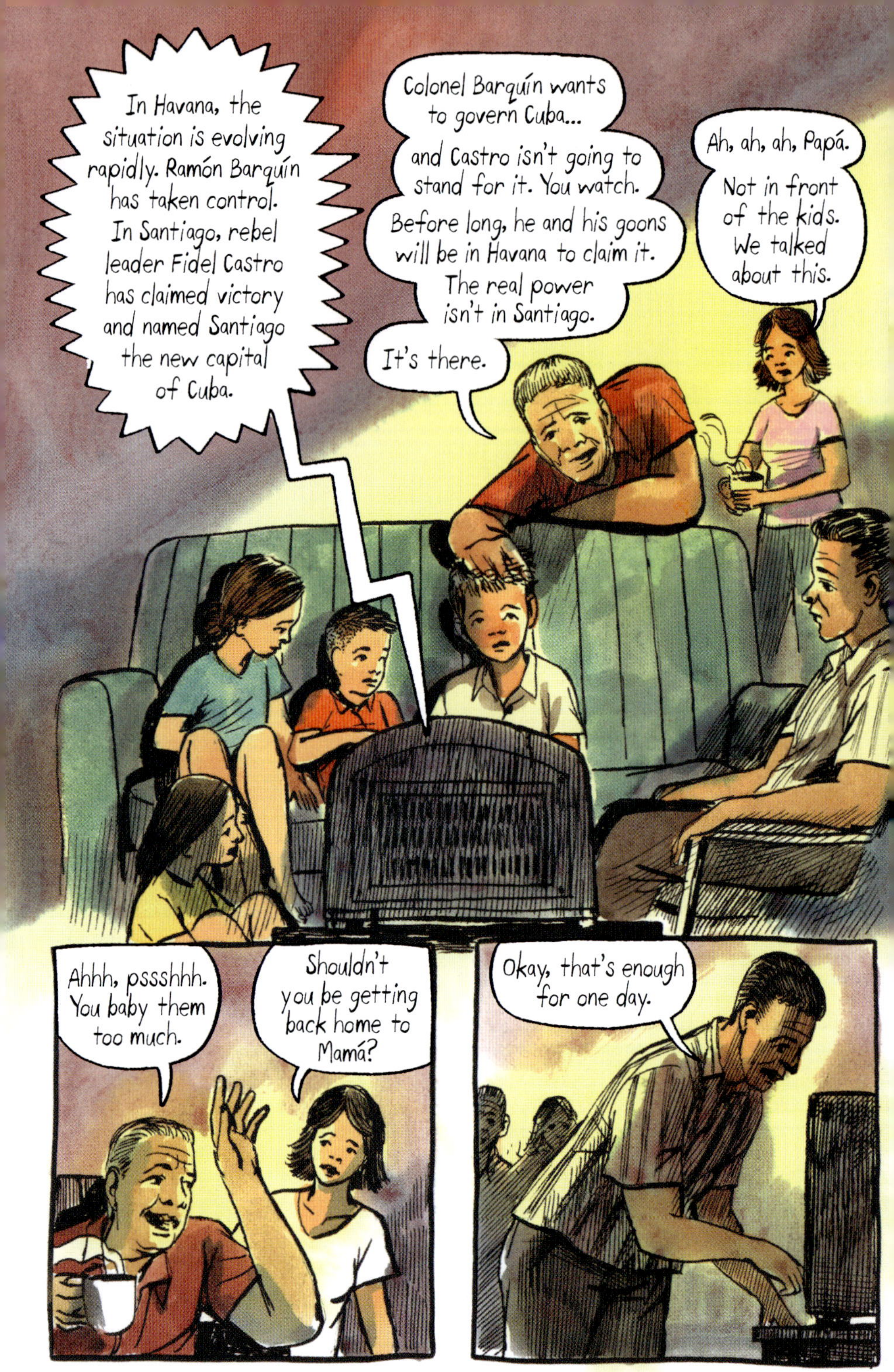
In Havana, the situation is evolving rapidly. Ramón Barquín has taken control. In Santiago, rebel leader Fidel Castro has claimed victory and named Santiago the new capital of Cuba.
Colonel Barquín wants to govern Cuba...
and Castro isn't going to stand for it. You watch.
Before long, he and his goons will be in Havana to claim it.
The real power isn't in Santiago.
It's there.
Ah, ah, ah, Papá.
Not in front of the kids. We talked about this.
Ahhh, pssshhh. You baby them too much.
Shouldn't you be getting back home to Mamá?
Okay, that's enough for one day.

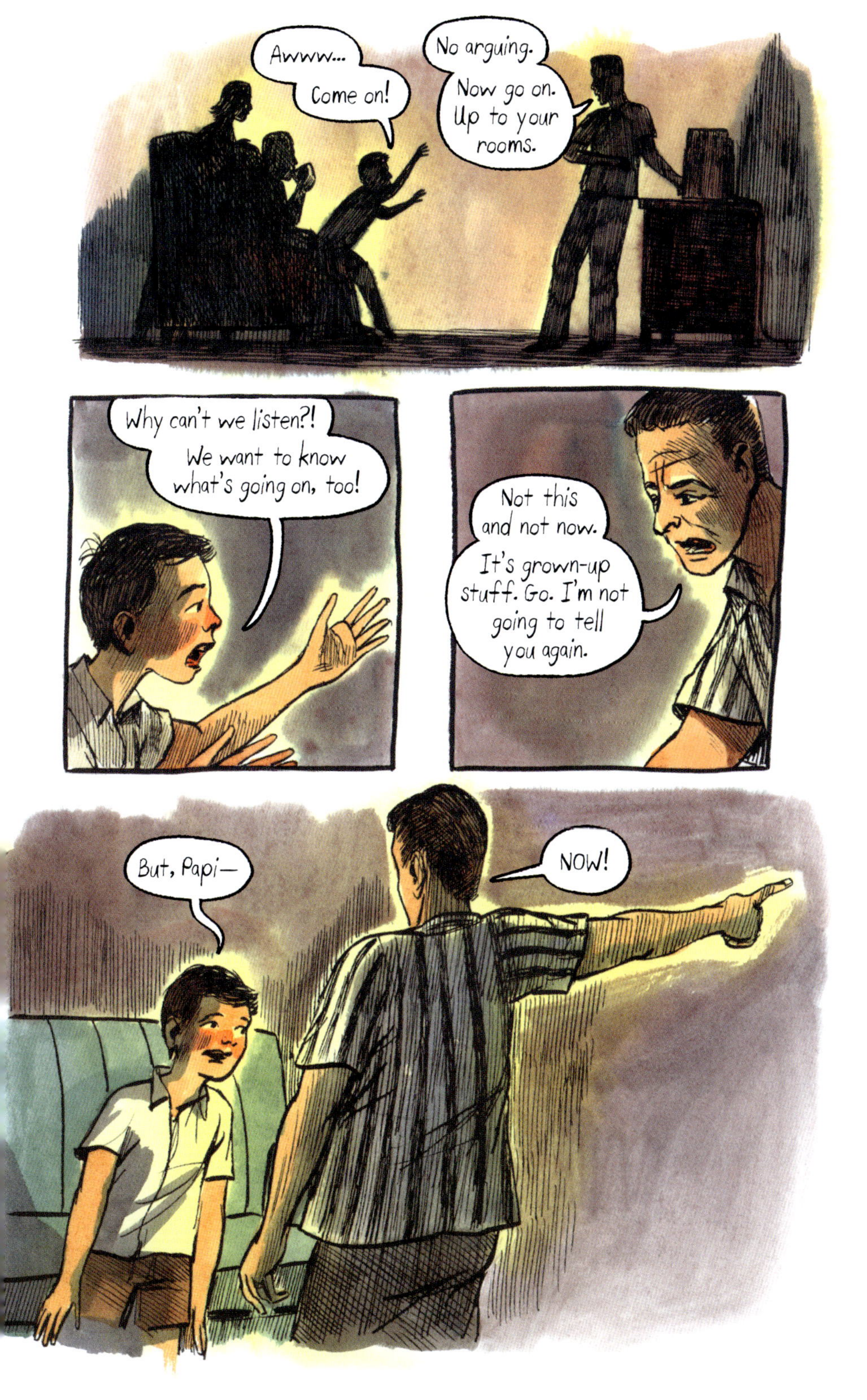
Awww...
Come on!
No arguing.
Now go on. Up to your rooms.
Why can't we listen?!
We want to know what's going on, too!
Not this and not now.
It's grown-up stuff. Go. I'm not going to tell you again.
But, Papi—
NOW!

Castro wants to shore up his power quickly. He postpones elections indefinitely, attacks the independent press, and begins to take control of factories, farms, private businesses, and homes.

Devil's Stew

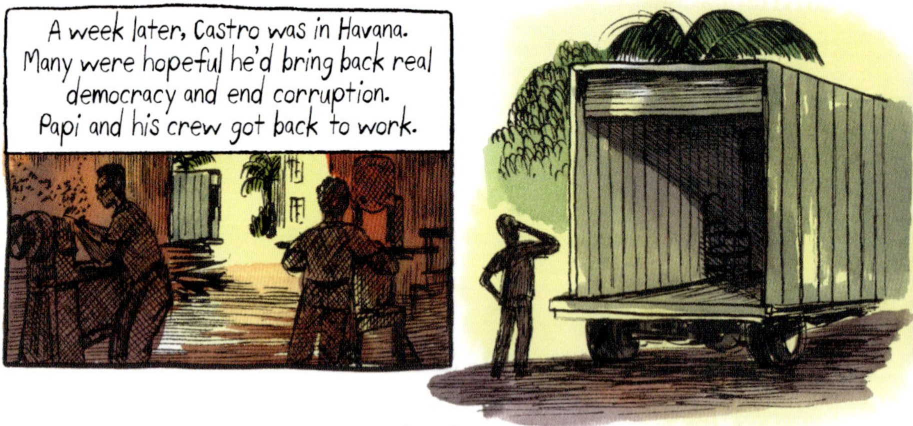
A week later, Castro was in Havana. Many were hopeful he'd bring back real democracy and end corruption. Papi and his crew got back to work.

But people also worried, and only spent money on stuff they needed to live—not sofas and chairs. Papi's orders dried up, and he earned barely enough to keep us afloat.

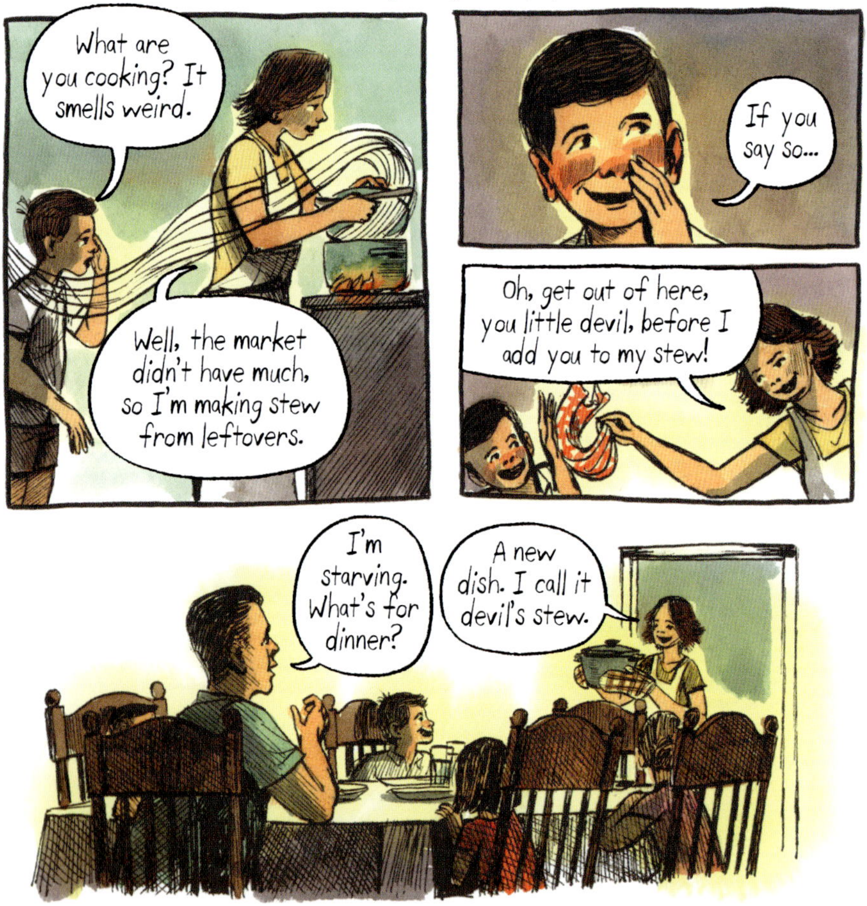
What are you cooking? It smells weird.
Well, the market didn't have much, so I'm making stew from leftovers.
If you say so...
Oh, get out of here, you little devil, before I add you to my stew!
I'm starving. What's for dinner?
A new dish. I call it devil's stew.

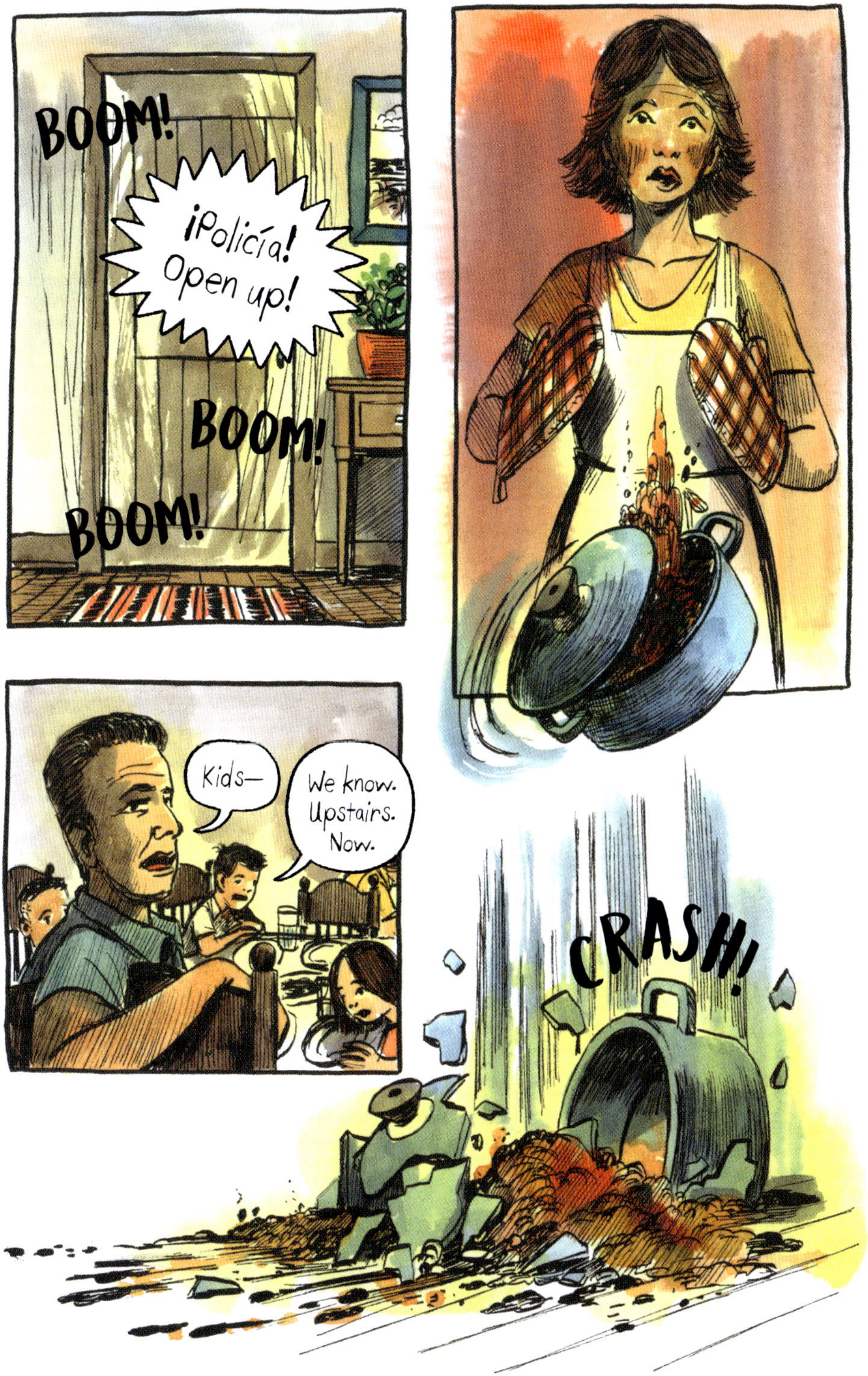
BOOM!
¡Policía! Open up!
BOOM!
BOOM!
Kids—
We know. Upstairs. Now.
CRASH!

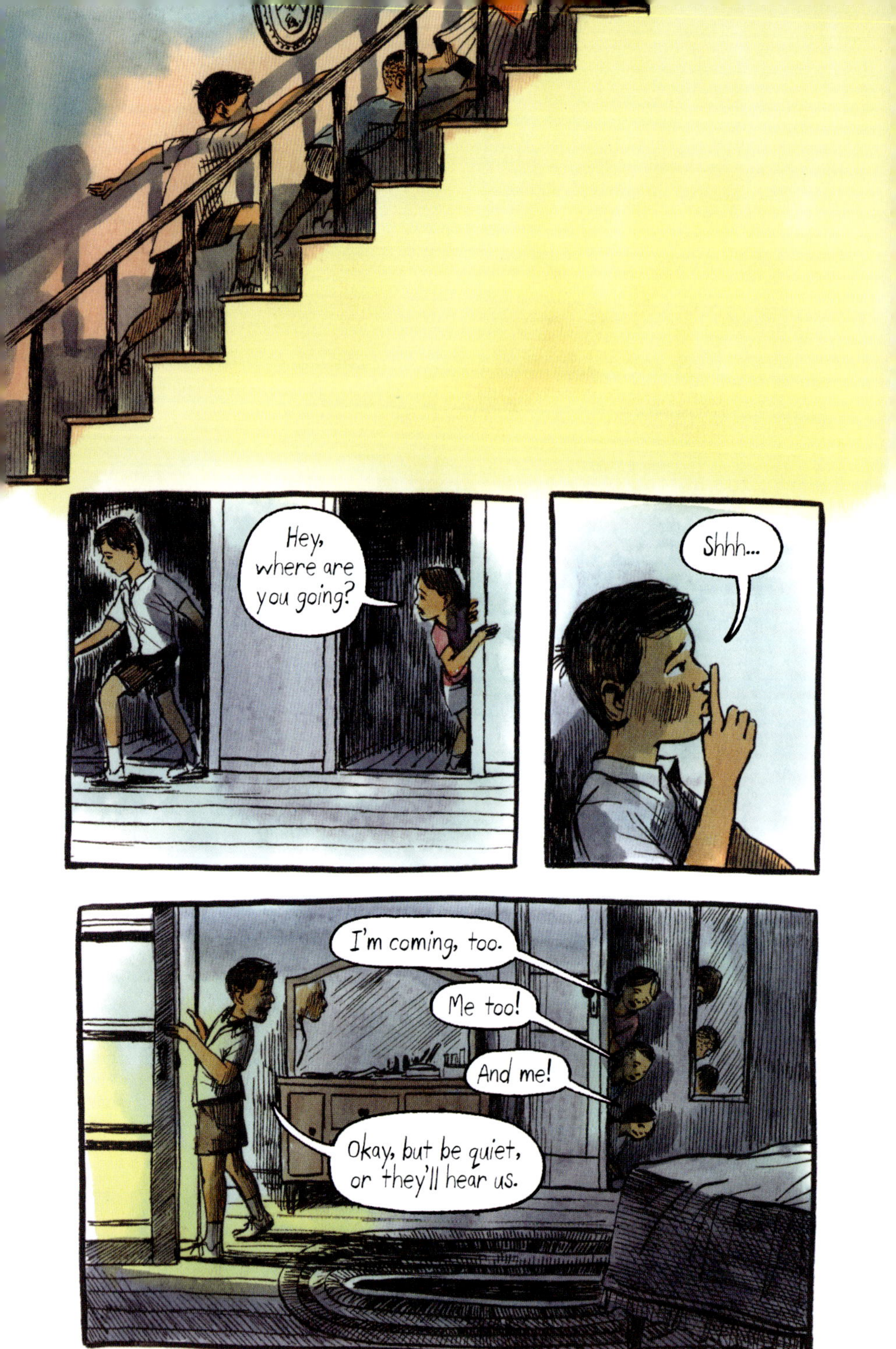
Hey, where are you going?
Shhh...
I'm coming, too.
Me too!
And me!
Okay, but be quiet, or they'll hear us.

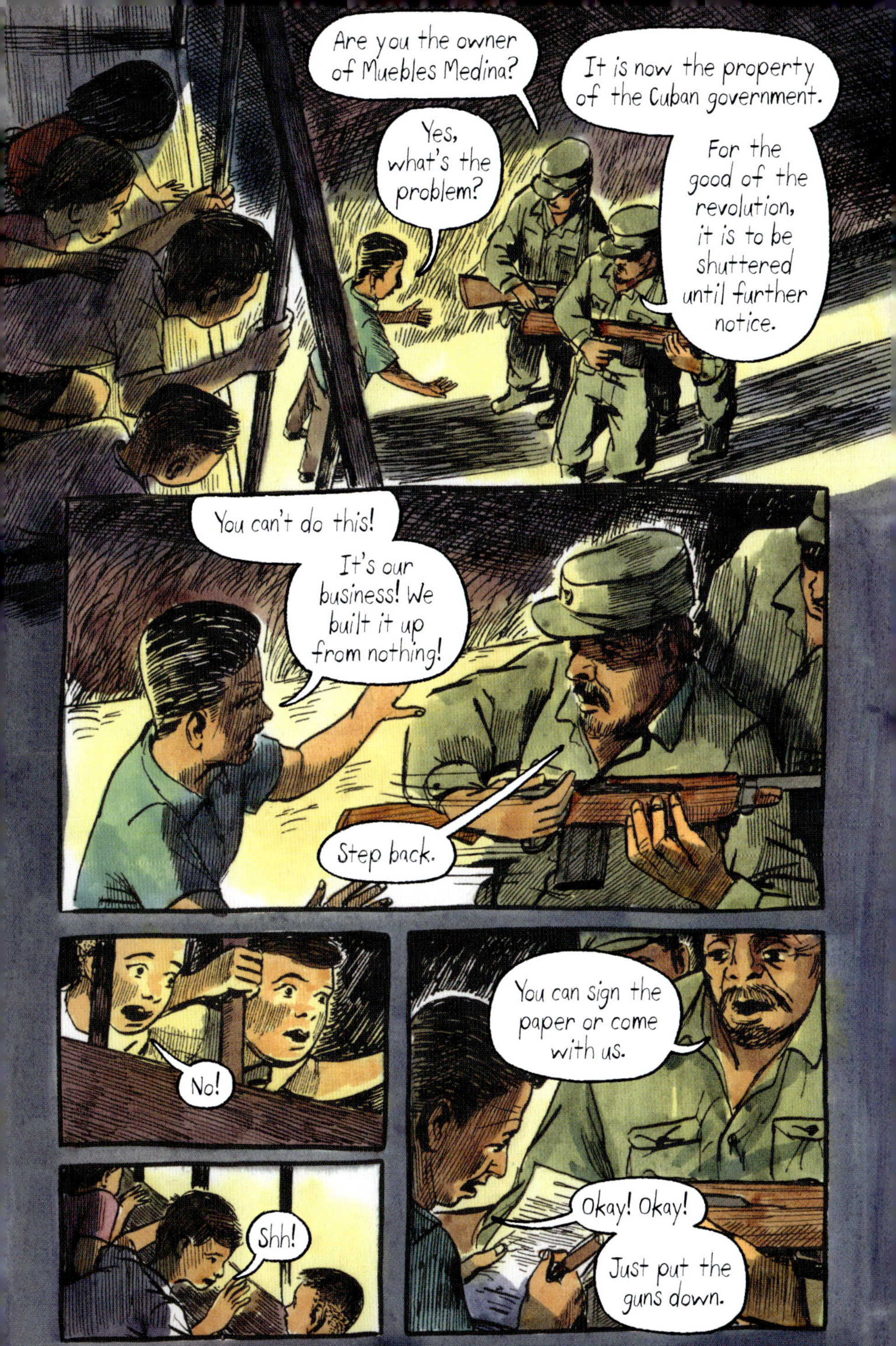
Are you the owner of Muebles Medina?
Yes, what's the problem?
It is now the property of the Cuban government.
For the good of the revolution, it is to be shuttered until further notice.
You can't do this!
It's our business! We built it up from nothing!
Step back.
No!
Shh!
You can sign the paper or come with us.
Okay! Okay!
Just put the guns down.

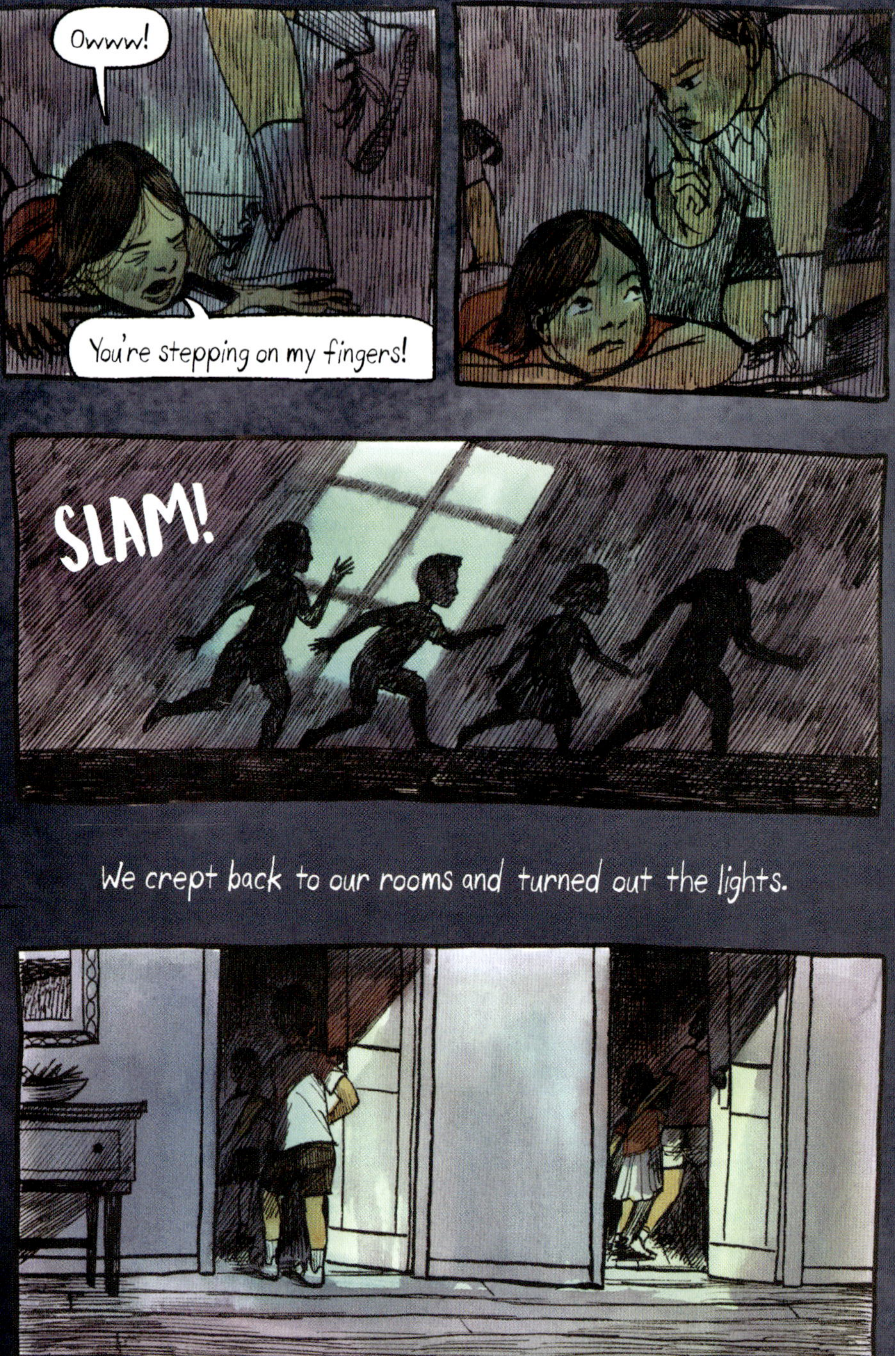
Owww!
You're stepping on my fingers!
SLAM!
We crept back to our rooms and turned out the lights.

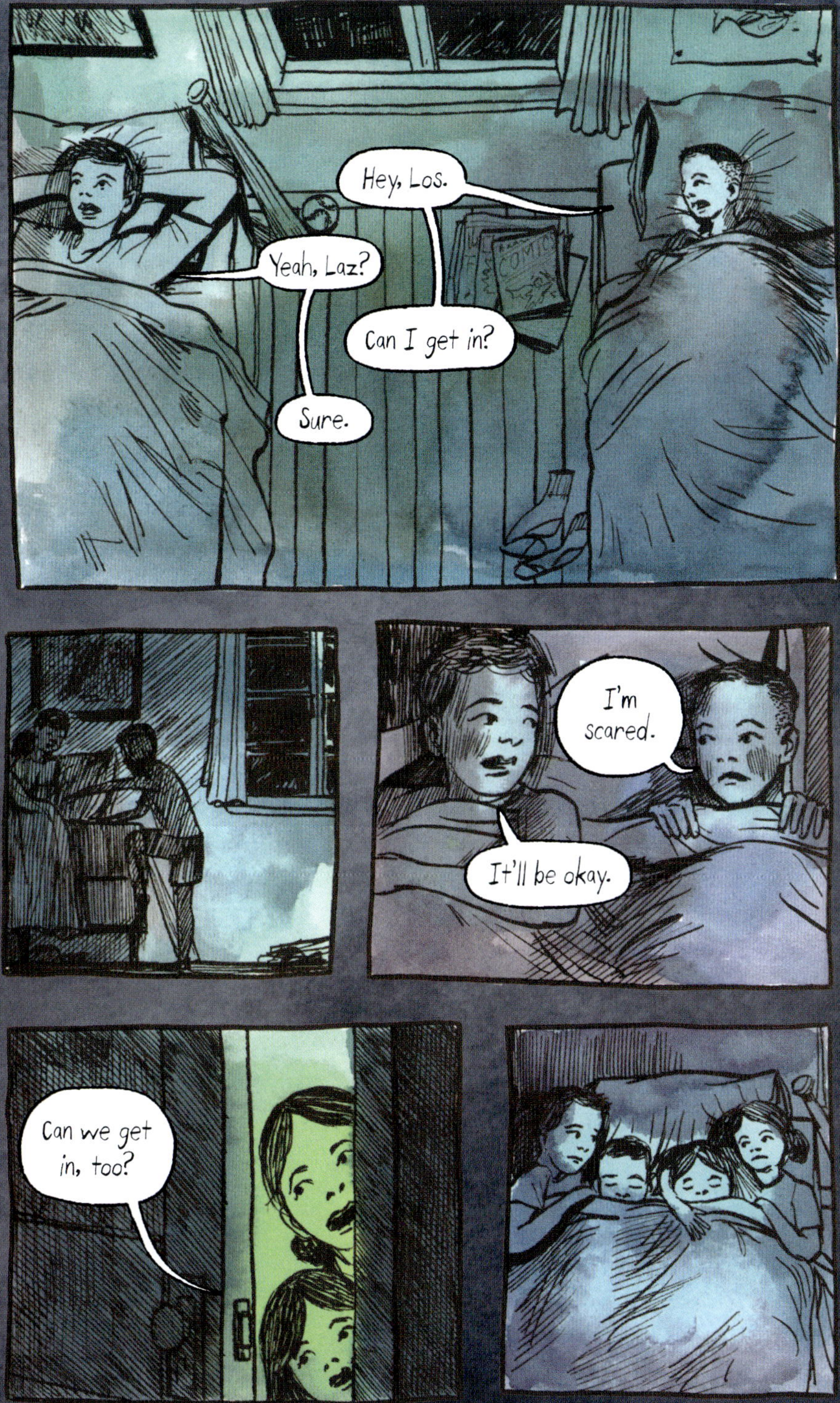
Hey, Los.
Yeah, Laz?
Can I get in?
Sure.
COMICS
I'm scared.
It'll be okay.
Can we get in, too?

con la guardia en alto

CDR

*with your guard up

The Committees for the Defense of the Revolution (CDR) are established in neighborhoods across the island. Their members are the eyes and ears of Castro's government, turning in anyone they suspect may be an "enemy of the Revolution."

For the Good of the Revolution

26 JULIO

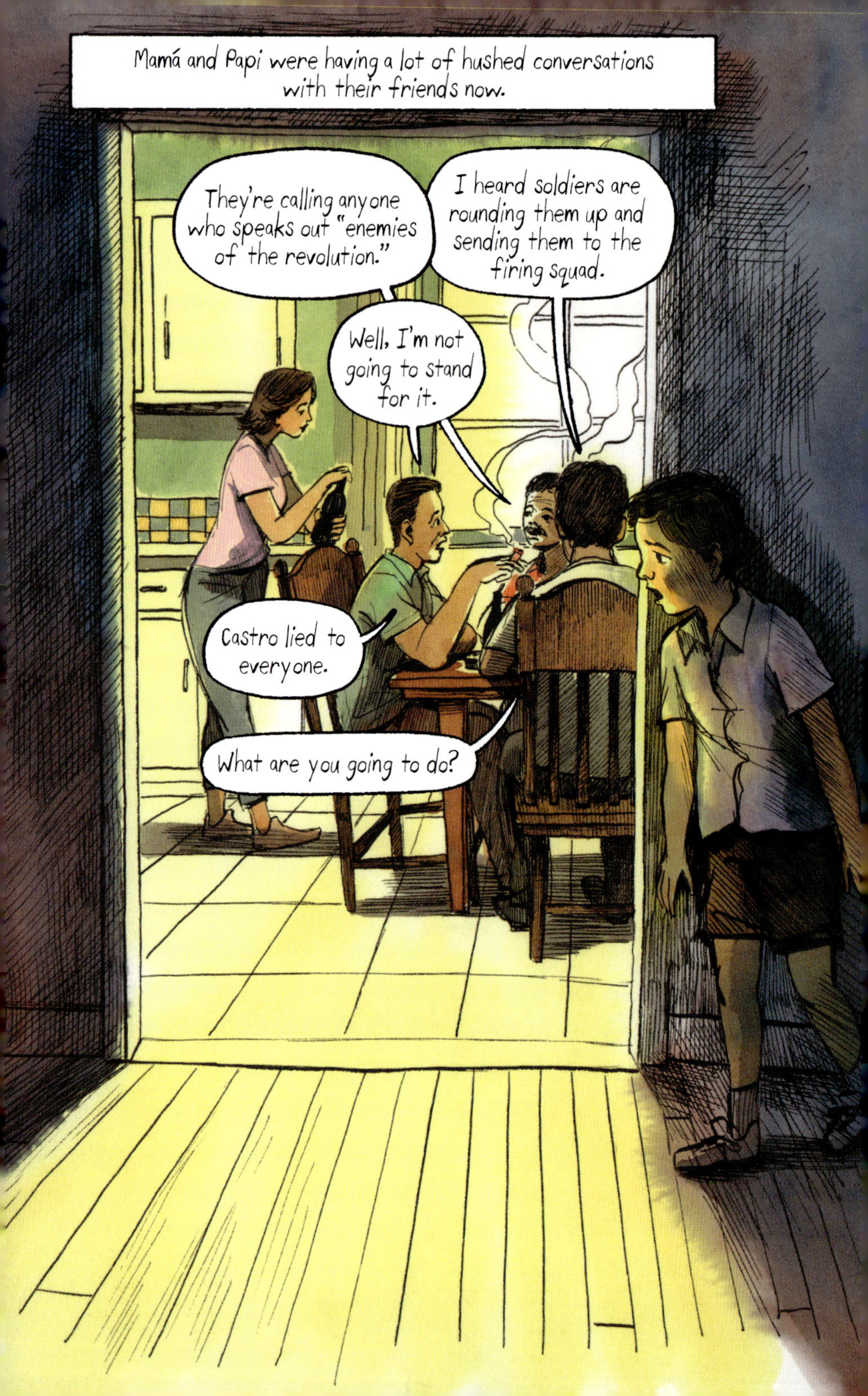
Mamá and Papi were having a lot of hushed conversations with their friends now.
They're calling anyone who speaks out "enemies of the revolution."
I heard soldiers are rounding them up and sending them to the firing squad.
Well, I'm not going to stand for it.
Castro lied to everyone.
What are you going to do?

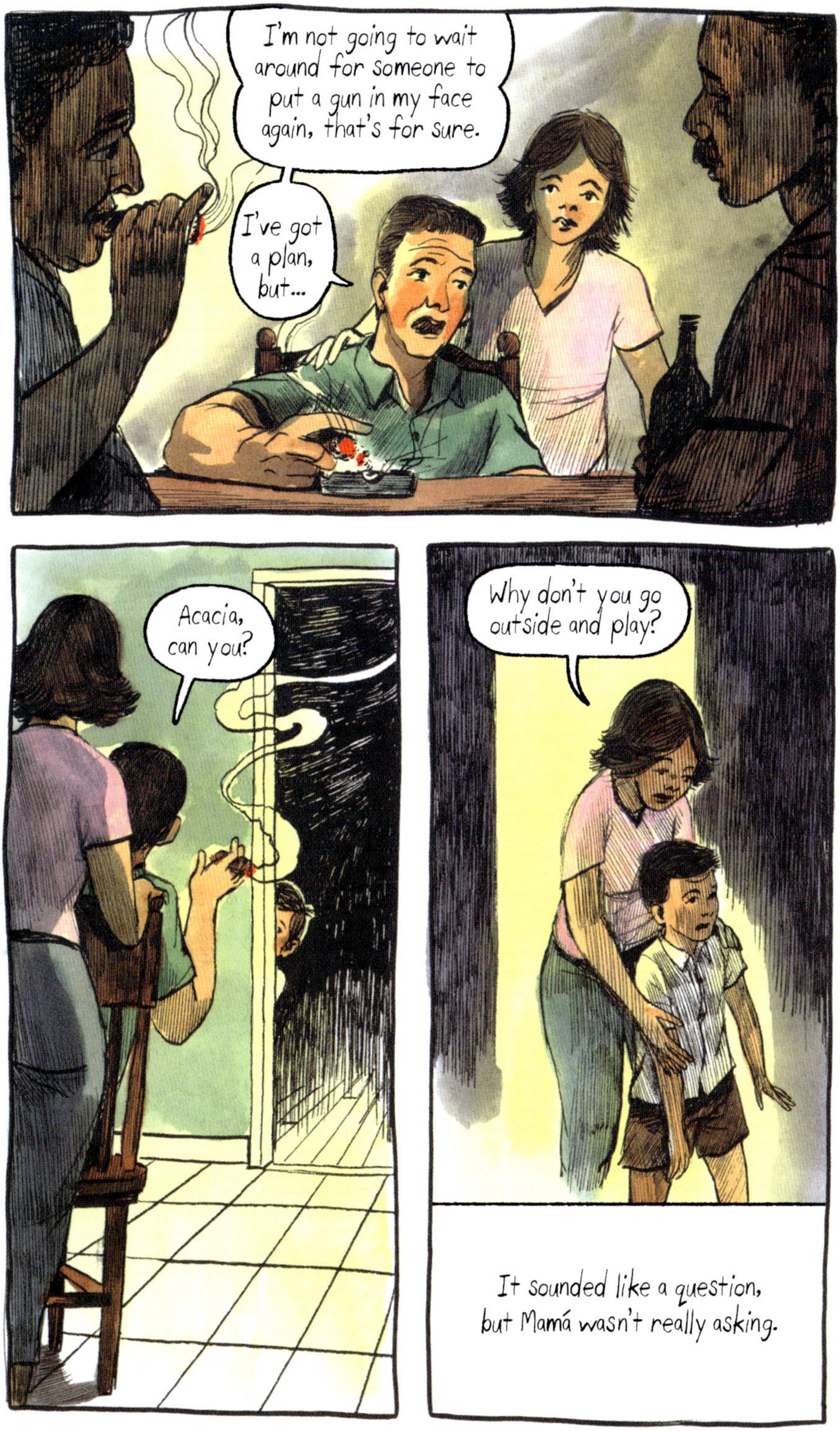
I'm not going to wait around for someone to put a gun in my face again, that's for sure.
I've got a plan, but...
Acacia, can you?
Why don't you go outside and play?
It sounded like a question, but Mamá wasn't really asking.

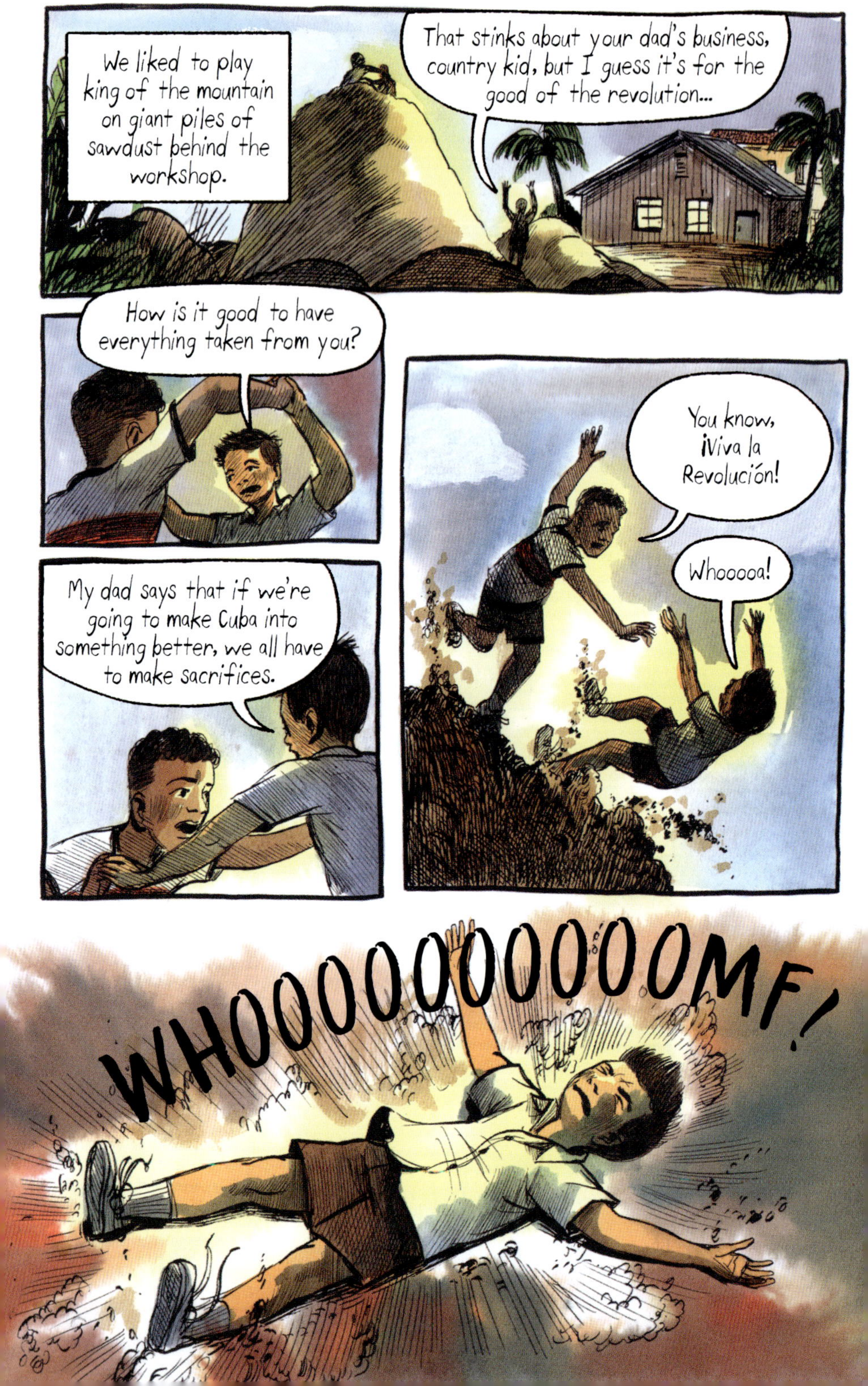
We liked to play king of the mountain on giant piles of sawdust behind the workshop.
That stinks about your dad's business, country kid, but I guess it's for the good of the revolution...
How is it good to have everything taken from you?
My dad says that if we're going to make Cuba into something better, we all have to make sacrifices.
You know, ¡Viva la Revolución!
Whooooa!
WHOOOOOOOOOOOMF!

121

(Panel 1)
"You're my friend and all, country kid, but your dad had better watch out."
"Oh yeah, why is that?"
"The neighborhood committee is keeping an eye out for enemies of the revolution."

(Panel 2)
"So just because someone doesn't agree with what's happening, they're an 'enemy of the revolution'?"
"Just watch out. That's all I'm saying."

(Panel 3)
"Oww, my back."
"You hurt?"
"I think I landed on something hard."

(Panel 4)
"What is it?"

(Panel 5)
"Something I don't think we were supposed to find."
"I gotta go."

"Hey, Papi."

"I thought we told you to play outside."

"You did... and I was... except I found this... in the sawdust."

"¡Ay, Dios mío!"

"Give me that. Did anyone else see it?"

"No. Just Diego and Luis."

"The boys from down the street?"

"Yeah, but why was there a gun in the sawdust pile?"

"It's mine. Now no more questions. And I don't want you hanging around those boys anymore."

"But they're my friends! And why do you have a gun?"

"I said NO MORE QUESTIONS!"

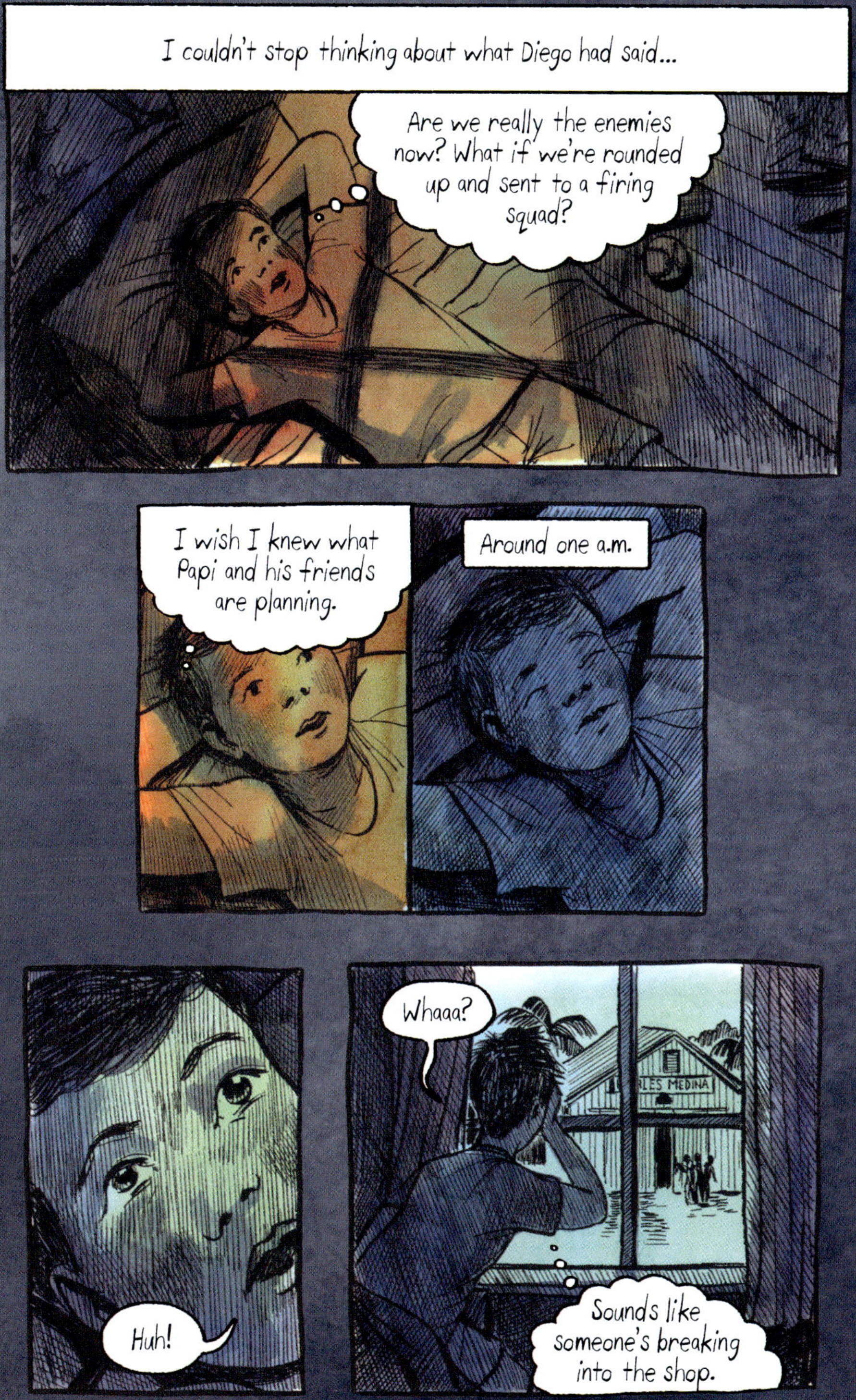
I couldn't stop thinking about what Diego had said...
Are we really the enemies now? What if we're rounded up and sent to a firing squad?
I wish I knew what Papi and his friends are planning.
Around one a.m.
Huh!
Whaaa?
Sounds like someone's breaking into the shop.

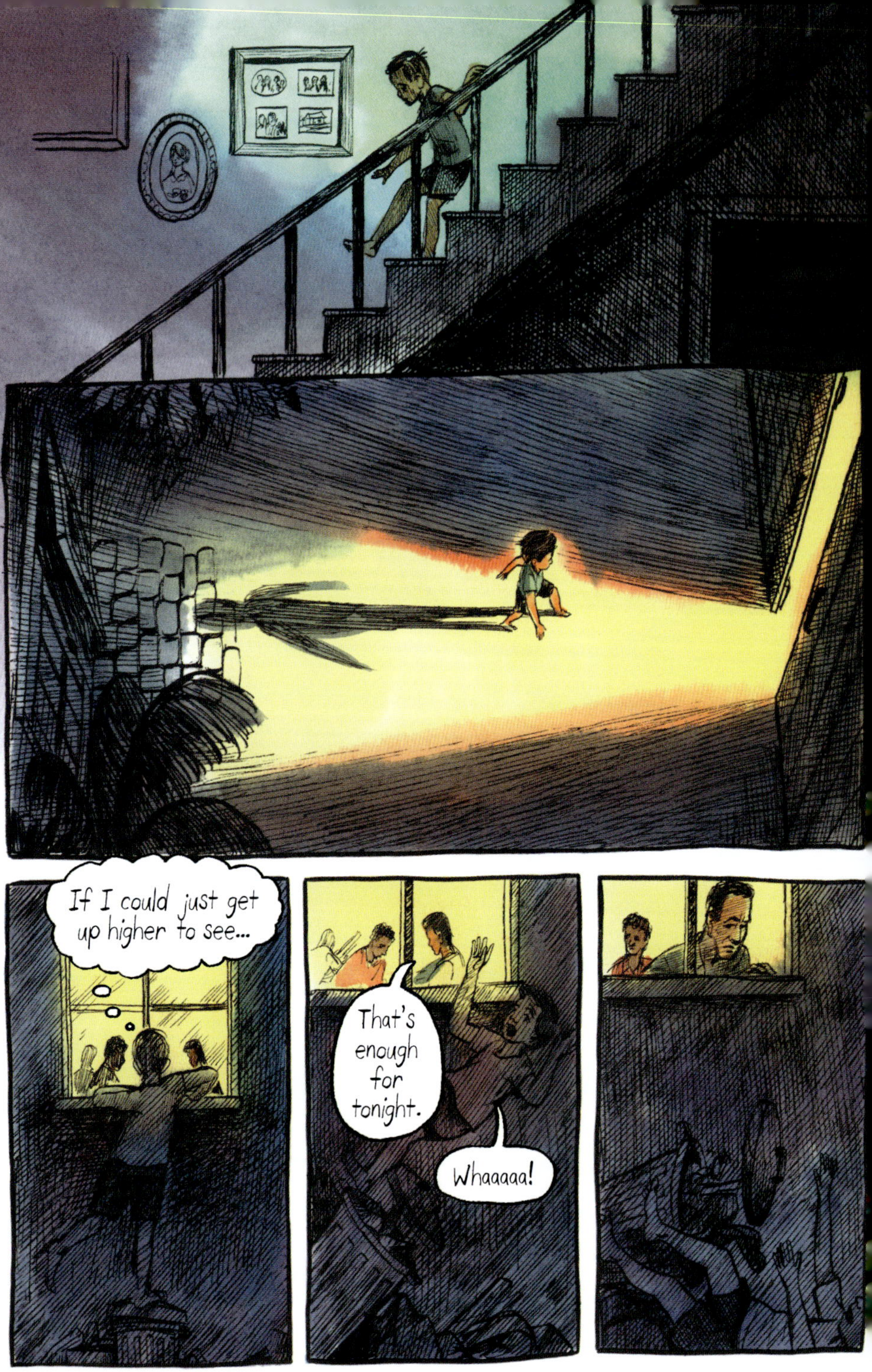
If I could just get up higher to see...
That's enough for tonight.
Whaaaaa!

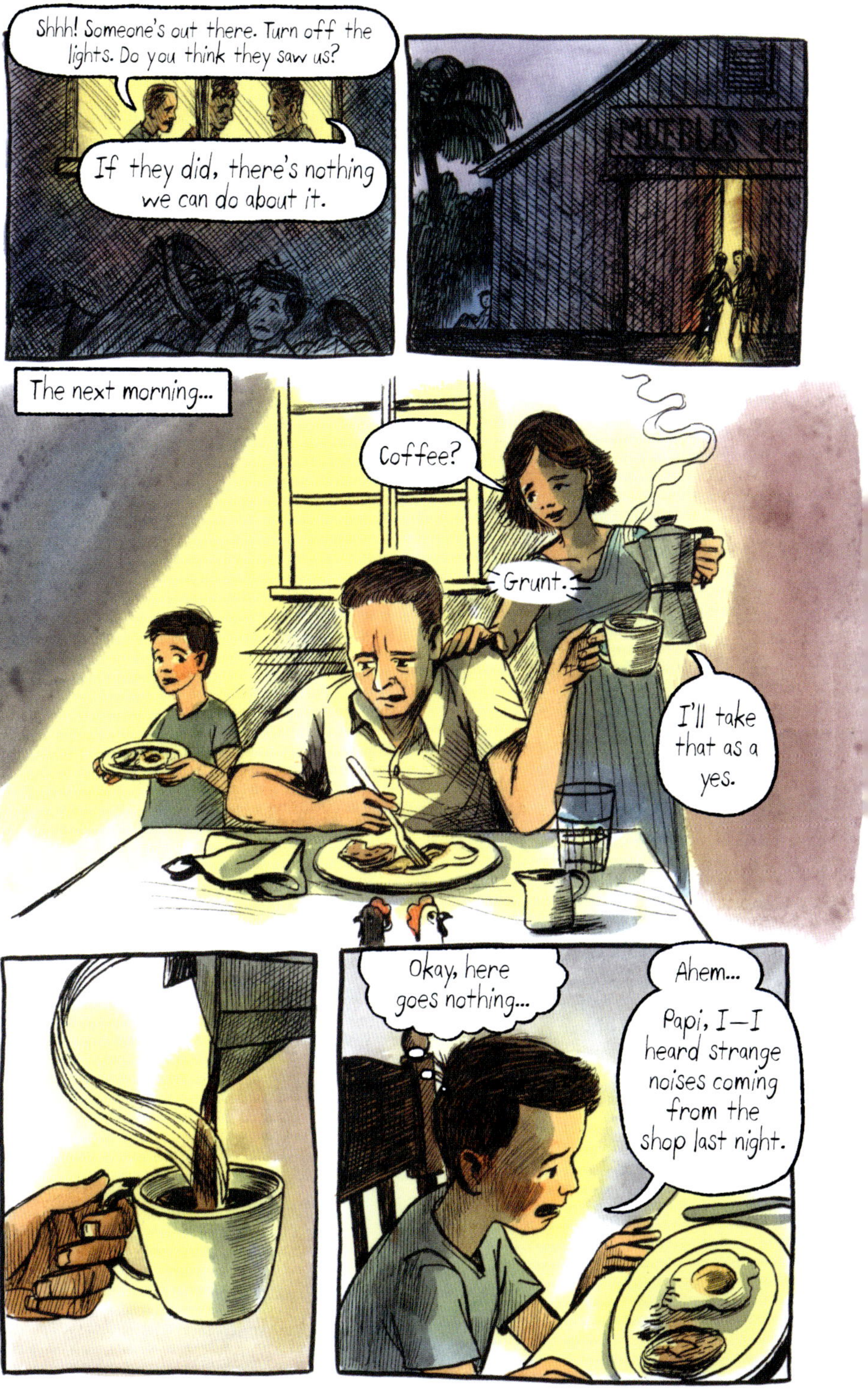
Shhh! Someone's out there. Turn off the lights. Do you think they saw us?
If they did, there's nothing we can do about it.
MUEBLES ME
The next morning...
Coffee?
Grunt.
I'll take that as a yes.
Okay, here goes nothing...
Ahem...
Papi, I—I heard strange noises coming from the shop last night.

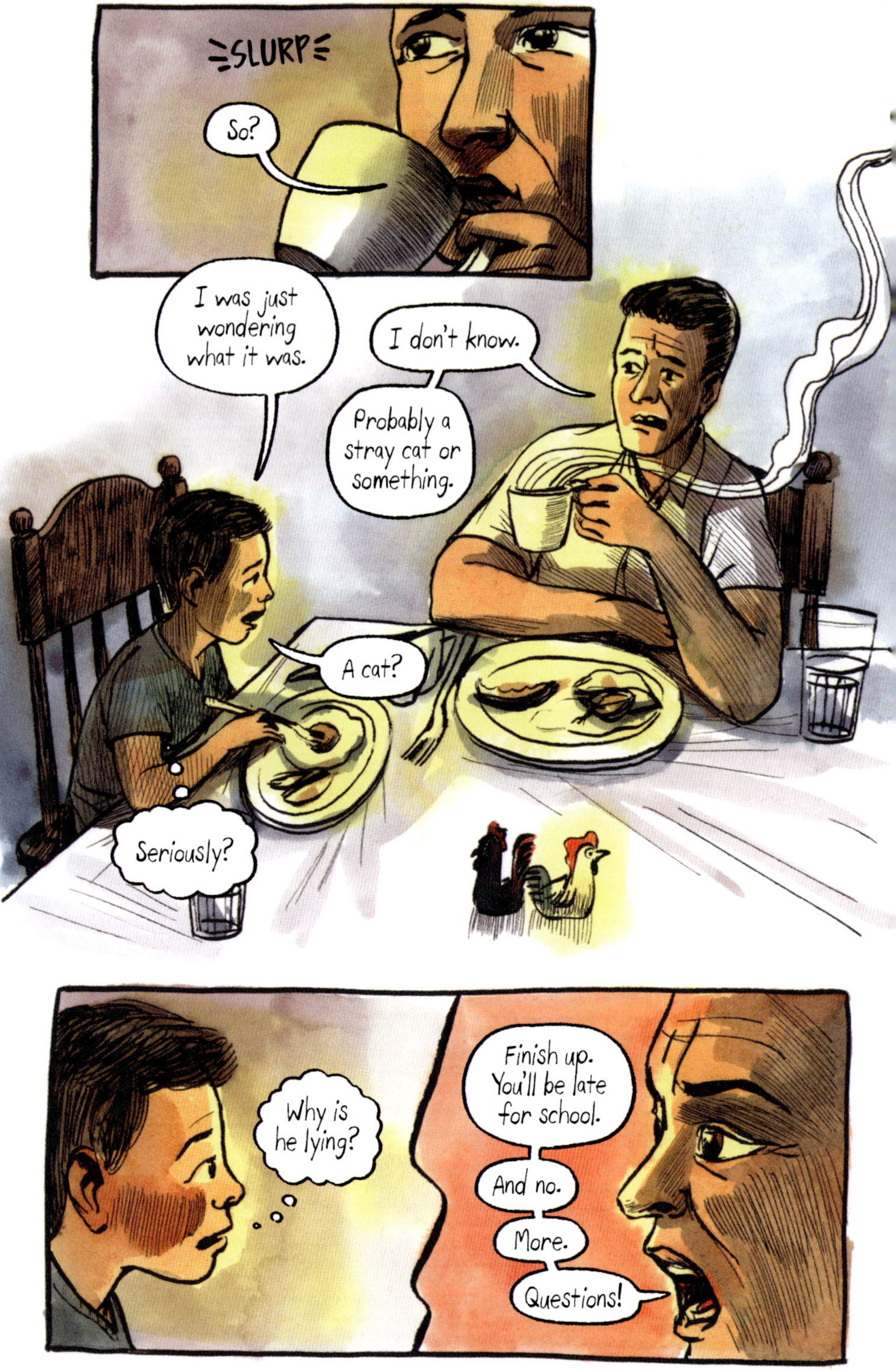
SLURP
So?
I was just wondering what it was.
I don't know.
Probably a stray cat or something.
A cat?
Seriously?
Why is he lying?
Finish up. You'll be late for school.
And no.
More.
Questions!

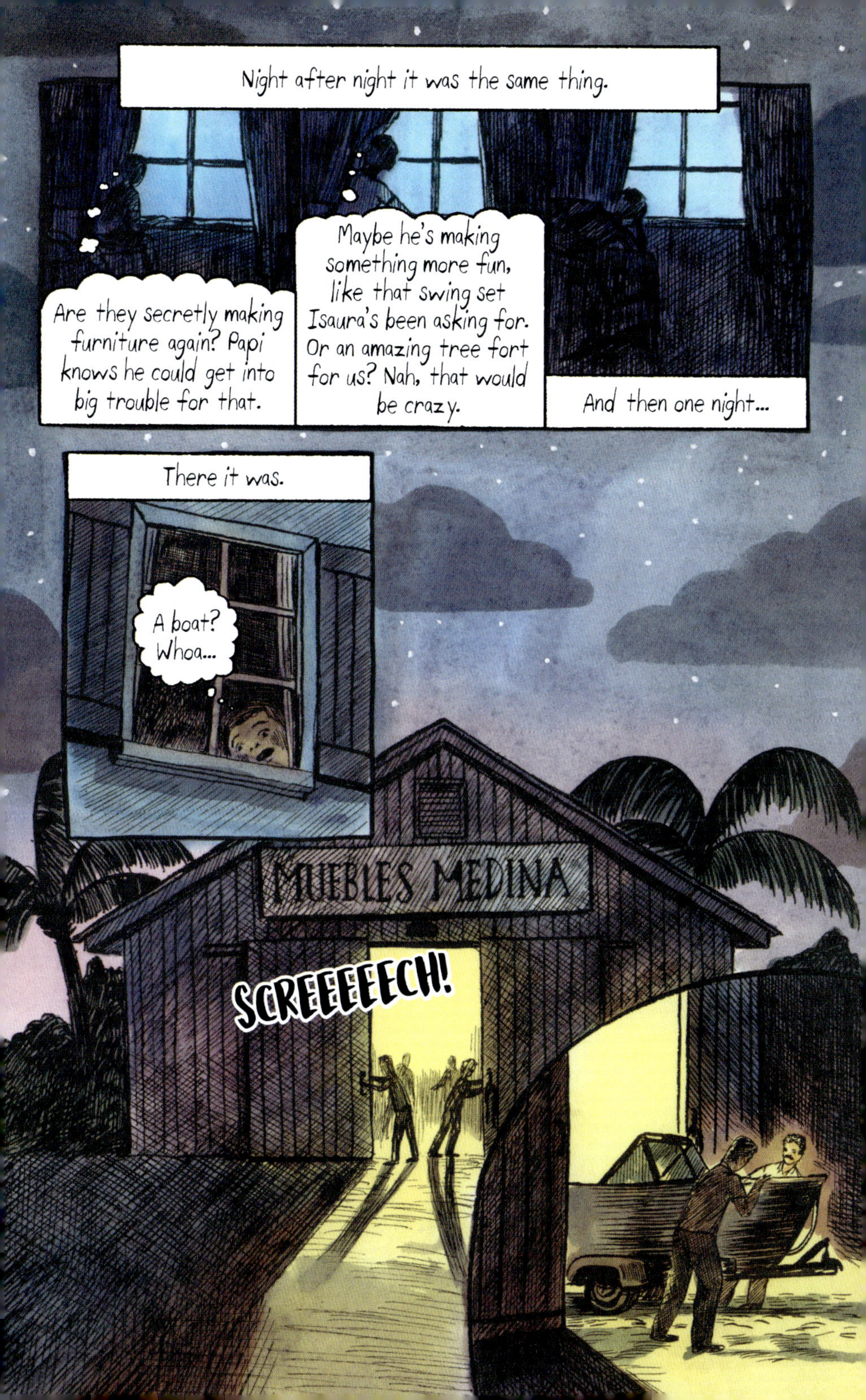
Night after night it was the same thing.
Are they secretly making furniture again? Papi knows he could get into big trouble for that.
Maybe he's making something more fun, like that swing set Isaura's been asking for. Or an amazing tree fort for us? Nah, that would be crazy.
And then one night...
There it was.
A boat? Whoa...
MUEBLES MEDINA
SCREEEEEECH!

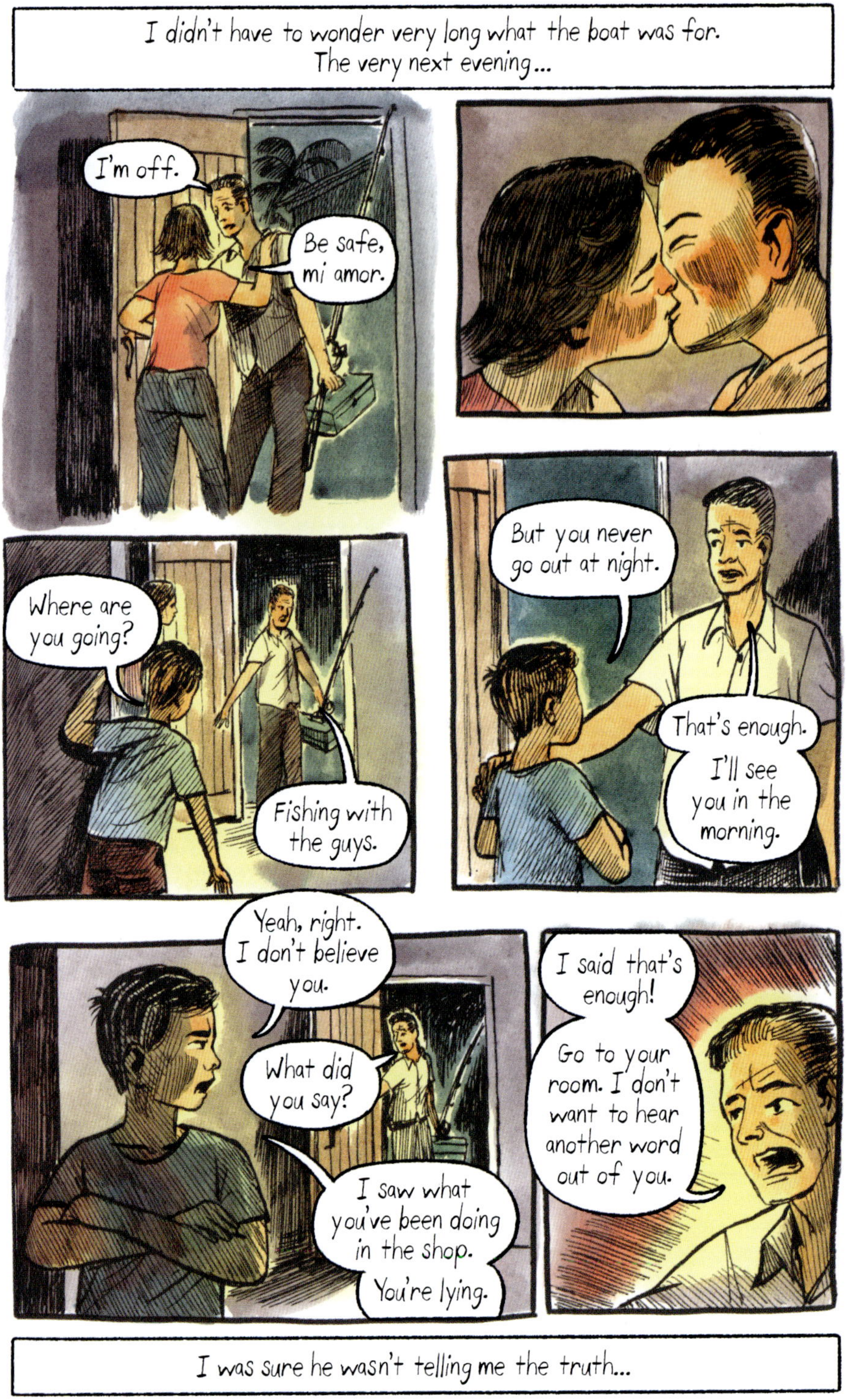
I didn't have to wonder very long what the boat was for. The very next evening...
I'm off.
Be safe, mi amor.
Where are you going?
Fishing with the guys.
But you never go out at night.
That's enough.
I'll see you in the morning.
Yeah, right. I don't believe you.
What did you say?
I saw what you've been doing in the shop.
You're lying.
I said that's enough!
Go to your room. I don't want to hear another word out of you.
I was sure he wasn't telling me the truth...

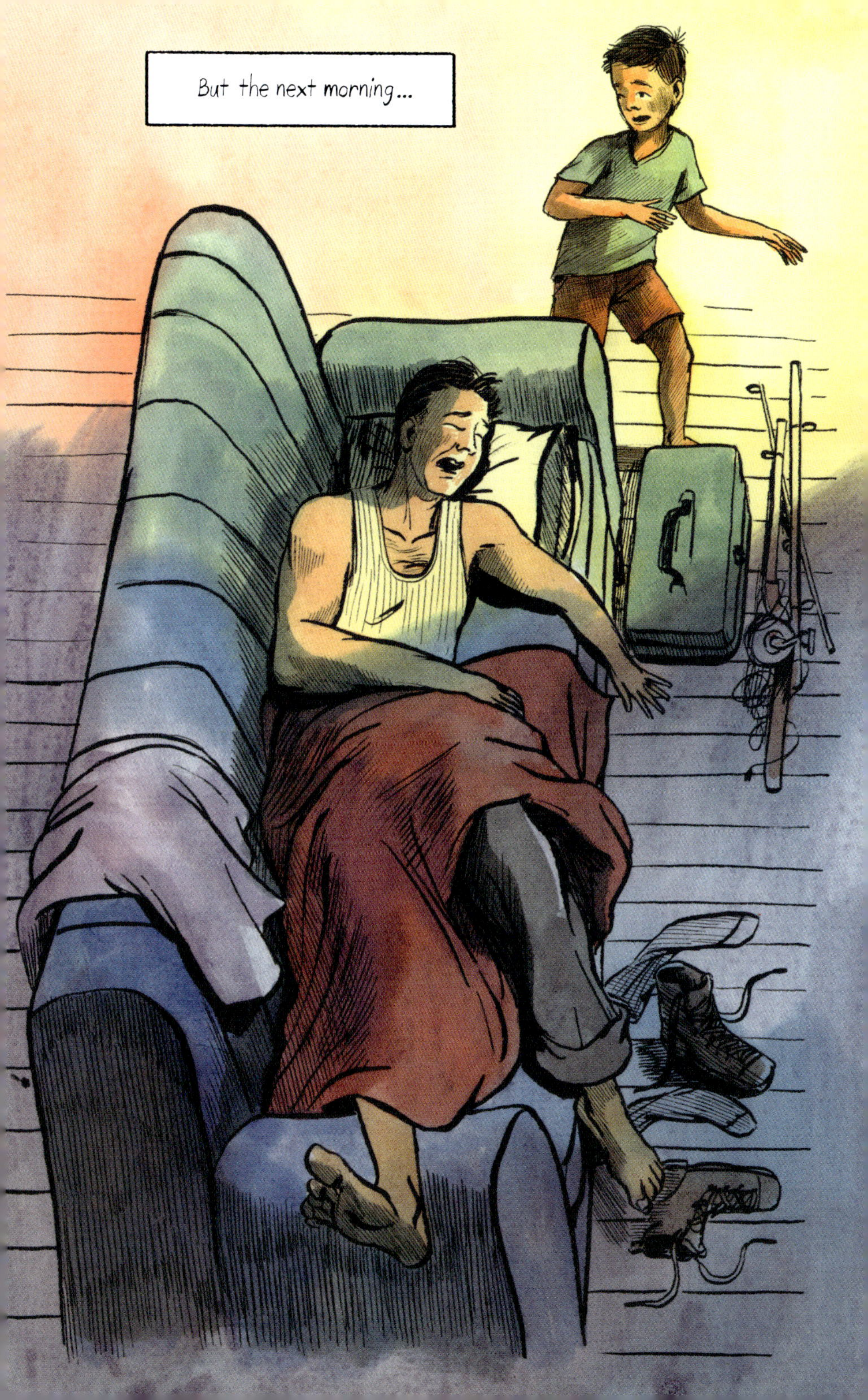
But the next morning...

Castro begins to align Cuba with the Soviet Union. The Soviets agree to buy Cuban sugar in exchange for their oil and weapons.

Gone Fishing

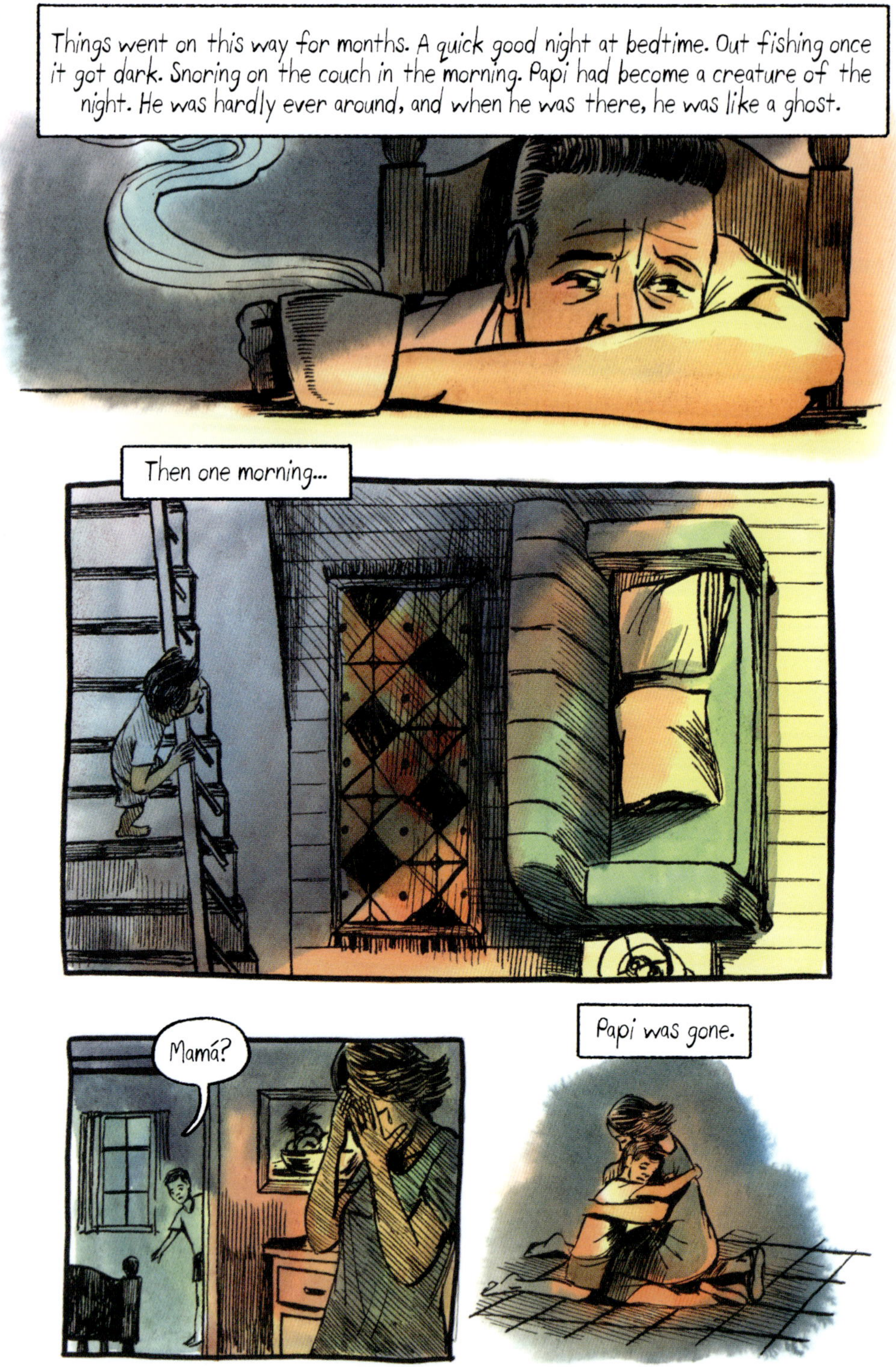
Things went on this way for months. A quick good night at bedtime. Out fishing once it got dark. Snoring on the couch in the morning. Papi had become a creature of the night. He was hardly ever around, and when he was there, he was like a ghost.
Then one morning...
Mamá?
Papi was gone.

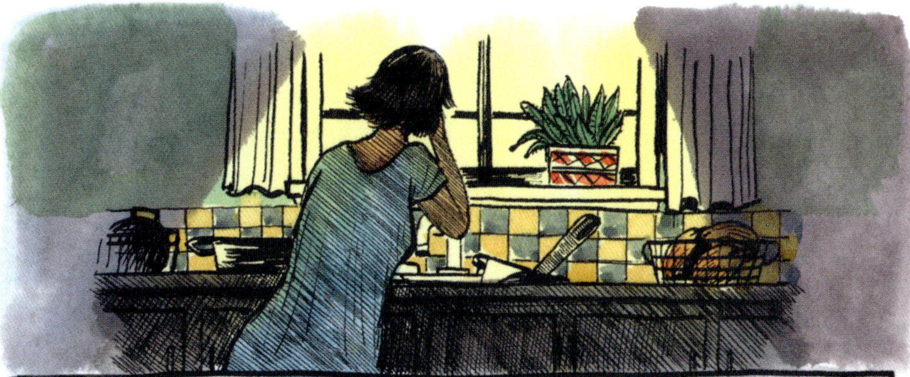

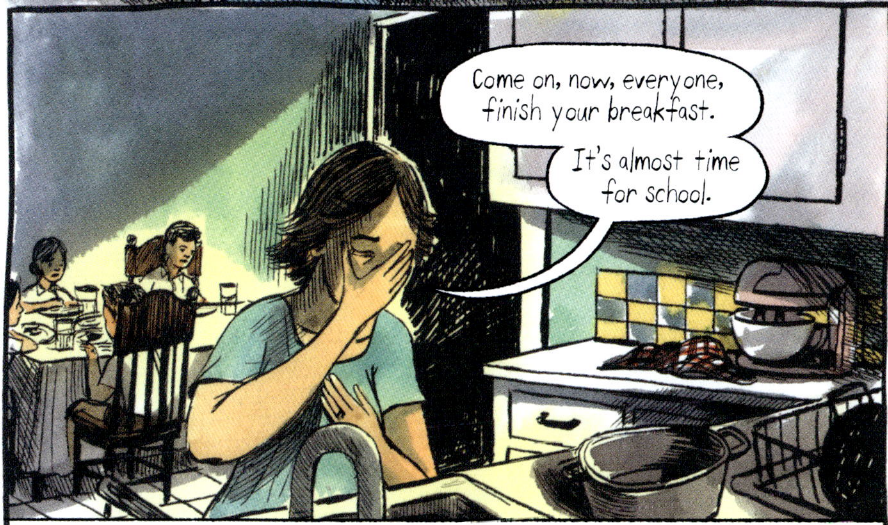
Come on, now, everyone, finish your breakfast.
It's almost time for school.

Mamá had her head turned away from us like she was doing the dishes, but she wasn't washing anything. Really, I think she just didn't want us to see her puffy red eyes—she must have been crying.

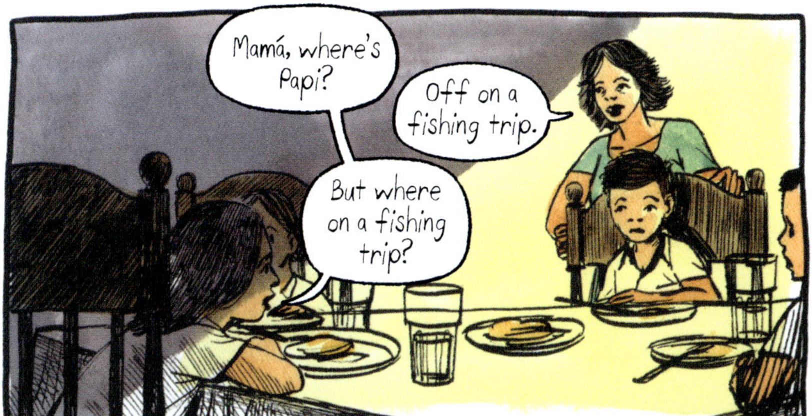
Mamá, where's Papi?
Off on a fishing trip.
But where on a fishing trip?

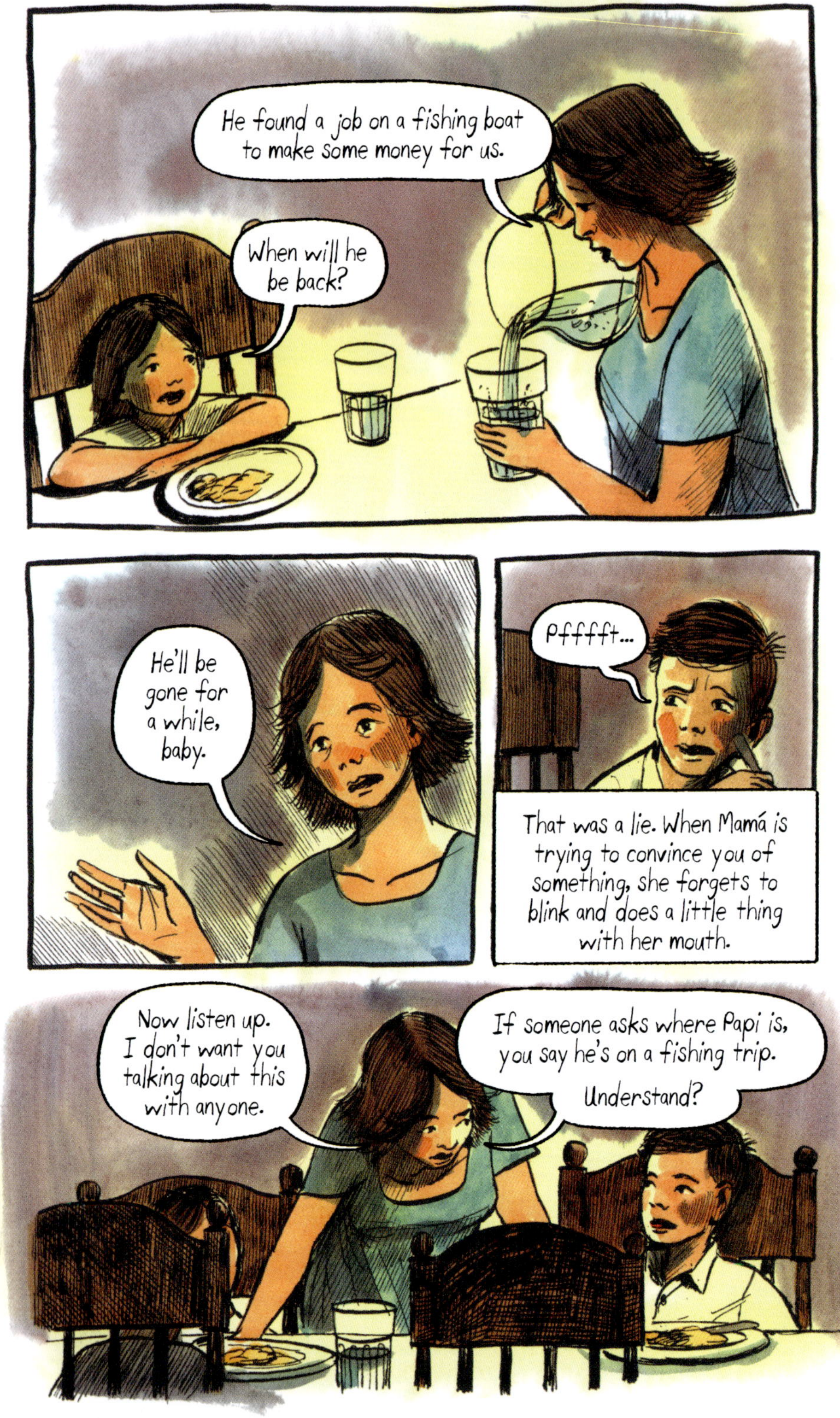
He found a job on a fishing boat to make some money for us.
When will he be back?
He'll be gone for a while, baby.
Pfffft...
That was a lie. When Mamá is trying to convince you of something, she forgets to blink and does a little thing with her mouth.
Now listen up. I don't want you talking about this with anyone.
If someone asks where Papi is, you say he's on a fishing trip.
Understand?

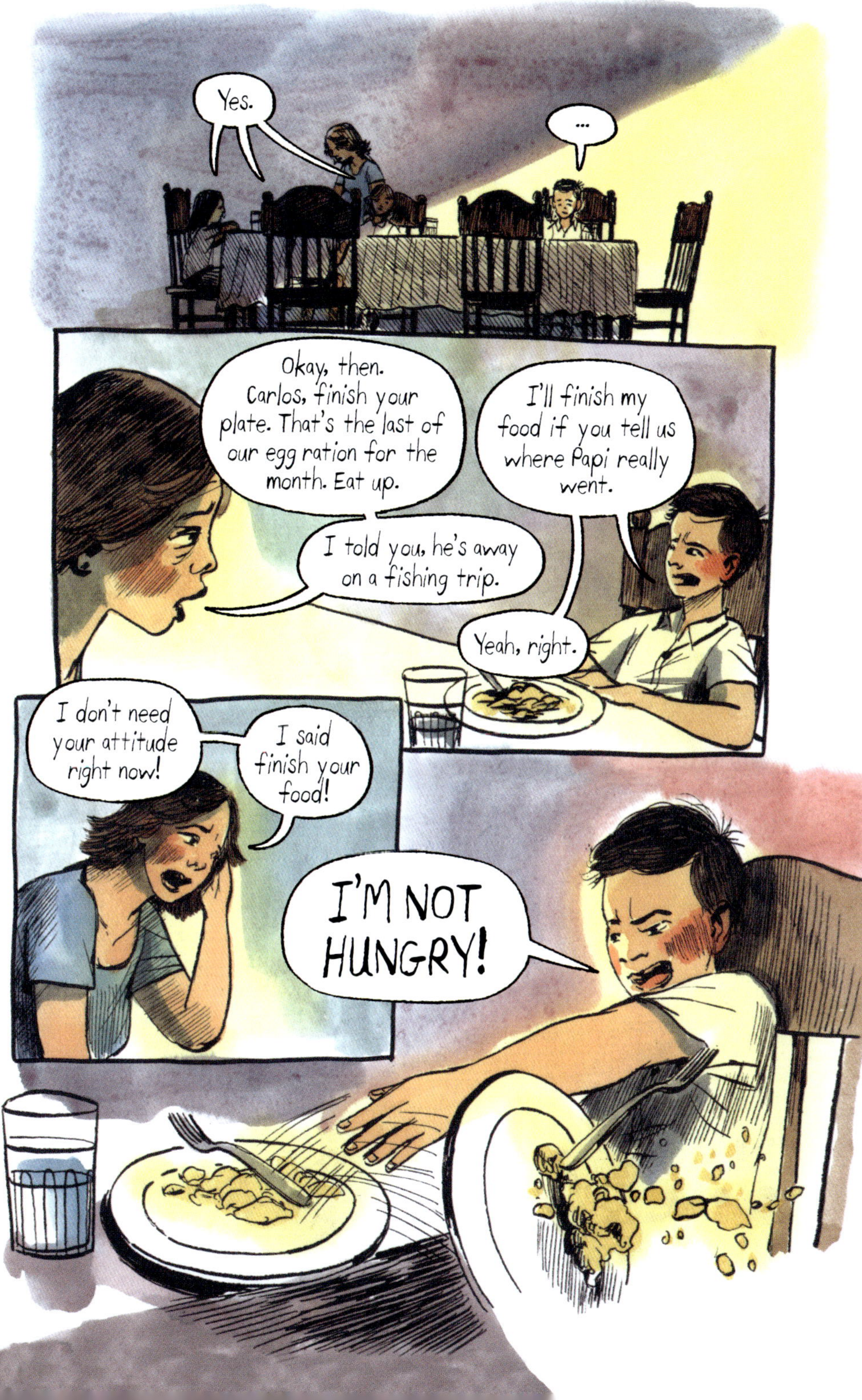
Yes.
...
Okay, then. Carlos, finish your plate. That's the last of our egg ration for the month. Eat up.
I'll finish my food if you tell us where Papi really went.
I told you, he's away on a fishing trip.
Yeah, right.
I don't need your attitude right now!
I said finish your food!
I'M NOT HUNGRY!

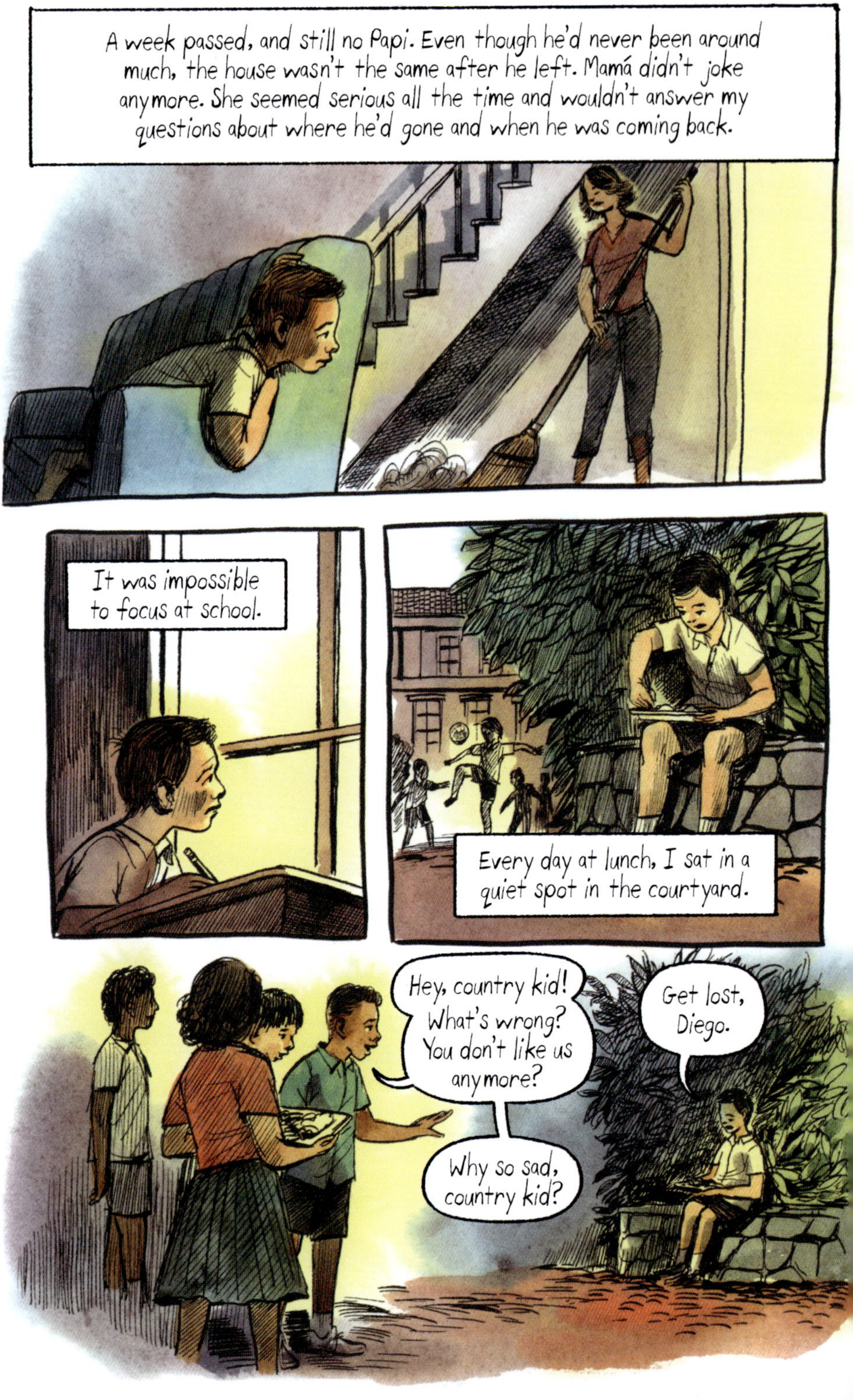
A week passed, and still no Papi. Even though he'd never been around much, the house wasn't the same after he left. Mamá didn't joke anymore. She seemed serious all the time and wouldn't answer my questions about where he'd gone and when he was coming back.
It was impossible to focus at school.
Every day at lunch, I sat in a quiet spot in the courtyard.
Hey, country kid! What's wrong? You don't like us anymore?
Why so sad, country kid?
Get lost, Diego.

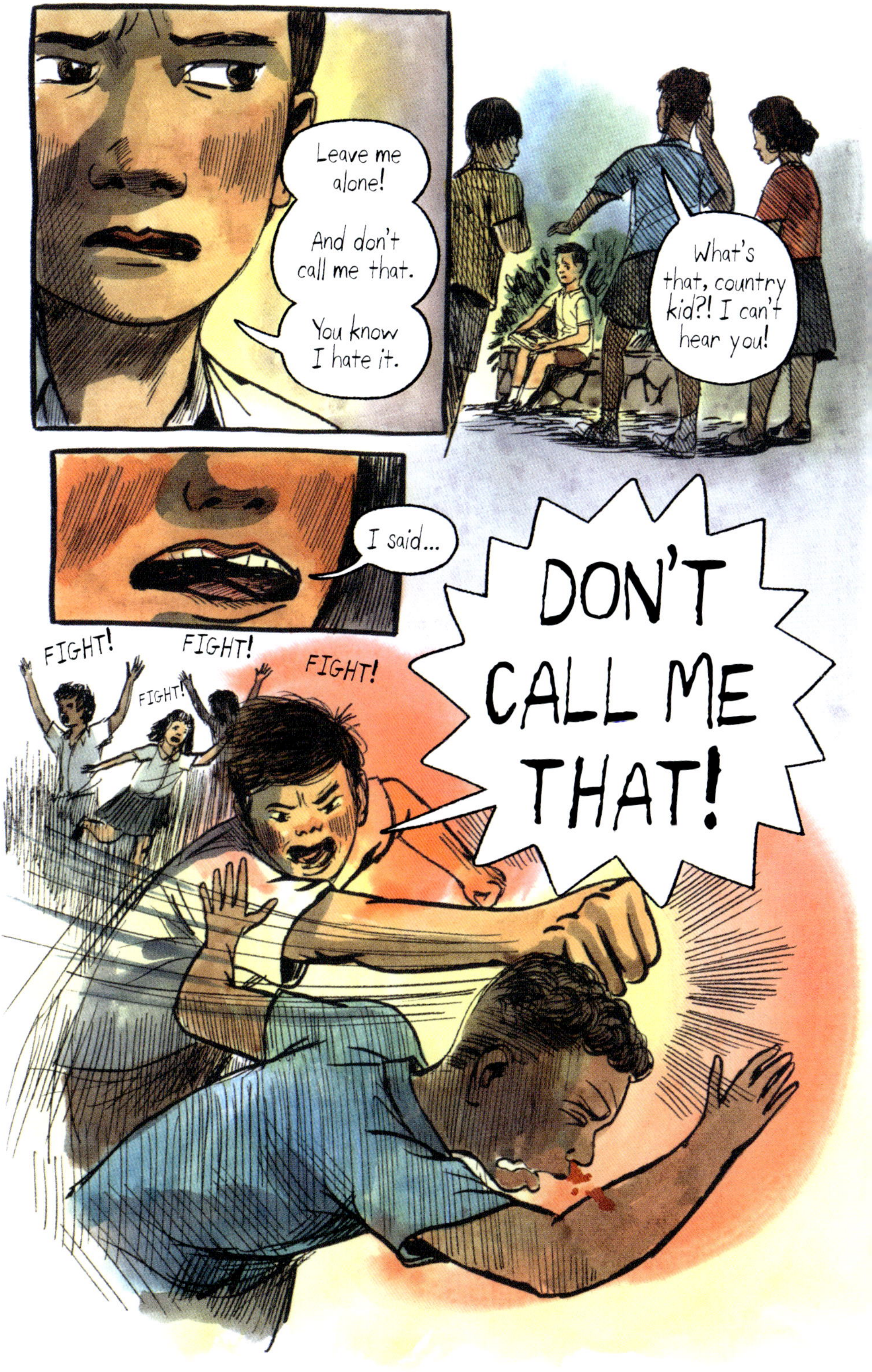
Leave me alone!
And don't call me that.
You know I hate it.
What's that, country kid?! I can't hear you!
I said...
DON'T CALL ME THAT!
FIGHT!
FIGHT!
FIGHT!
FIGHT!

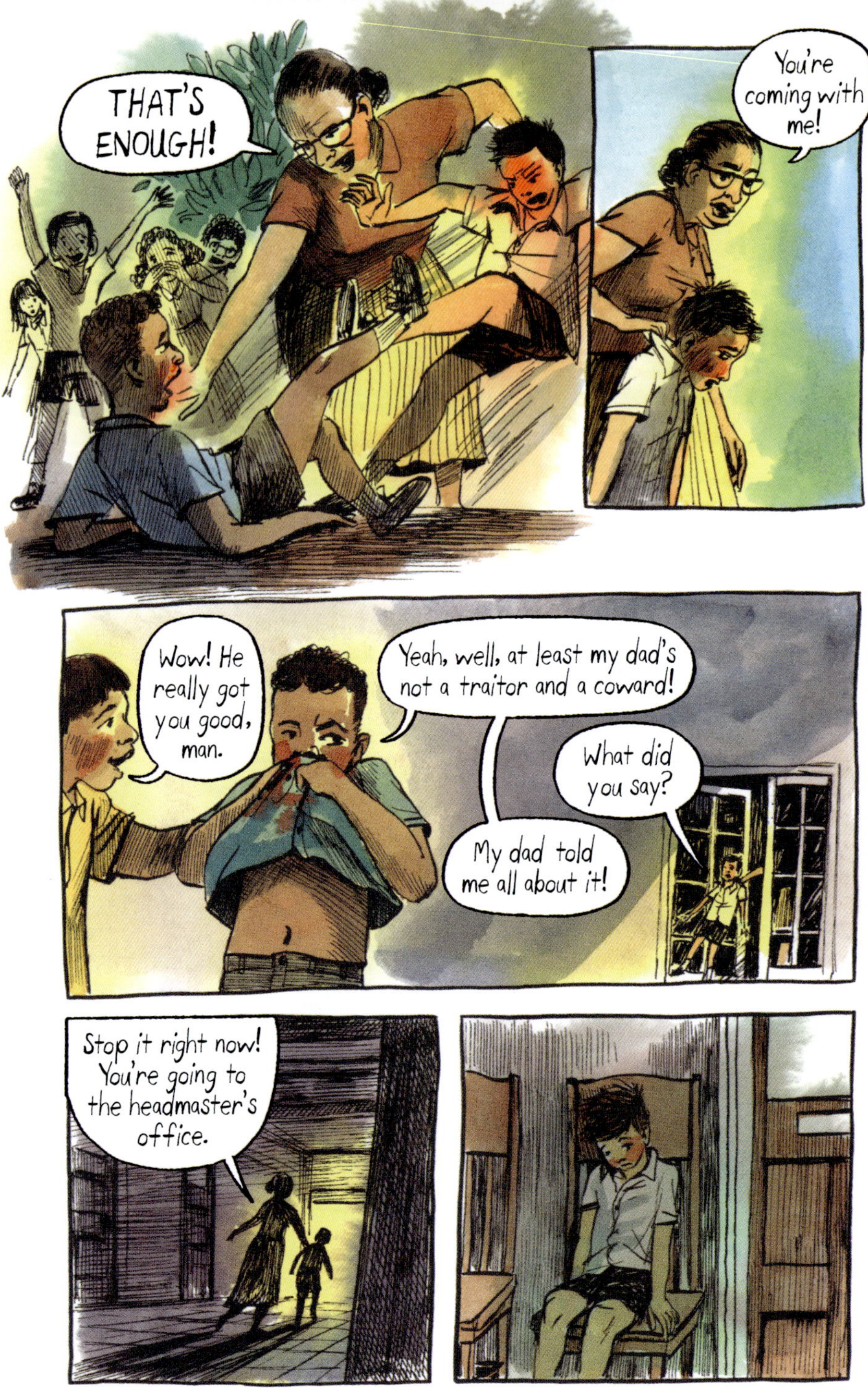
THAT'S ENOUGH!
You're coming with me!
Wow! He really got you good, man.
Yeah, well, at least my dad's not a traitor and a coward!
My dad told me all about it!
What did you say?
Stop it right now! You're going to the headmaster's office.

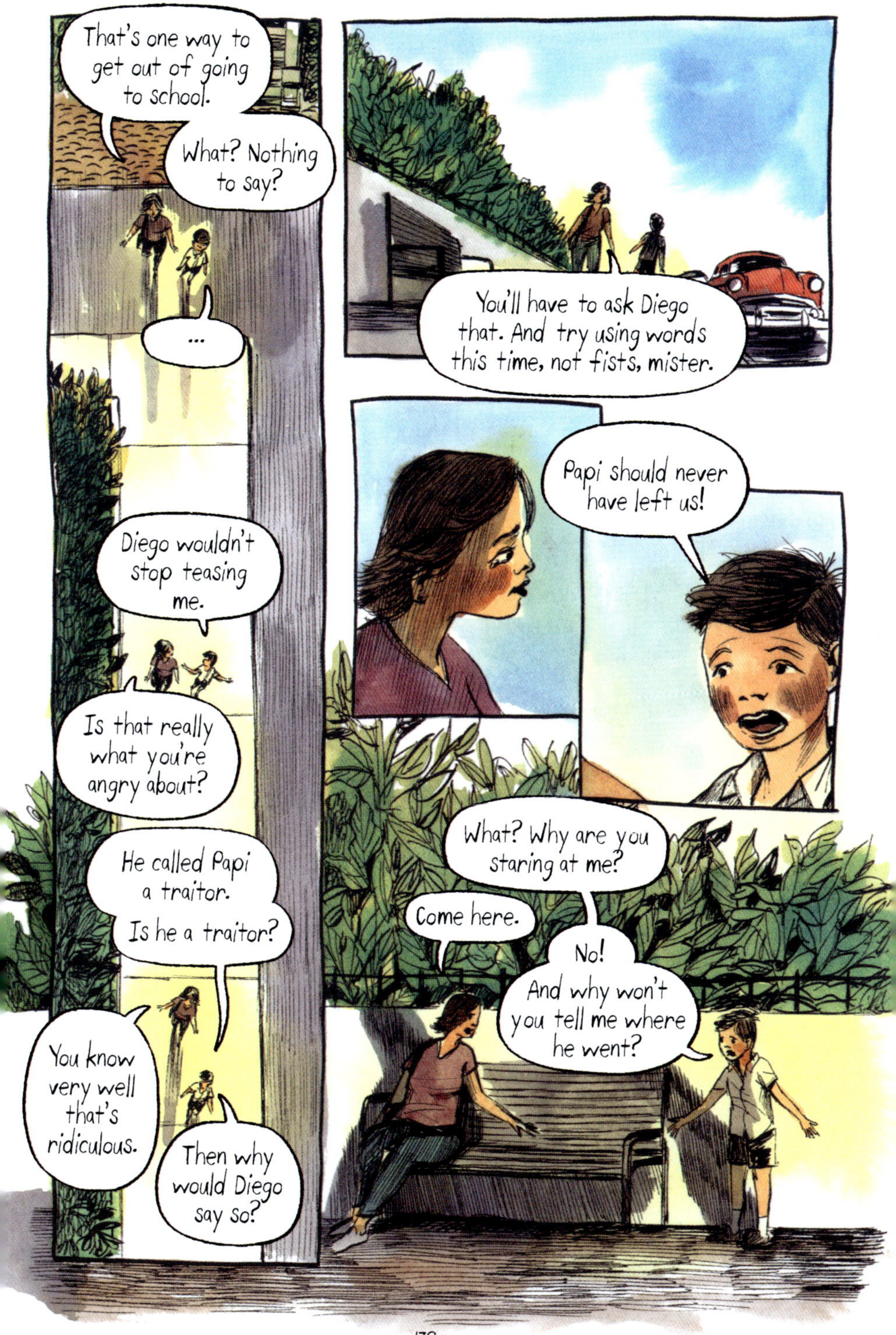
That's one way to get out of going to school.
What? Nothing to say?
...
Diego wouldn't stop teasing me.
Is that really what you're angry about?
He called Papi a traitor.
Is he a traitor?
You know very well that's ridiculous.
Then why would Diego say so?
You'll have to ask Diego that. And try using words this time, not fists, mister.
Papi should never have left us!
What? Why are you staring at me?
Come here.
No!
And why won't you tell me where he went?

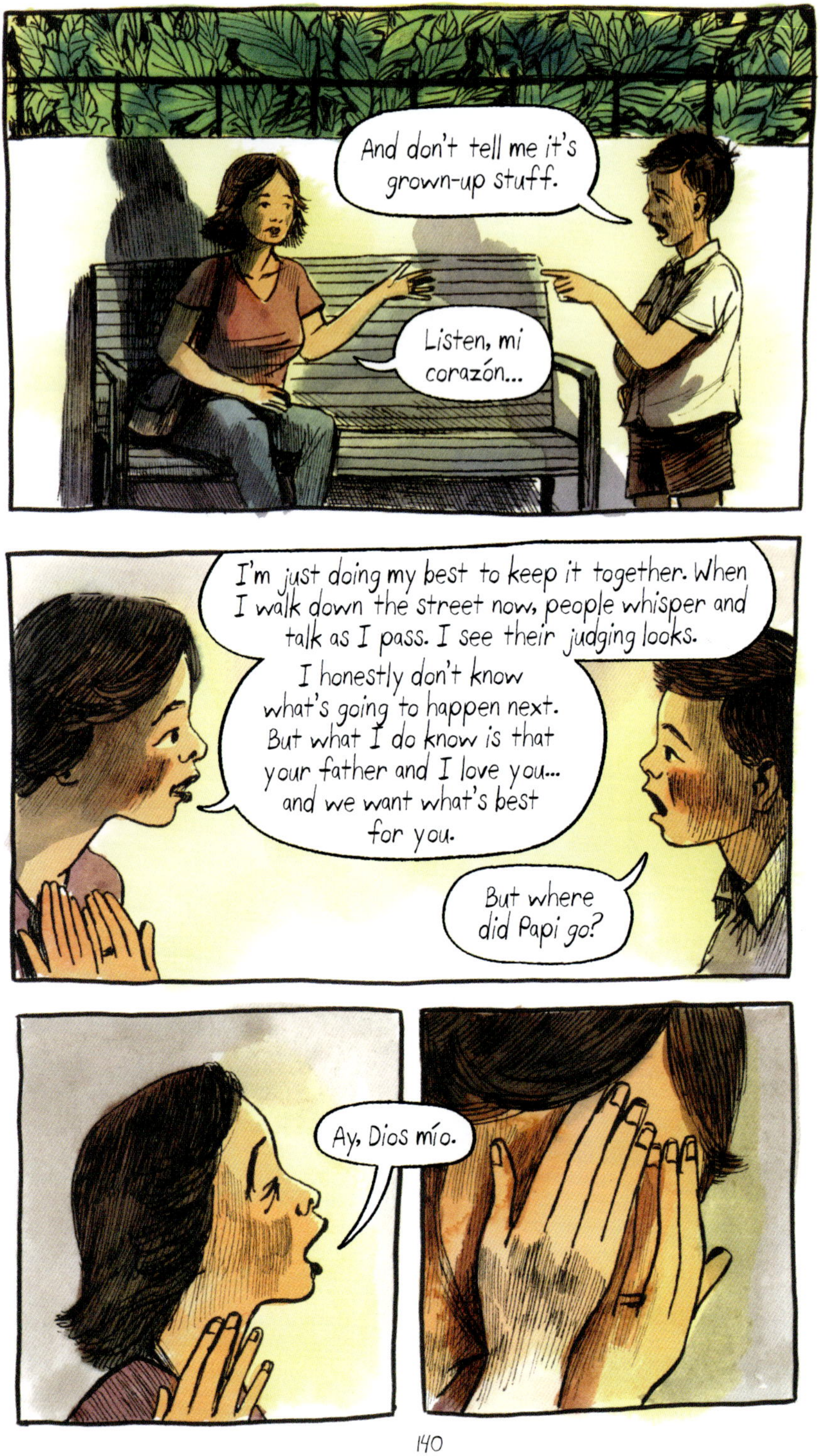
And don't tell me it's grown-up stuff.
Listen, mi corazón...
I'm just doing my best to keep it together. When I walk down the street now, people whisper and talk as I pass. I see their judging looks.
I honestly don't know what's going to happen next. But what I do know is that your father and I love you... and we want what's best for you.
But where did Papi go?
Ay, Dios mío.

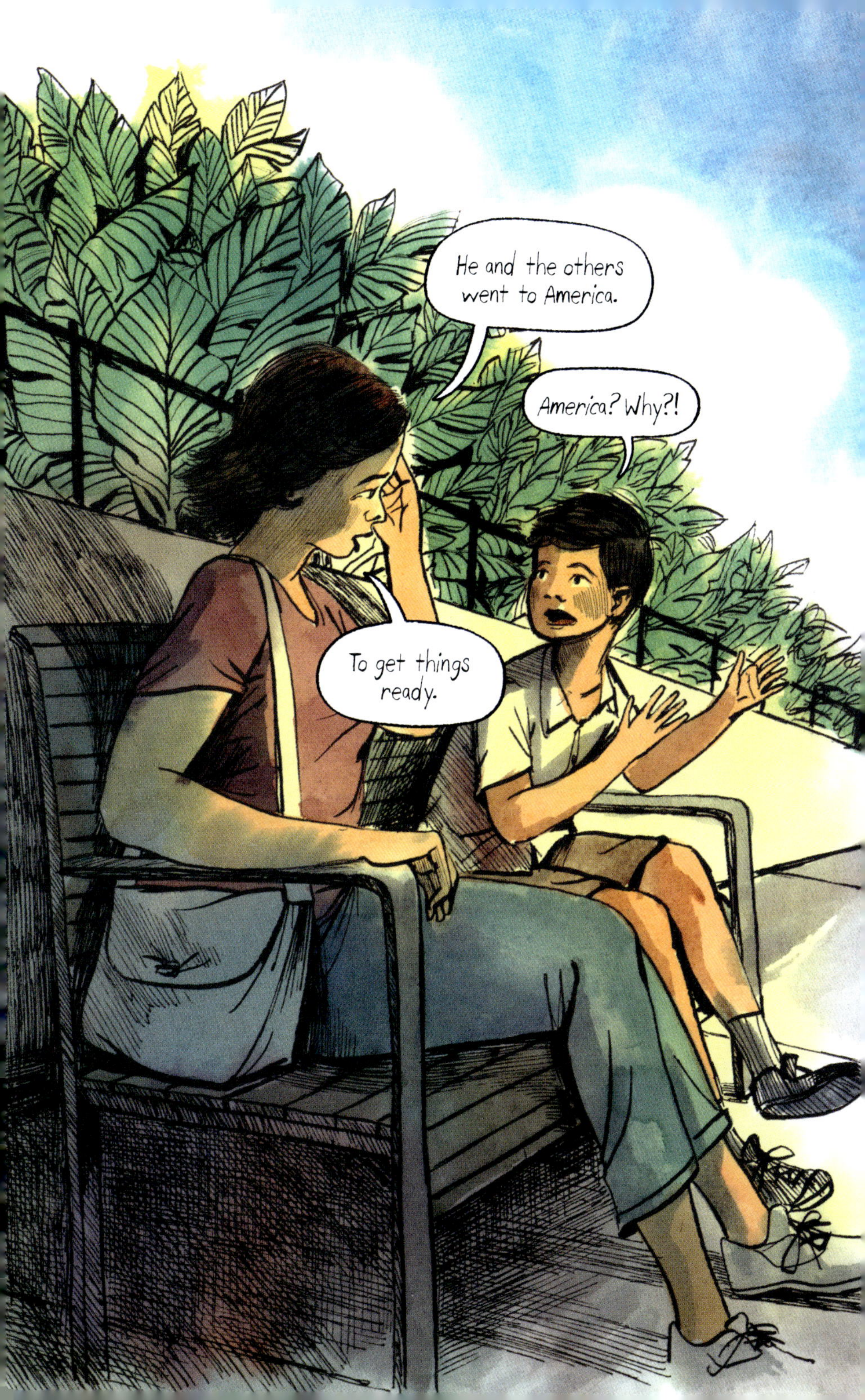
He and the others went to America.
America? Why?!
To get things ready.

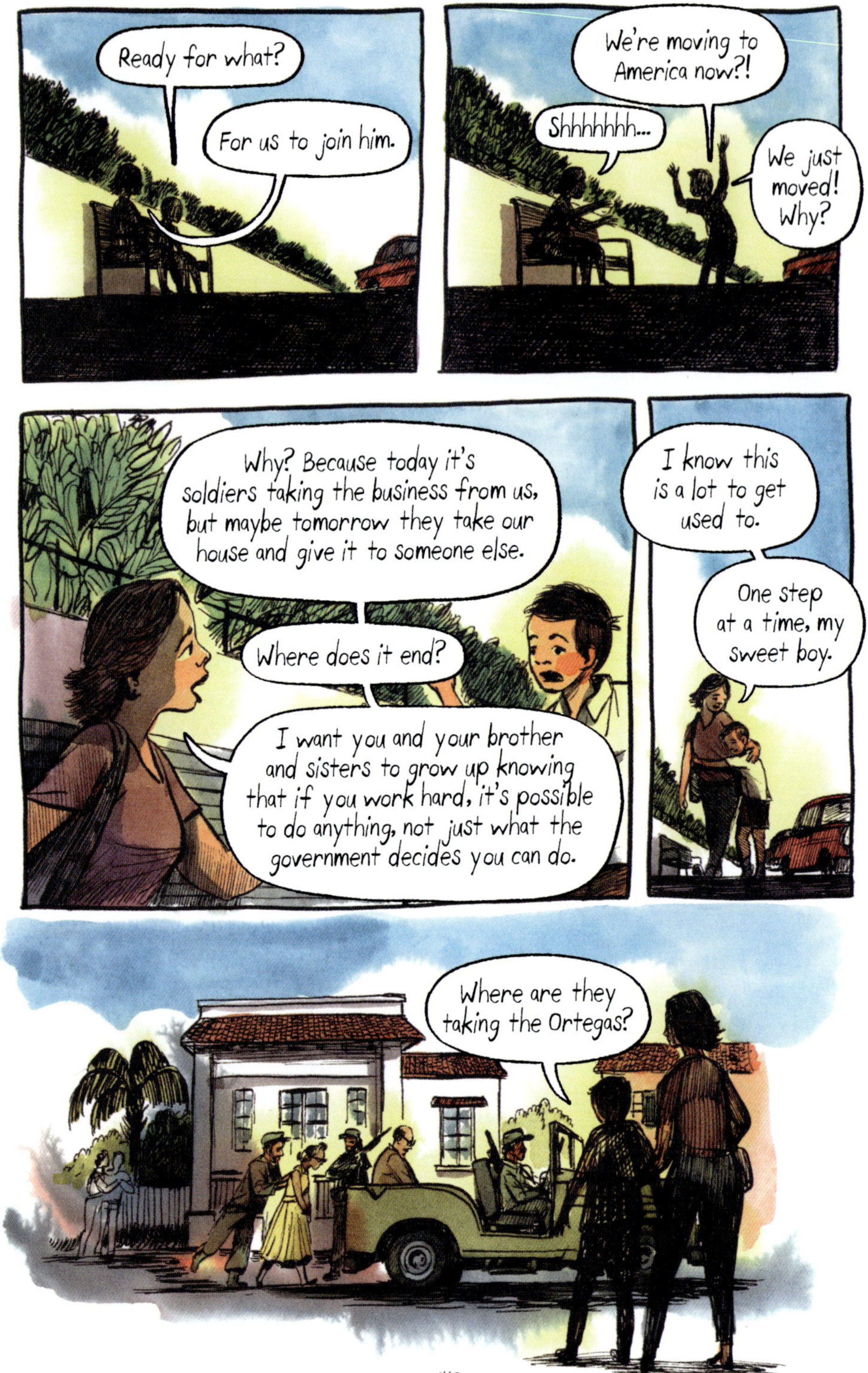
Ready for what?
For us to join him.
We're moving to America now?!
Shhhhhhh...
We just moved! Why?
Why? Because today it's soldiers taking the business from us, but maybe tomorrow they take our house and give it to someone else.
Where does it end?
I want you and your brother and sisters to grow up knowing that if you work hard, it's possible to do anything, not just what the government decides you can do.
I know this is a lot to get used to.
One step at a time, my sweet boy.
Where are they taking the Ortegas?

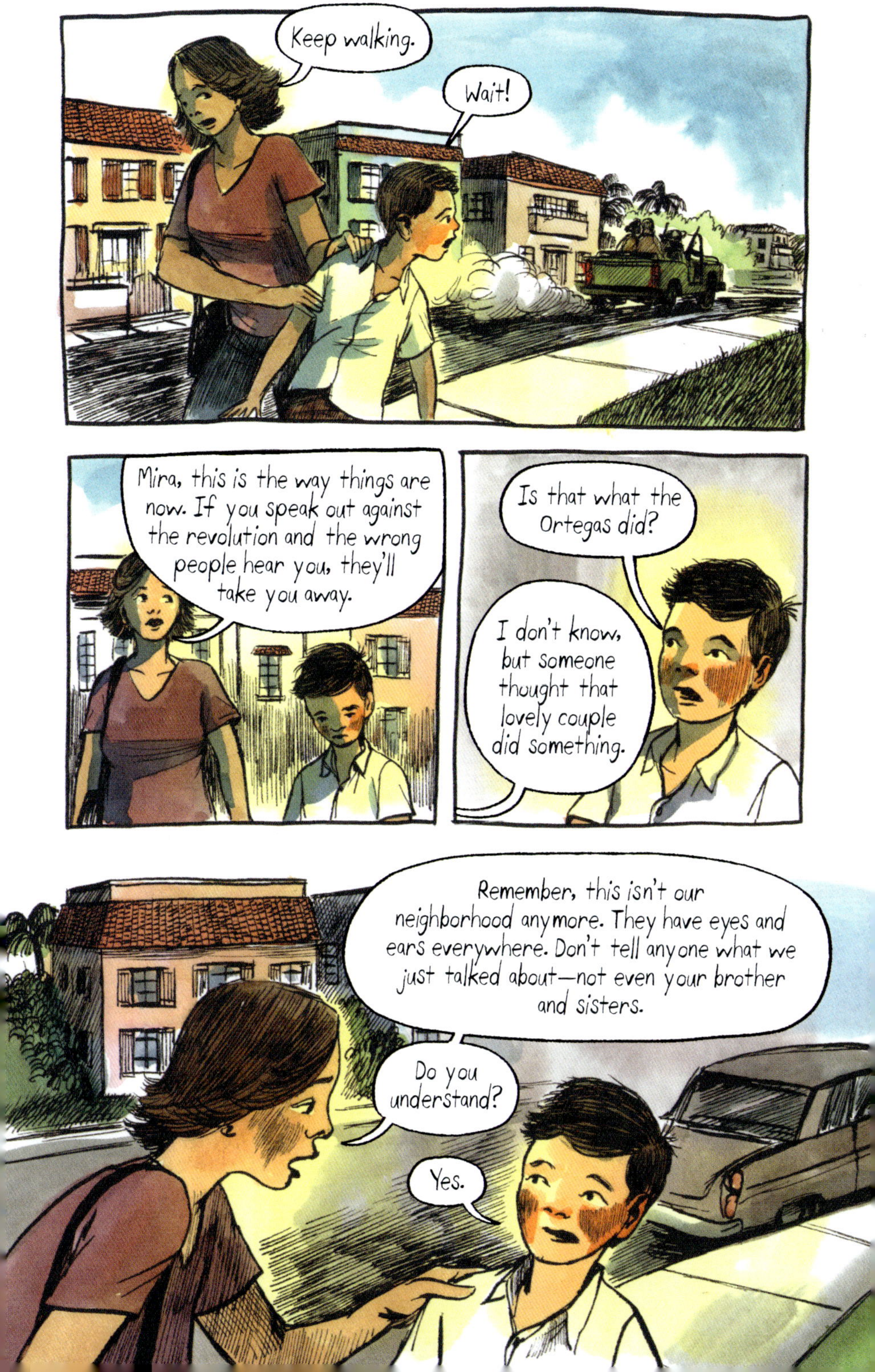
Keep walking.
Wait!
Mira, this is the way things are now. If you speak out against the revolution and the wrong people hear you, they'll take you away.
Is that what the Ortegas did?
I don't know, but someone thought that lovely couple did something.
Remember, this isn't our neighborhood anymore. They have eyes and ears everywhere. Don't tell anyone what we just talked about—not even your brother and sisters.
Do you understand?
Yes.

Trying to topple Castro's government, the American CIA trains Cuban exiles in preparation for invading Cuba's southern coast.

Bay of Pigs

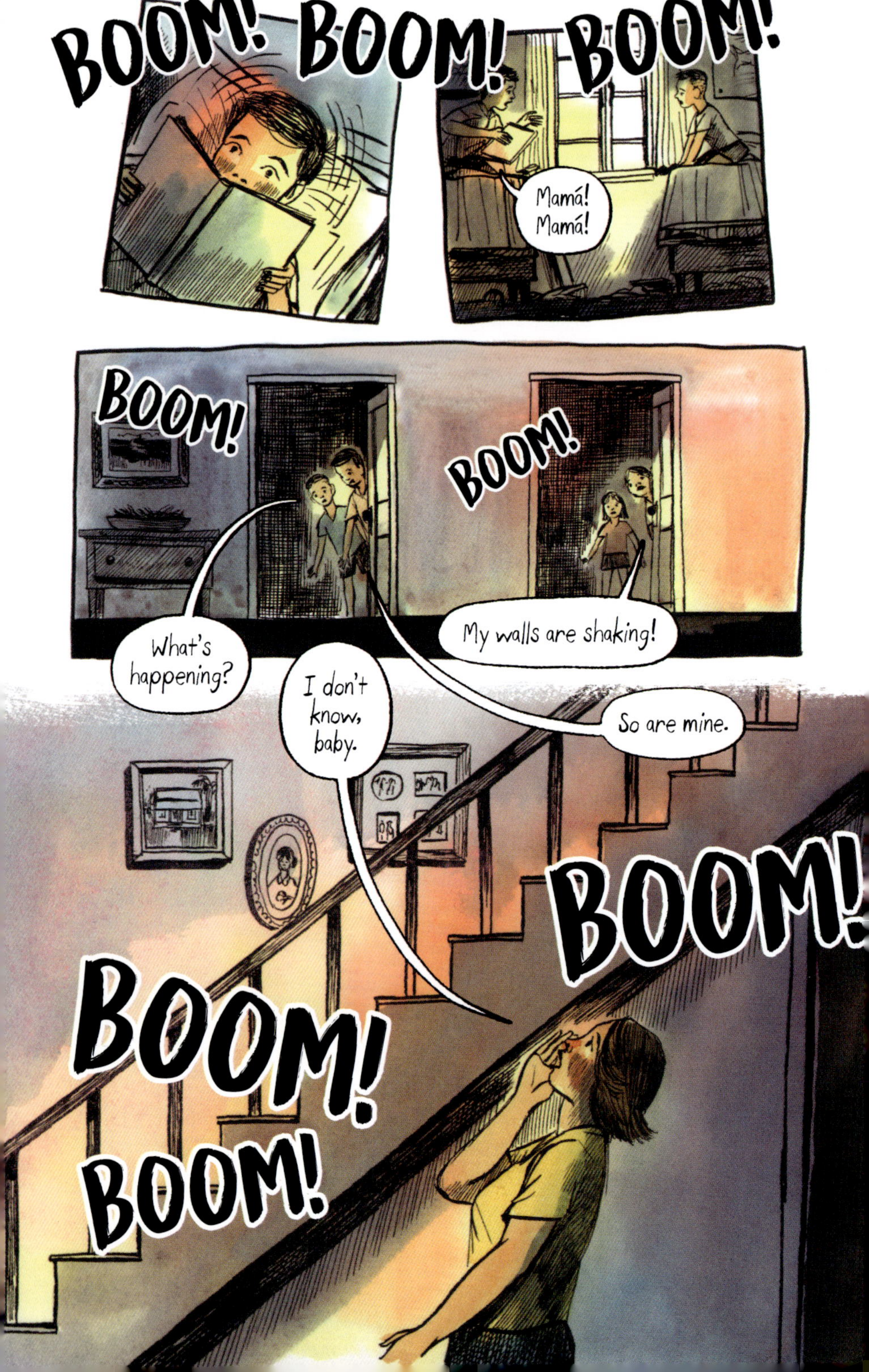
BOOM! BOOM! BOOM!
Mamá! Mamá!
BOOM!
BOOM!
What's happening?
My walls are shaking!
I don't know, baby.
So are mine.
BOOM!
BOOM!
BOOM!

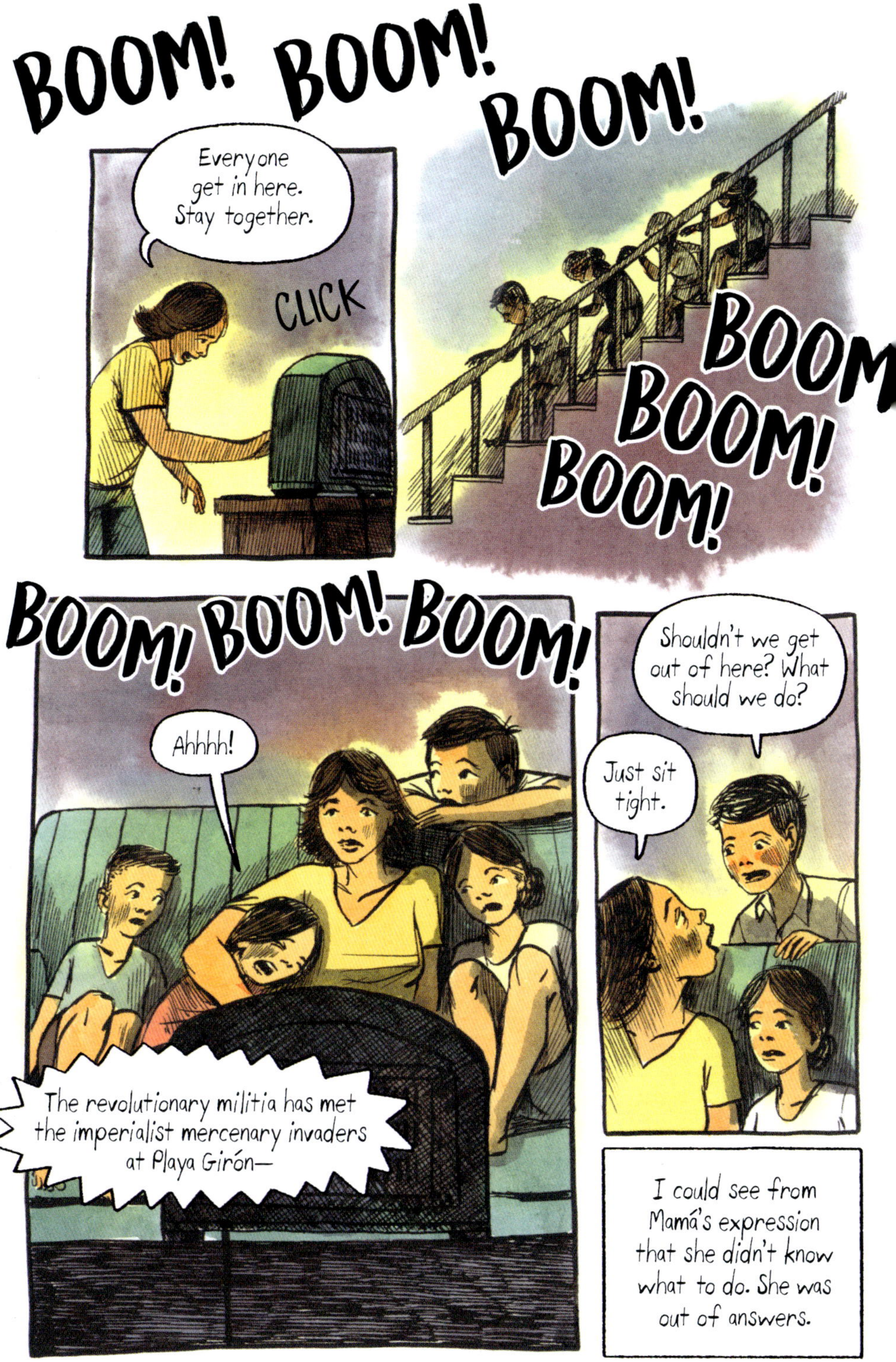
BOOM! BOOM! BOOM!
Everyone get in here. Stay together.
CLICK
BOOM BOOM! BOOM!
BOOM! BOOM! BOOM!
Ahhhh!
The revolutionary militia has met the imperialist mercenary invaders at Playa Girón—
Shouldn't we get out of here? What should we do?
Just sit tight.
I could see from Mamá's expression that she didn't know what to do. She was out of answers.

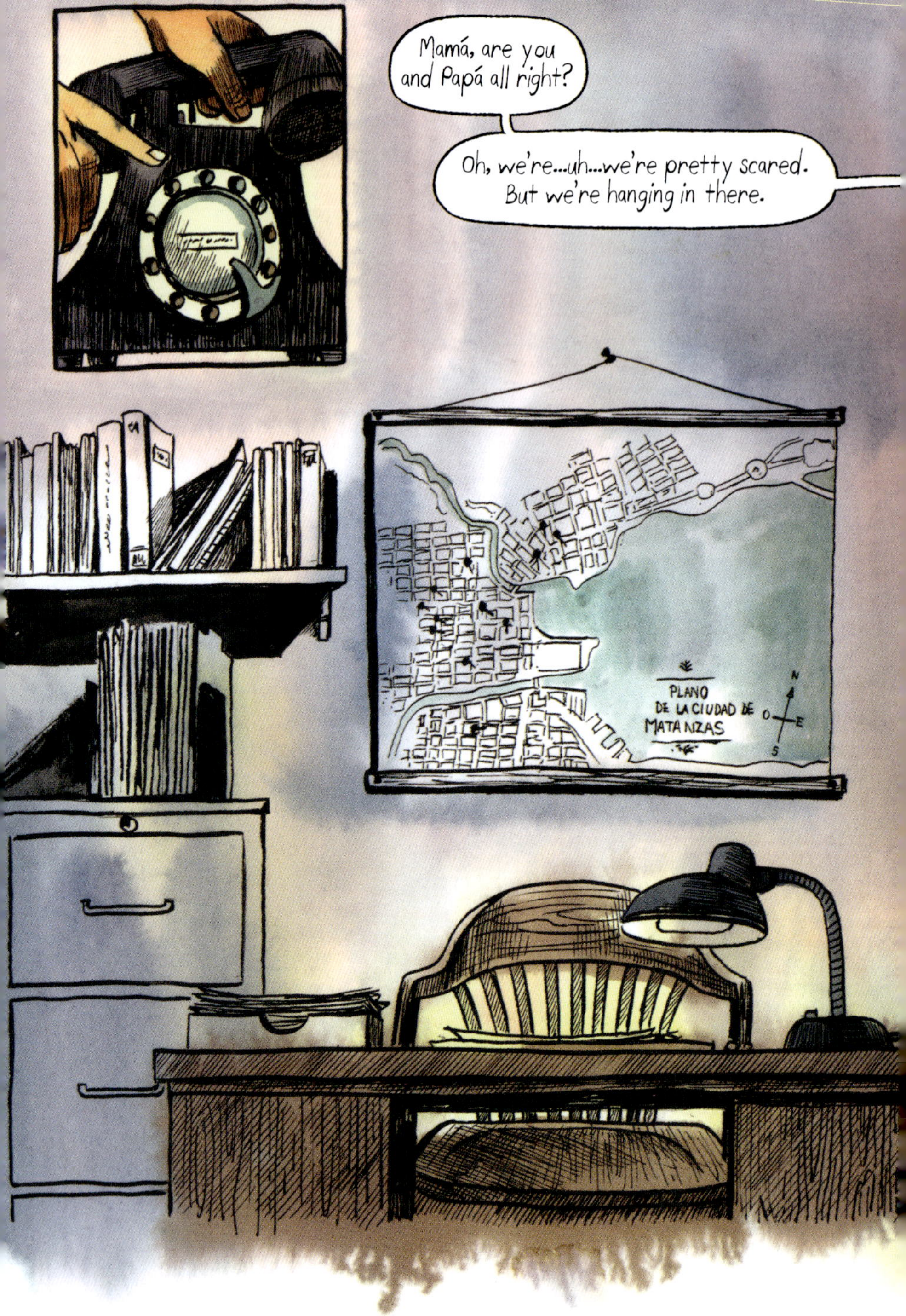
Mamá, are you and Papá all right?
Oh, we're...uh...we're pretty scared. But we're hanging in there.
PLANO DE LA CIUDAD DE MATANZAS
N
O
E
S

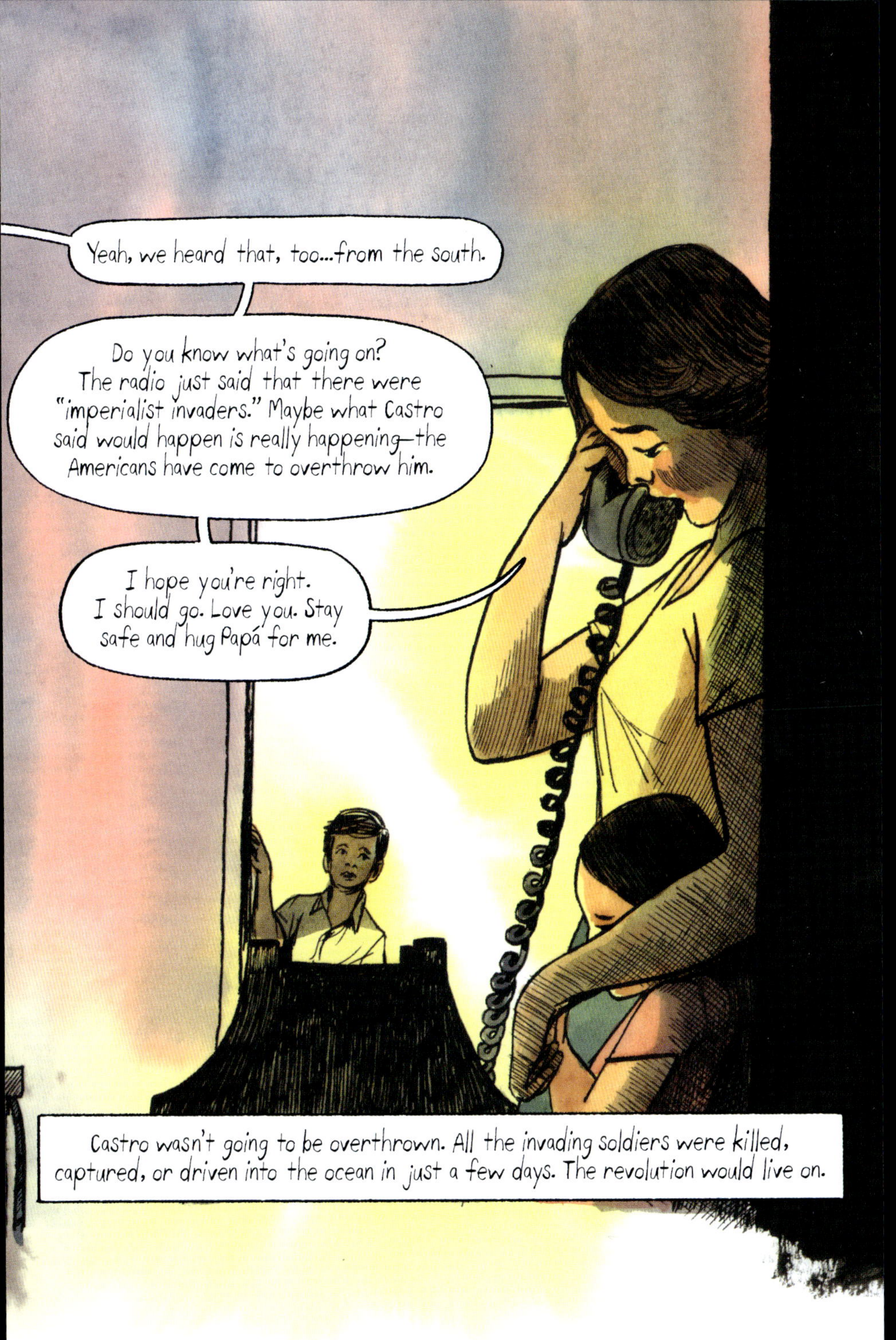
Yeah, we heard that, too...from the south.
Do you know what's going on? The radio just said that there were "imperialist invaders." Maybe what Castro said would happen is really happening—the Americans have come to overthrow him.
I hope you're right. I should go. Love you. Stay safe and hug Papá for me.
Castro wasn't going to be overthrown. All the invading soldiers were killed, captured, or driven into the ocean in just a few days. The revolution would live on.

CONTROL DE VENTAS PARA
PRODUCTOS ALIMENTICIOS

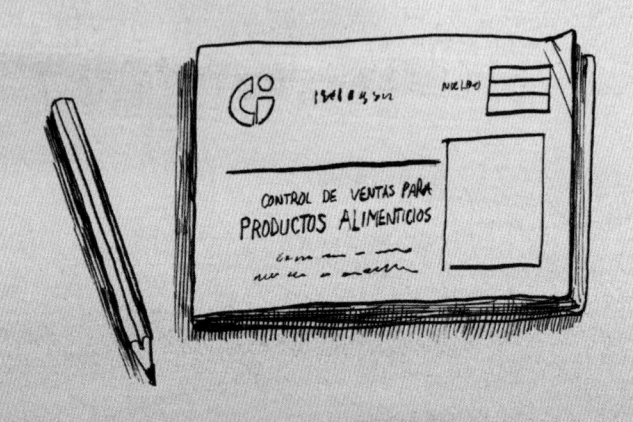

Castro declares that he is a Marxist-Leninist, cementing Cuba's relationship with the Soviet Union.

In response, US President John F. Kennedy bans all trade with Cuba, which results in fewer essentials like food and household goods being available. Rationing begins, limiting the amount of goods Cuban families can buy.

Worms

COLOR
de
AEROSOL

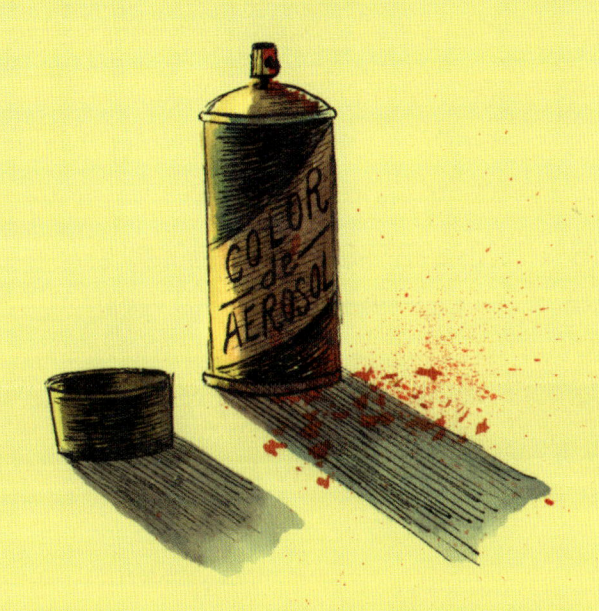

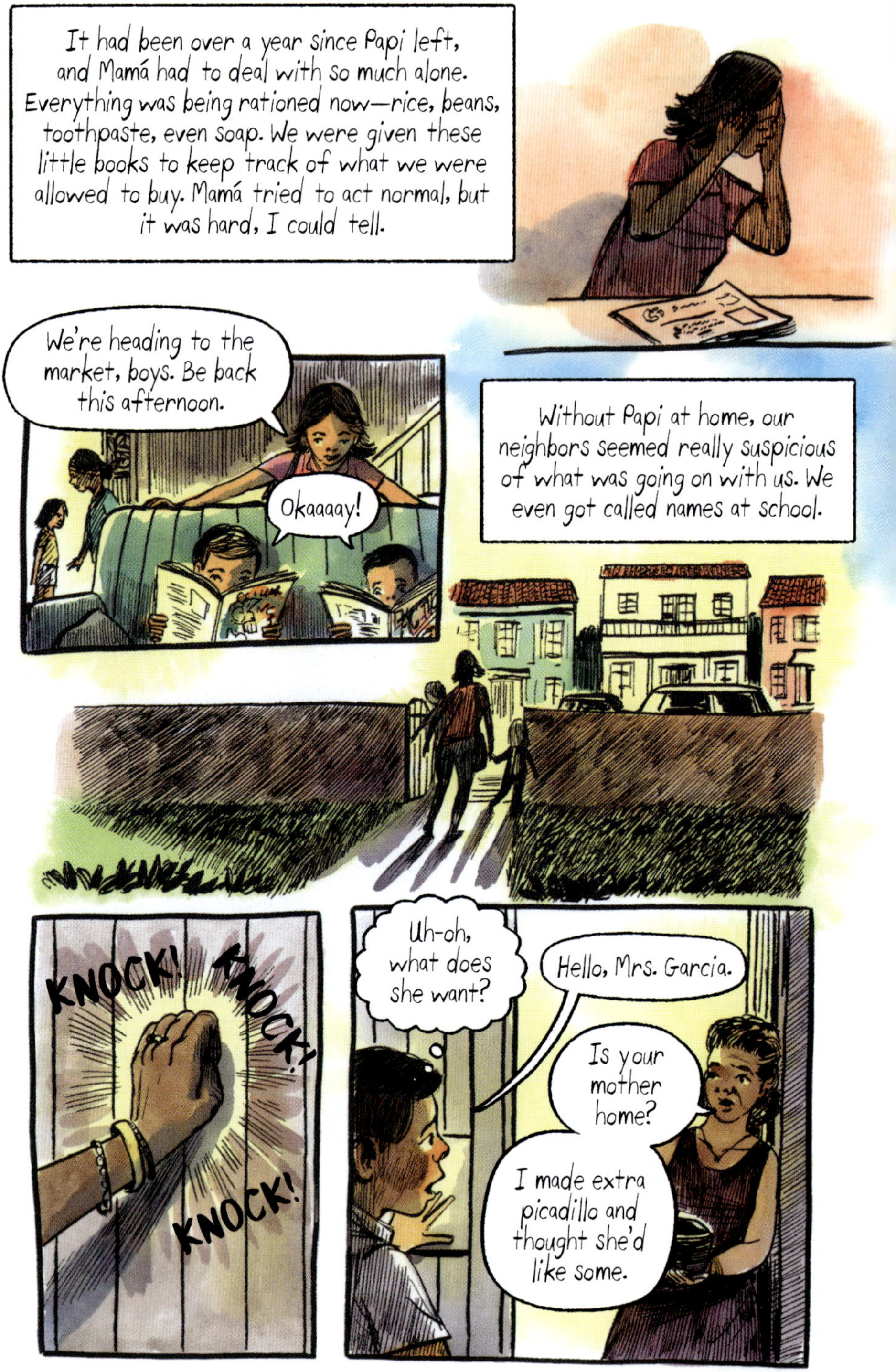
It had been over a year since Papi left, and Mamá had to deal with so much alone. Everything was being rationed now—rice, beans, toothpaste, even soap. We were given these little books to keep track of what we were allowed to buy. Mamá tried to act normal, but it was hard, I could tell.
We're heading to the market, boys. Be back this afternoon.
Okaaaay!
Without Papi at home, our neighbors seemed really suspicious of what was going on with us. We even got called names at school.
KNOCK! KNOCK! KNOCK!
Uh-oh, what does she want?
Hello, Mrs. Garcia.
Is your mother home?
I made extra picadillo and thought she'd like some.

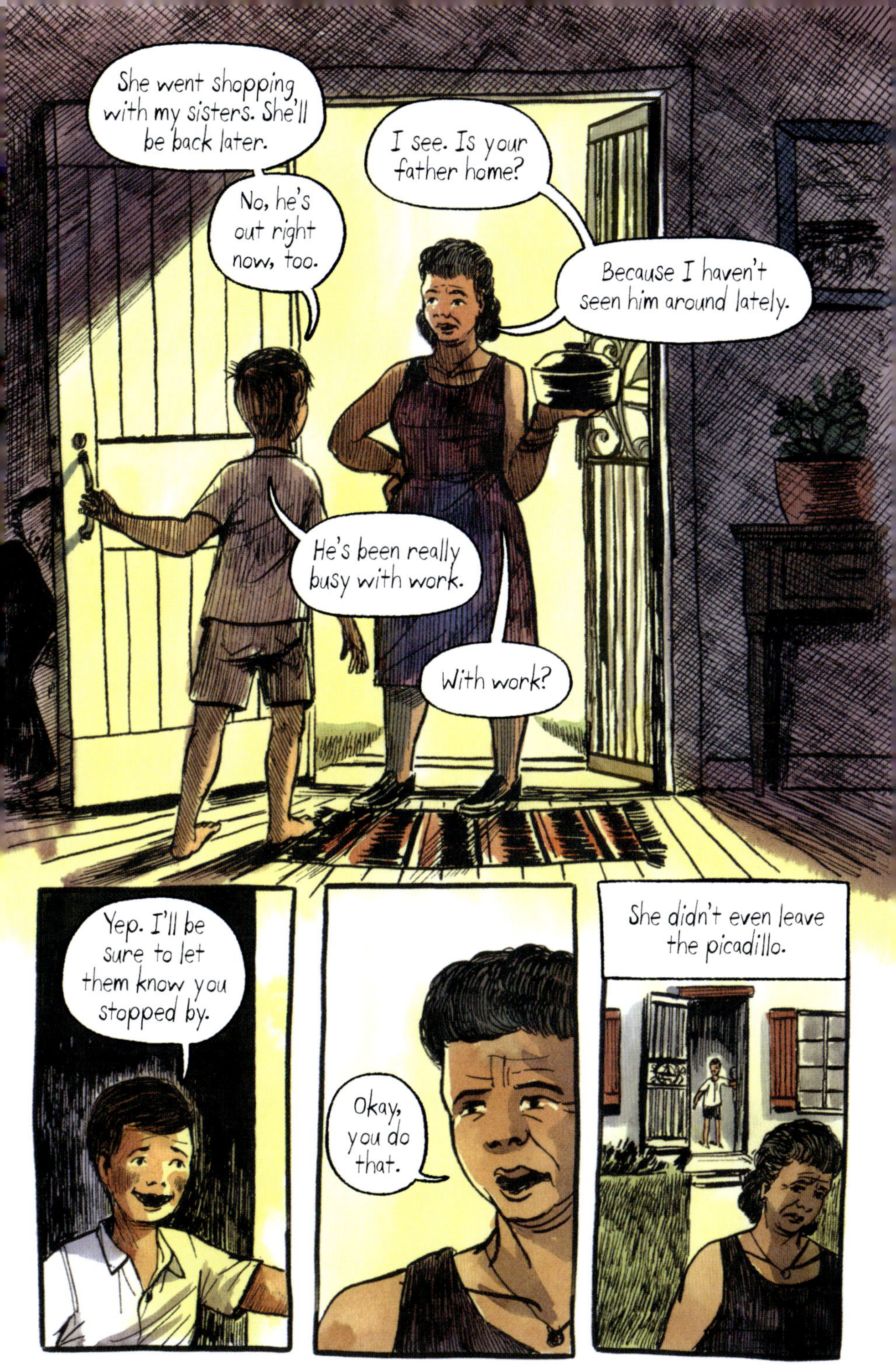
She went shopping with my sisters. She'll be back later.
I see. Is your father home?
No, he's out right now, too.
Because I haven't seen him around lately.
He's been really busy with work.
With work?
Yep. I'll be sure to let them know you stopped by.
Okay, you do that.
She didn't even leave the picadillo.

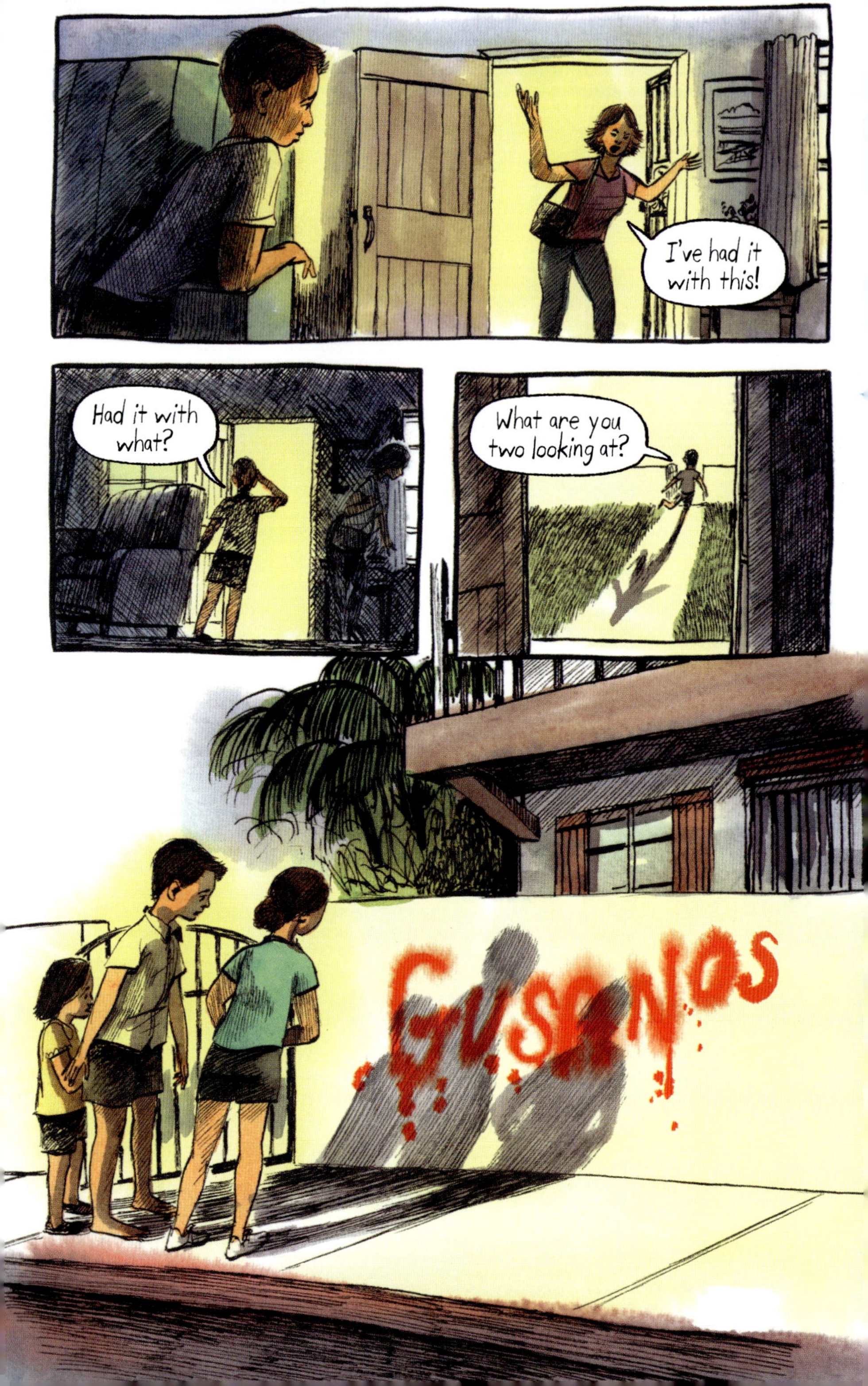
I've had it with this!
Had it with what?
What are you two looking at?
GUSANOS

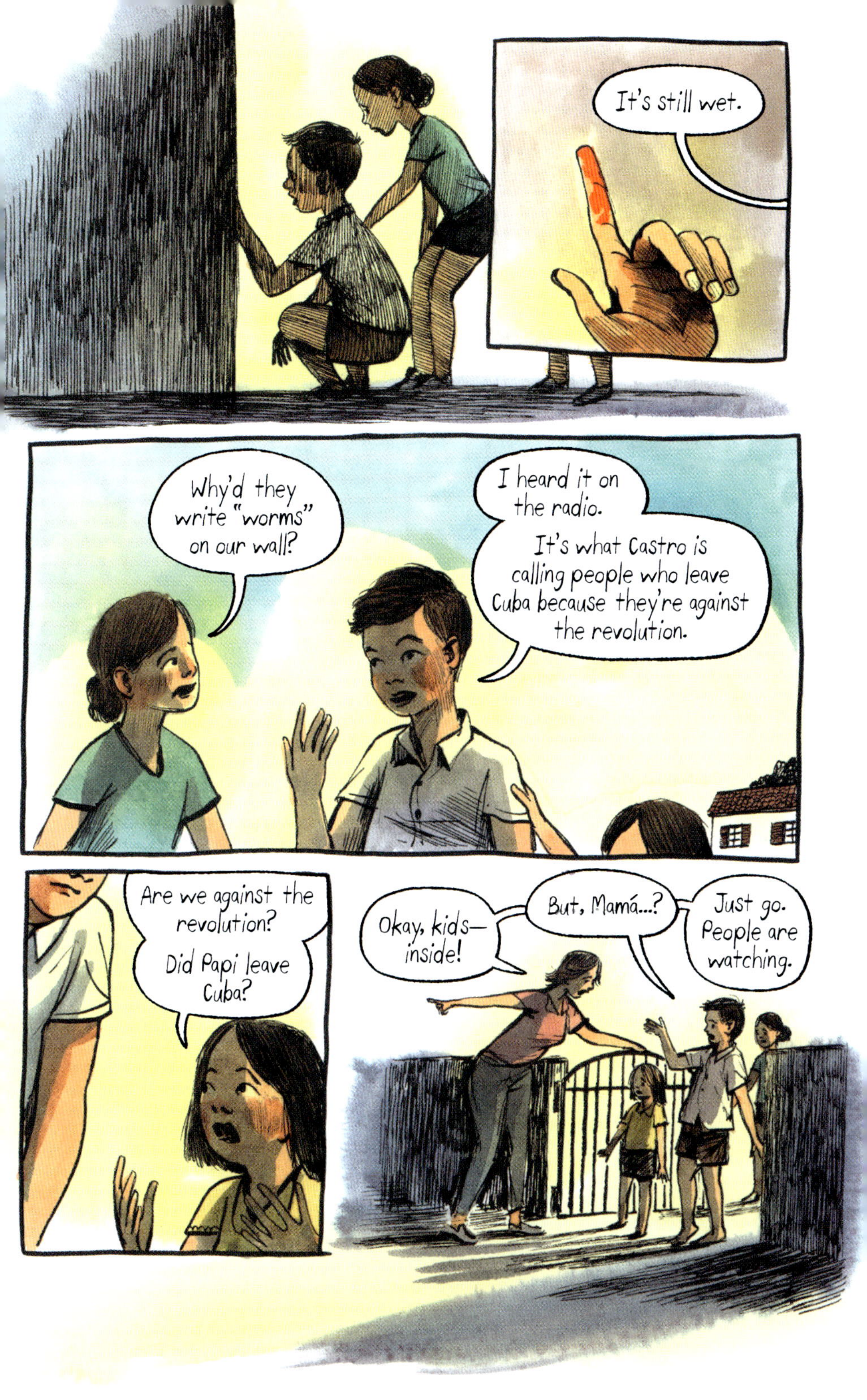
It's still wet.
Why'd they write "worms" on our wall?
I heard it on the radio.
It's what Castro is calling people who leave Cuba because they're against the revolution.
Are we against the revolution?
Did Papi leave Cuba?
Okay, kids—inside!
But, Mamá...?
Just go. People are watching.

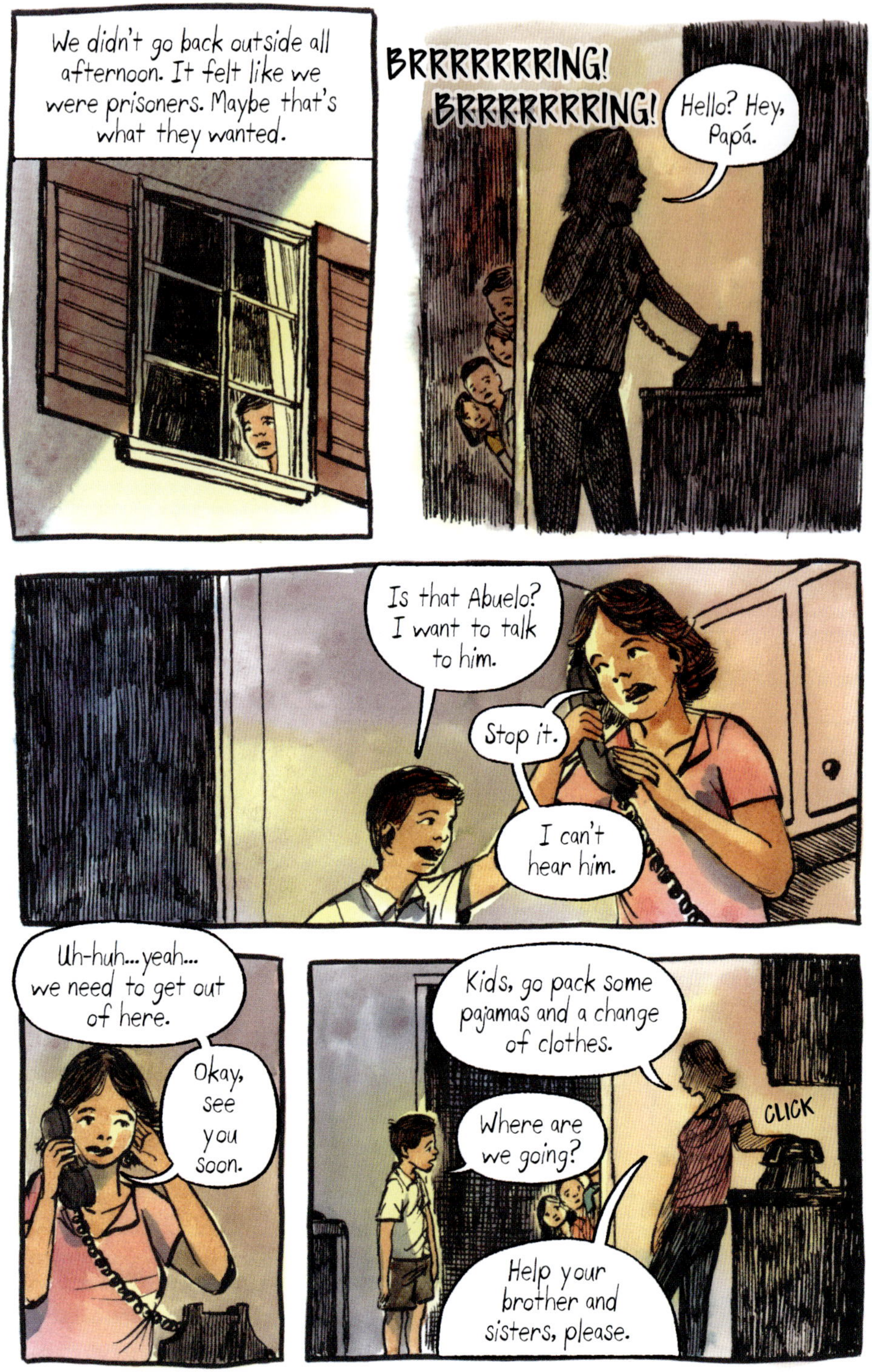
We didn't go back outside all afternoon. It felt like we were prisoners. Maybe that's what they wanted.
BRRRRRRRING!
BRRRRRRRING!
Hello? Hey, Papá.
Is that Abuelo? I want to talk to him.
Stop it.
I can't hear him.
Uh-huh... yeah... we need to get out of here.
Okay, see you soon.
Kids, go pack some pajamas and a change of clothes.
CLICK
Where are we going?
Help your brother and sisters, please.

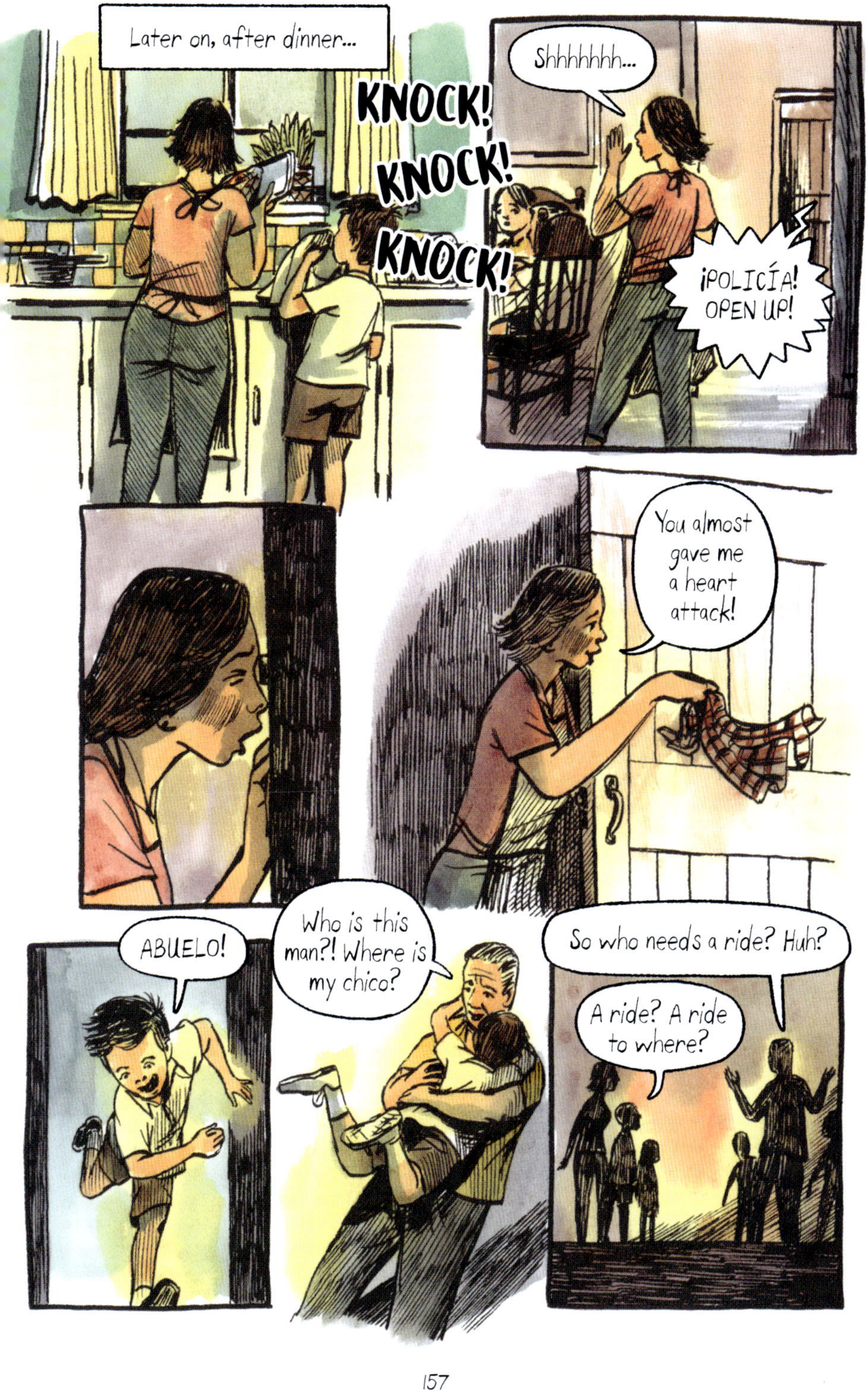
Later on, after dinner...
KNOCK!
KNOCK!
KNOCK!
Shhhhhhh...
¡POLICÍA! OPEN UP!
You almost gave me a heart attack!
ABUELO!
Who is this man?! Where is my chico?
So who needs a ride? Huh?
A ride? A ride to where?

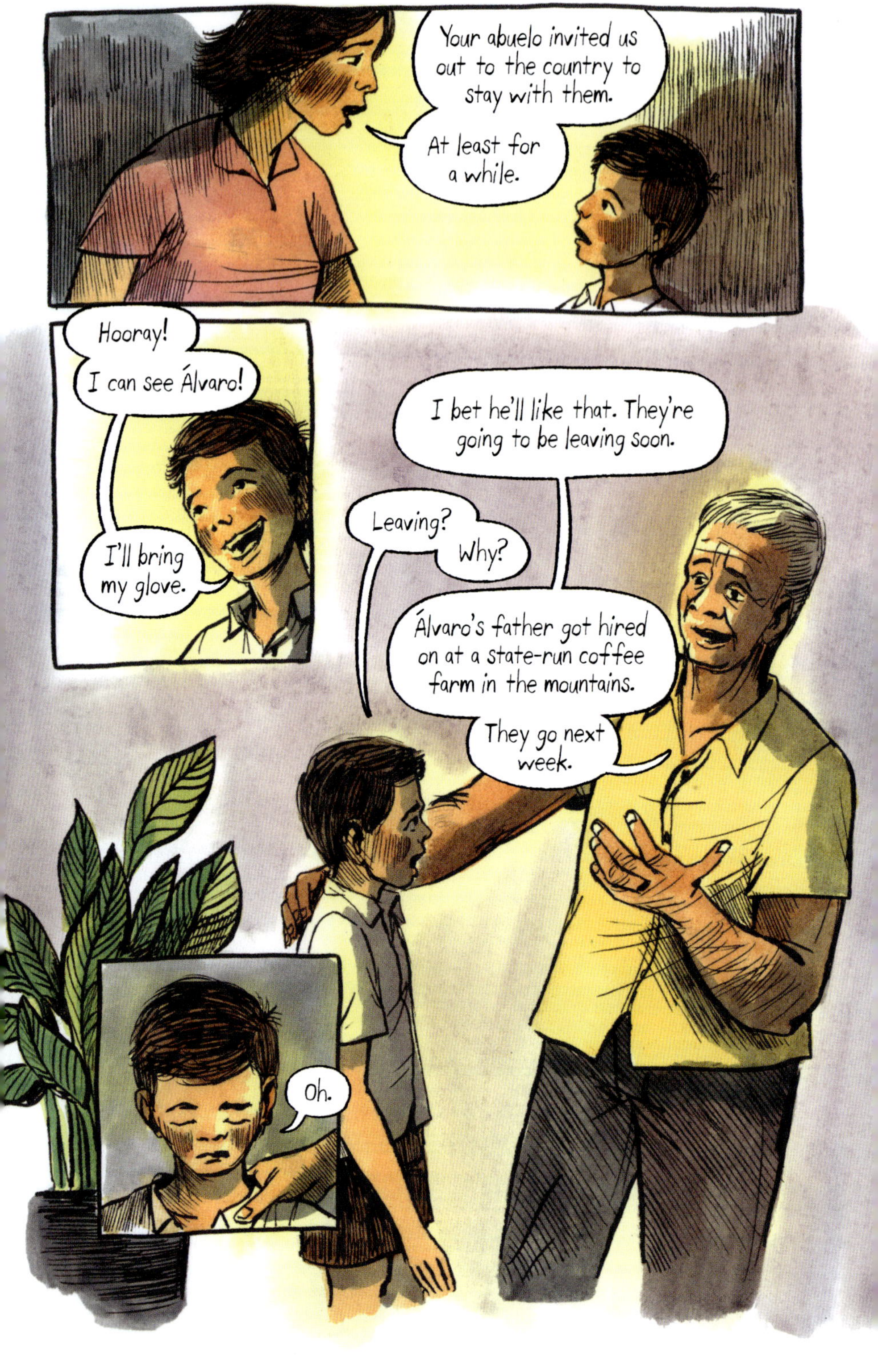
Your abuelo invited us out to the country to stay with them.
At least for a while.
Hooray!
I can see Álvaro!
I'll bring my glove.
I bet he'll like that. They're going to be leaving soon.
Leaving?
Why?
Álvaro's father got hired on at a state-run coffee farm in the mountains.
They go next week.
Oh.

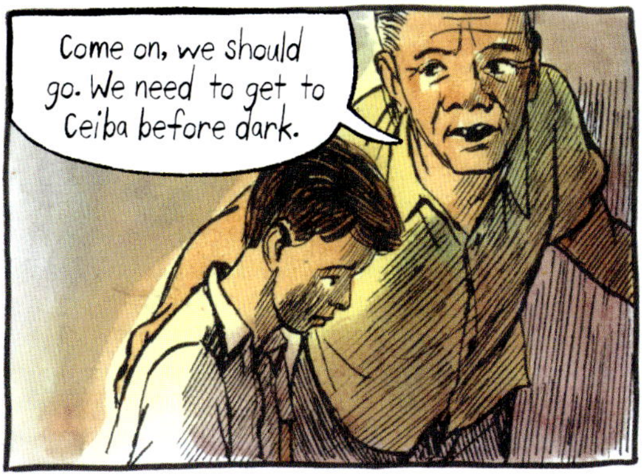
Come on, we should go. We need to get to Ceiba before dark.

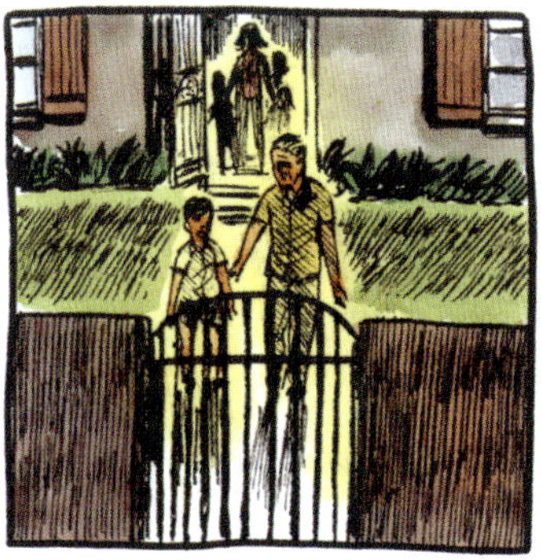

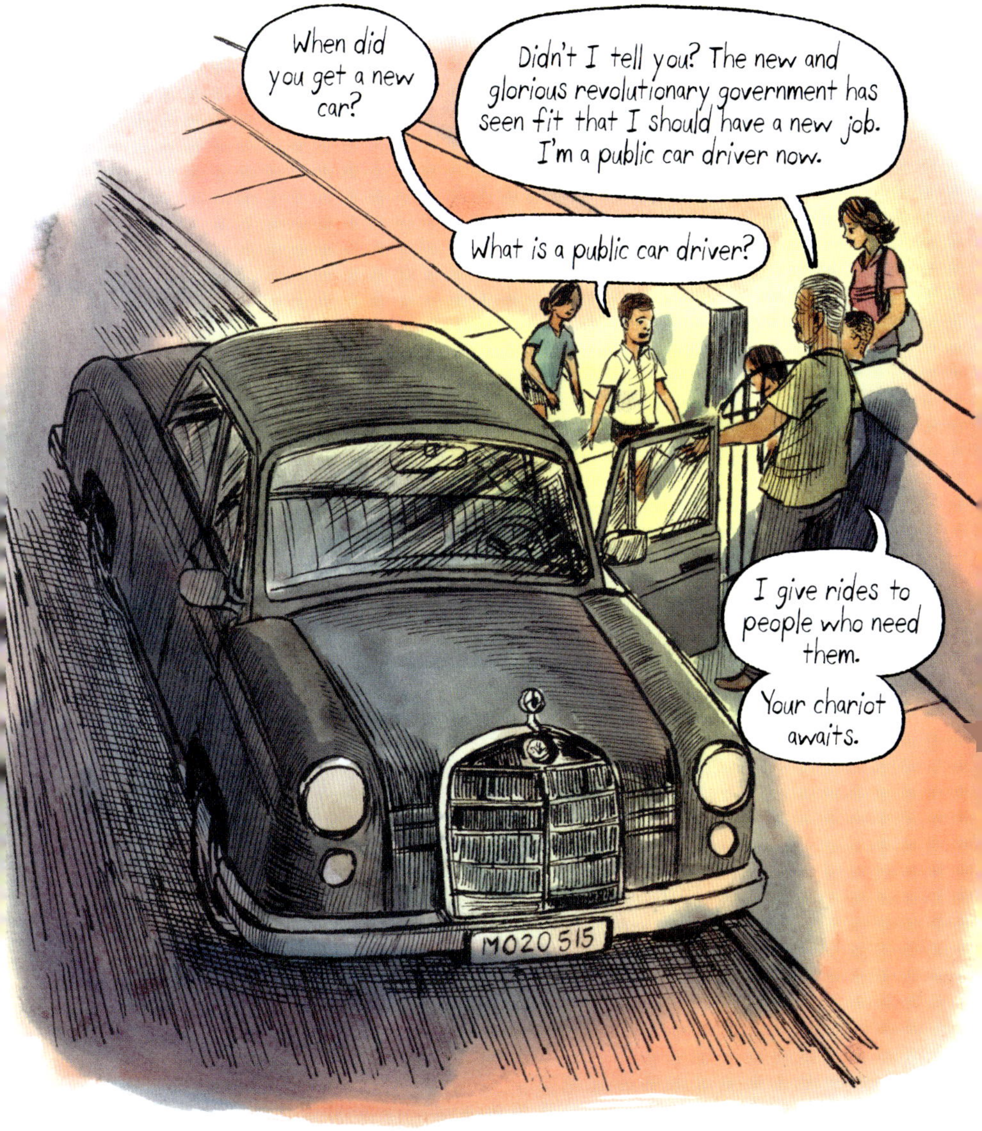
When did you get a new car?
Didn't I tell you? The new and glorious revolutionary government has seen fit that I should have a new job. I'm a public car driver now.
What is a public car driver?
I give rides to people who need them.
Your chariot awaits.
MO20 515

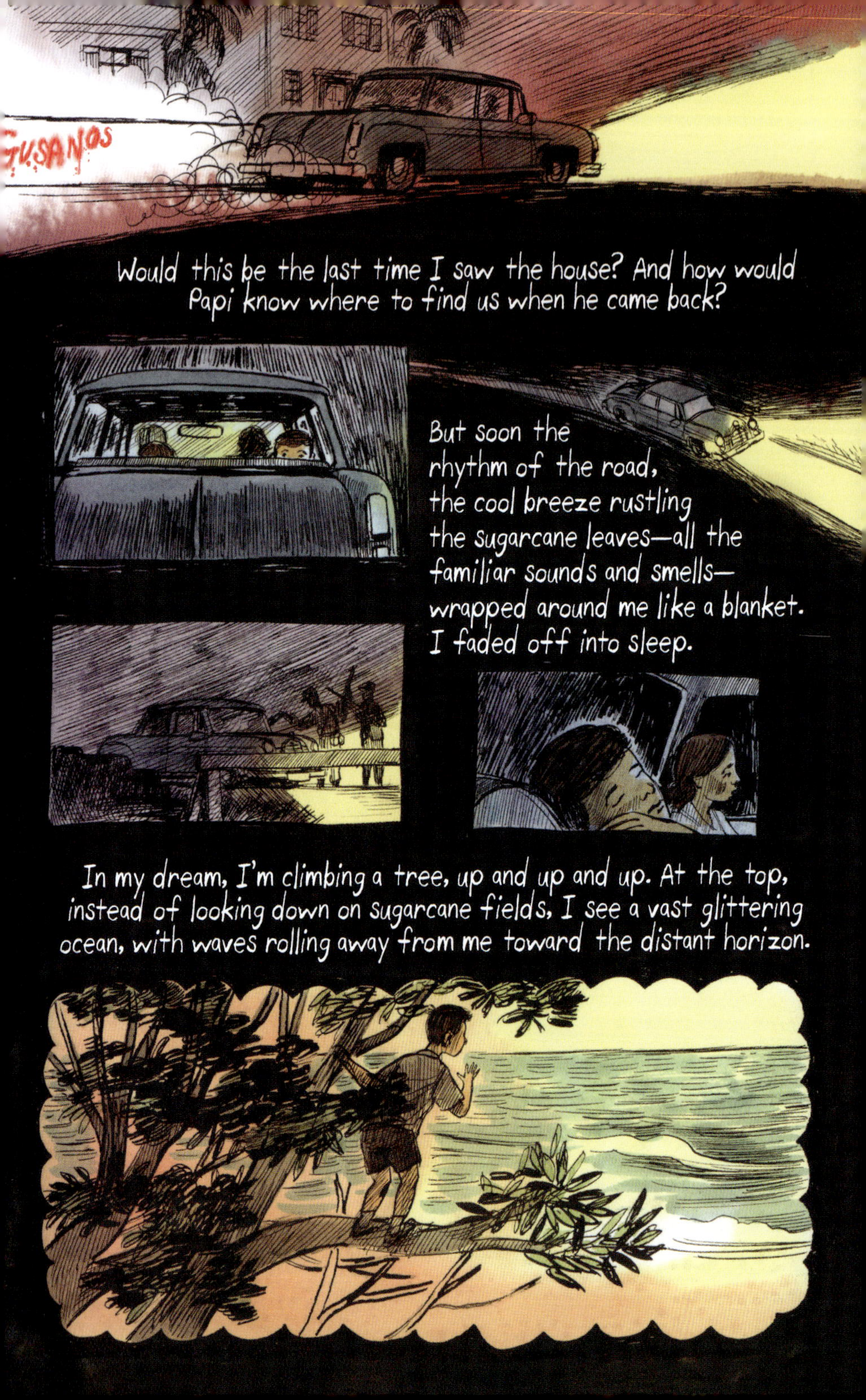
GUSANOS
Would this be the last time I saw the house? And how would Papi know where to find us when he came back?
But soon the rhythm of the road, the cool breeze rustling the sugarcane leaves—all the familiar sounds and smells—wrapped around me like a blanket. I faded off into sleep.
In my dream, I'm climbing a tree, up and up and up. At the top, instead of looking down on sugarcane fields, I see a vast glittering ocean, with waves rolling away from me toward the distant horizon.

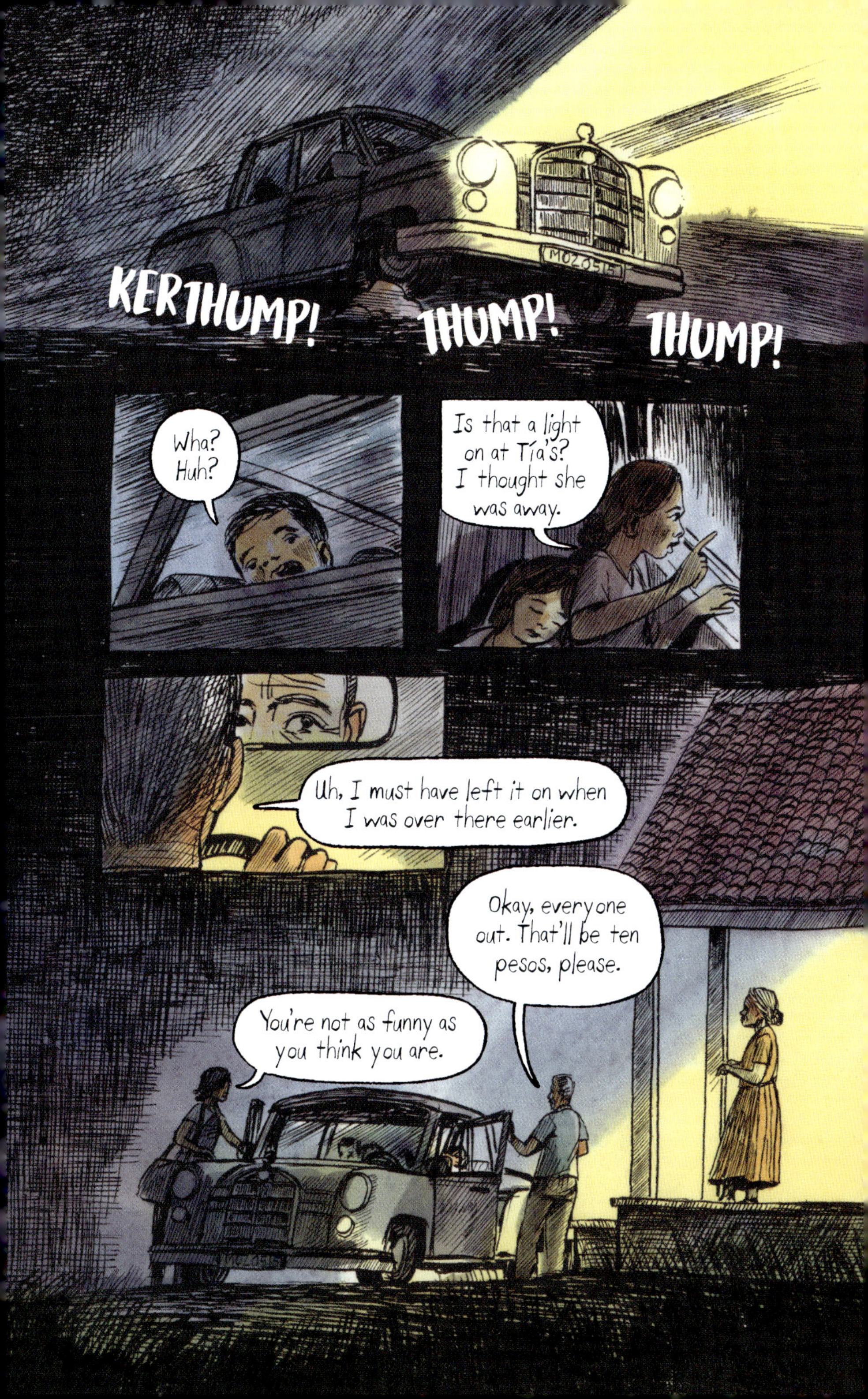
KERTHUMP!
THUMP!
THUMP!
Wha? Huh?
Is that a light on at Tía's? I thought she was away.
Uh, I must have left it on when I was over there earlier.
Okay, everyone out. That'll be ten pesos, please.
You're not as funny as you think you are.

Because of Castro's agricultural reforms, working-class people have new opportunities. Some are given their own land, which the government had taken from wealthier citizens. Others find work on state-owned farms.

Going, Going, Gone!

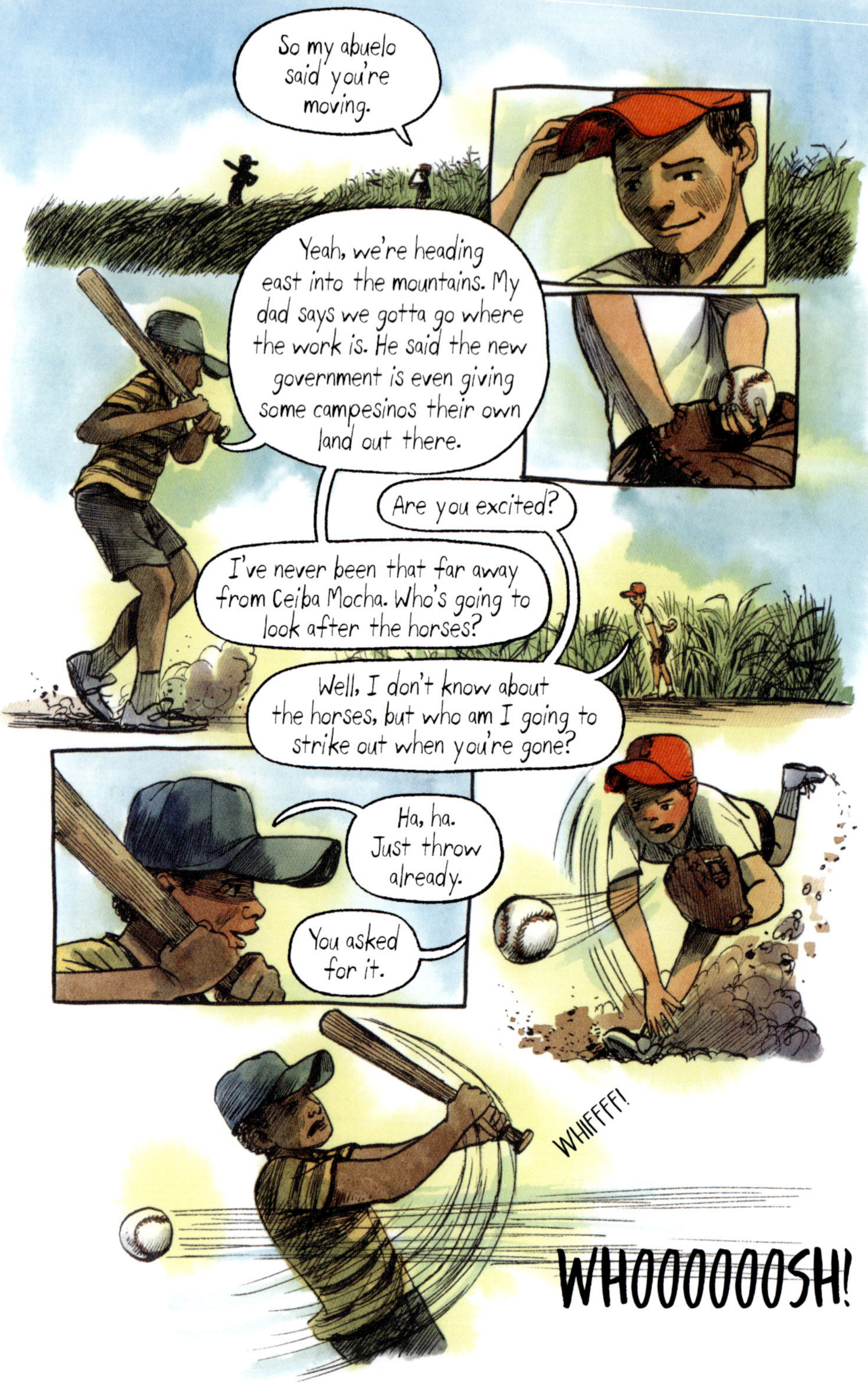
So my abuelo said you're moving.
Yeah, we're heading east into the mountains. My dad says we gotta go where the work is. He said the new government is even giving some campesinos their own land out there.
Are you excited?
I've never been that far away from Ceiba Mocha. Who's going to look after the horses?
Well, I don't know about the horses, but who am I going to strike out when you're gone?
Ha, ha. Just throw already.
You asked for it.
WHIFFFF!
WHOOOOOOSH!

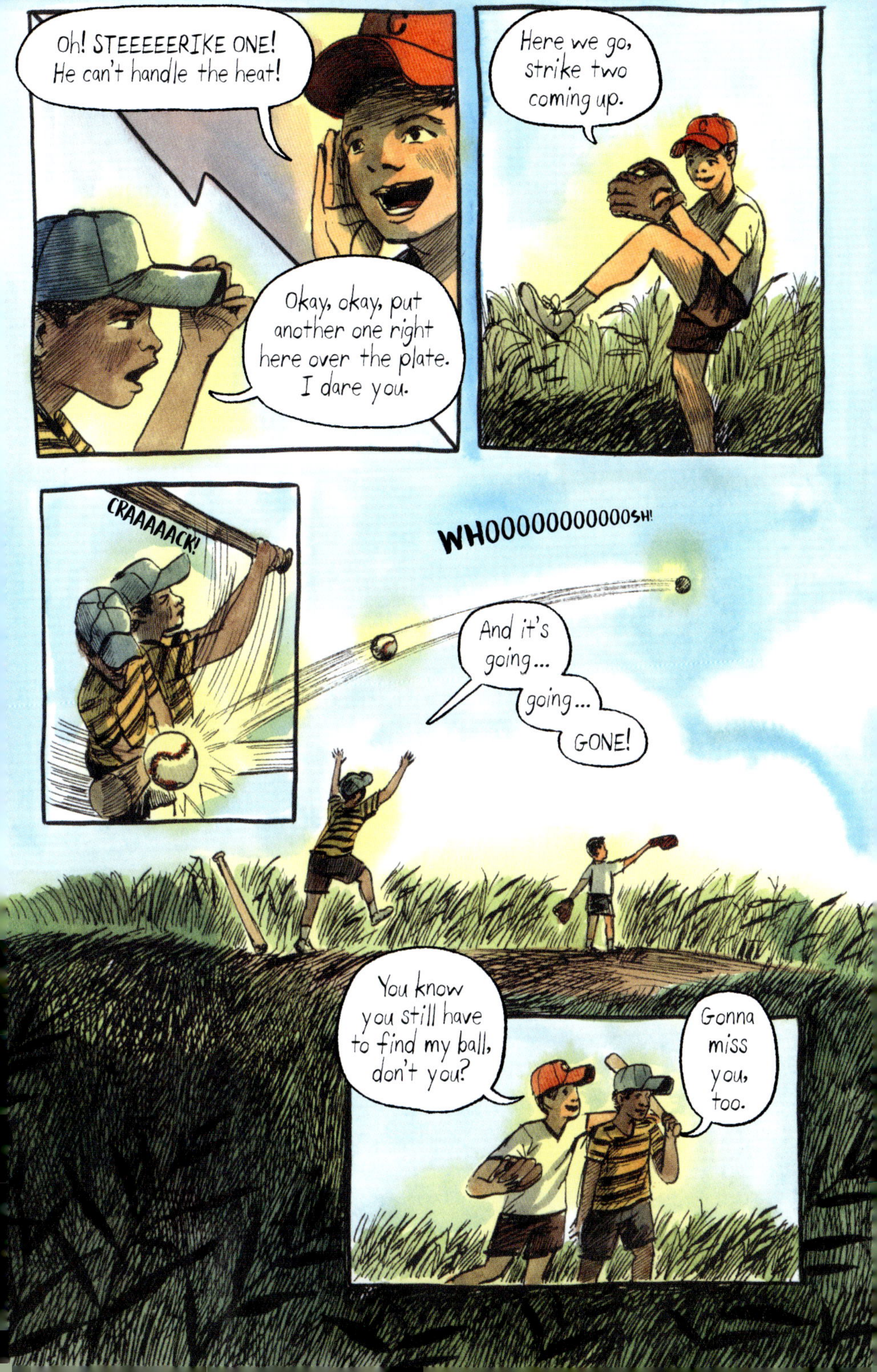
Oh! STEEEEERIKE ONE! He can't handle the heat!
Okay, okay, put another one right here over the plate. I dare you.
Here we go, strike two coming up.
CRAAAAACK!
WHOOOOOOOOOOOSH!
And it's going...
going...
GONE!
You know you still have to find my ball, don't you?
Gonna miss you, too.

Due to Castro's severe travel restrictions, it is difficult for Cubans to leave the country legally.

Breakfast

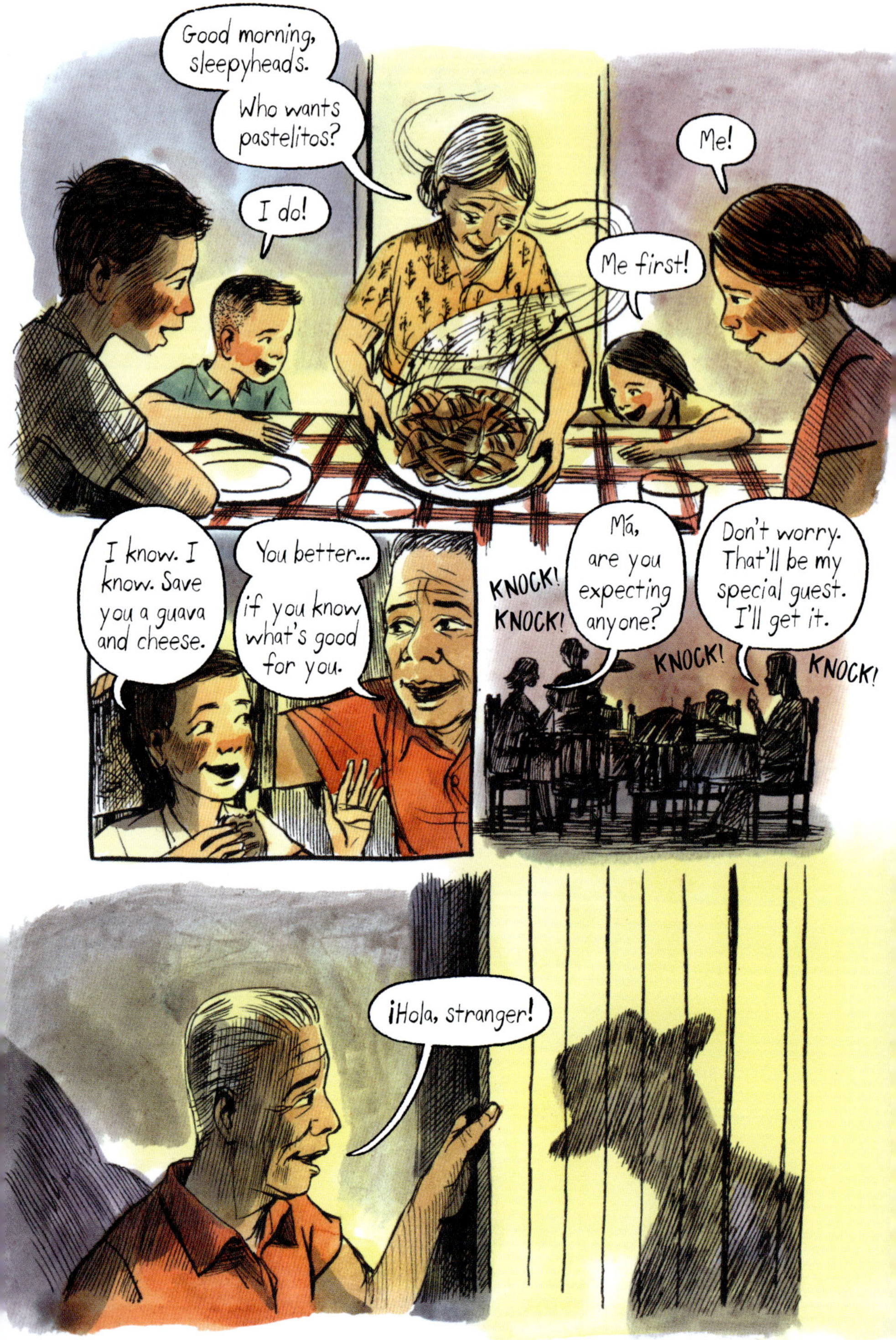
Good morning, sleepyheads.
Who wants pastelitos?
I do!
Me!
Me first!
I know. I know. Save you a guava and cheese.
You better...
if you know what's good for you.
KNOCK! KNOCK!
Má, are you expecting anyone?
KNOCK!
Don't worry. That'll be my special guest. I'll get it.
KNOCK!
¡Hola, stranger!

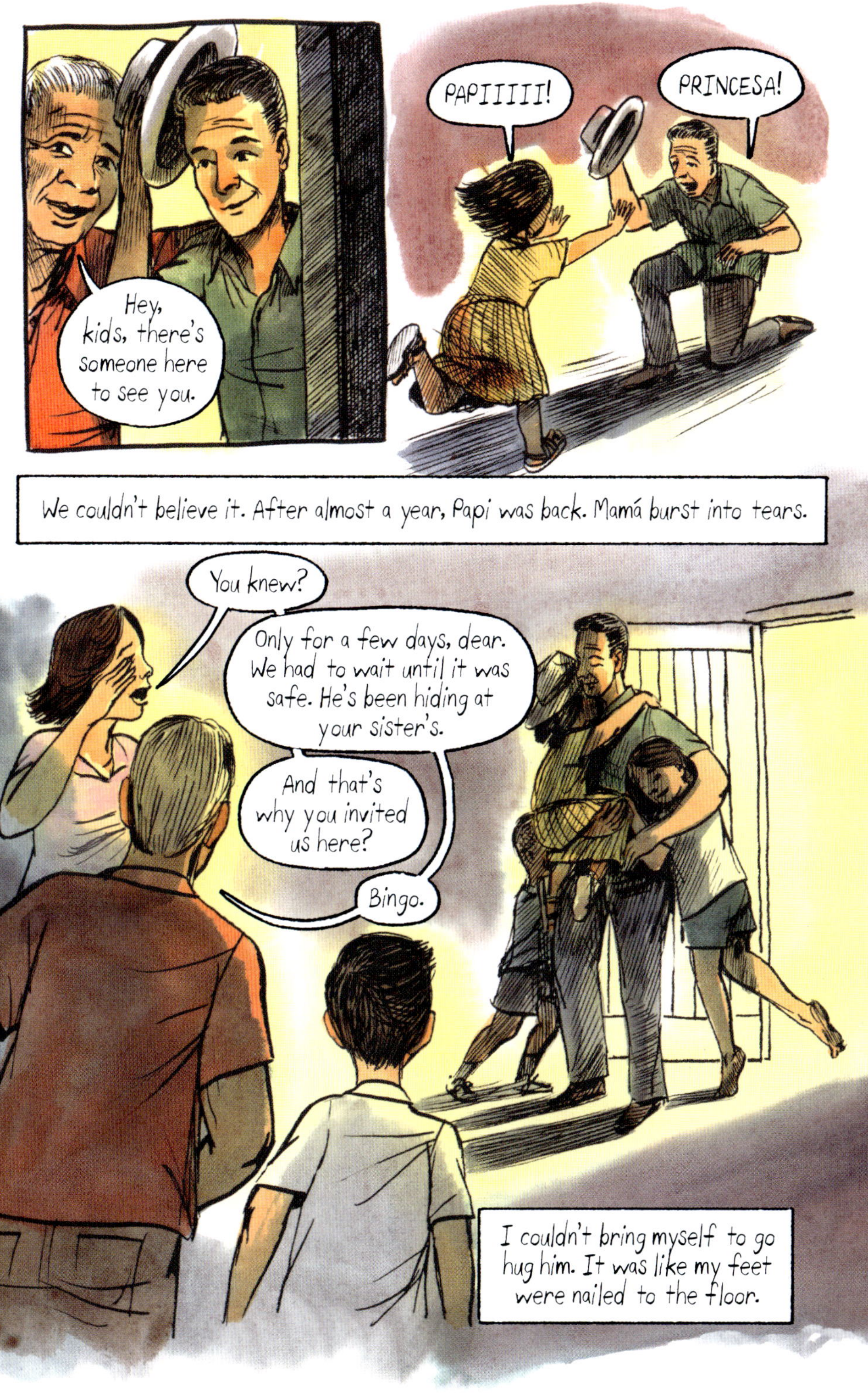
Hey, kids, there's someone here to see you.
PAPIIIII!
PRINCESA!
We couldn't believe it. After almost a year, Papi was back. Mamá burst into tears.
You knew?
Only for a few days, dear. We had to wait until it was safe. He's been hiding at your sister's.
And that's why you invited us here?
Bingo.
I couldn't bring myself to go hug him. It was like my feet were nailed to the floor.

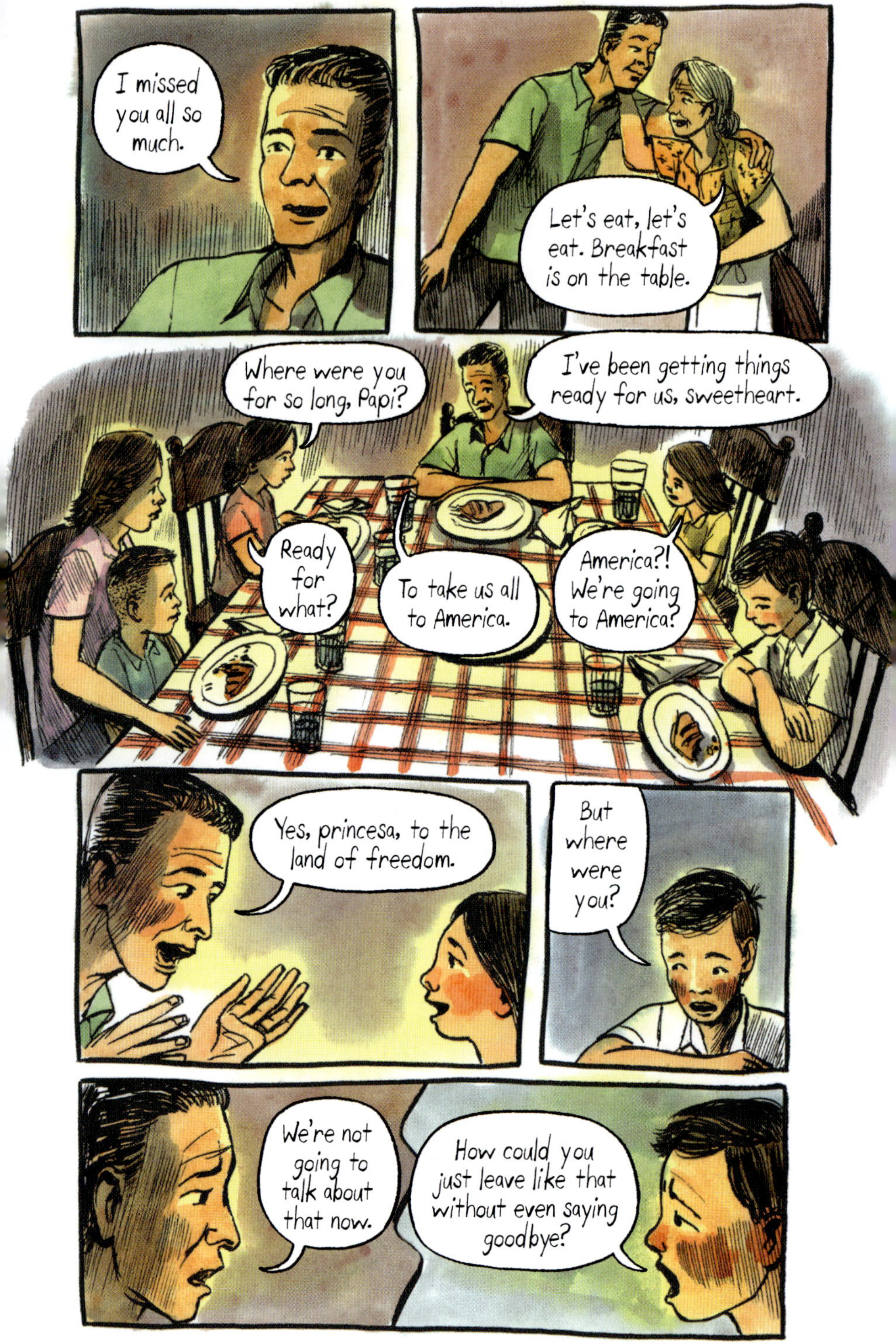
I missed you all so much.
Let's eat, let's eat. Breakfast is on the table.
Where were you for so long, Papi?
I've been getting things ready for us, sweetheart.
Ready for what?
To take us all to America.
America?! We're going to America?
Yes, princesa, to the land of freedom.
But where were you?
We're not going to talk about that now.
How could you just leave like that without even saying goodbye?

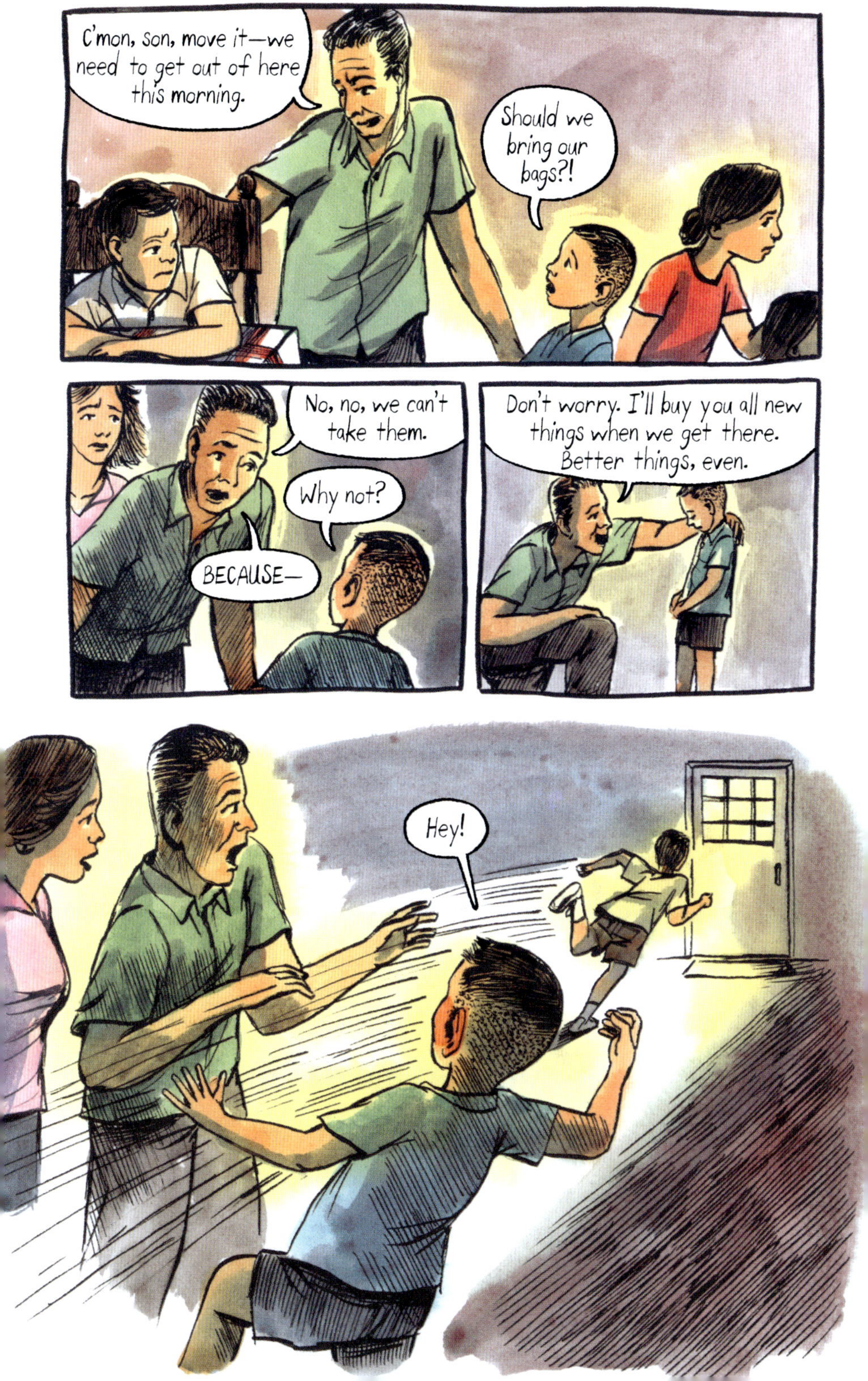
C'mon, son, move it—we need to get out of here this morning.
Should we bring our bags?!
No, no, we can't take them.
Why not?
BECAUSE—
Don't worry. I'll buy you all new things when we get there. Better things, even.
Hey!

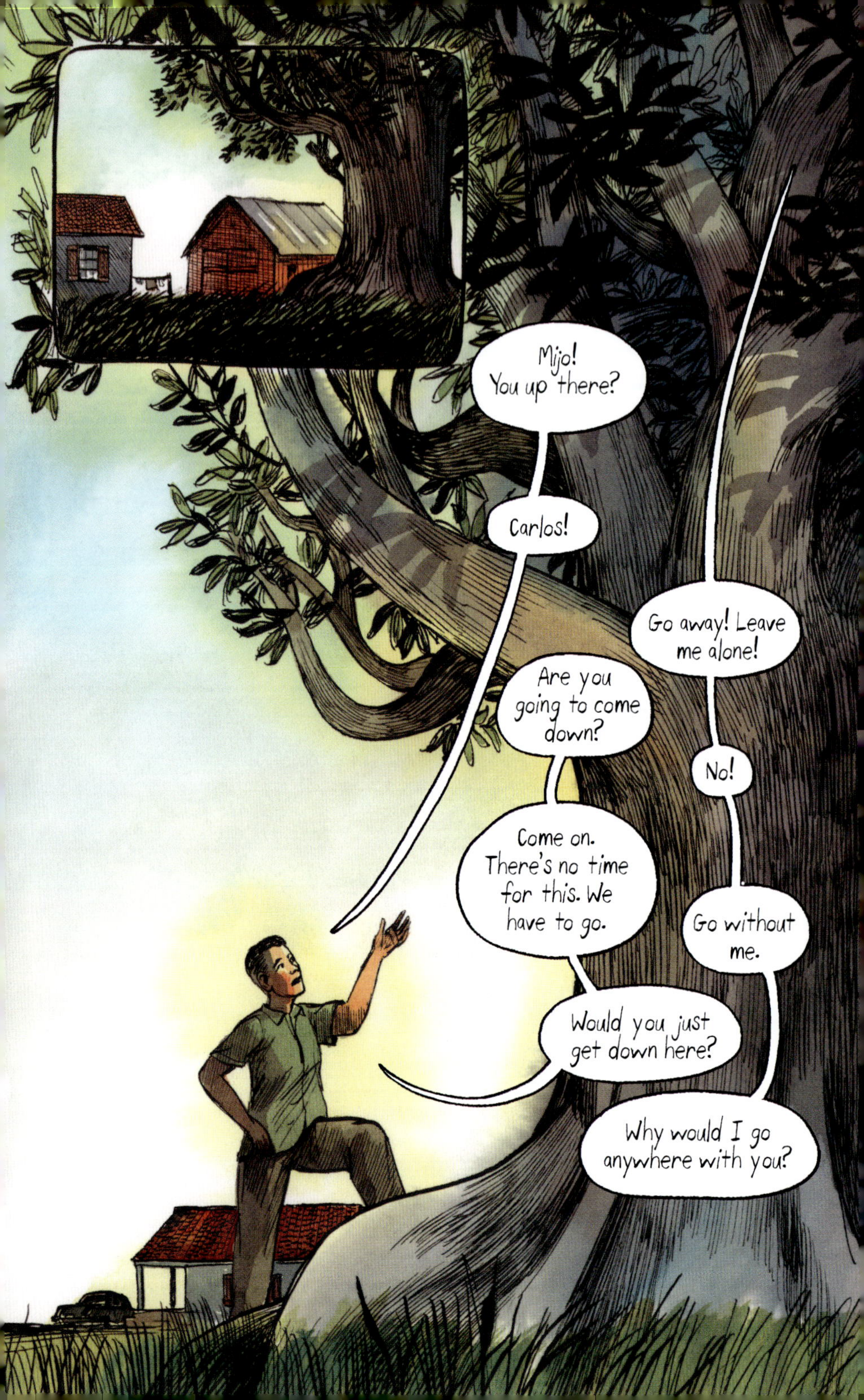
Mijo! You up there?
Carlos!
Go away! Leave me alone!
Are you going to come down?
No!
Come on. There's no time for this. We have to go.
Go without me.
Would you just get down here?
Why would I go anywhere with you?

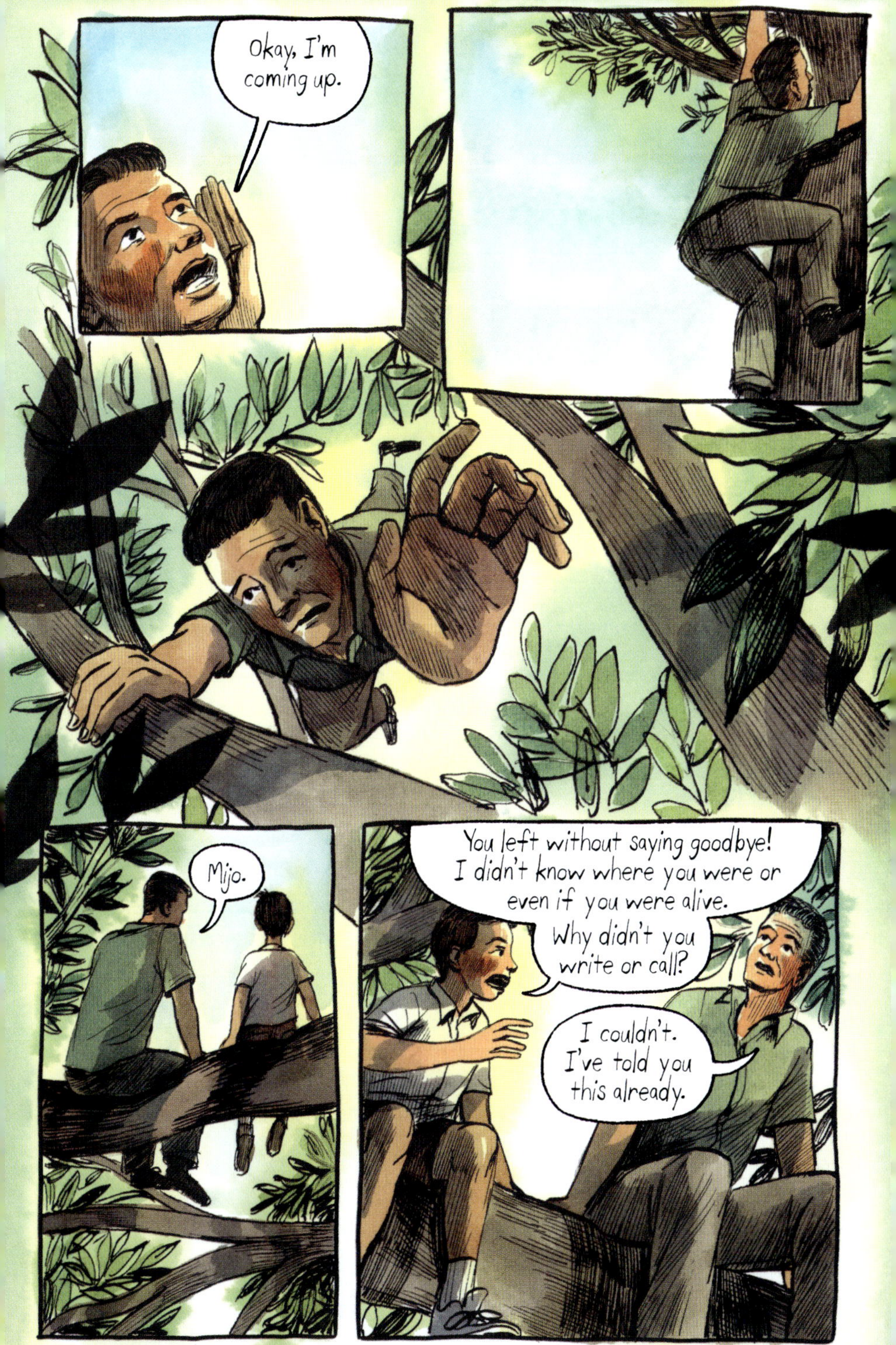

Okay, I'm coming up.
Mijo.
You left without saying goodbye! I didn't know where you were or even if you were alive.
Why didn't you write or call?
I couldn't. I've told you this already.

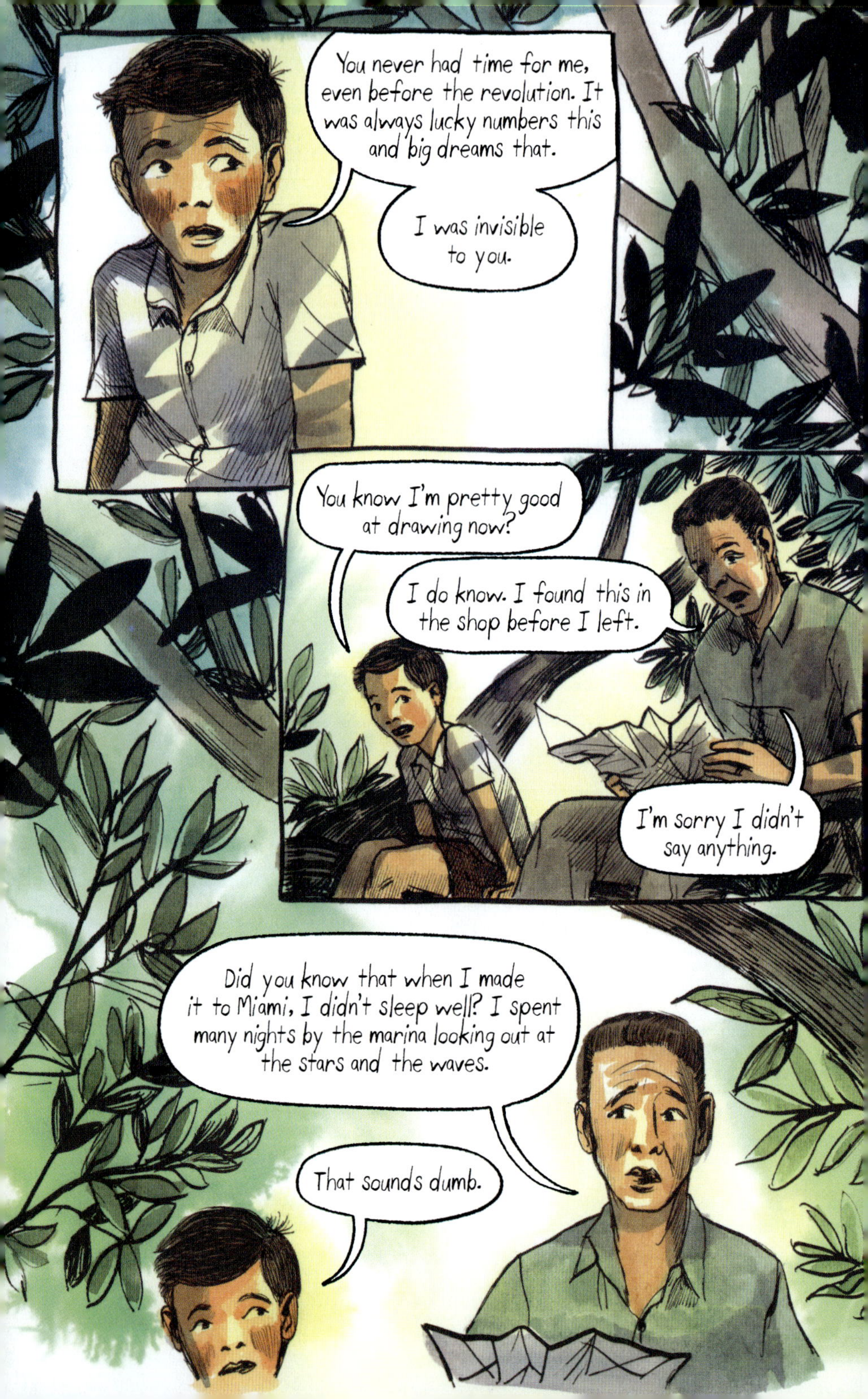
You never had time for me, even before the revolution. It was always lucky numbers this and big dreams that.
I was invisible to you.
You know I'm pretty good at drawing now?
I do know. I found this in the shop before I left.
I'm sorry I didn't say anything.
Did you know that when I made it to Miami, I didn't sleep well? I spent many nights by the marina looking out at the stars and the waves.
That sounds dumb.

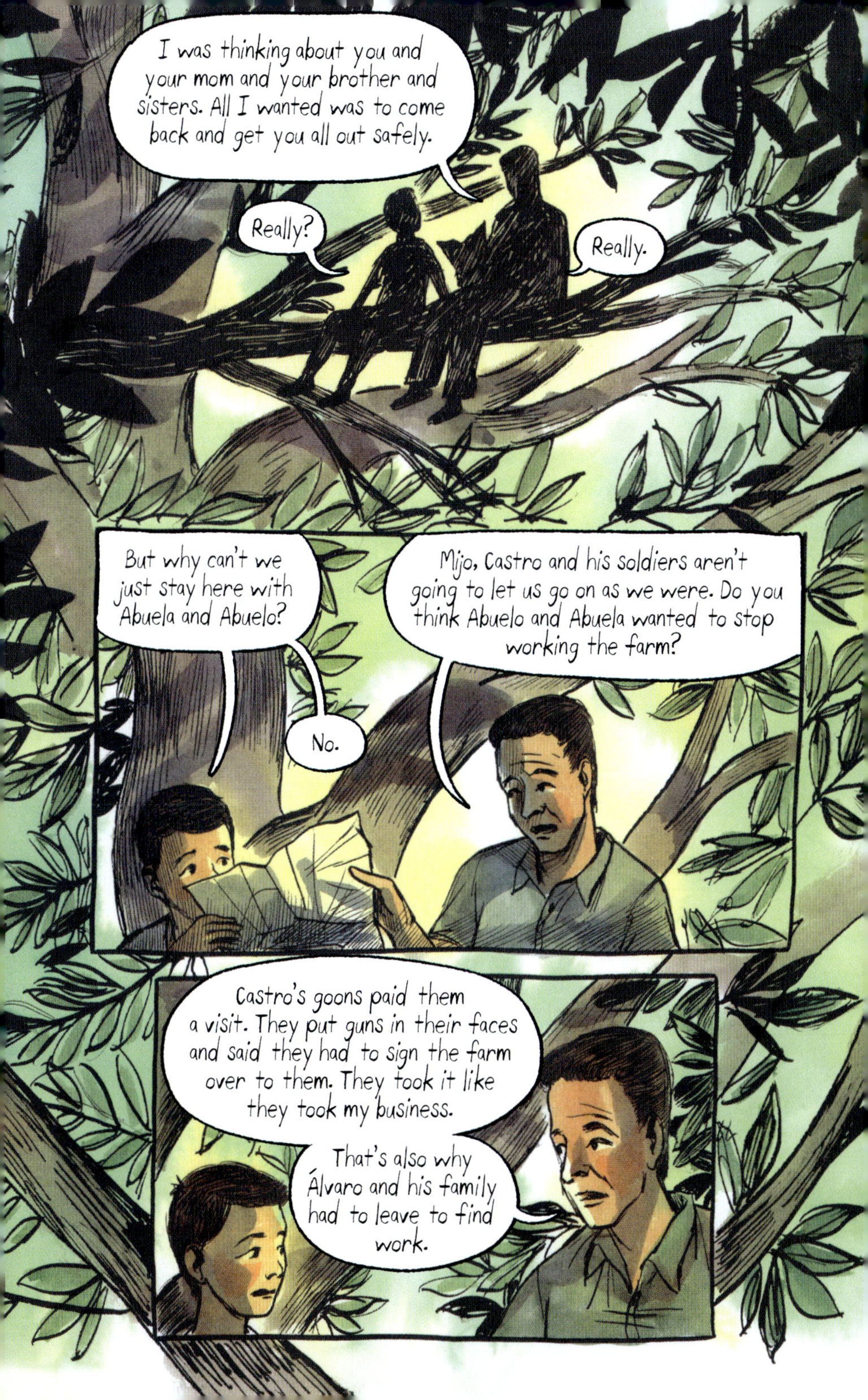
I was thinking about you and your mom and your brother and sisters. All I wanted was to come back and get you all out safely.
Really?
Really.
But why can't we just stay here with Abuela and Abuelo?
Mijo, Castro and his soldiers aren't going to let us go on as we were. Do you think Abuelo and Abuela wanted to stop working the farm?
No.
Castro's goons paid them a visit. They put guns in their faces and said they had to sign the farm over to them. They took it like they took my business.
That's also why Álvaro and his family had to leave to find work.

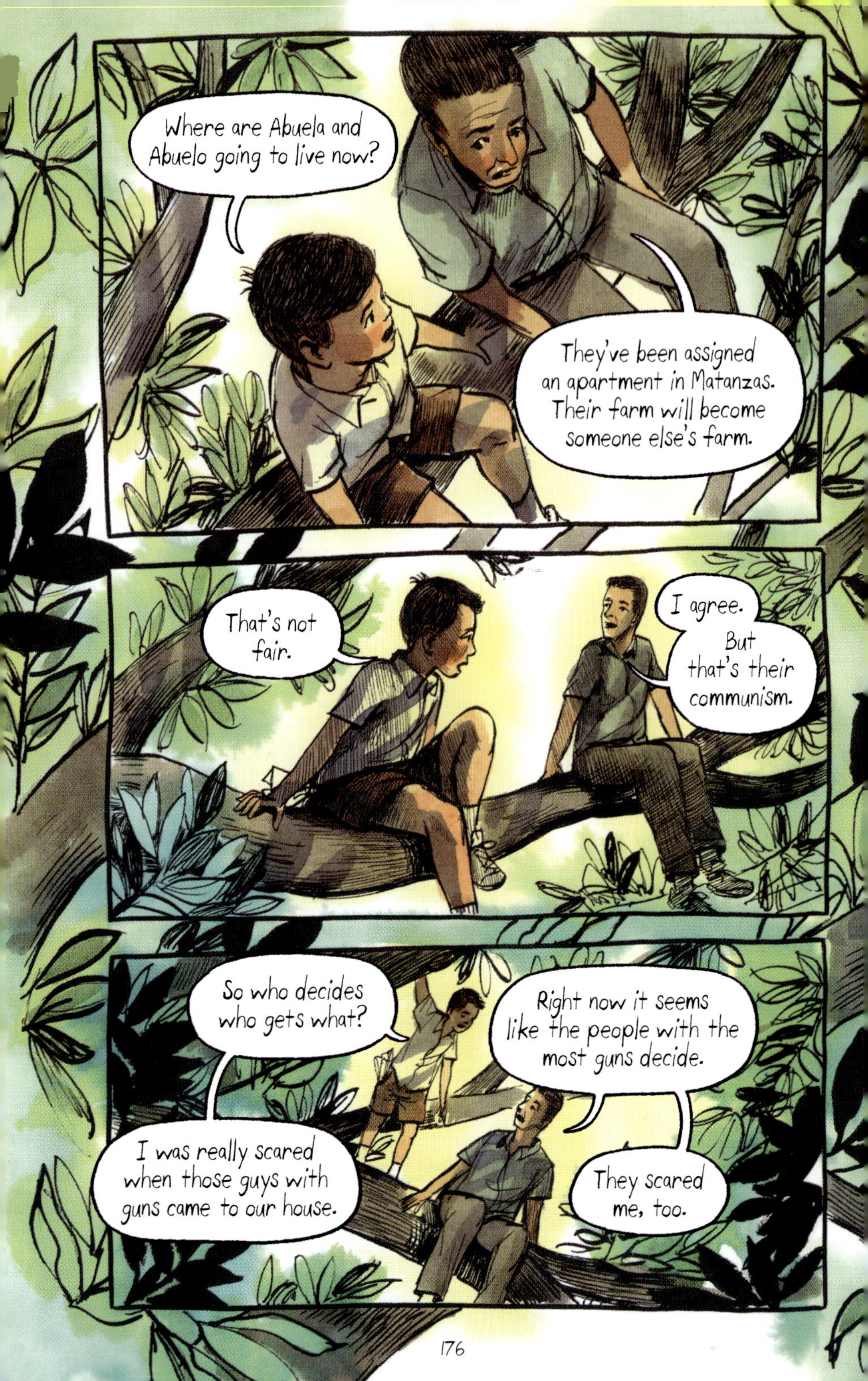
Where are Abuela and Abuelo going to live now?
They've been assigned an apartment in Matanzas. Their farm will become someone else's farm.
That's not fair.
I agree.
But that's their communism.
So who decides who gets what?
Right now it seems like the people with the most guns decide.
I was really scared when those guys with guns came to our house.
They scared me, too.

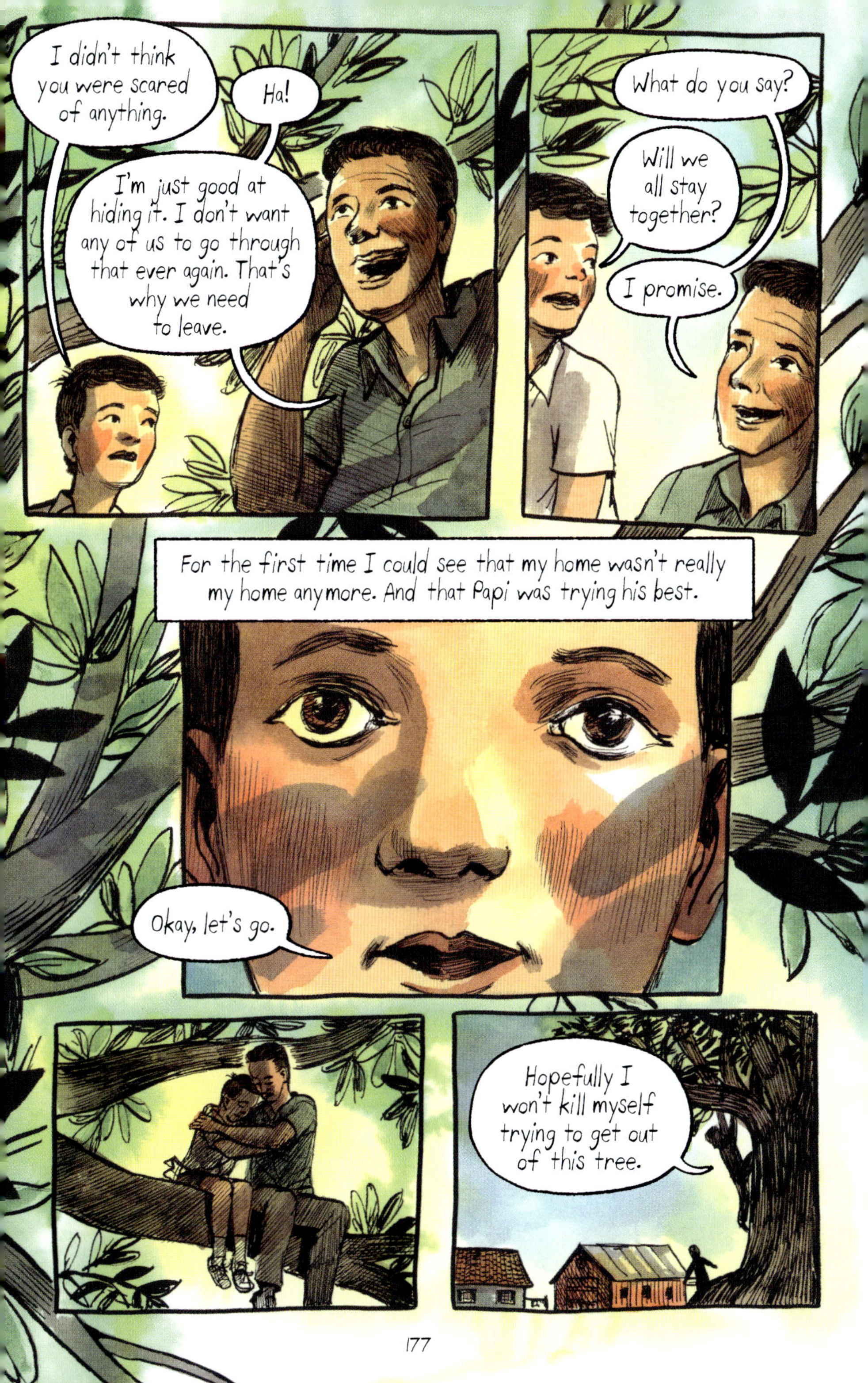
I didn't think you were scared of anything.
Ha!
I'm just good at hiding it. I don't want any of us to go through that ever again. That's why we need to leave.
What do you say?
Will we all stay together?
I promise.
For the first time I could see that my home wasn't really my home anymore. And that Papi was trying his best.
Okay, let's go.
Hopefully I won't kill myself trying to get out of this tree.

And so we left everything we had.

"Why is everyone crying? Abuelo? Abuela?"

"Aren't you coming, too?"

"No, dear, we're staying in Matanzas."

"But I'll be giving you all a ride today."

"Why? Don't you want to come with us?"

"I wish we could, but this is where we belong."

"We've been working this land since before your mamá was born."

"Did you know I bought this farm with my own money?"

"You did?"

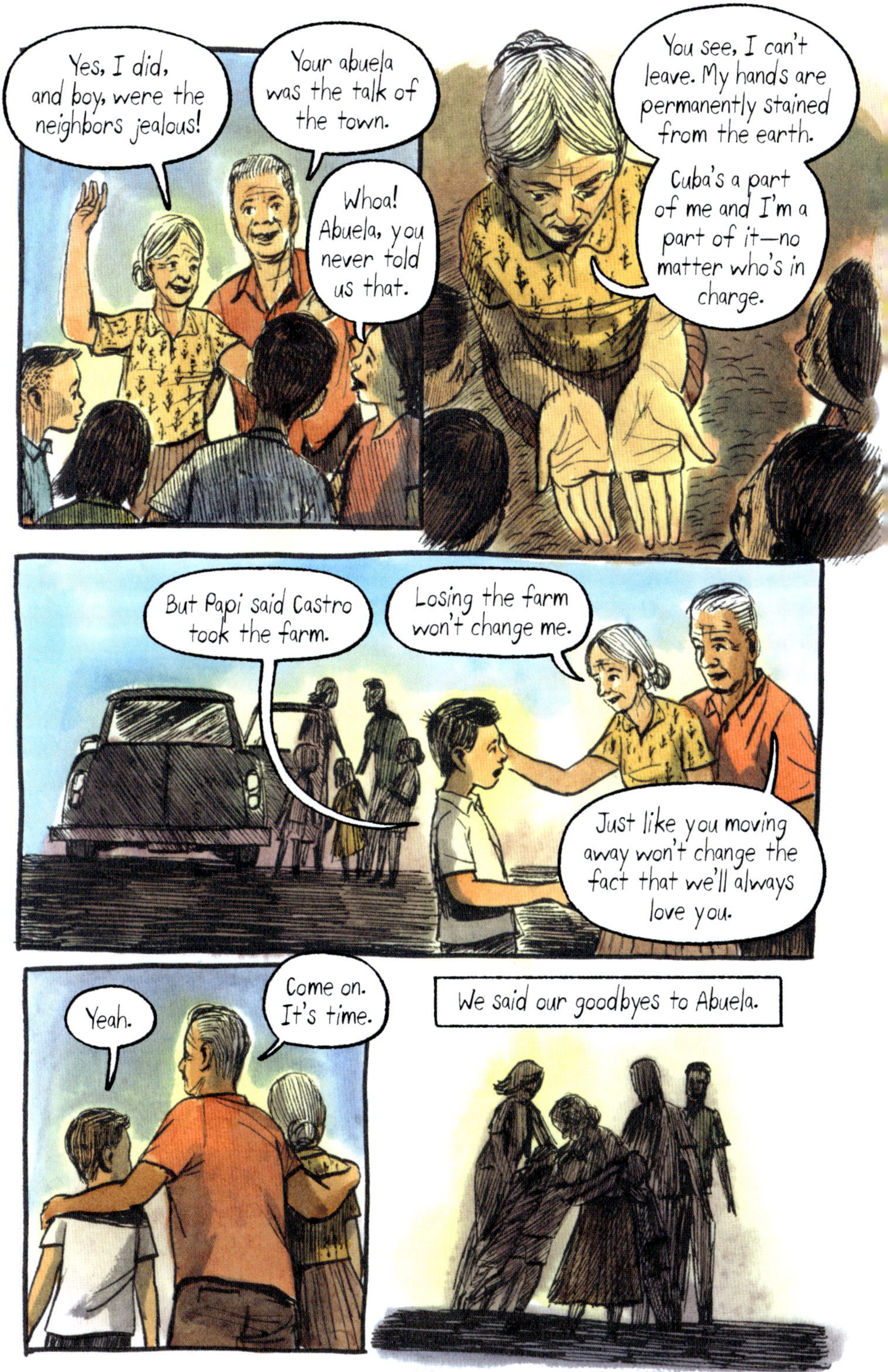
Yes, I did, and boy, were the neighbors jealous!
Your abuela was the talk of the town.
Whoa! Abuela, you never told us that.
You see, I can't leave. My hands are permanently stained from the earth.
Cuba's a part of me and I'm a part of it—no matter who's in charge.
But Papi said Castro took the farm.
Losing the farm won't change me.
Just like you moving away won't change the fact that we'll always love you.
Yeah.
Come on. It's time.
We said our goodbyes to Abuela.

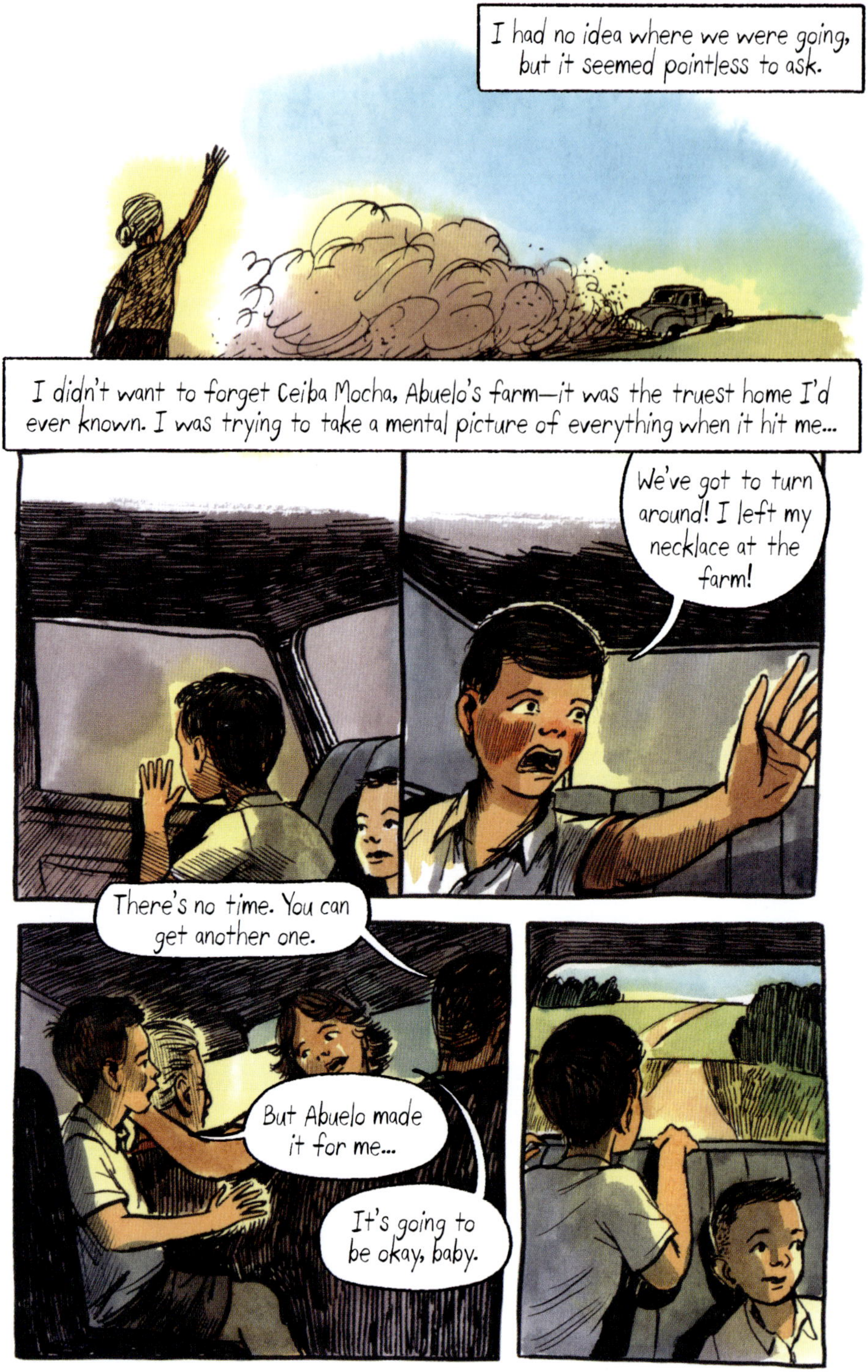
I had no idea where we were going, but it seemed pointless to ask.
I didn't want to forget Ceiba Mocha, Abuelo's farm—it was the truest home I'd ever known. I was trying to take a mental picture of everything when it hit me...
We've got to turn around! I left my necklace at the farm!
There's no time. You can get another one.
But Abuelo made it for me...
It's going to be okay, baby.

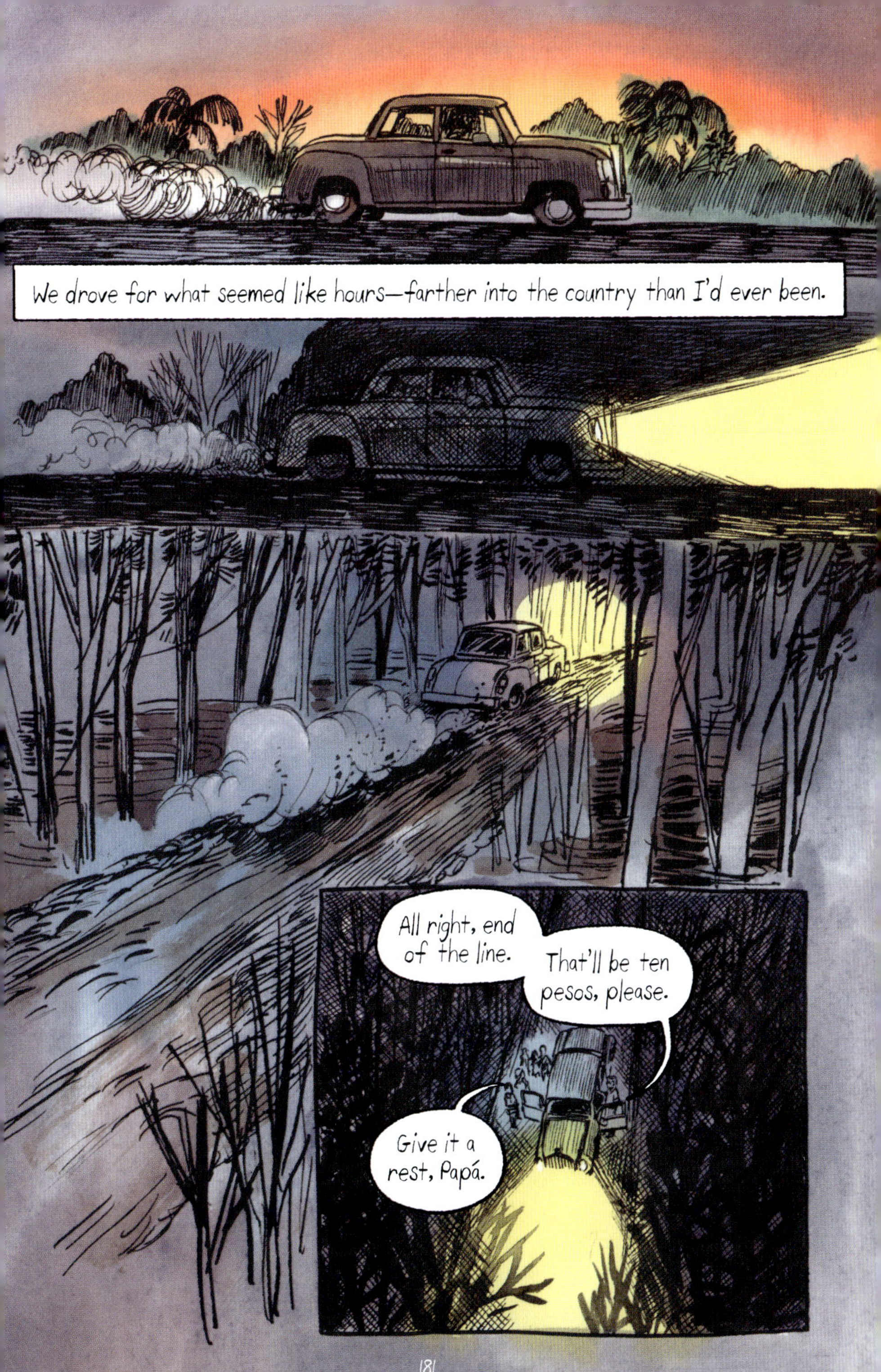
We drove for what seemed like hours—farther into the country than I'd ever been.
All right, end of the line.
That'll be ten pesos, please.
Give it a rest, Papá.

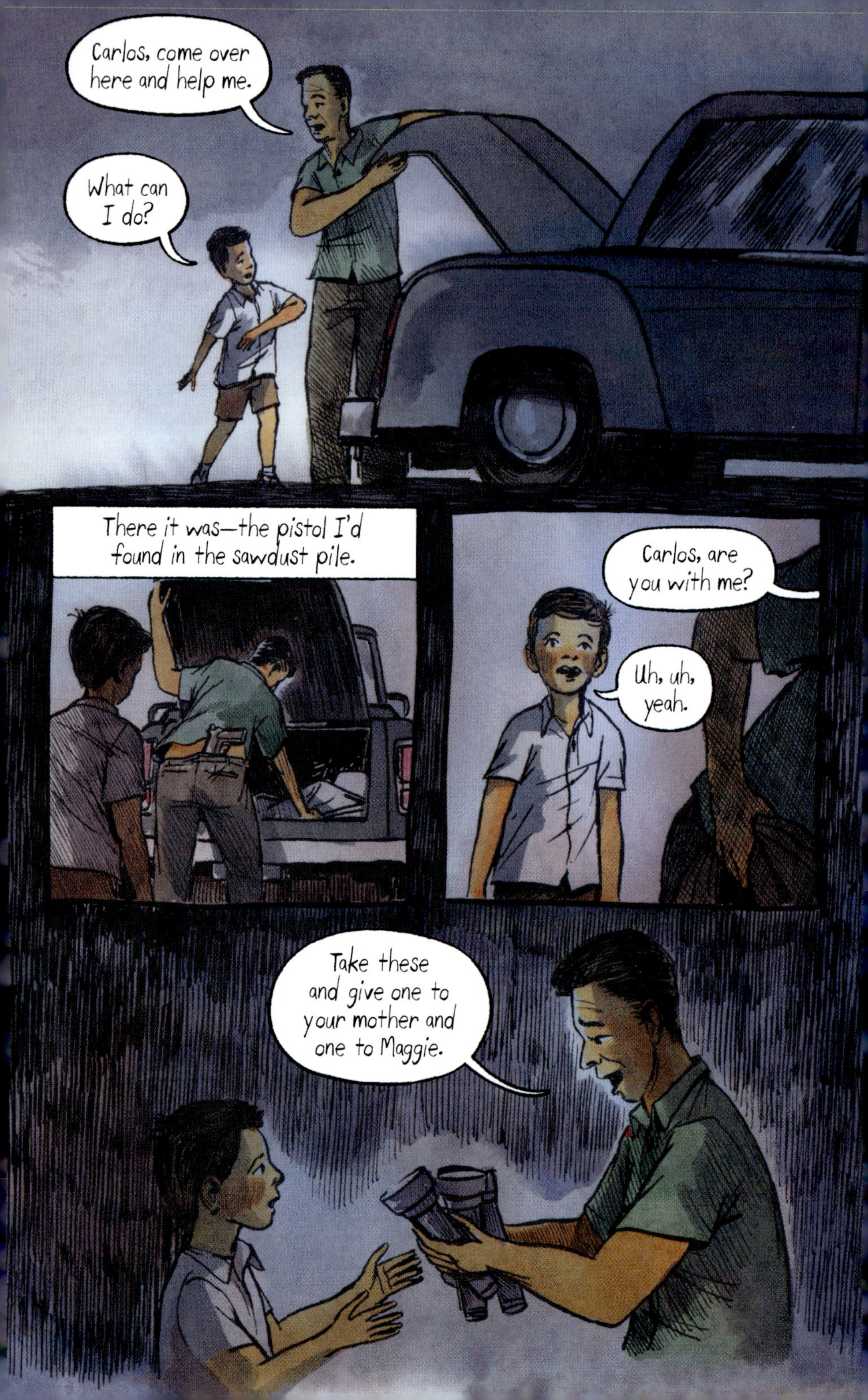
Carlos, come over here and help me.
What can I do?
There it was—the pistol I'd found in the sawdust pile.
Carlos, are you with me?
Uh, uh, yeah.
Take these and give one to your mother and one to Maggie.

"Come here, family. Give me a hug."

"I don't want to go, Abuelo."

"I know, chico."

"I'm scared."

"That's okay."

"Being scared doesn't mean you can't do the hard things.

Just remember where you come from and be strong for your family."

"Can you do that?"

"Yes?"

"Yes."

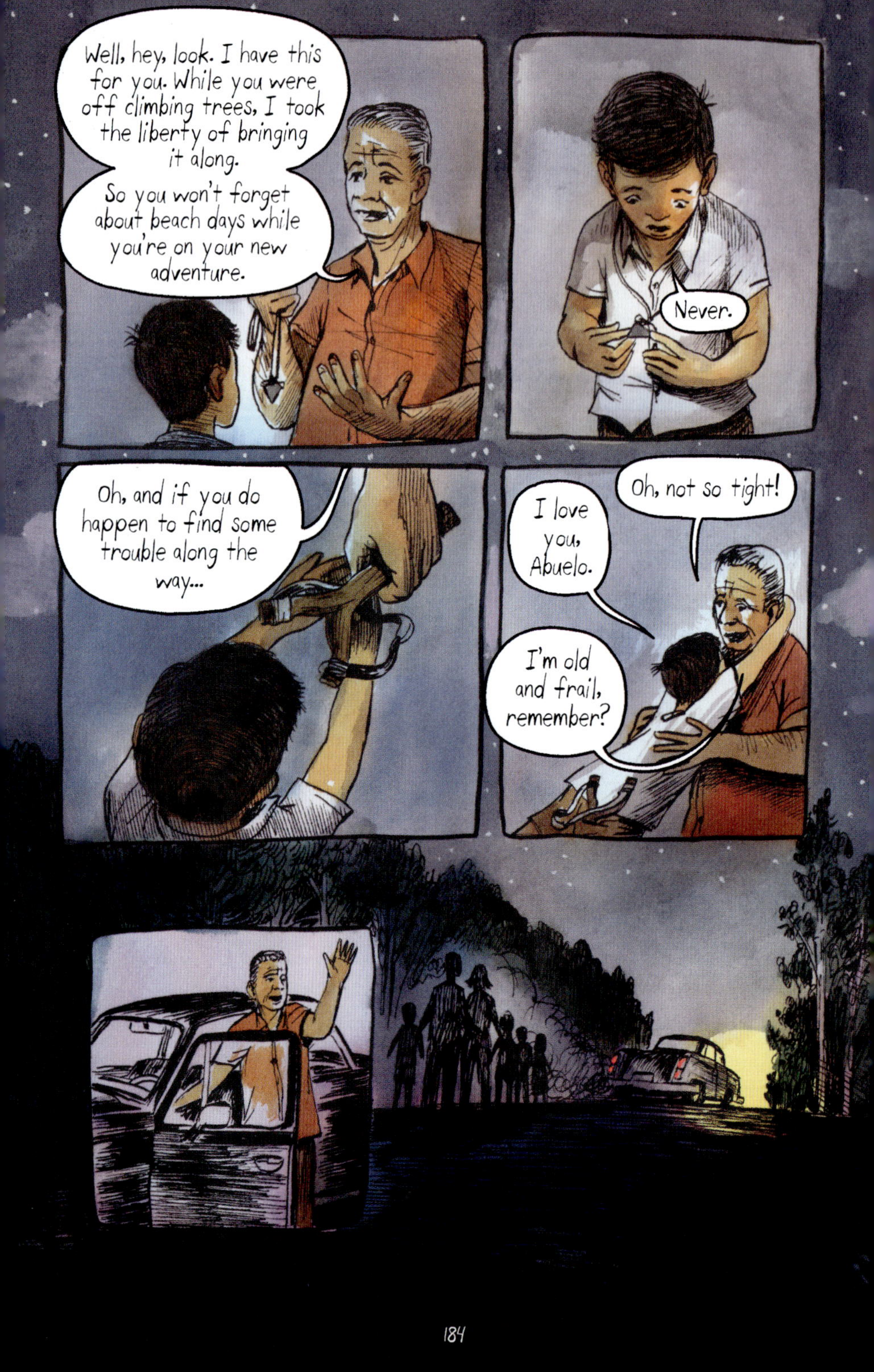
Well, hey, look. I have this for you. While you were off climbing trees, I took the liberty of bringing it along.
So you won't forget about beach days while you're on your new adventure.
Never.
Oh, and if you do happen to find some trouble along the way...
I love you, Abuelo.
Oh, not so tight!
I'm old and frail, remember?

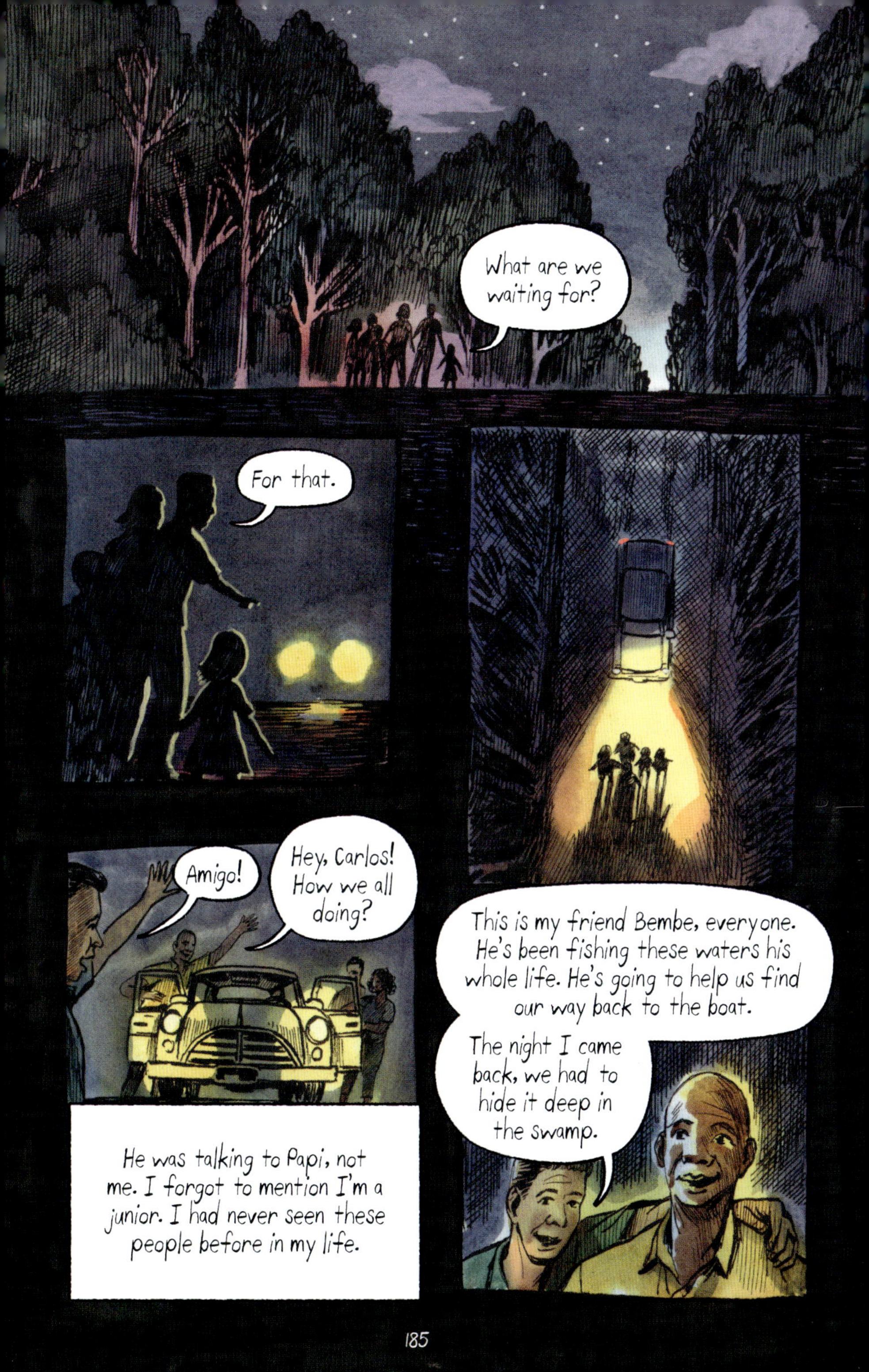
What are we waiting for?
For that.
Amigo!
Hey, Carlos! How we all doing?
He was talking to Papi, not me. I forgot to mention I'm a junior. I had never seen these people before in my life.
This is my friend Bembe, everyone. He's been fishing these waters his whole life. He's going to help us find our way back to the boat.
The night I came back, we had to hide it deep in the swamp.

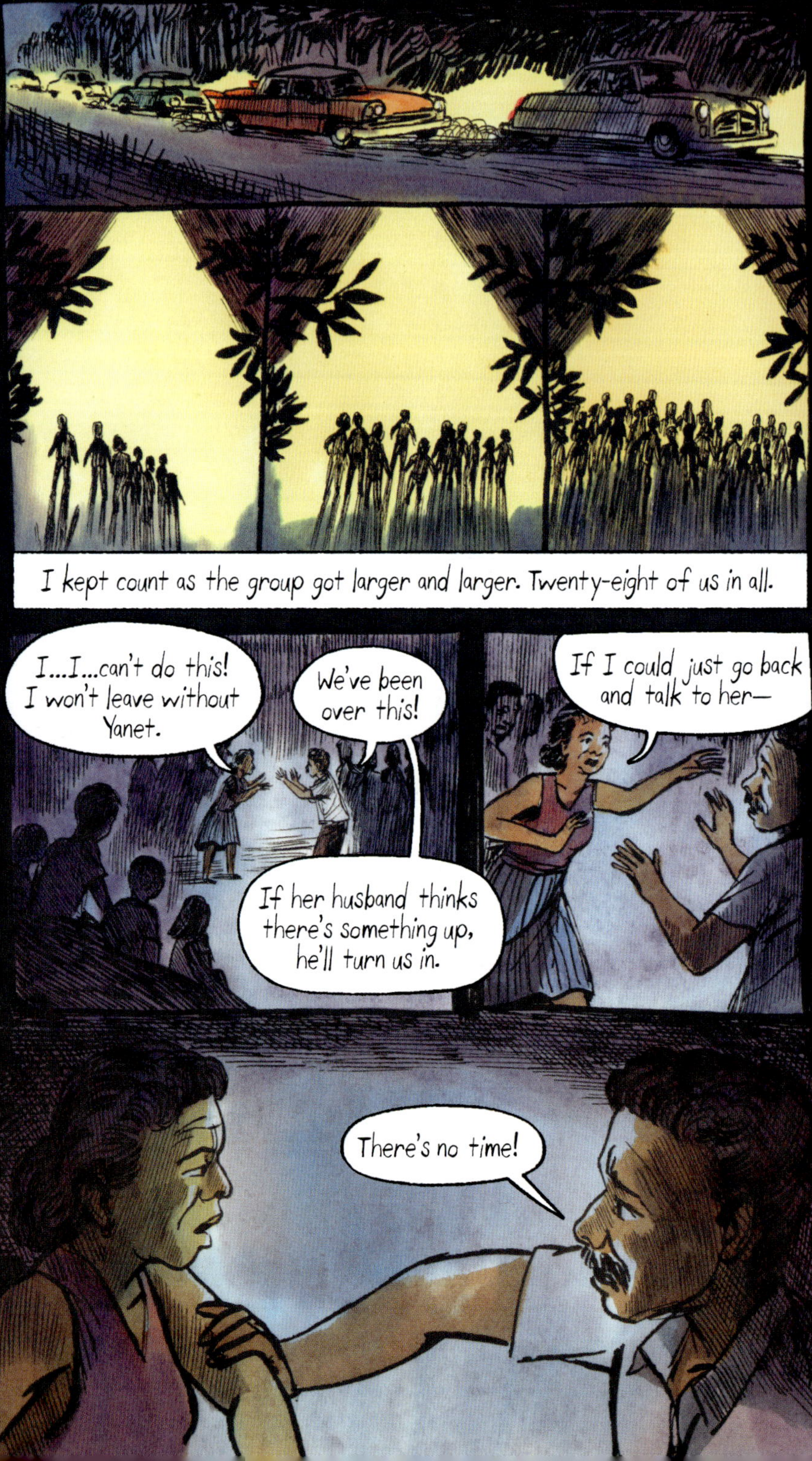
I kept count as the group got larger and larger. Twenty-eight of us in all.
I...I...can't do this! I won't leave without Yanet.
We've been over this!
If her husband thinks there's something up, he'll turn us in.
If I could just go back and talk to her—
There's no time!

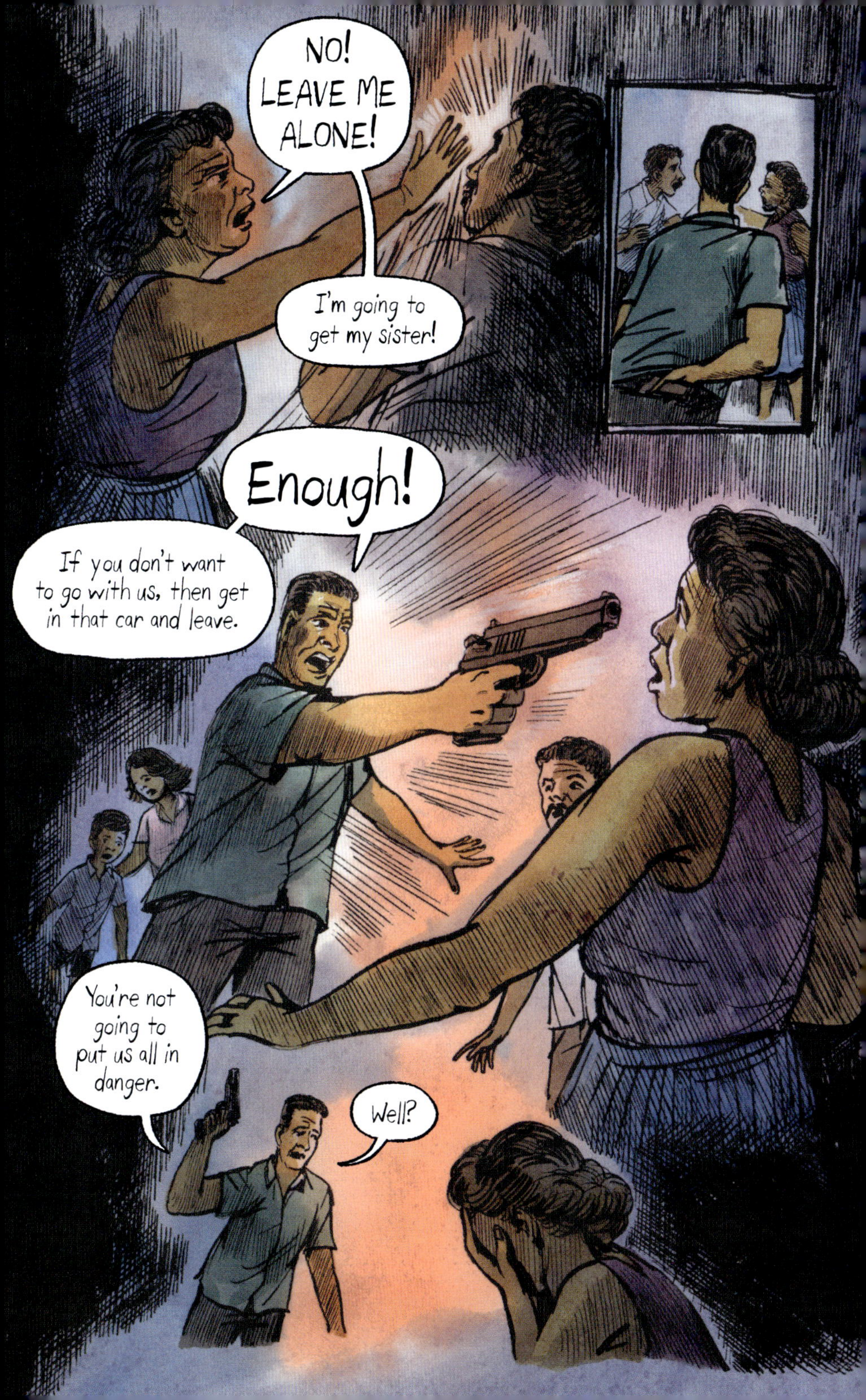
NO! LEAVE ME ALONE!
I'm going to get my sister!
Enough!
If you don't want to go with us, then get in that car and leave.
You're not going to put us all in danger.
Well?

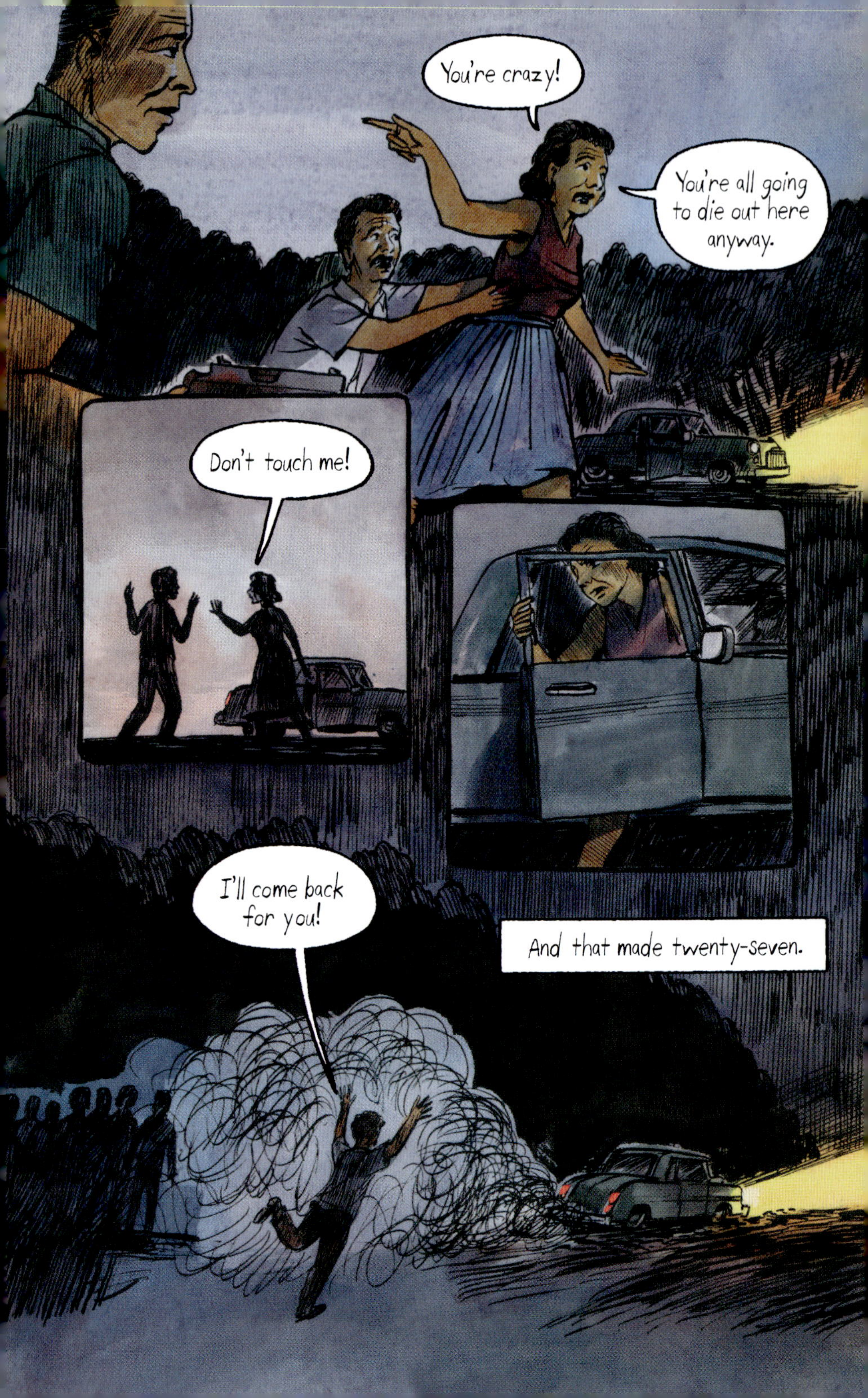
You're crazy!
You're all going to die out here anyway.
Don't touch me!
I'll come back for you!
And that made twenty-seven.

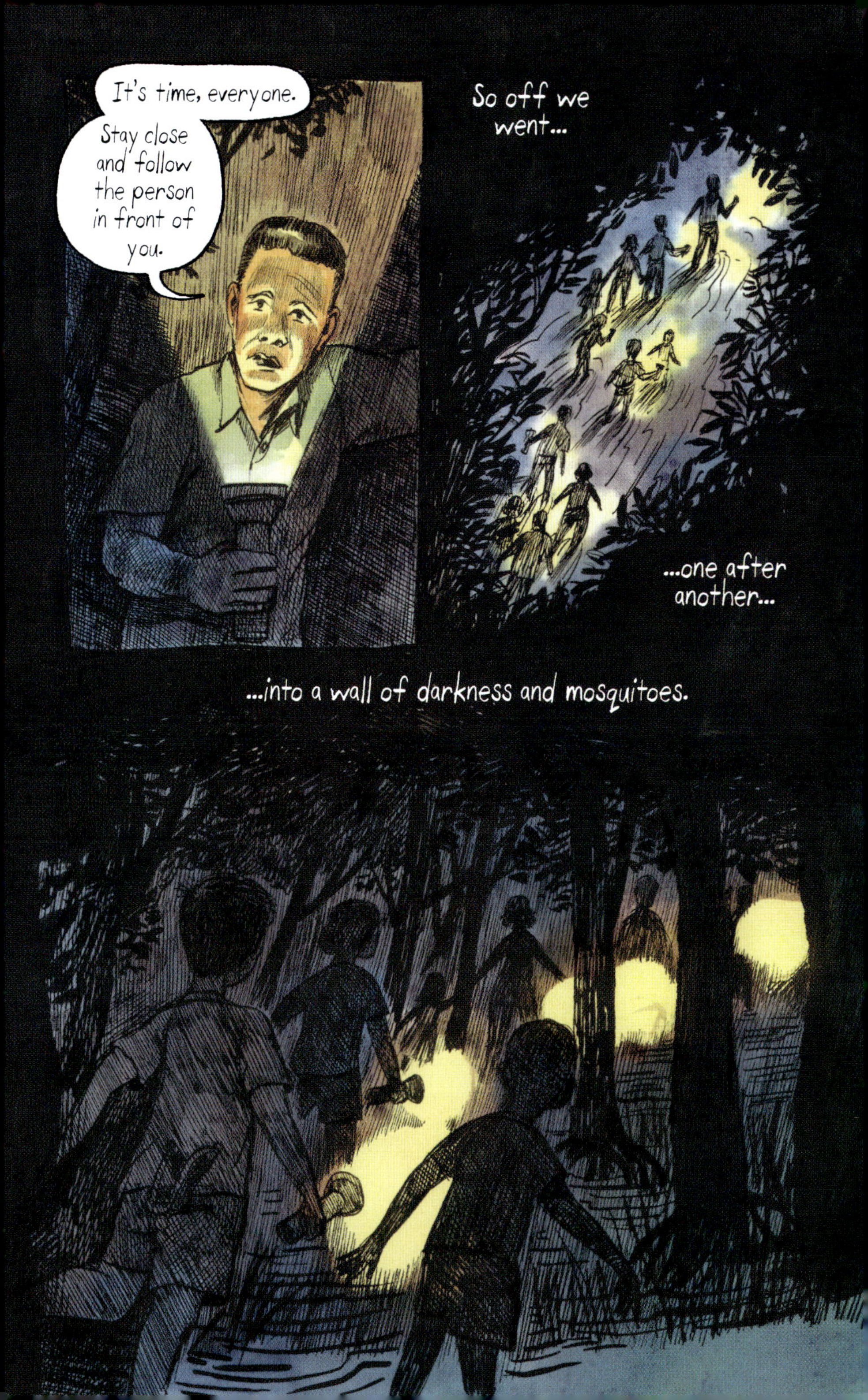
It's time, everyone.
Stay close and follow the person in front of you.
So off we went...
...one after another...
...into a wall of darkness and mosquitoes.

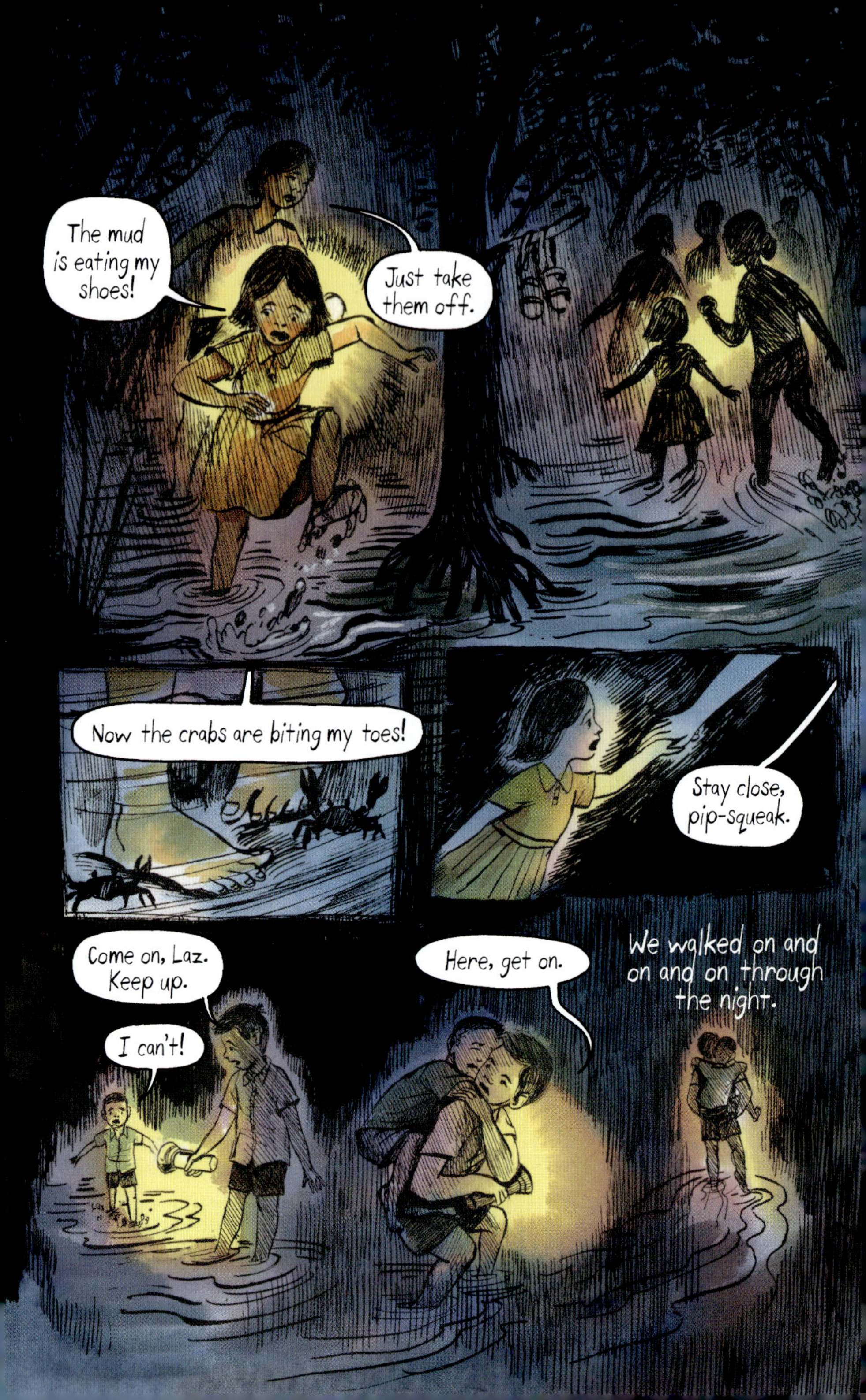
The mud is eating my shoes!
Just take them off.
Now the crabs are biting my toes!
Stay close, pip-squeak.
Come on, Laz. Keep up.
I can't!
Here, get on.
We walked on and on and on through the night.

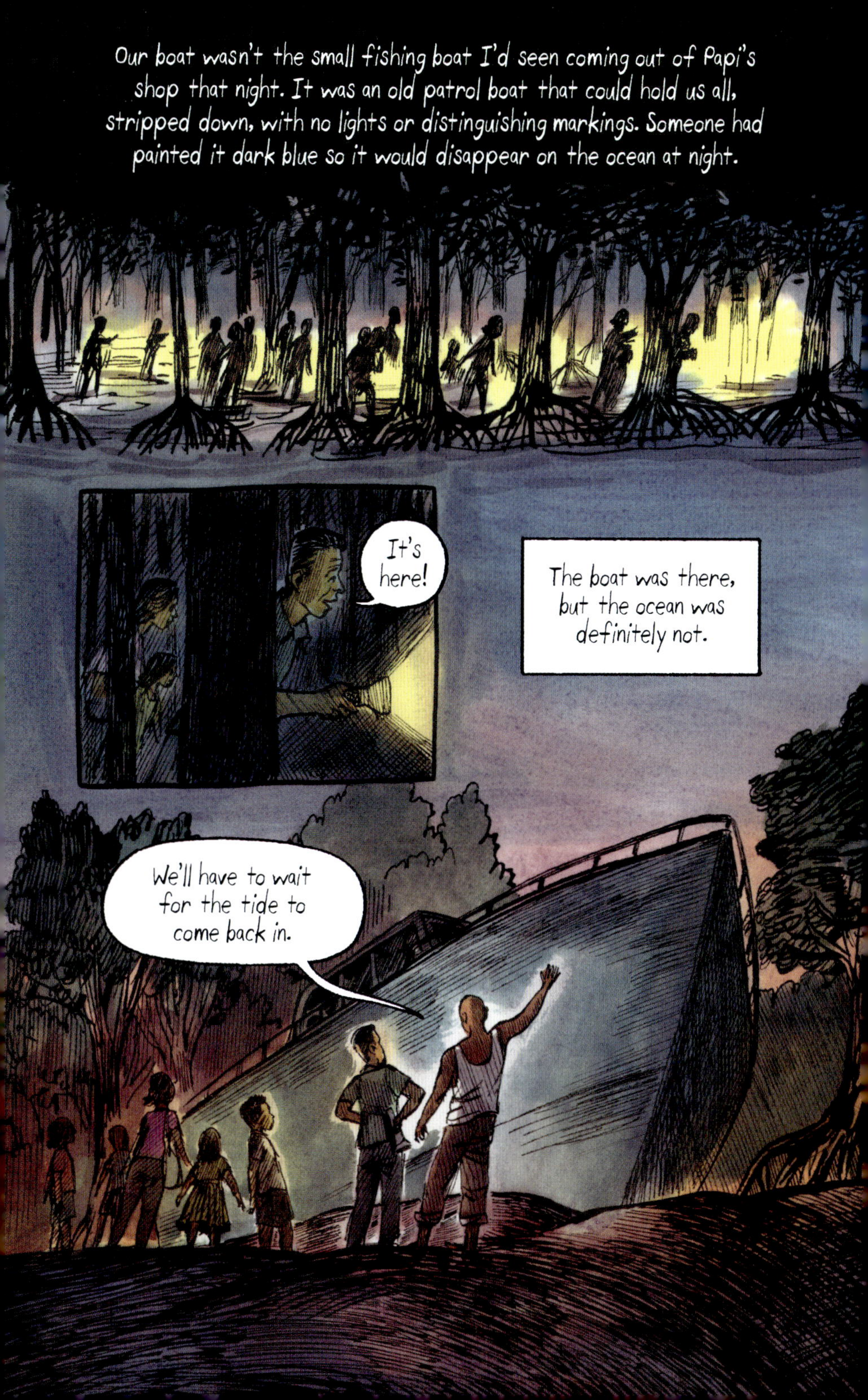
Our boat wasn't the small fishing boat I'd seen coming out of Papi's shop that night. It was an old patrol boat that could hold us all, stripped down, with no lights or distinguishing markings. Someone had painted it dark blue so it would disappear on the ocean at night.
It's here!
The boat was there, but the ocean was definitely not.
We'll have to wait for the tide to come back in.

Those who try to flee by boat may be shot at or arrested by the Cuban coast guard. They face long jail sentences and forced labor. Their family members are also punished harshly.

The Missing Ocean

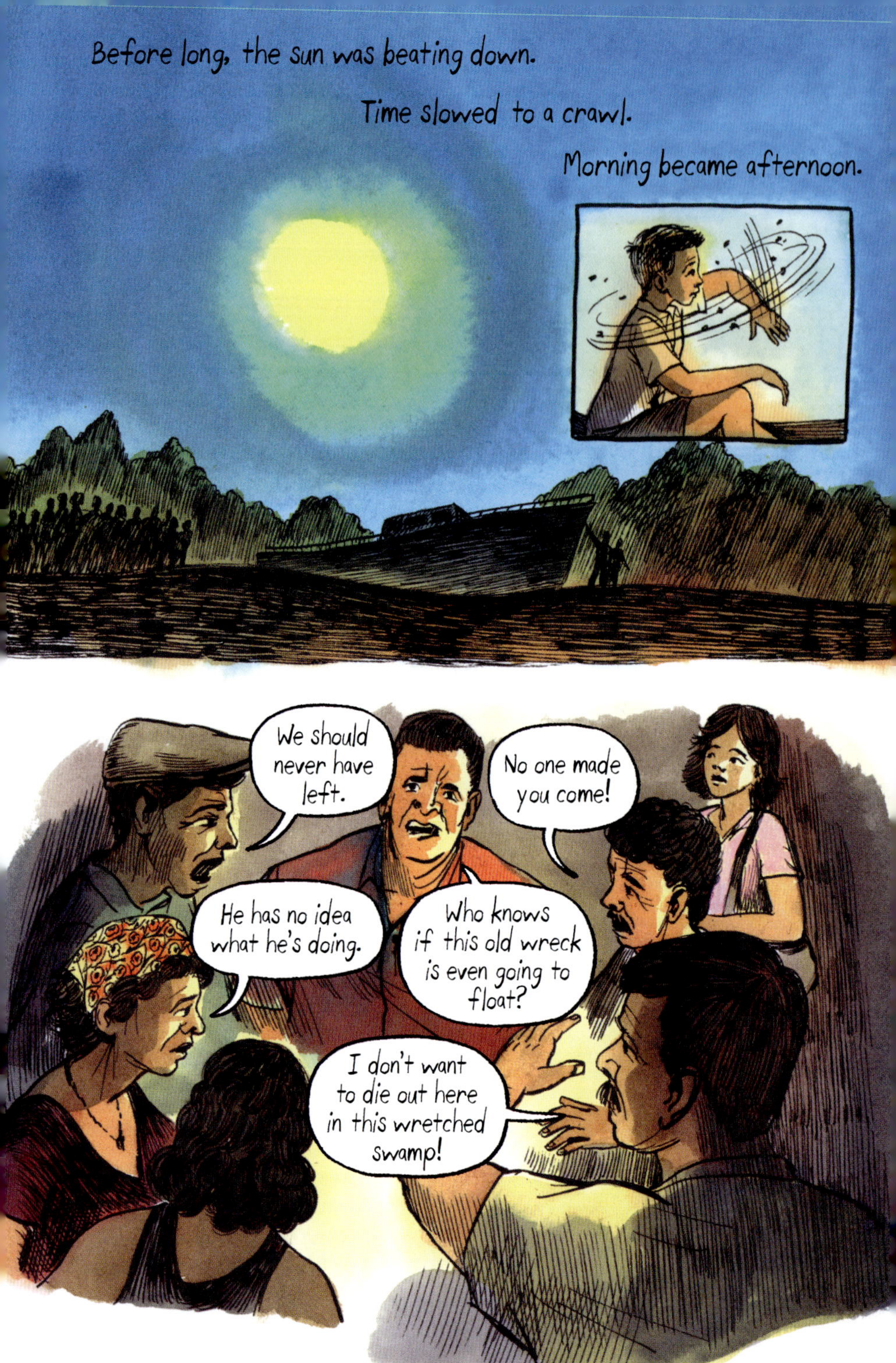
Before long, the sun was beating down.
Time slowed to a crawl.
Morning became afternoon.
We should never have left.
No one made you come!
He has no idea what he's doing.
Who knows if this old wreck is even going to float?
I don't want to die out here in this wretched swamp!

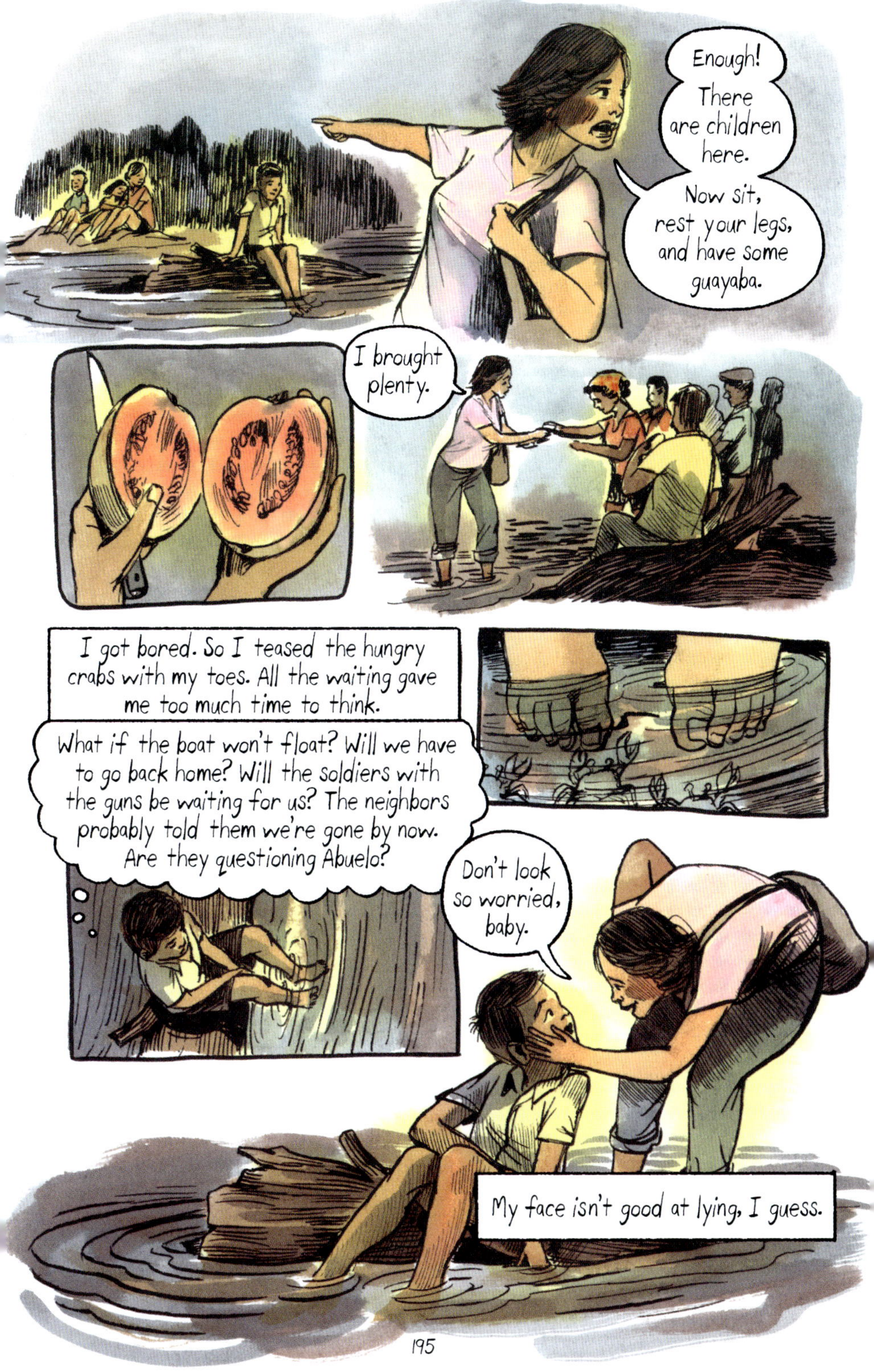
Enough!
There are children here.
Now sit, rest your legs, and have some guayaba.
I brought plenty.
I got bored. So I teased the hungry crabs with my toes. All the waiting gave me too much time to think.
What if the boat won't float? Will we have to go back home? Will the soldiers with the guns be waiting for us? The neighbors probably told them we're gone by now. Are they questioning Abuelo?
Don't look so worried, baby.
My face isn't good at lying, I guess.

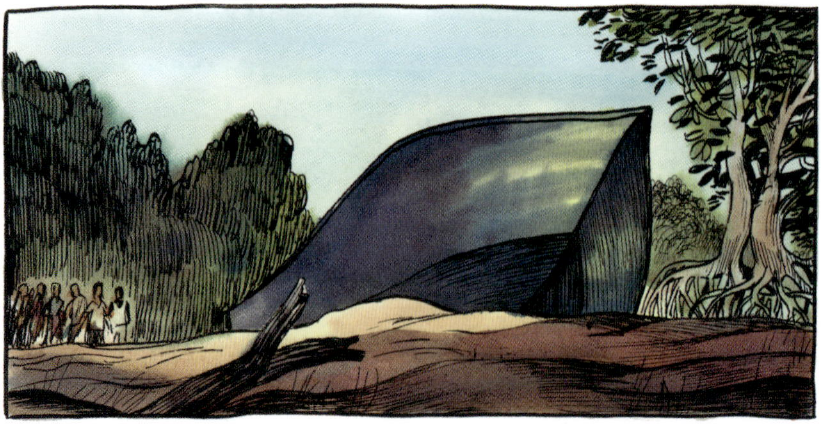

The afternoon dragged on into the evening.

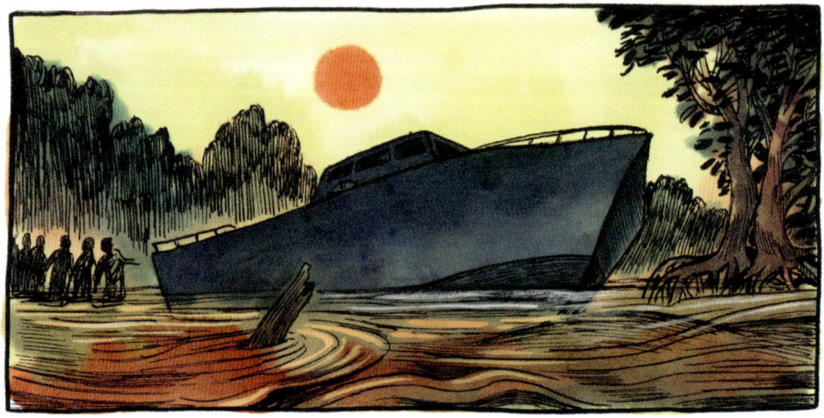

The sun was getting orangey and low in the sky...

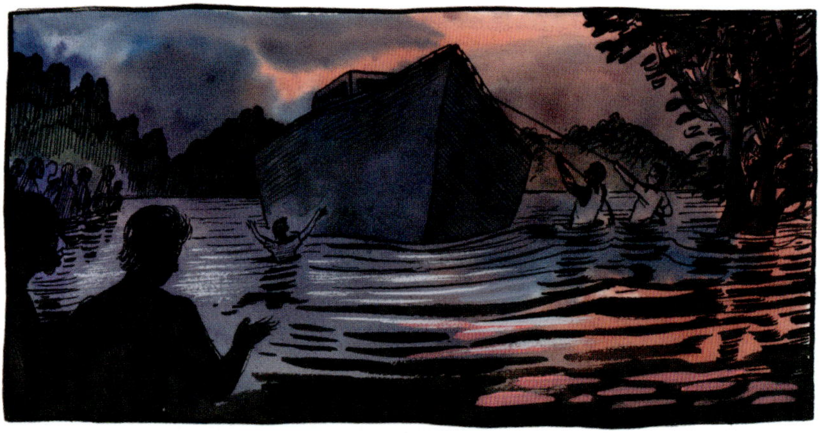

And the water level rose.

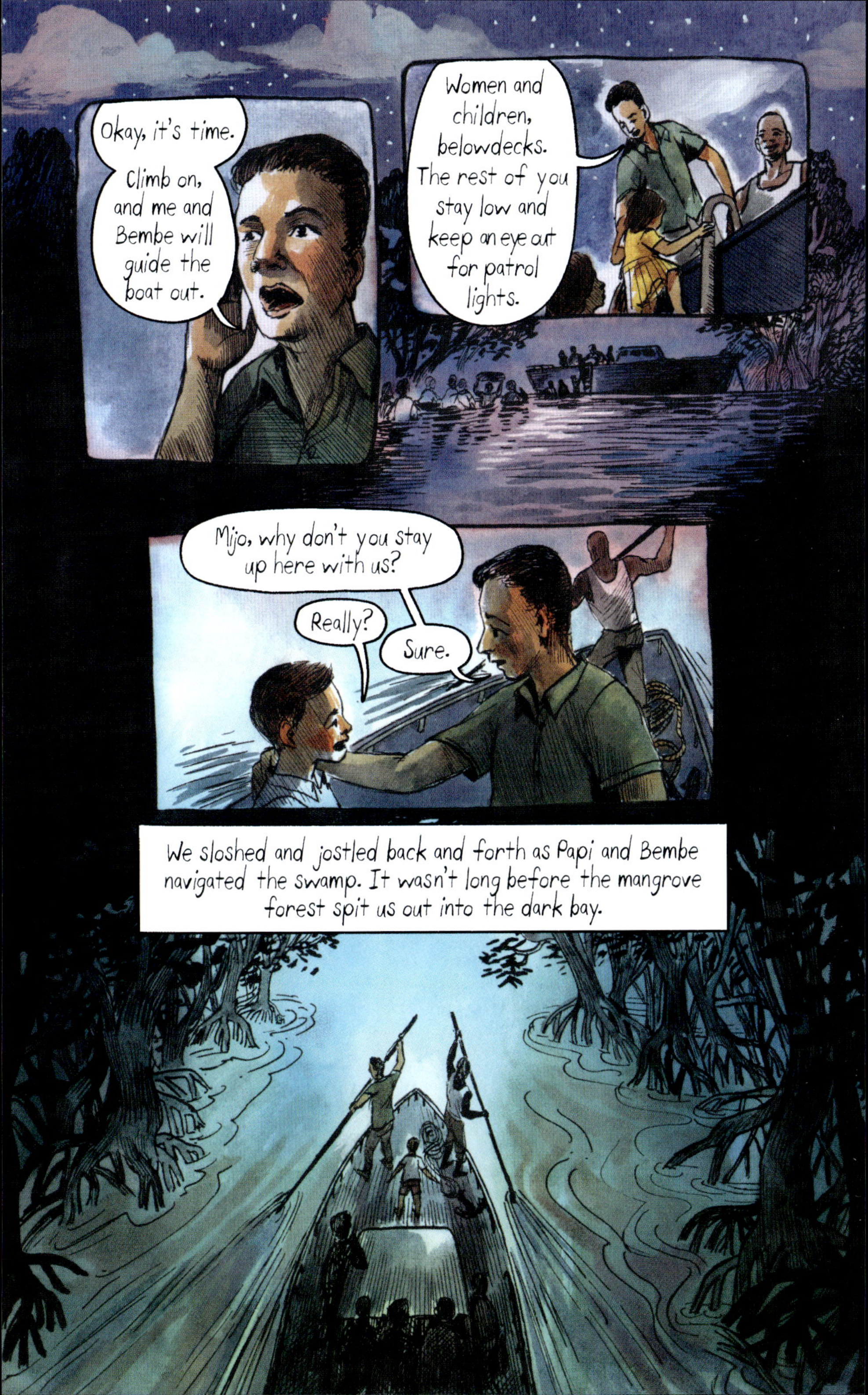
Okay, it's time.
Climb on, and me and Bembe will guide the boat out.
Women and children, belowdecks. The rest of you stay low and keep an eye out for patrol lights.
Mijo, why don't you stay up here with us?
Really?
Sure.
We sloshed and jostled back and forth as Papi and Bembe navigated the swamp. It wasn't long before the mangrove forest spit us out into the dark bay.

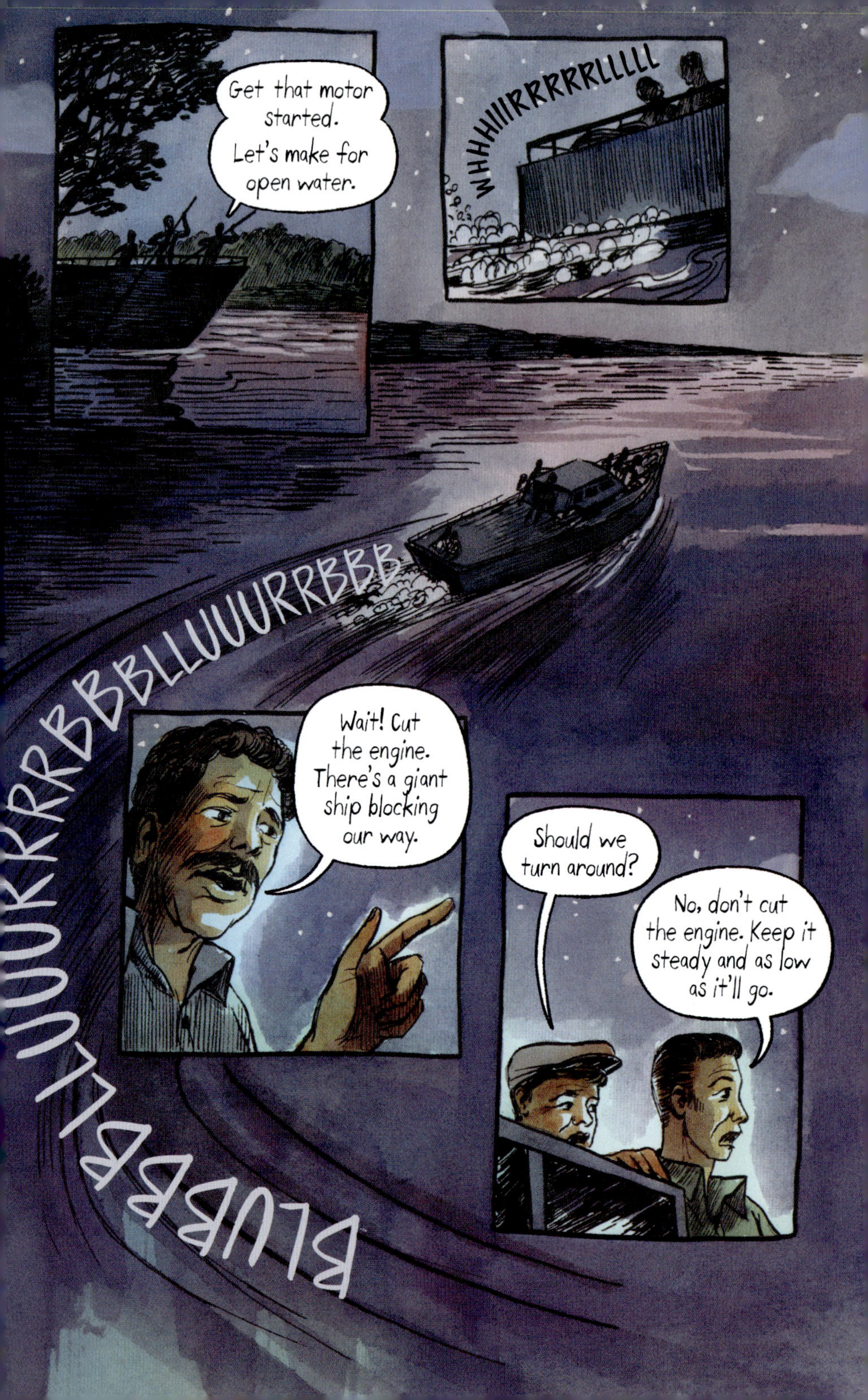
Get that motor started. Let's make for open water.
WHHHIIIRRRRRLLLLL
BLUBBLUUUURRRBBBLLUUUURRBBB
Wait! Cut the engine. There's a giant ship blocking our way.
Should we turn around?
No, don't cut the engine. Keep it steady and as low as it'll go.

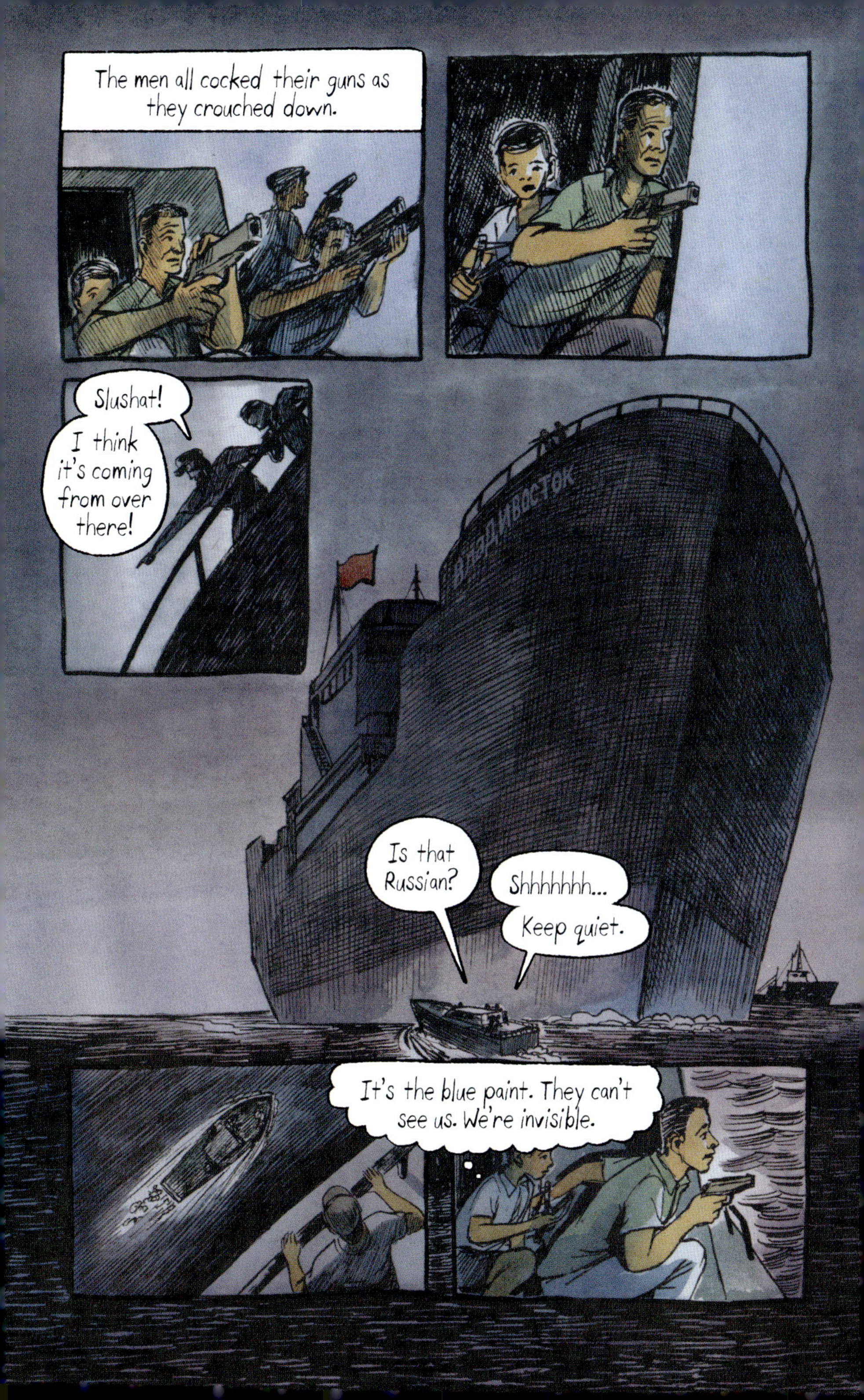
The men all cocked their guns as they crouched down.
Slushat!
I think it's coming from over there!
Is that Russian?
Shhhhhhh... Keep quiet.
It's the blue paint. They can't see us. We're invisible.

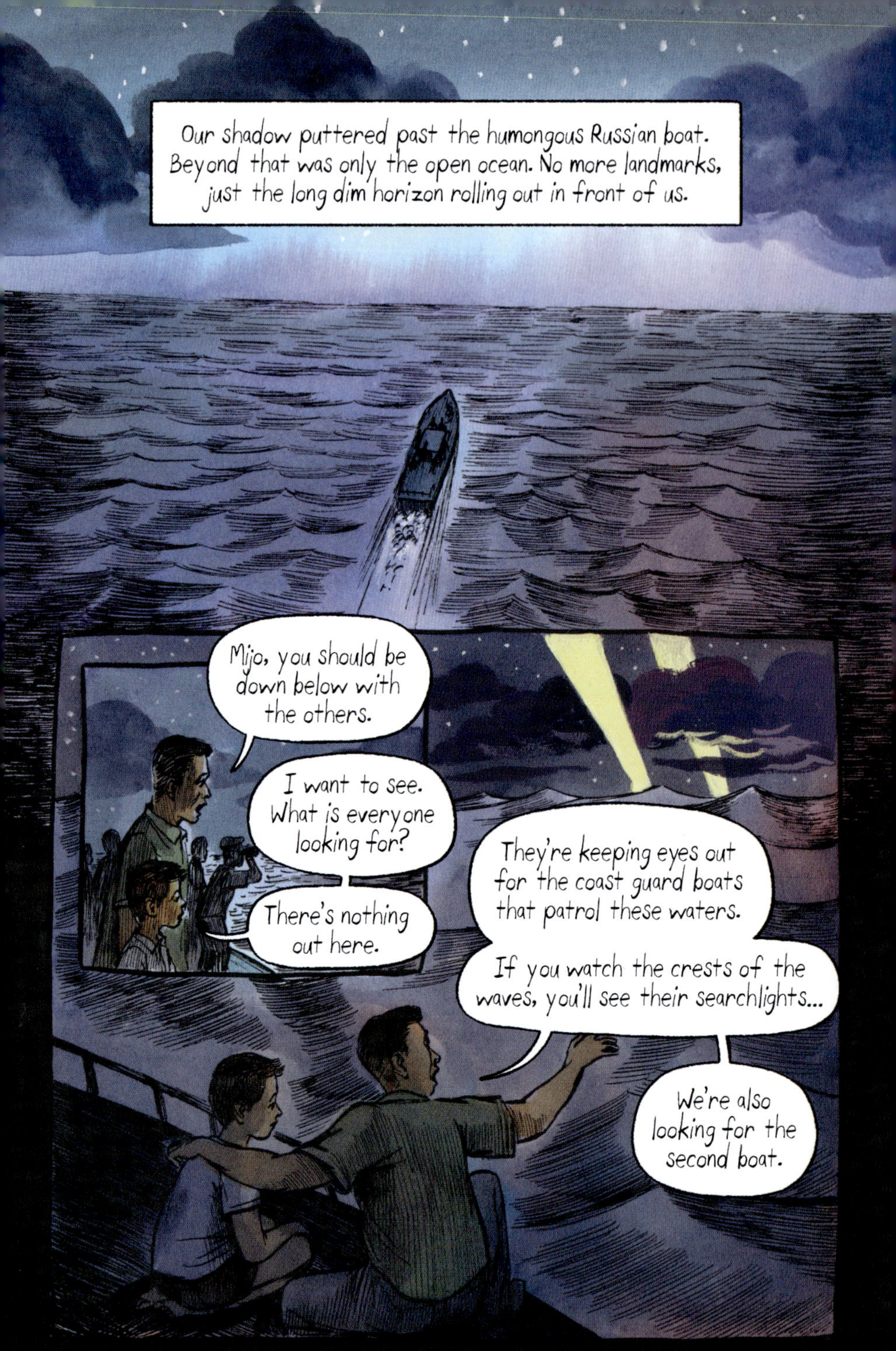
Our shadow puttered past the humongous Russian boat. Beyond that was only the open ocean. No more landmarks, just the long dim horizon rolling out in front of us.
Mijo, you should be down below with the others.
I want to see. What is everyone looking for?
There's nothing out here.
They're keeping eyes out for the coast guard boats that patrol these waters.
If you watch the crests of the waves, you'll see their searchlights...
We're also looking for the second boat.

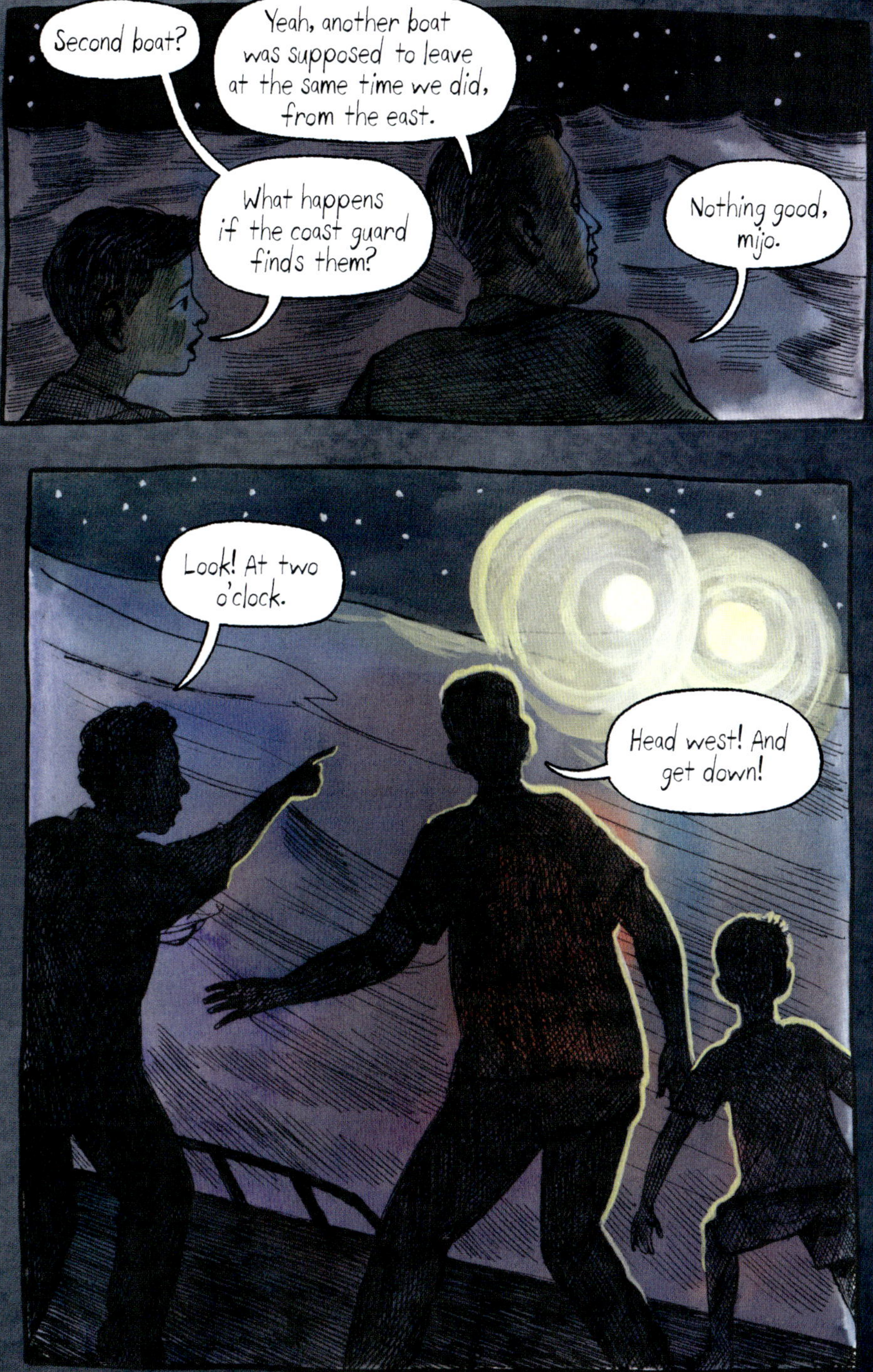
Second boat?
Yeah, another boat was supposed to leave at the same time we did, from the east.
What happens if the coast guard finds them?
Nothing good, mijo.
Look! At two o'clock.
Head west! And get down!

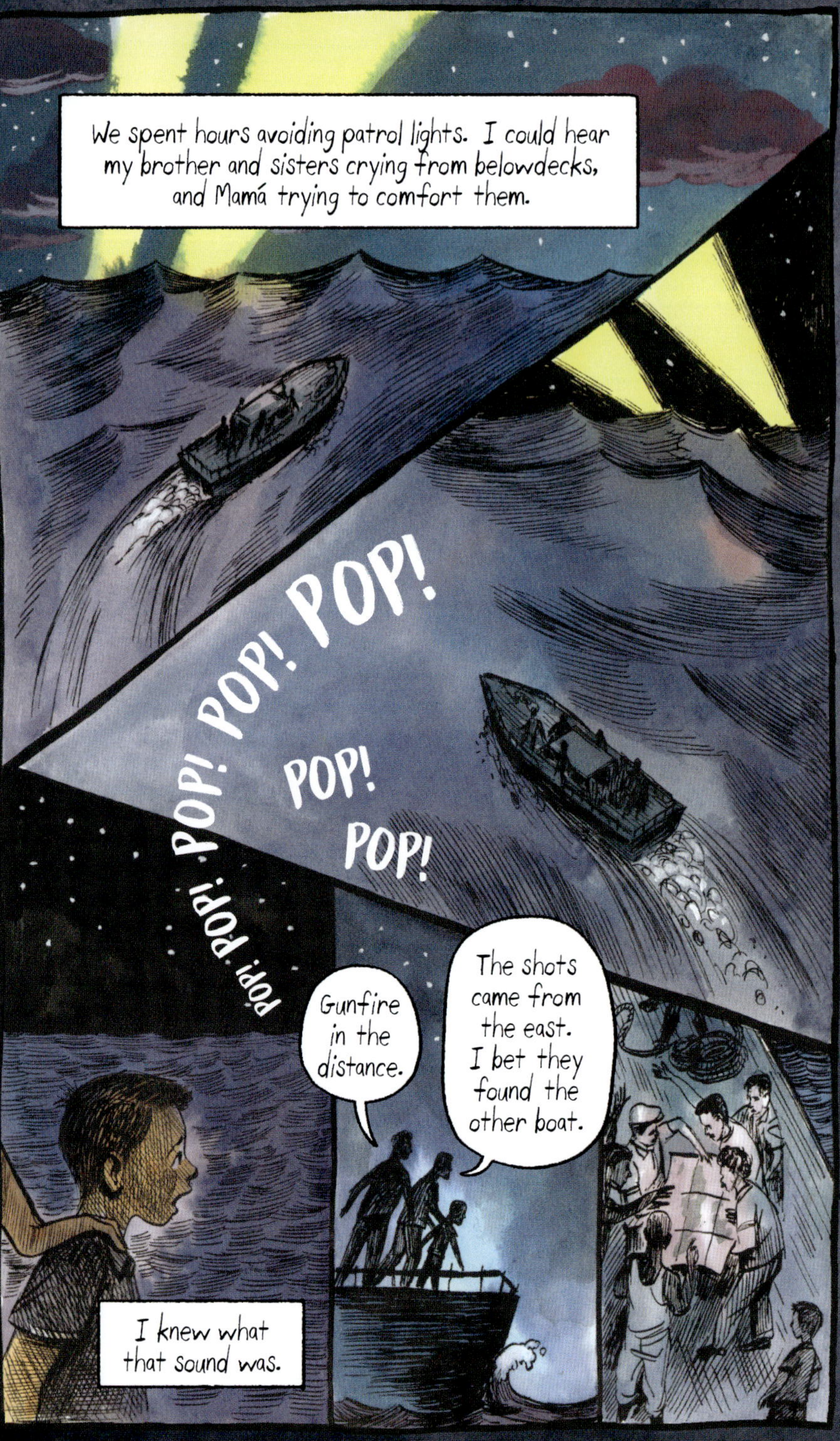
We spent hours avoiding patrol lights. I could hear my brother and sisters crying from belowdecks, and Mamá trying to comfort them.
POP! POP! POP! POP! POP! POP! POP!
I knew what that sound was.
Gunfire in the distance.
The shots came from the east. I bet they found the other boat.

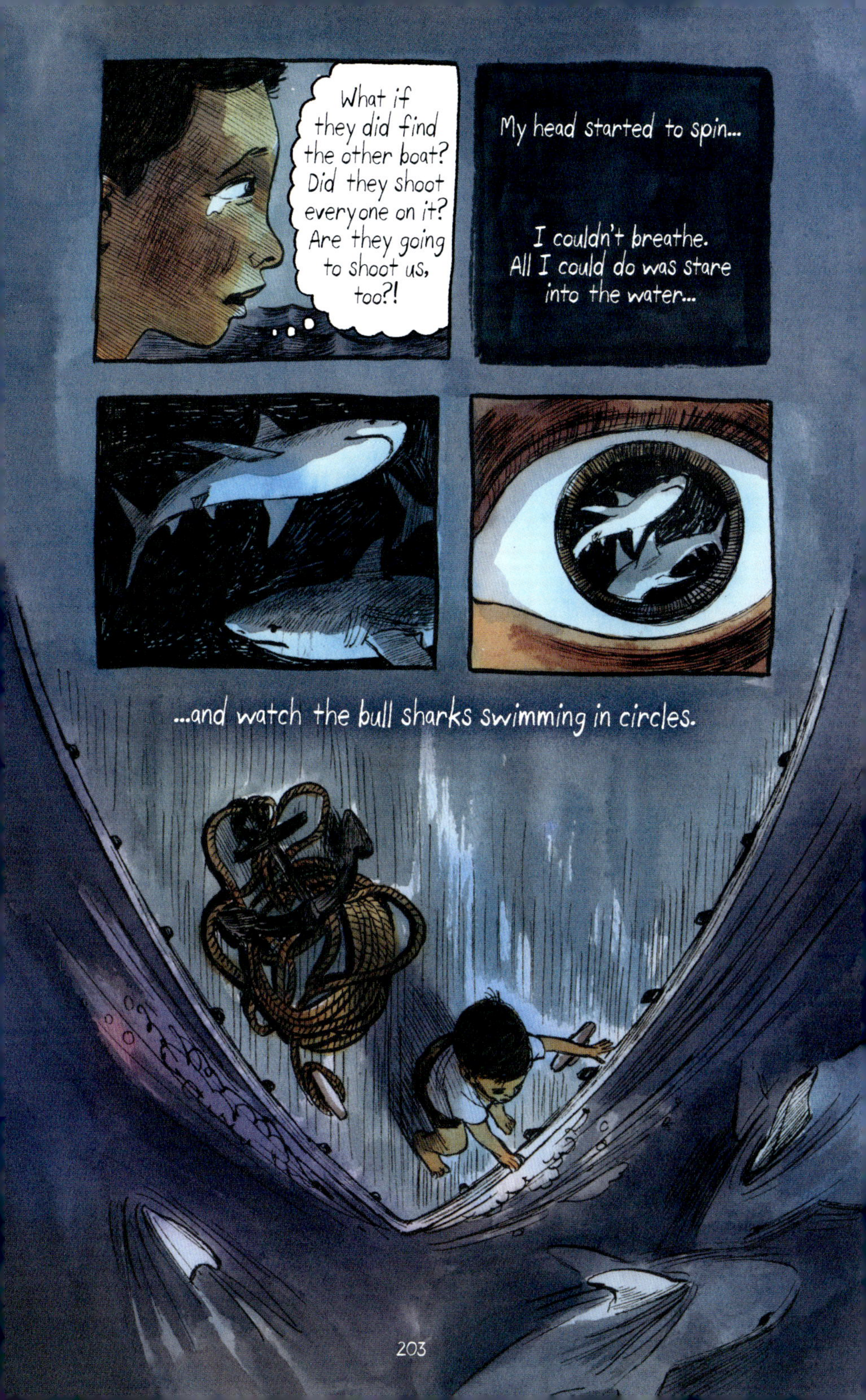
What if they did find the other boat? Did they shoot everyone on it? Are they going to shoot us, too?!
My head started to spin...
I couldn't breathe. All I could do was stare into the water...
...and watch the bull sharks swimming in circles.

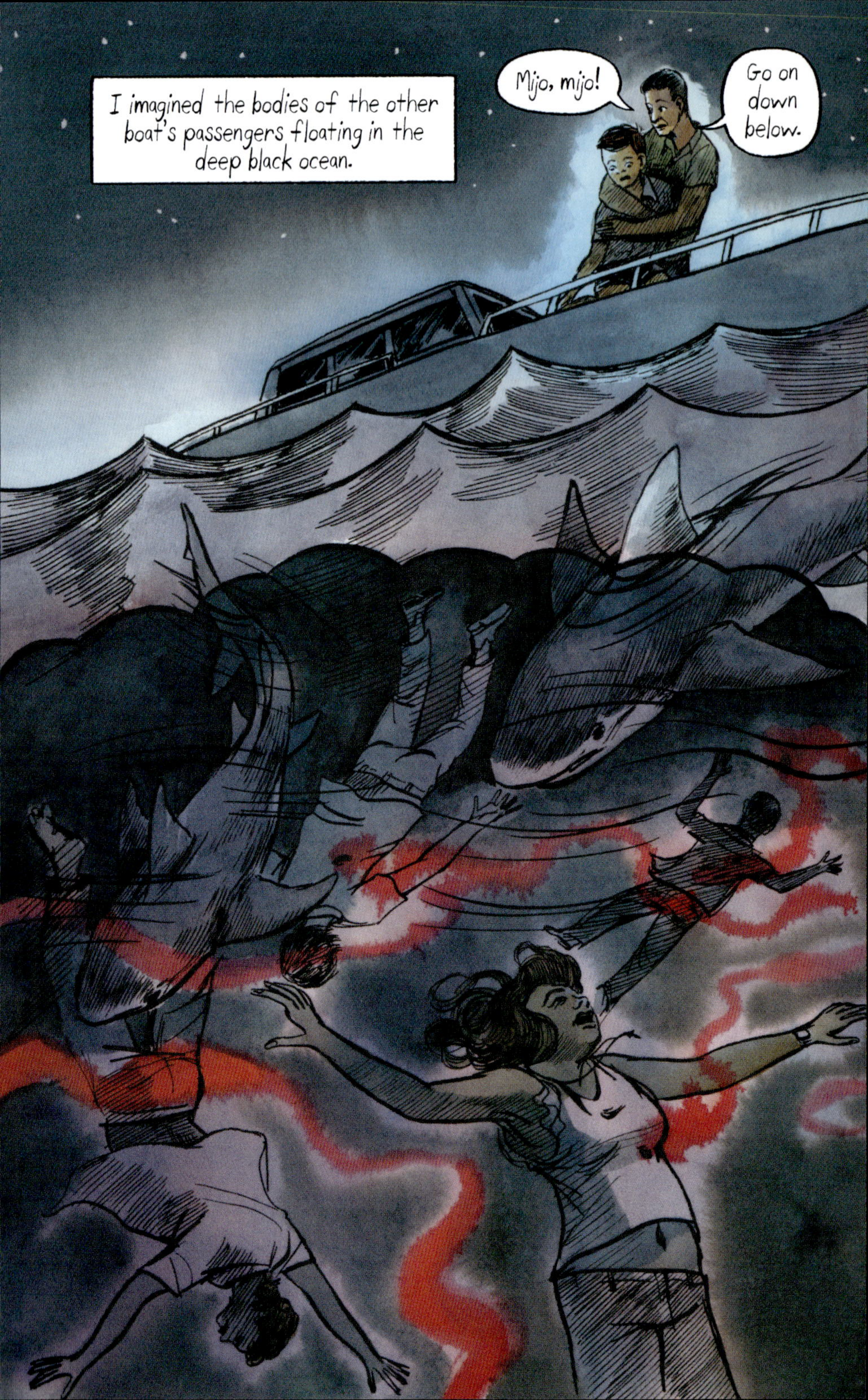
I imagined the bodies of the other boat's passengers floating in the deep black ocean.
Mijo, mijo!
Go on down below.

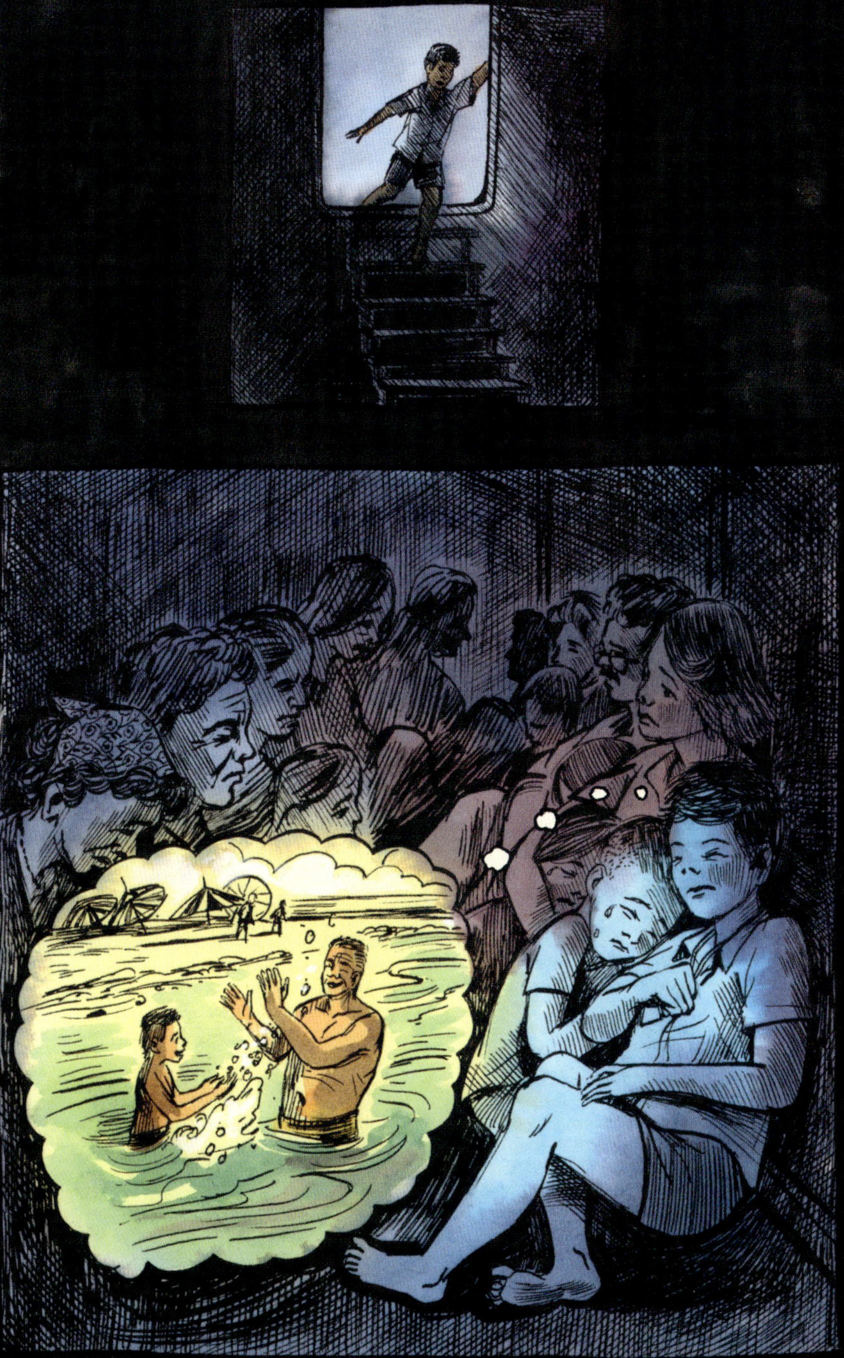

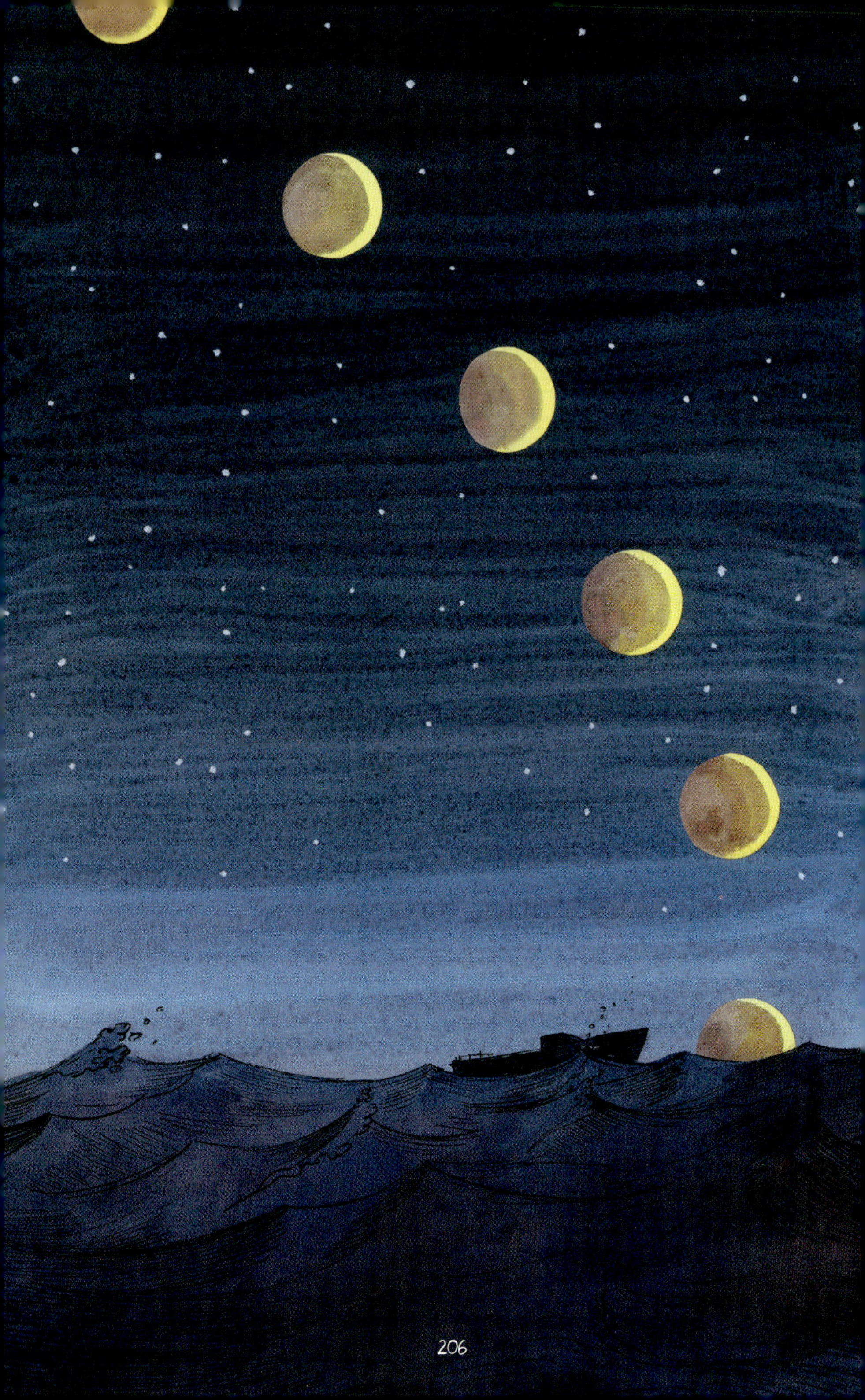

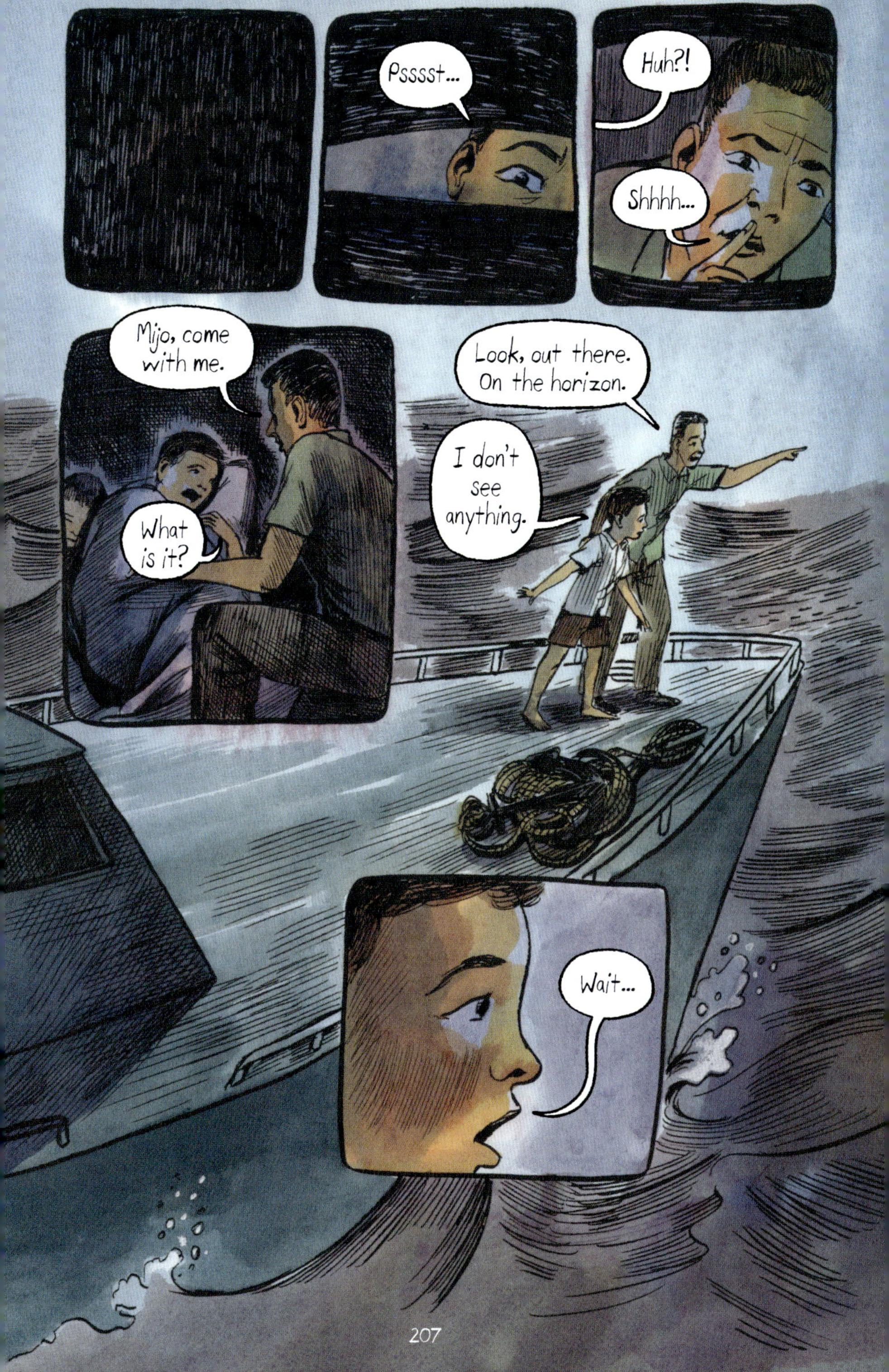
Psssst...
Huh?!
Shhhh...
Mijo, come with me.
What is it?
Look, out there. On the horizon.
I don't see anything.
Wait...

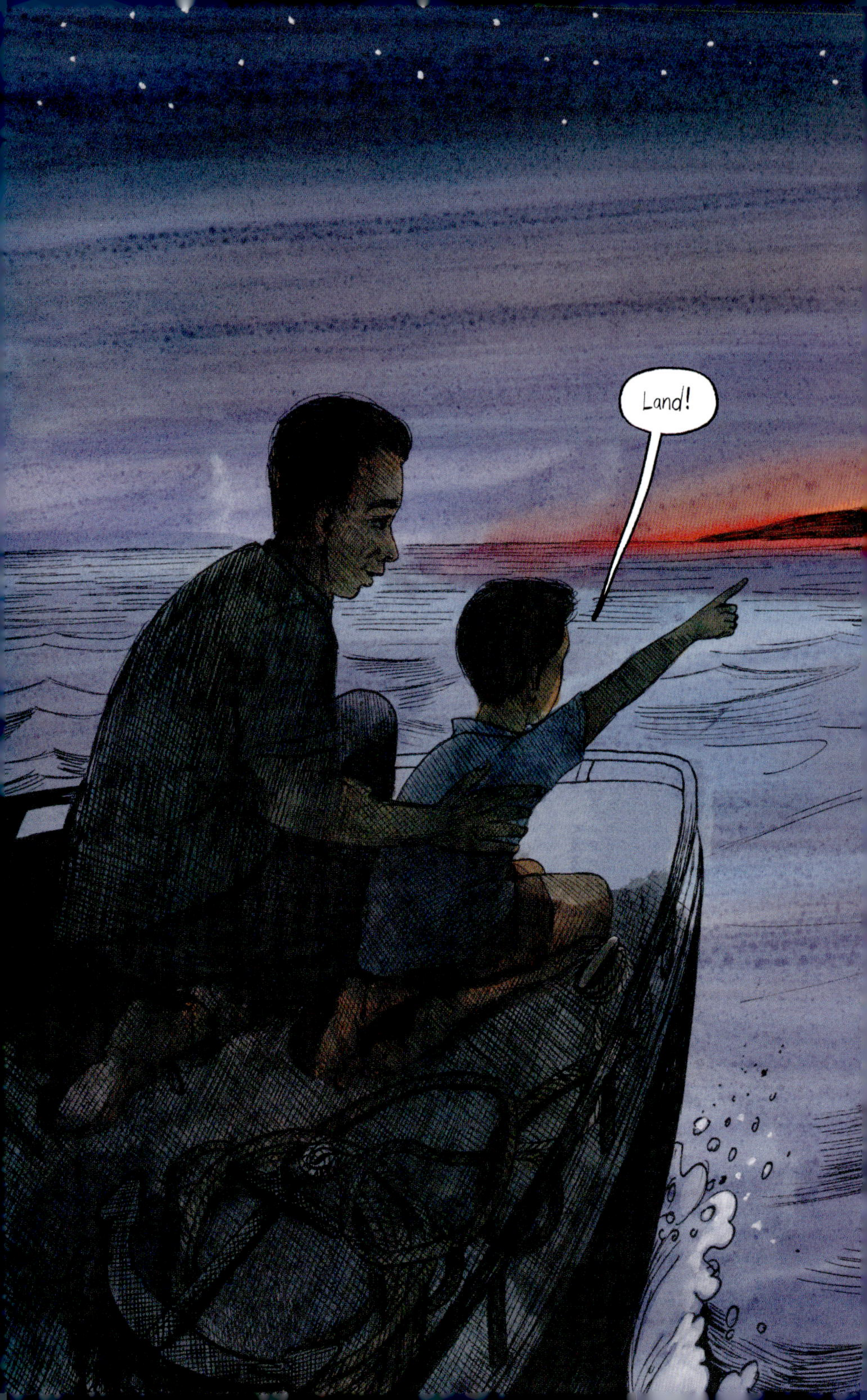
Land!

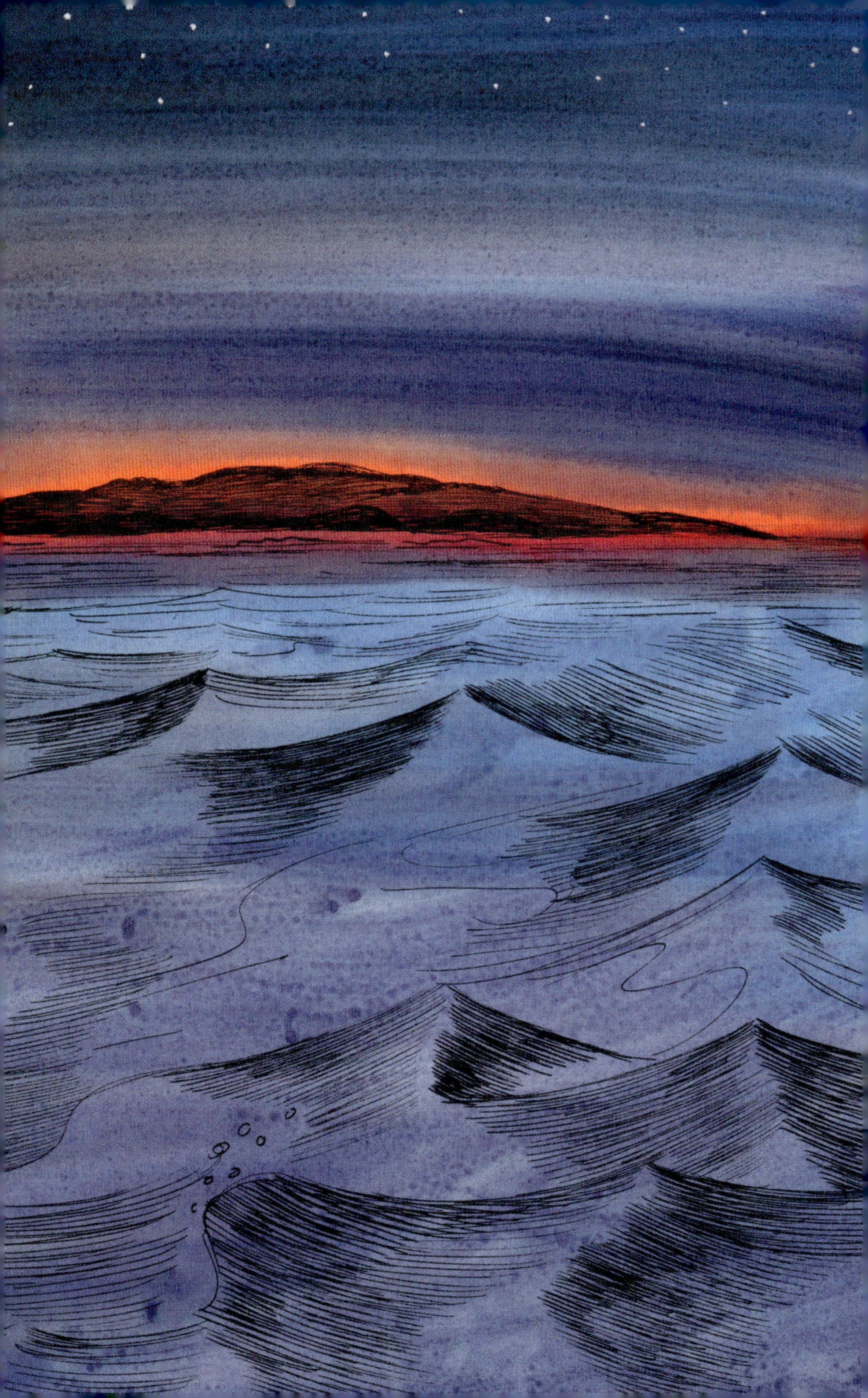

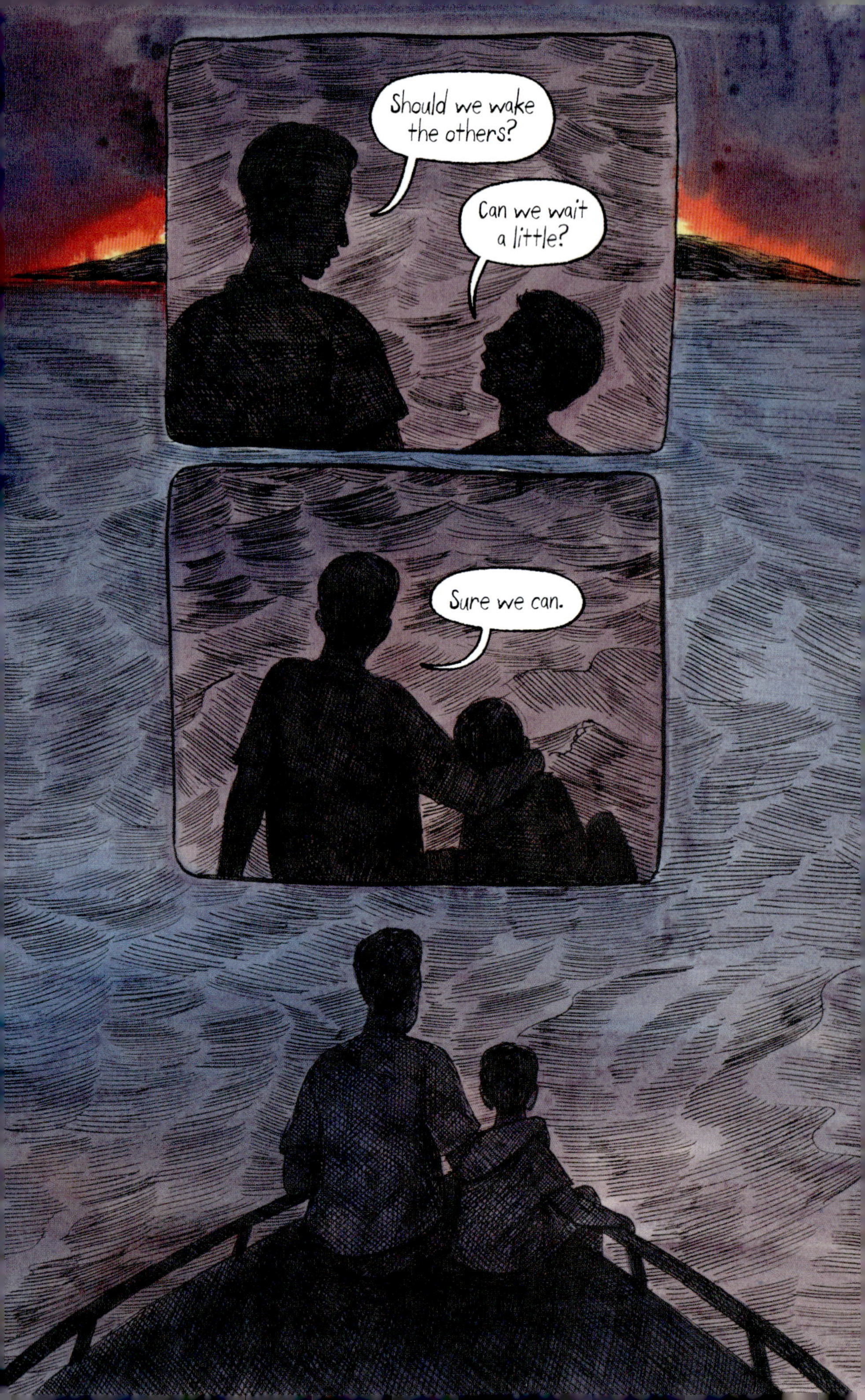
Should we wake the others?
Can we wait a little?
Sure we can.

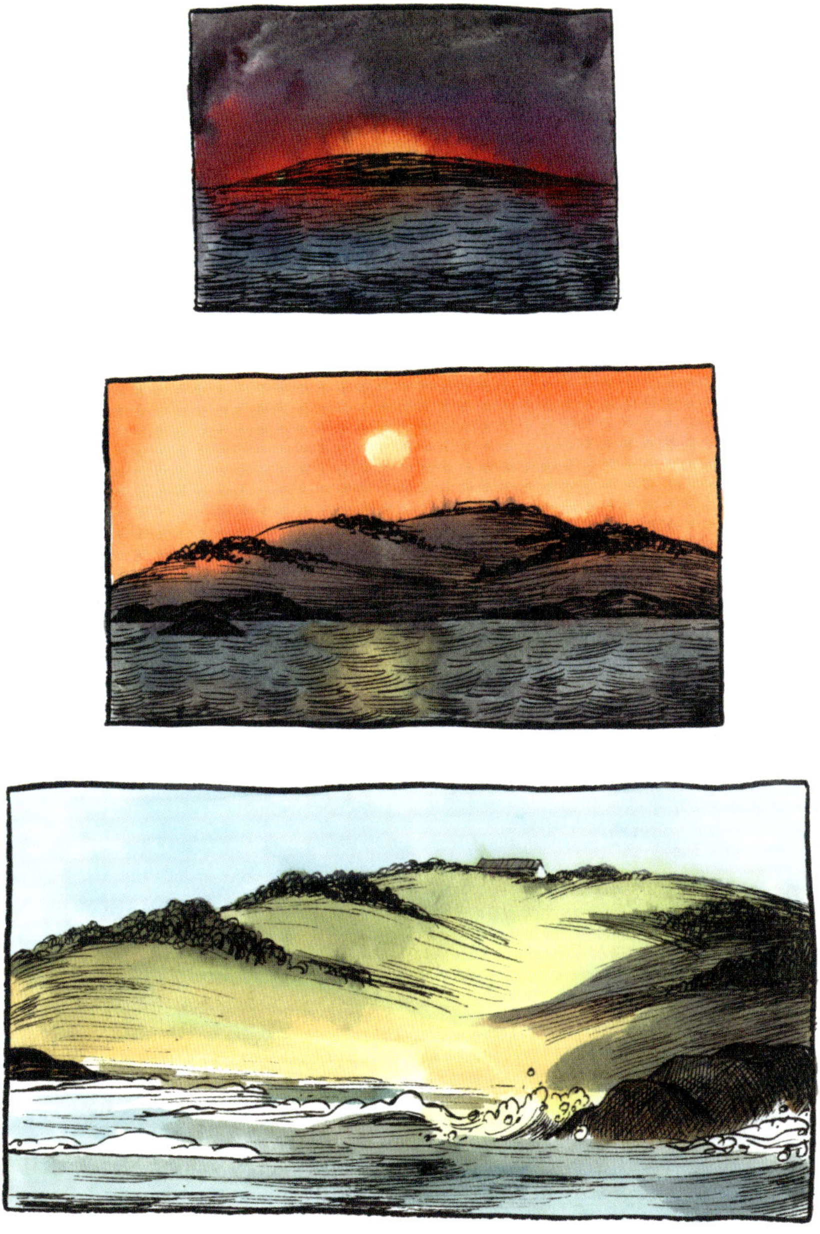

In the twenty-year period after the revolution, more than one million Cubans flee to the United States.

New Day, New Shore

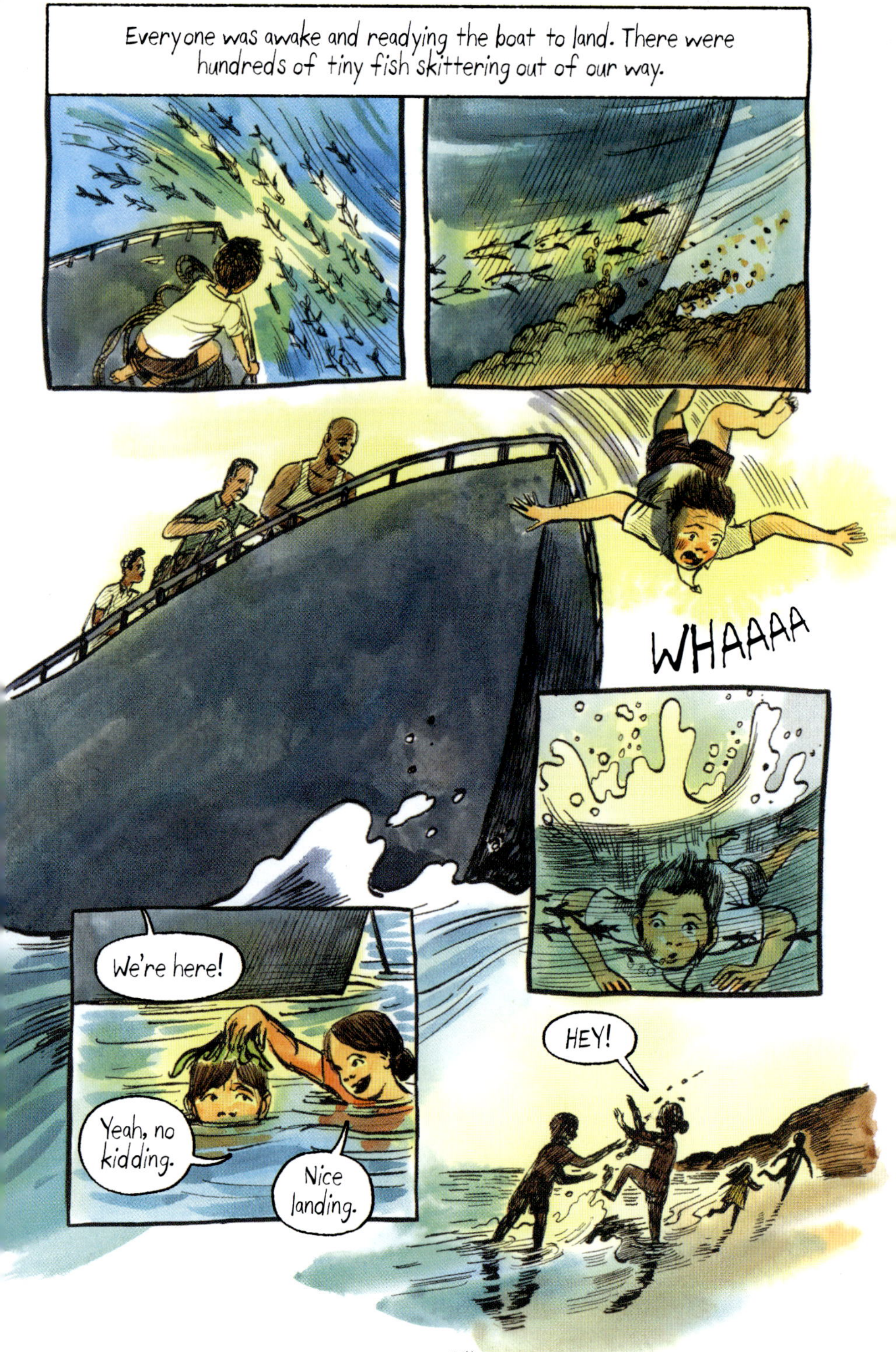
Everyone was awake and readying the boat to land. There were hundreds of tiny fish skittering out of our way.
WHAAAA
We're here!
Yeah, no kidding.
Nice landing.
HEY!

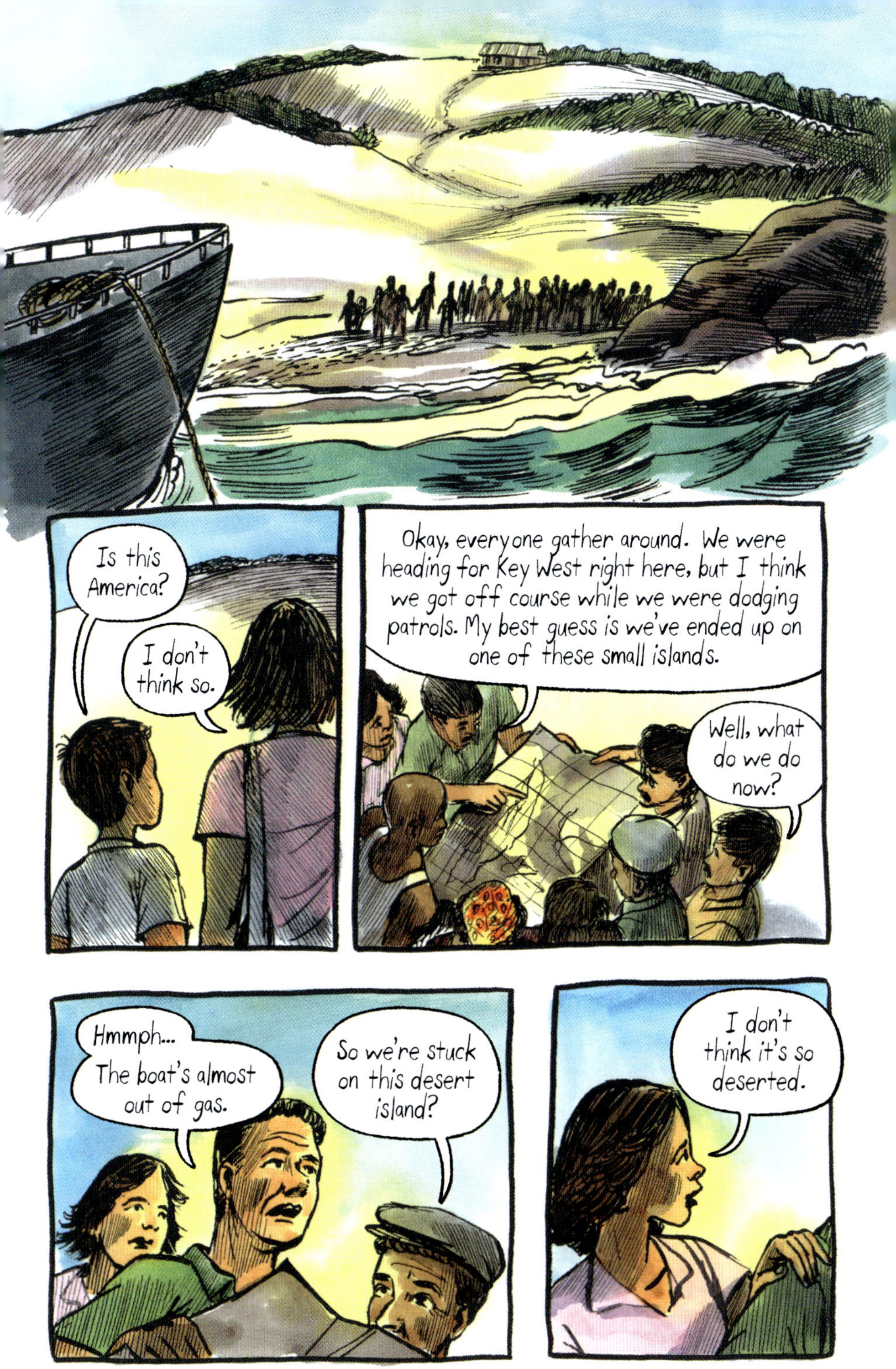
Is this America?
I don't think so.
Okay, everyone gather around. We were heading for Key West right here, but I think we got off course while we were dodging patrols. My best guess is we've ended up on one of these small islands.
Well, what do we do now?
Hmmph... The boat's almost out of gas.
So we're stuck on this desert island?
I don't think it's so deserted.

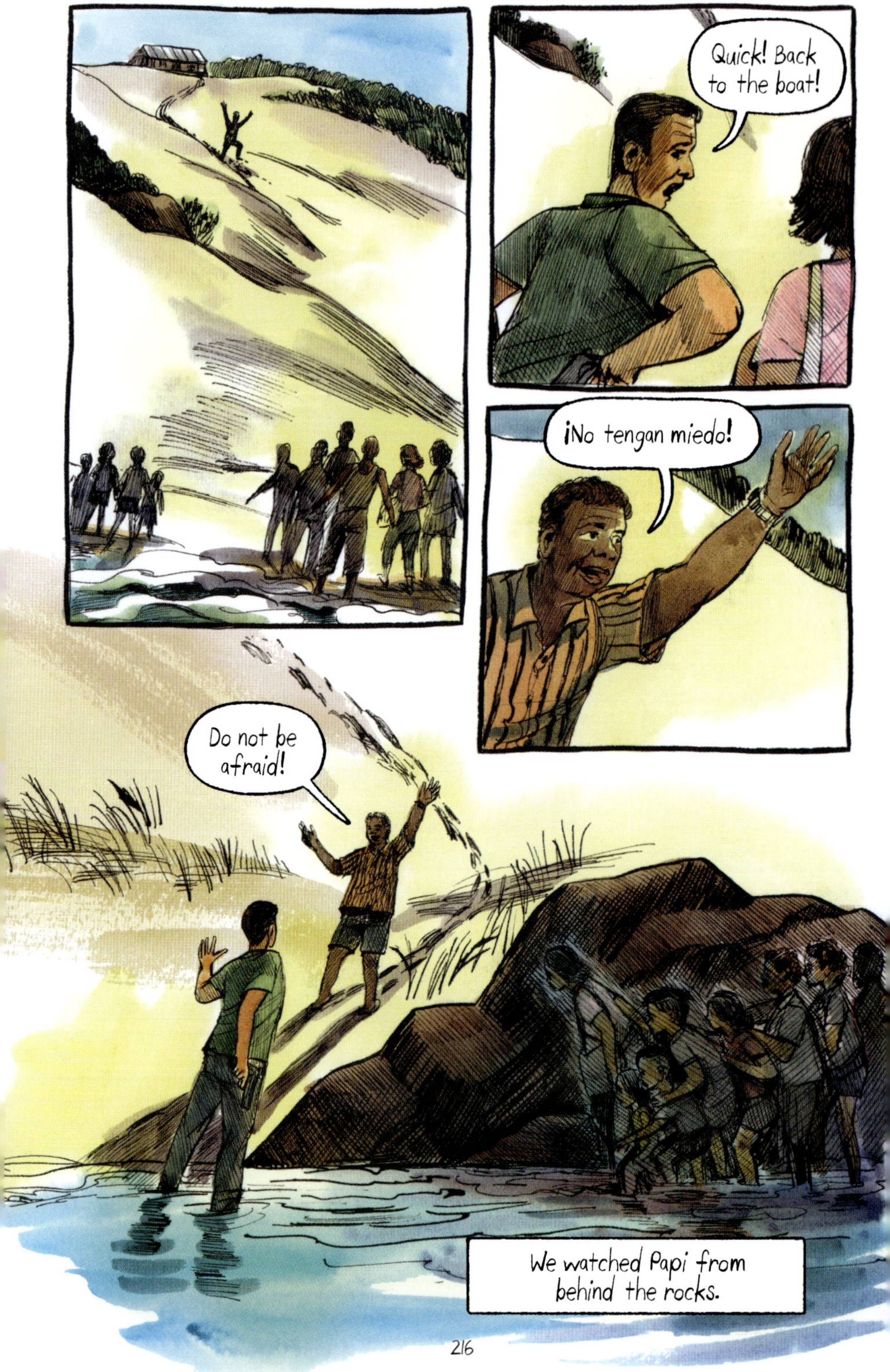
Quick! Back to the boat!
¡No tengan miedo!
Do not be afraid!
We watched Papi from behind the rocks.

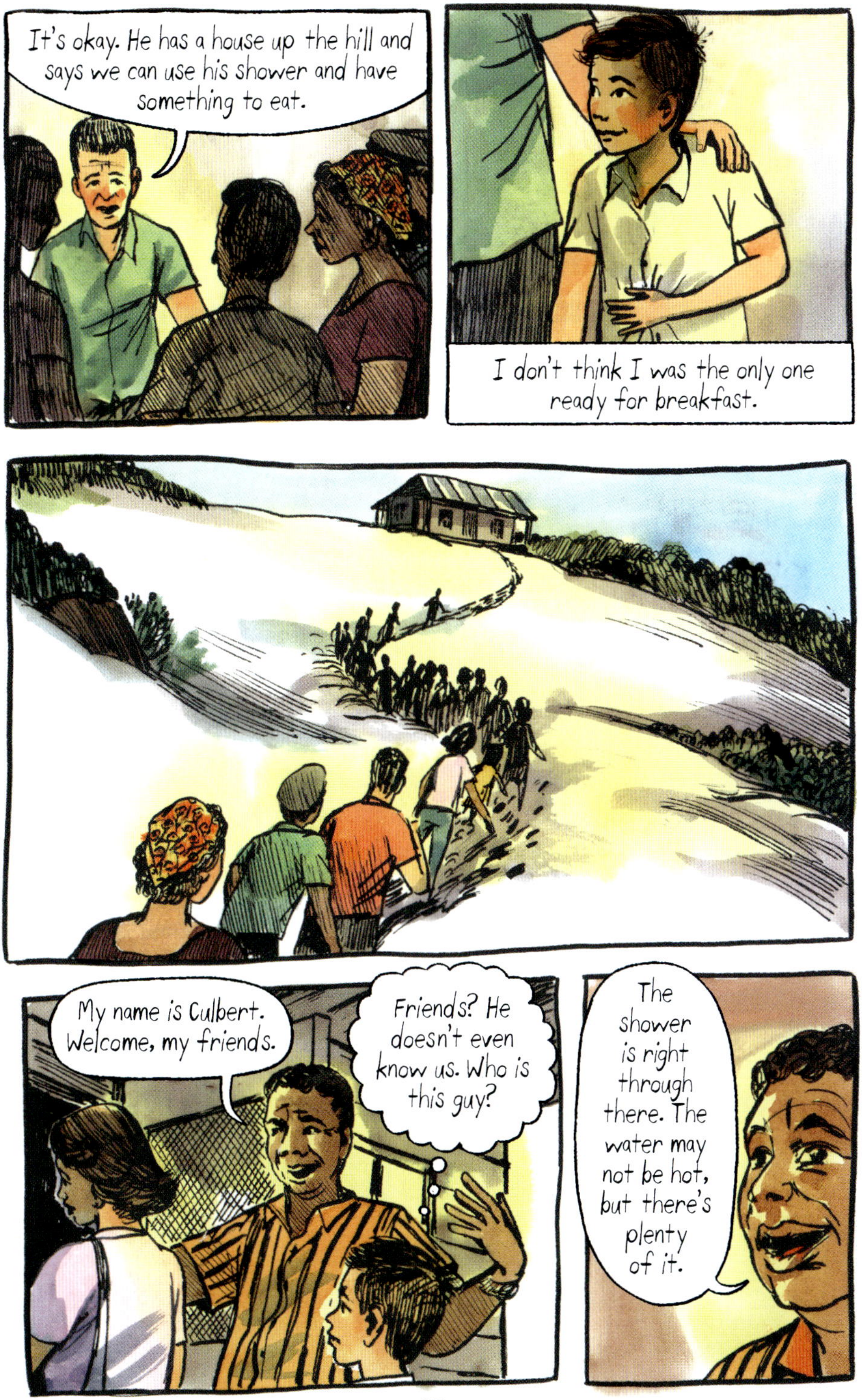
It's okay. He has a house up the hill and says we can use his shower and have something to eat.
I don't think I was the only one ready for breakfast.
My name is Culbert. Welcome, my friends.
Friends? He doesn't even know us. Who is this guy?
The shower is right through there. The water may not be hot, but there's plenty of it.

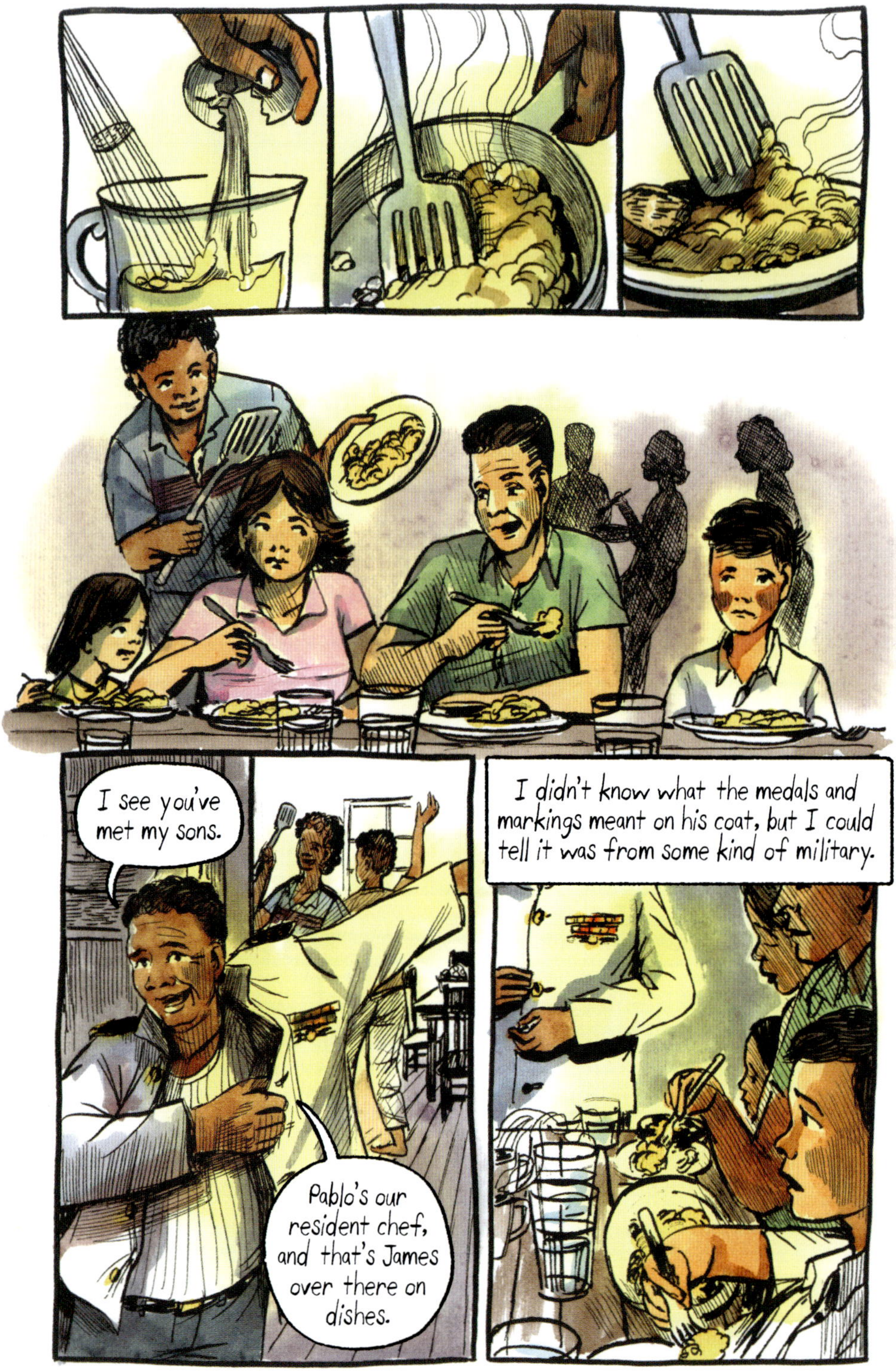
I see you've met my sons.
Pablo's our resident chef, and that's James over there on dishes.
I didn't know what the medals and markings meant on his coat, but I could tell it was from some kind of military.

"So I've got a radio in the other room. I took the liberty of calling you a ride."

CLANNNG!

"Okay, time to go. Everybody up! Back down to the boat."

"Quickly now."

AWWWWOOOOOOOOOOOOGAAAA!

All of a sudden it didn't matter if we made it to our boat or not.

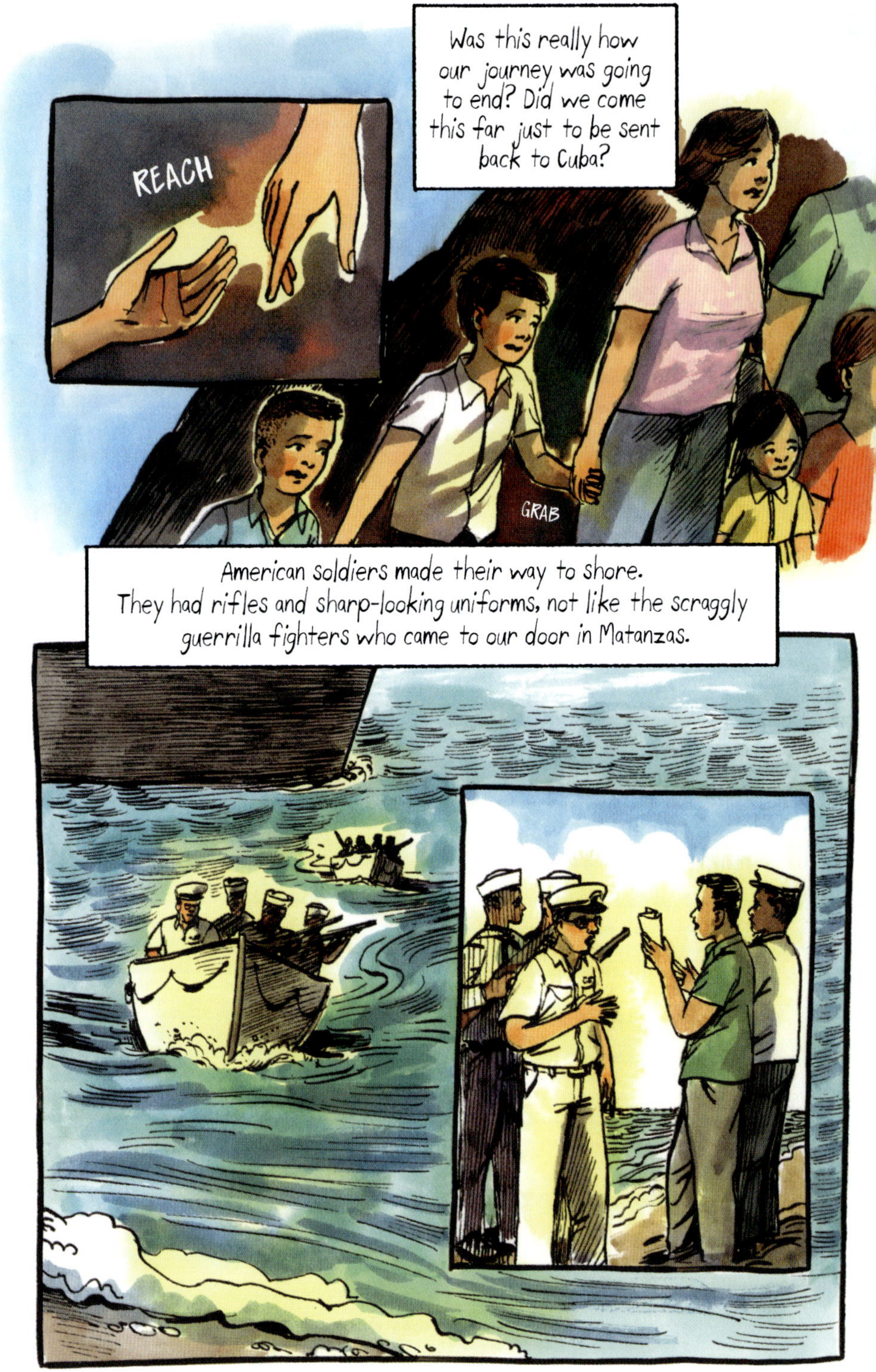
Was this really how our journey was going to end? Did we come this far just to be sent back to Cuba?
REACH
GRAB
American soldiers made their way to shore. They had rifles and sharp-looking uniforms, not like the scraggly guerrilla fighters who came to our door in Matanzas.

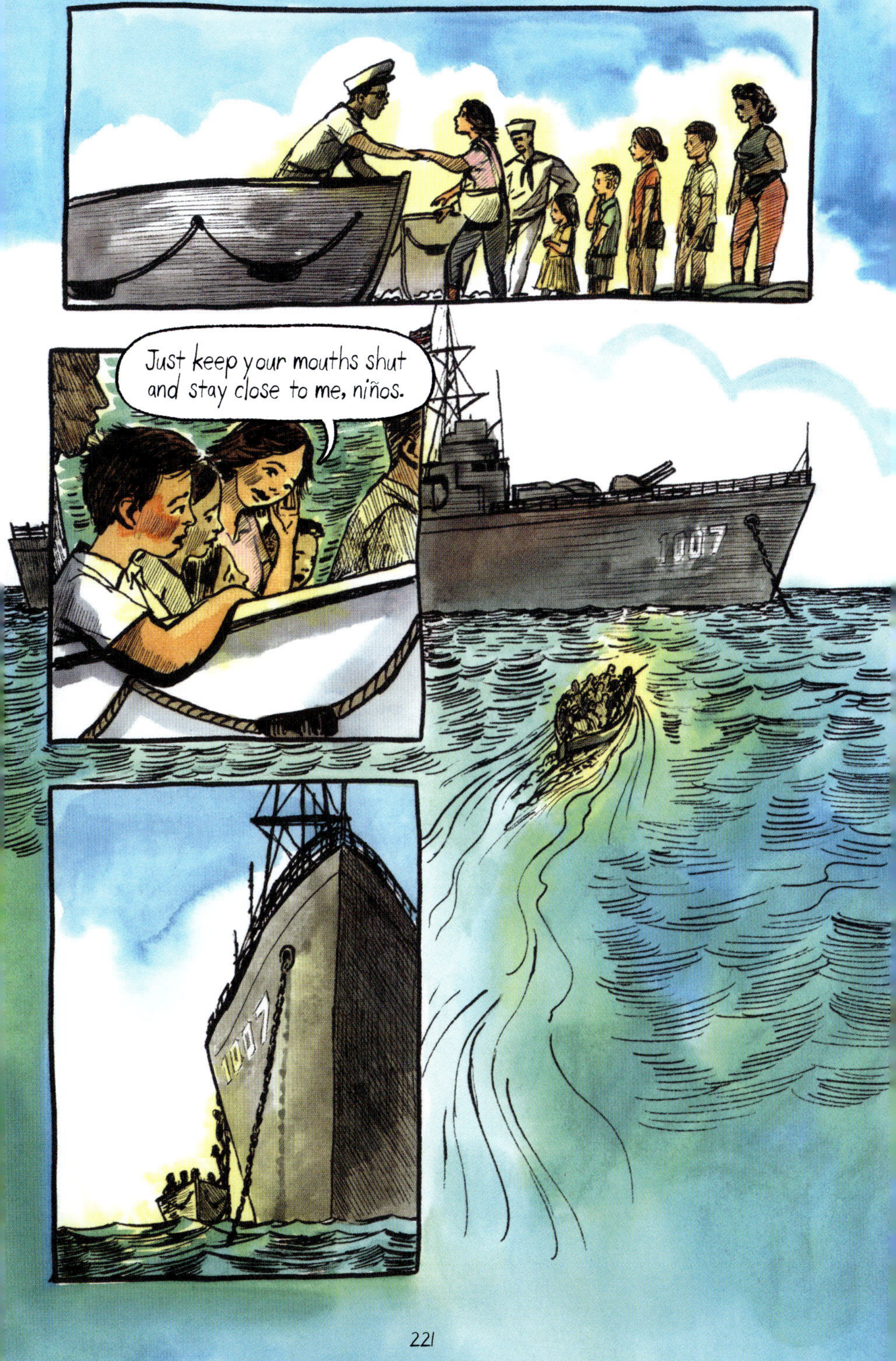
Just keep your mouths shut and stay close to me, niños.
1007
1007

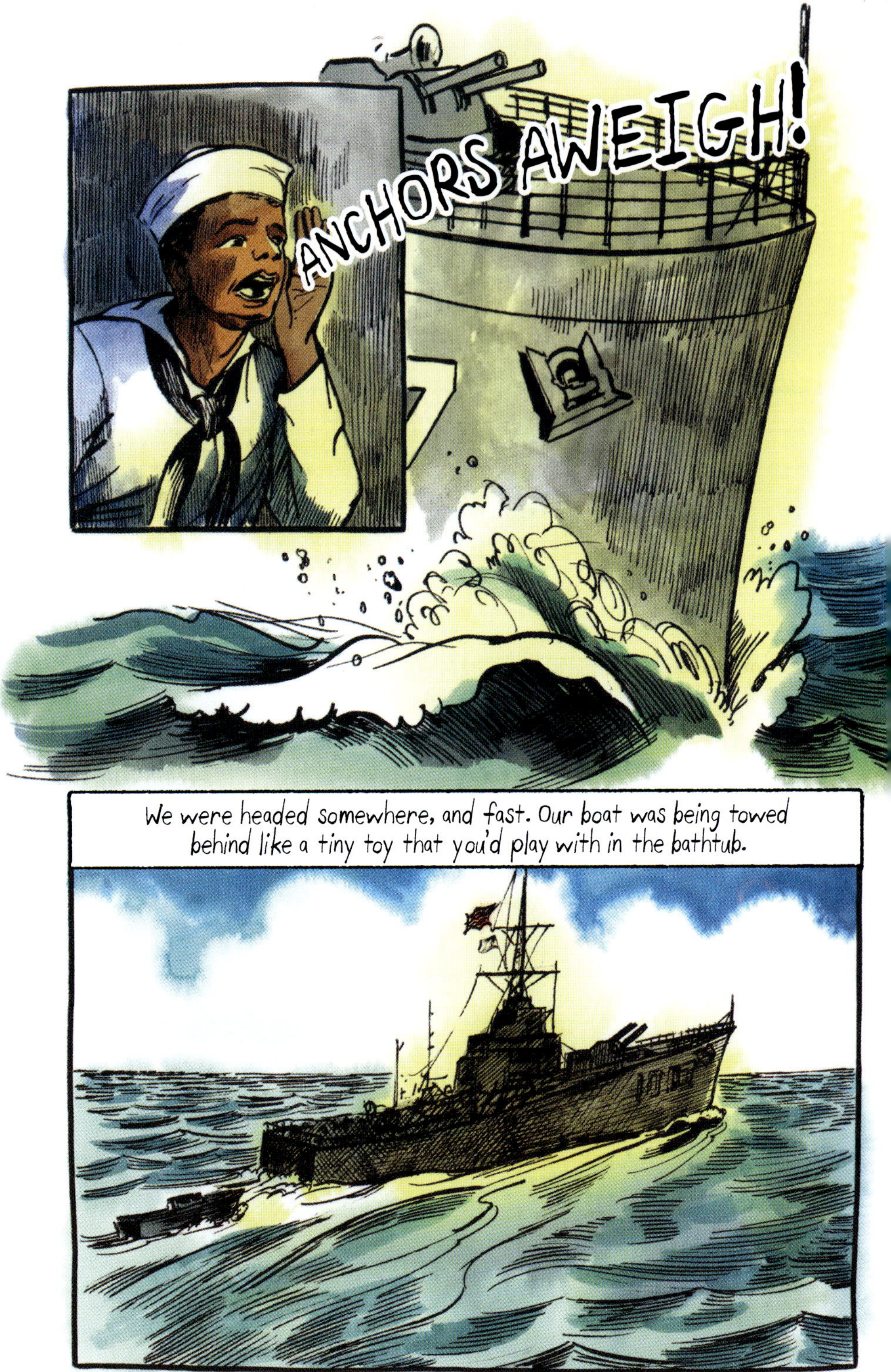
ANCHORS AWEIGH!
We were headed somewhere, and fast. Our boat was being towed behind like a tiny toy that you'd play with in the bathtub.

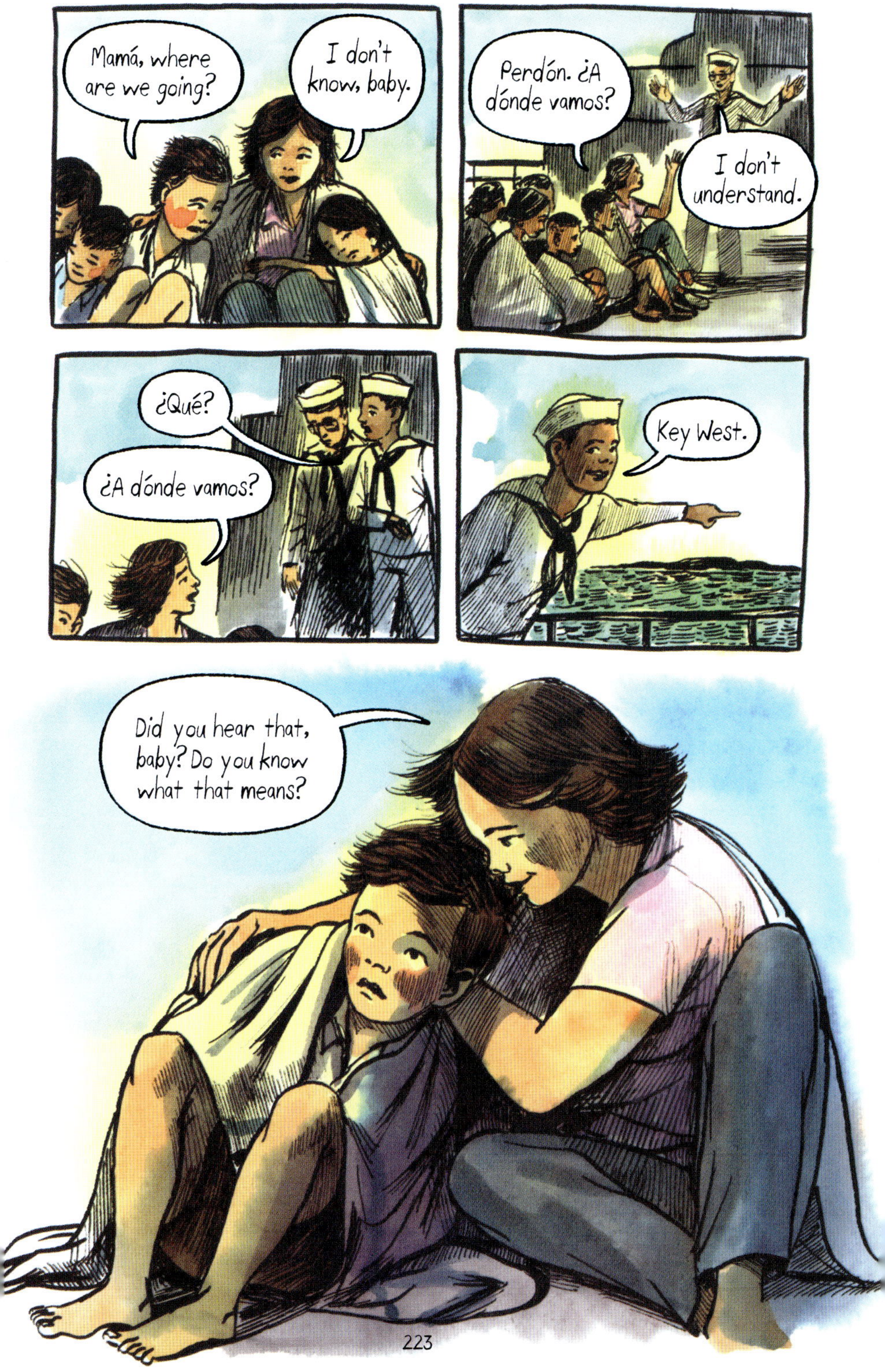
Mamá, where are we going?
I don't know, baby.
Perdón. ¿A dónde vamos?
I don't understand.
¿Qué?
¿A dónde vamos?
Key West.
Did you hear that, baby? Do you know what that means?

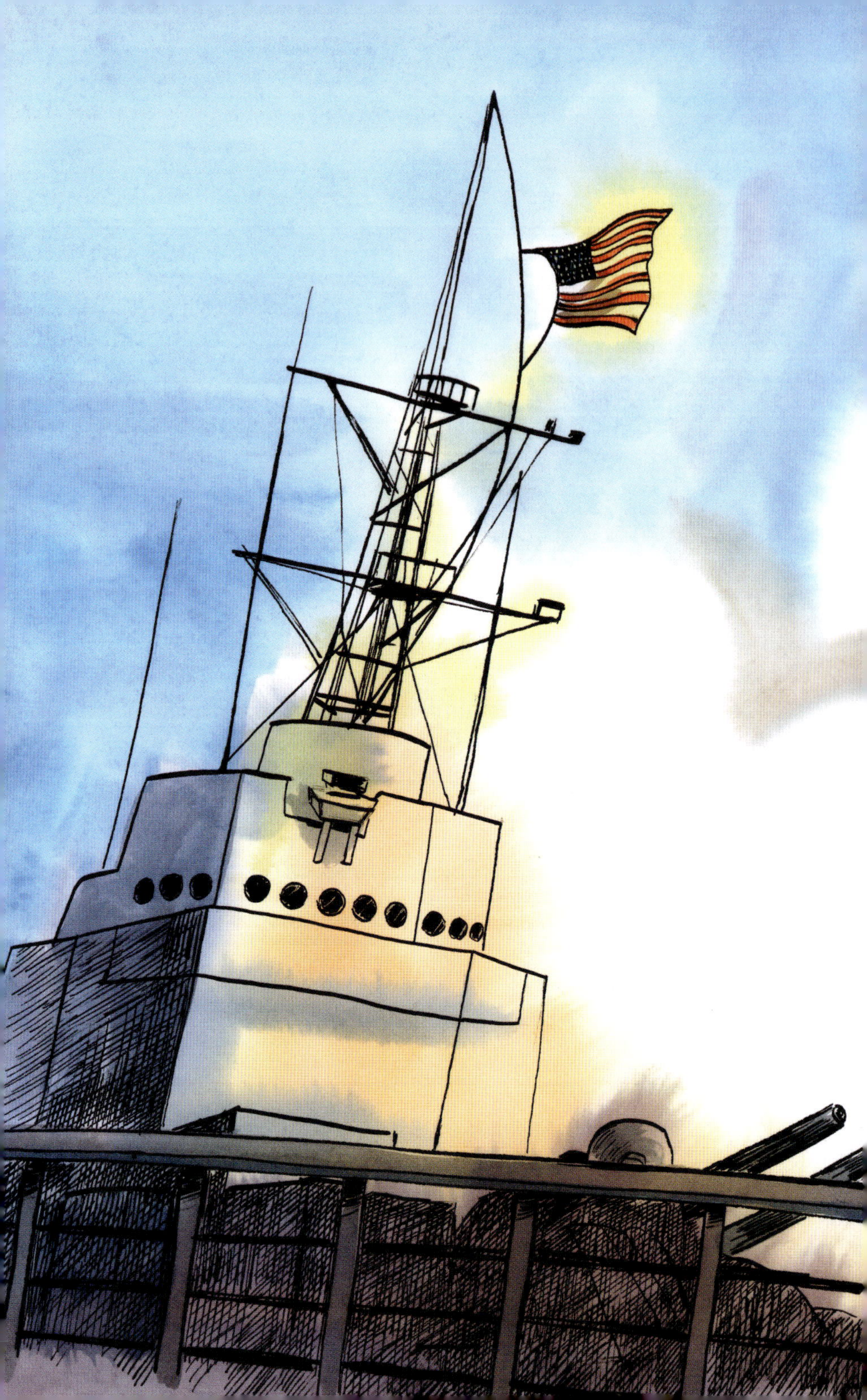

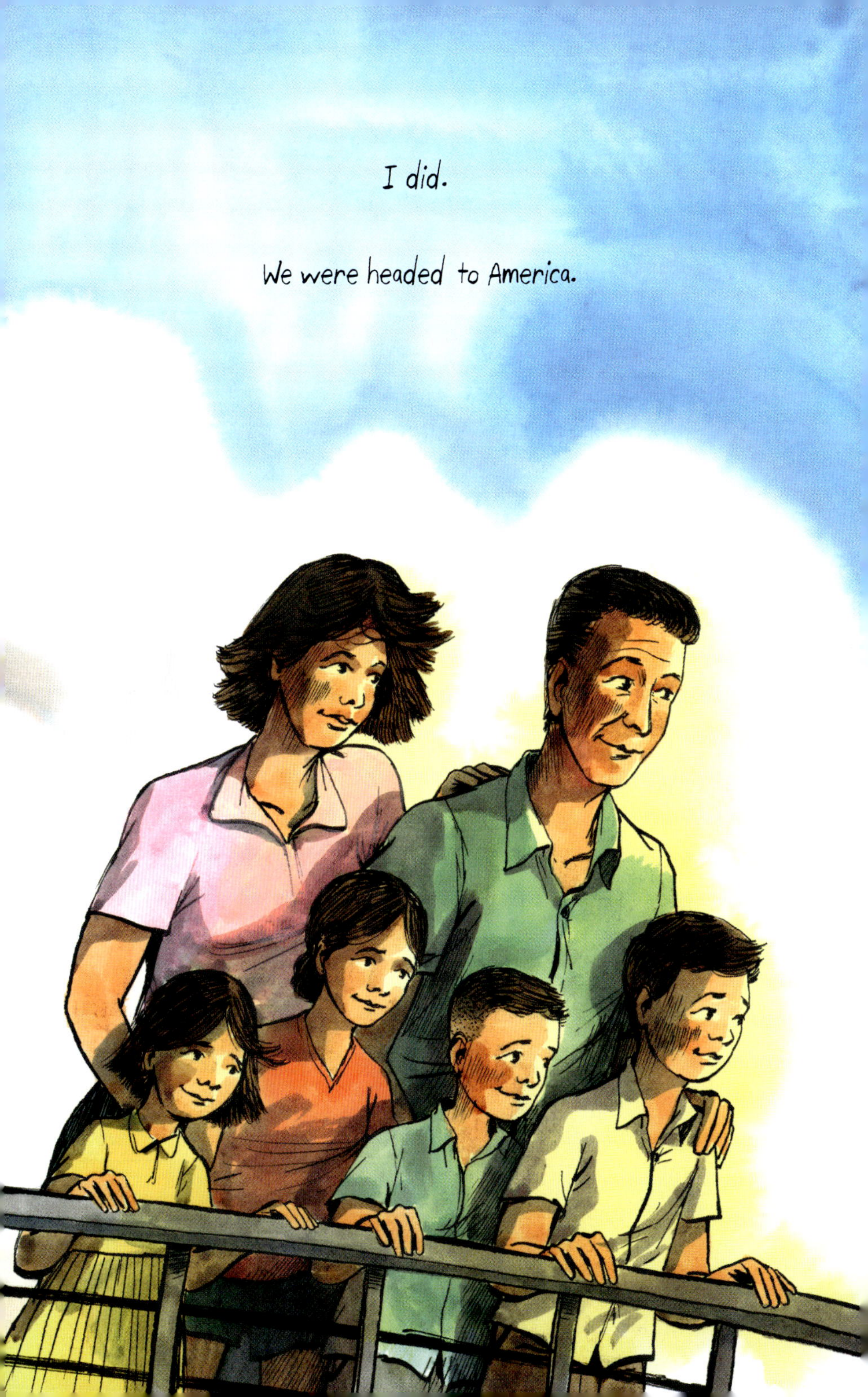
I did.
We were headed to America.

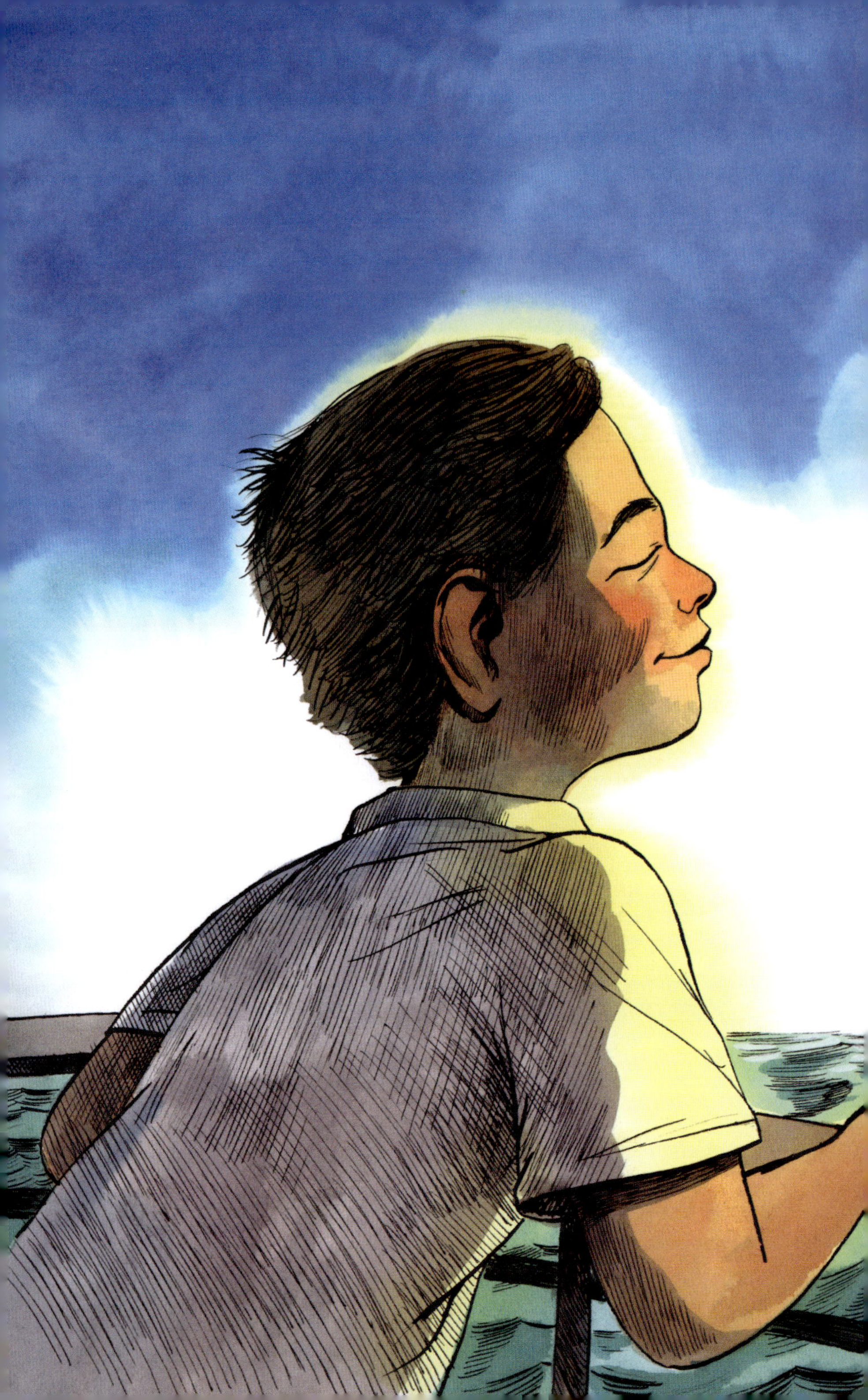

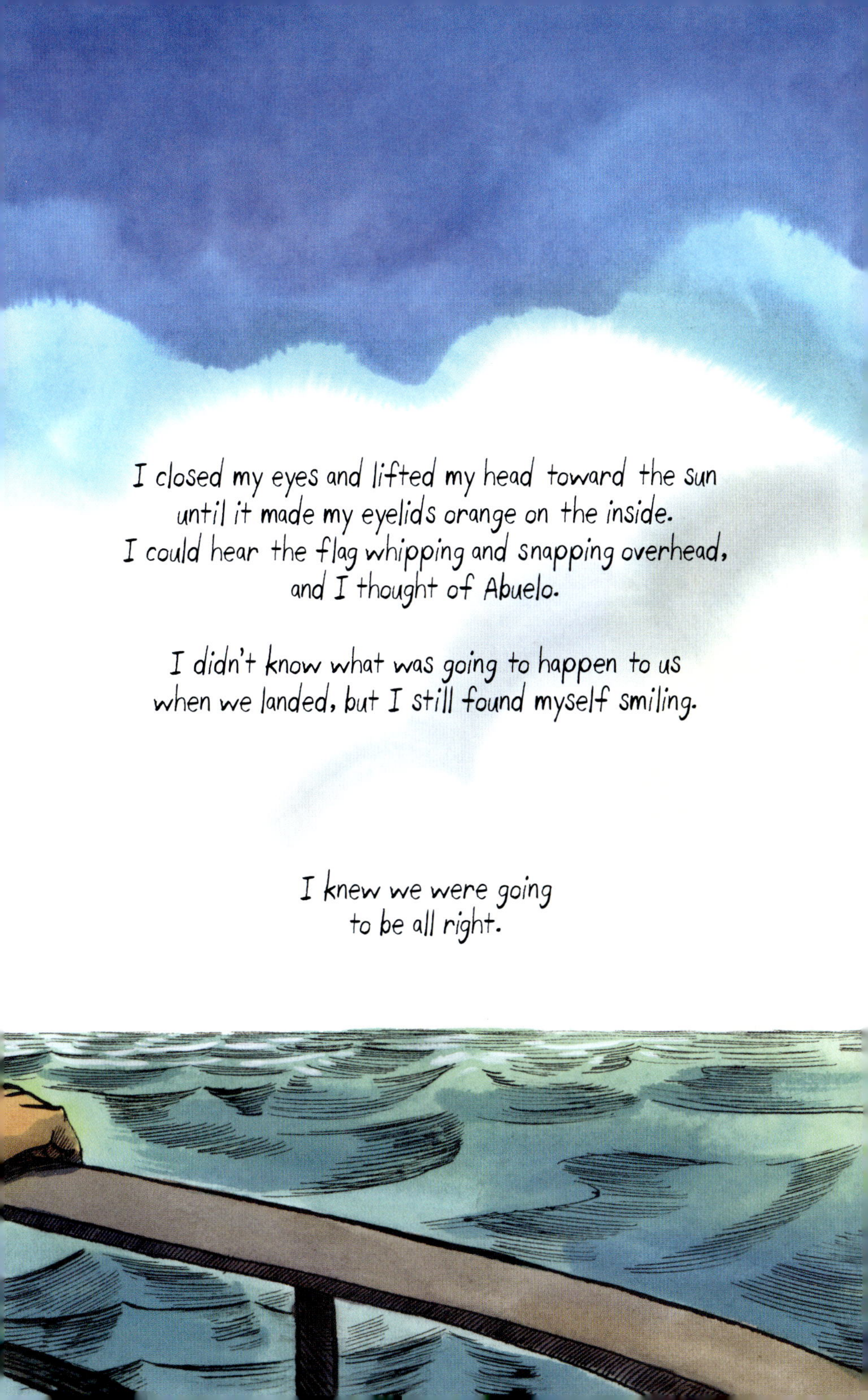
I closed my eyes and lifted my head toward the sun
until it made my eyelids orange on the inside.
I could hear the flag whipping and snapping overhead,
and I thought of Abuelo.
I didn't know what was going to happen to us
when we landed, but I still found myself smiling.
I knew we were going
to be all right.

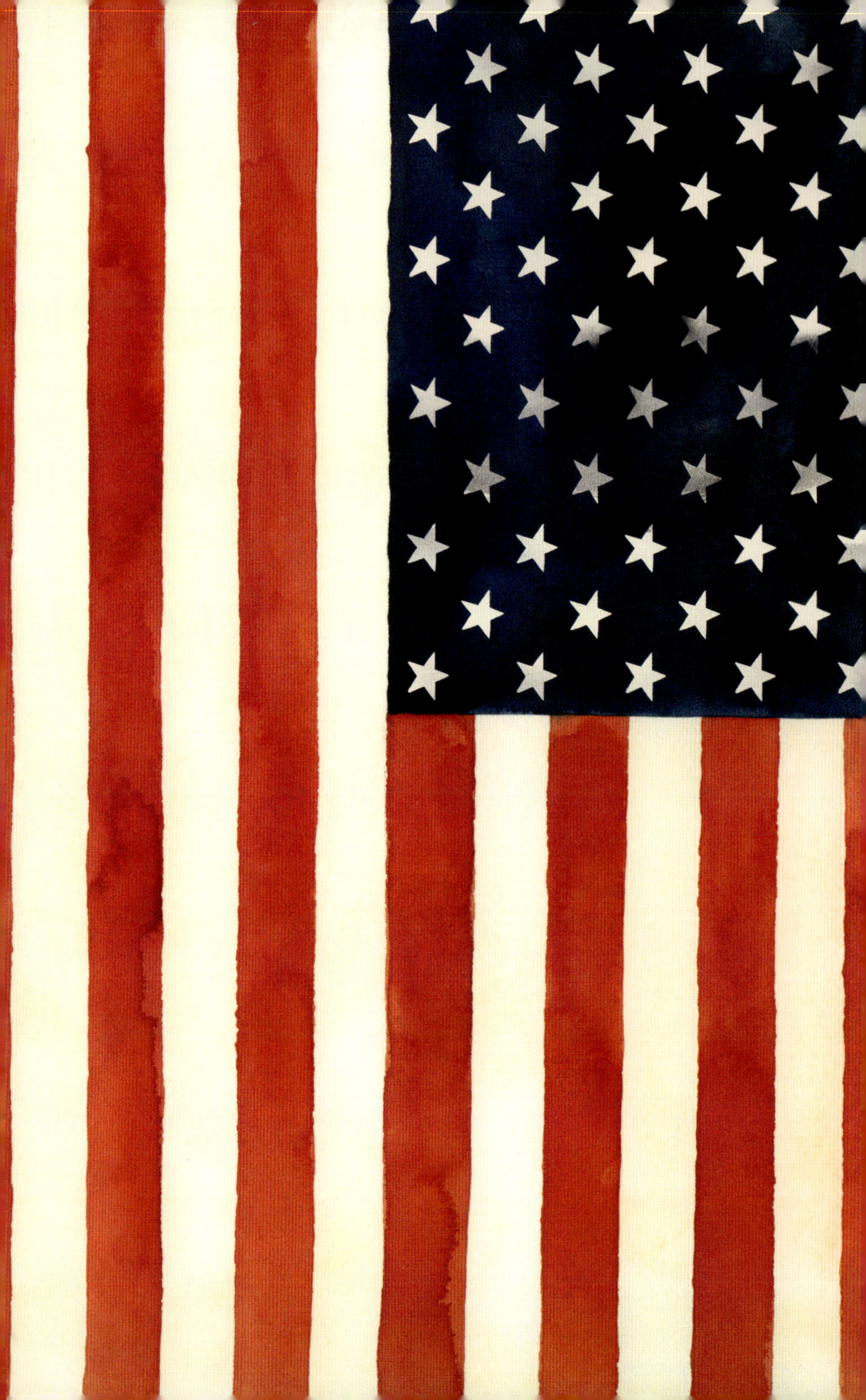

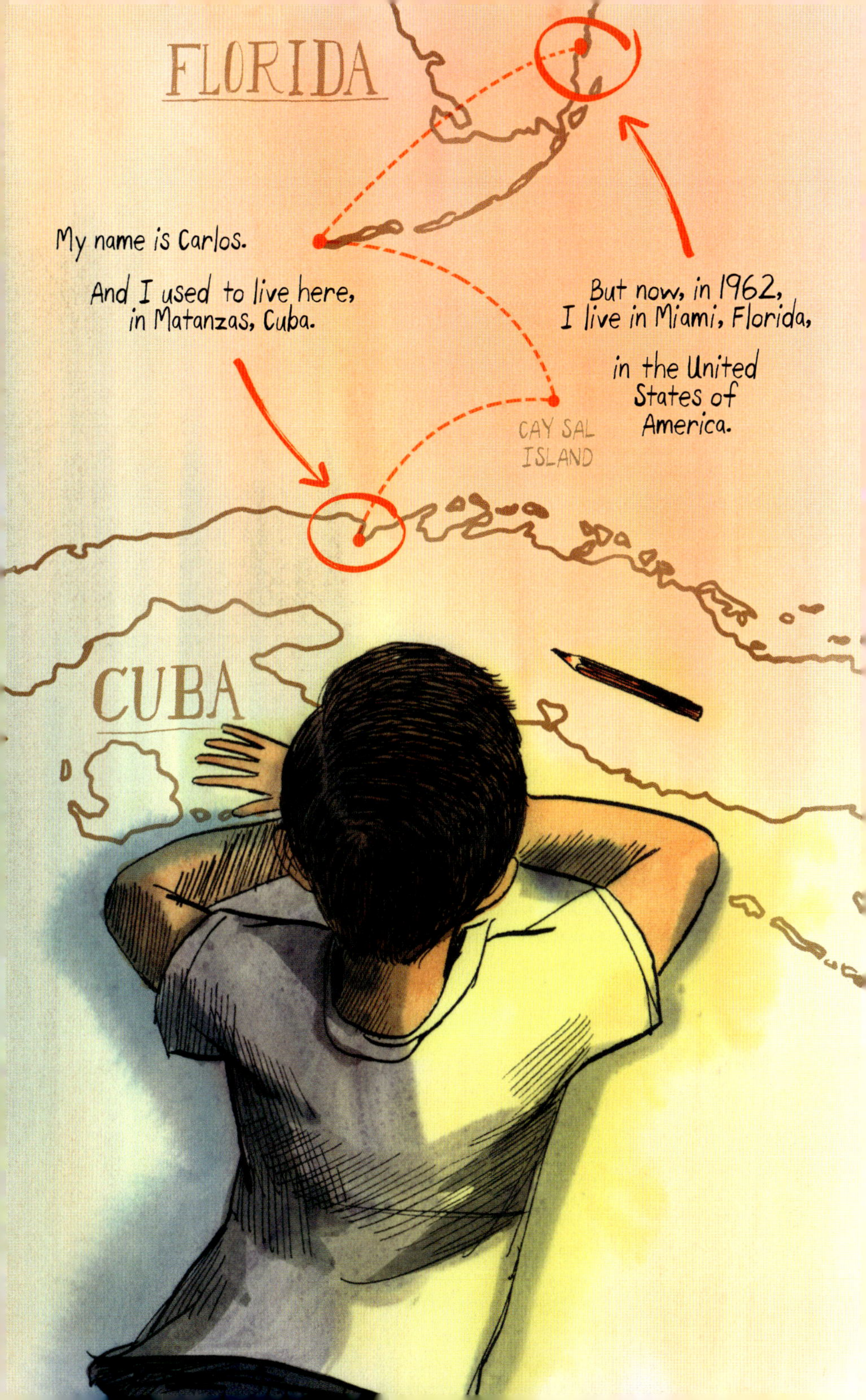
FLORIDA
My name is Carlos.
And I used to live here, in Matanzas, Cuba.
But now, in 1962, I live in Miami, Florida,
in the United States of America.
CAY SAL ISLAND
CUBA

AUTHOR'S NOTE

Over twenty years ago, my phone rang in the middle of the night. It was my dad, Carlos, calling to see how I was adjusting to the new city where I'd moved for my first job. While I appreciated him checking on me, I was surprised—he didn't call often, and we weren't close. He told me he knew what it felt like to move to a new place. Then he started to share the story of how he and his family fled to the United States from Cuba when he was a kid, just after the Revolution. This was the first time I'd ever heard it.

Isaura (far left), Carlos (with candle in hand), Maggie (second from right), Lázaro (far right), and friends, celebrating Carlos's birthday.

In my half-awake state, I fumbled around for a notebook and feverishly began scribbling. It felt like if I didn't write everything down, my dad's story might evaporate into thin air. He fondly recalled riding horses with his abuelo at their farm and catching tarantulas with his friends in the woods of Matanzas. But when Castro took over, everything changed. Castro's soldiers seized the farm and my grandfather's furniture business, all in the name of the Revolution. The life my family had built was gone.

From left to right: Lázaro, Mamá, Isaura, Papi, and Maggie, pictured just after they arrived in the United States. Carlos took the photo!

My dad went on to tell me about the impossible decision my grandfather made: to uproot his family and flee their beloved Cuba. In the early 1960s, Cubans weren't allowed to leave the country freely, so many escaped by boat. The journey was extremely dangerous. Of course, there was the ocean to contend with, and if Castro's soldiers caught them, they could be imprisoned, forced to work in labor camps, or even shot.

I couldn't imagine having to make that choice as a parent or going on such a perilous journey as a kid. I grew up in an American suburb. My friends and I rode bikes and played in the woods. I didn't have to worry about anyone coming to take my home from me.

For years after that night, I asked my dad questions about his life and jotted down his answers; it felt like a way to make up for lost time between us.

It took me almost two decades to summon the courage to turn my dad's words into a book—this book. At first, I wasn't even sure how to approach it. What should I include? What should I leave out? I did lots of research and started having weekly phone calls with my dad. Soon I realized that there were some things he didn't remember or had been too young to understand—I'd have to fill in the gaps.

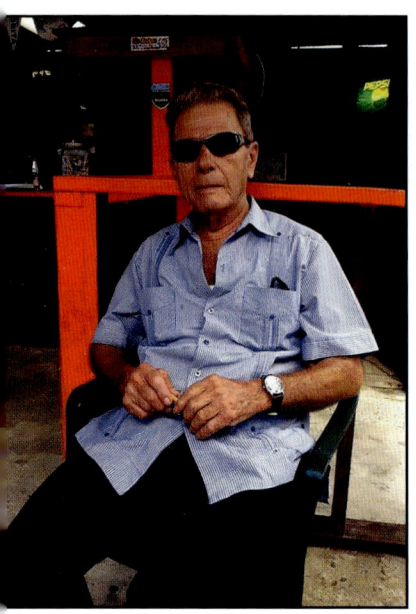

Papi in Puerto Rico in 2019, a few years before he passed away. I never got to meet him.

I decided to narrate the story from my dad's perspective at the time, but I aged him up a few years so my audience could connect with him better. Above all, I wanted to show a boy, not so different from any of us, trying to make sense of the big churning world around him, as his old life crumbled and a new one began to take shape.

Abuela and Abuelo in Cuba.

From left to right: Carlos, Lázaro, Isaura, Maggie, and two other kids from their neighborhood, celebrating their first Christmas in the United States.

    Weeks and months went by. My dad and I both looked forward to our check-ins, and he was excited to see my work progressing. But in September 2022, I got another phone call in the middle of the night. My dad had died unexpectedly. As I grieved, I wasn't sure how to proceed with the book, or even if I should. But I sensed that my dad would have wanted me to complete it.

    Reflecting on his life, I've come to realize how important our family stories are. They show us where we come from, who we are, and who we might become. They need to be told. By retelling my dad's story in a new way—in my own way—I've gained a renewed appreciation for my family and a deeper understanding of who I am.

    Thank you for joining me on this journey.

Hasta luego,

Daniel

Carlos and Daniel

Daniel Miyares's father (the real-life Carlos) loved to draw and encouraged his son to become an artist. Now a father himself, Daniel has illustrated numerous books for young readers, including *That Is My Dream!* by Langston Hughes, which received two starred reviews; *Nell Plants a Tree* by Anne Wynter, which *Kirkus Reviews* hailed as a "future classic"; and *Hope at Sea* and *Night Out*, both of which he also wrote. *The New York Times* has lauded Daniel's work as "stunning" and "versatile." He lives in Lenexa, Kansas, with his family.

danielmiyares.com